Oracle Certified Professional Java SE 8 Programmer Exam 1Z0-809

A Comprehensive OCPJP 8 Certification Guide

S G Ganesh

Hari Kiran

Tushar Sharma

Apress®

Oracle Certified Professional Java SE 8 Programmer Exam 1Z0-809: A Comprehensive OCPJP 8 Certification Guide

ISBN-13 (pbk): 978-1-4842-1835-8

ISBN-13 (electronic): 978-1-4842-1836-5

Trademarked names, logos, and images may appear in this book. Rather than use a trademark symbol with every occurrence of a trademarked name, logo, or image we use the names, logos, and images only in an editorial fashion and to the benefit of the trademark owner, with no intention of infringement of the trademark.

The use in this publication of trade names, trademarks, service marks, and similar terms, even if they are not identified as such, is not to be taken as an expression of opinion as to whether or not they are subject to proprietary rights.

While the advice and information in this book are believed to be true and accurate at the date of publication, neither the authors nor the editors nor the publisher can accept any legal responsibility for any errors or omissions that may be made. The publisher makes no warranty, express or implied, with respect to the material contained herein.

Managing Director: Welmoed Spahr
Acquisitions Editor: Celestin Suresh John
Developmental Editor: Douglas Pundick
Technical Reviewer: Vishal Biyani
Editorial Board: Steve Anglin, Pramila Balan, Louise Corrigan, James DeWolf, Jonathan Gennick, Robert Hutchinson, Celestin Suresh John, Michelle Lowman, James Markham, Susan McDermott, Matthew Moodie, Jeffrey Pepper, Douglas Pundick, Ben Renow-Clarke, Gwenan Spearing
Coordinating Editor: Rita Fernando
Copy Editor: Lori Cavanaugh, Tiffany Taylor
Compositor: SPi Global
Indexer: SPi Global

Distributed to the book trade worldwide by Springer Science+Business Media New York, 233 Spring Street, 6th Floor, New York, NY 10013. Phone 1-800-SPRINGER, fax (201) 348-4505, e-mail orders-ny@springer-sbm.com, or visit www.springer.com. Apress Media, LLC is a California LLC and the sole member (owner) is Springer Science + Business Media Finance Inc (SSBM Finance Inc). SSBM Finance Inc is a Delaware corporation.

For information on translations, please e-mail rights@apress.com, or visit www.apress.com.

Apress and friends of ED books may be purchased in bulk for academic, corporate, or promotional use. eBook versions and licenses are also available for most titles. For more information, reference our Special Bulk Sales–eBook Licensing web page at www.apress.com/bulk-sales.

Any source code or other supplementary materials referenced by the author in this text is available to readers at www.apress.com. For detailed information about how to locate your book's source code, go to www.apress.com/source-code/.

To my little princess Tanmaye

—Ganesh

To my wonderful parents and amazing friends

—Hari Kiran

To my caring parents, loving wife, and cute son

—Tushar

Contents at a Glance

Contents

About the Authors

S G Ganesh has Oracle Certified Professional, Java SE 8 Programmer (OCPJP 8) certification. He has 12+ years of working experience in the IT industry. He is currently a corporate trainer and independent consultant based in Bangalore, India. He quit his well-paying job to pursue his passion for sharing knowledge through corporate training and writing books. He worked for Siemens (Corporate Research and Technologies, Bangalore) in "Software Architecture and Development" team for 6+ years. Before Siemens, he worked in Hewlett-Packard's C++ compiler team, Bangalore for 4.5 years. He also has IEEE Software Engineering Certified Instructor (SECI) and IEEE Professional Software Engineering Master (PSEM) certifications. He has authored/co-authored many articles, research papers, and books. For more information, visit his LinkedIn page: `http://bit.ly/sgganesh`.

Hari Kiran is an independent consultant based in Bangalore, India. He has 12+ years of experience in the IT industry. He has worked for large IT companies including HCL Technologies, CSC, and Cisco Systems. He is an experienced Java developer. Throughout his career, he has worked on various technologies related to Java.

Tushar Sharma is currently a researcher at Athens University of Economics and Business. Earlier, he worked with Siemens Research and Technology Center, Bangalore, India for more than 7 years. His career interests include software design, refactoring, design smells, code and design quality, technical debt, design patterns, and change impact analysis. He has an MS (by research) degree in Computer Science from the Indian Institute of Technology-Madras (IIT-M), Chennai, India, where he specialized in design patterns and refactoring. He co-authored the book *Refactoring for Software Design Smells: Managing Technical Debt* published by Morgan Kaufmann in November 2014. He has Oracle Certified Professional, Java SE 7 Programmer (OCPJP 7) certification. He is an IEEE Senior Member. He can be reached at `tusharsharma@ieee.org`.

About the Technical Reviewer

Vishal Biyani started his career working on Java 1.3 and he is excited that Java8 finally has streams and closures. Over the years he has performed various roles in technology projects for large as well as smaller companies. Biyani's current focus is helping organizations implement DevOps and continuous delivery principles. Biyani writes some of his thoughts at www.vishalbiyani.com and can be reached at vrbiyani@gmail.com.

Acknowledgements

We would like to convey our sincere thanks to the entire Apress team for making this book possible.

Our first and foremost thanks go to our acquisitions editor Celestin Suresh John who played a key role from the conceptualization to the production stage of the book.

Our special thanks to Jeffrey Pepper for his support for our initial proposal to revise the earlier OCPJP 7 book, to coordinating editor Rita Fernando for her excellent coordination of this book project, and to developmental editor Douglas Pundick for improving the quality of the chapters. Thank you Jeff, Rita, and Douglas for your help!

A special thanks to our technical reviewer Vishal Biyani for his help in improving the quality of the book.

We convey our thanks to Anindya Bandopadhyay for sharing his feedback on improving the date and time API chapter in this book.

We would like to convey our sincere thanks to the following readers who reported errors in the earlier OCPJP 7 book: Sheila Weiss, Sebastiaan Heunis, John Doe, Steve Tarlton, Beto Montejo, Michael Klenk, Luca Aliberti, Mikael Strand, Jonathan S. Weissman, Bob, Gaël Jaffré, EpicWestern, John Stark, FlyTrap, Bruno Soares Bravo, Jaymoid, Denis Talochkin, Souvik Goswami, and Pawel K. We have corrected the reported mistakes in this book for a better reading/learning experience.

We take this opportunity to express our gratitude to friends and family for their continued support and encouragement.

—S G Ganesh, Hari Kiran, and Tushar Sharma

Introduction

This book is a comprehensive guide to prepare for the OCPJP 8 exam. This book covers all the exam objectives for *Oracle Certified Professional, Java SE 8 Programmer* certification (1Z0-809 exam).

The book covers all of the exam topics for *Java SE 8 Programmer II* (1Z0-809) exam. The chapters and sections in this book map one-to-one to the exam objectives and subtopics. This one-to-one mapping between chapters and the exam objectives ensures that we cover only the topics to the required breadth and depth—no more, no less.

This book follows an example-driven approach to improve your reading and study experience. Additionally, in each chapter we use visual cues (such as notes, caution signs, and exam tips) to help you prepare for the OCPJP 8 exam.

Prerequisites

Since the OCAJP 8 (a.k.a. *Java SE 8 Programmer 1/ 1Z0-808*) exam is a prerequisite for the more comprehensive OCPJP 8 exam (1Z0-809), we assume that you are already familiar with the fundamentals of the language. We focus only on the OCPJP 8 exam objectives, assuming that you have working knowledge in Java.

Target Audience

This book is for you:

- If you are a student or a programmer aspiring to crack the OCPJP 8 exam.

- If you want to learn new features added in Java 8 (especially on functional programming).

- If you're a trainer for OCPJP 8 exam. You can use this book as training material for OCPJP 8 exam preparation.

- If you just want to refresh your knowledge of Java programming or gain a better understanding of various Java APIs.

Please note, however, that this book is neither a tutorial for learning Java nor a comprehensive reference book for Java.

Roadmap for Reading This Book

To get the most out of reading this book, we recommend you follow these steps:

Step 0: Make sure you have JDK 8 installed on your machine and you're able to compile and run Java programs.

Step 1: First read the FAQs in Chapter 1 and become familiar with the exam (you may want to skip irrelevant questions or questions for which you already know the answers).

Step 2: Check the exam topics given in the beginning of each chapter and mark the topics you're not familiar or comfortable with. Read the chapters or sections corresponding to the topics you've marked for preparation.

Step 3: Try out as many sample programs as possible when you read the chapters.

Step 4: Once you feel you are ready to take the exam, take the mock exam (Chapter 14). If you don't pass it, go back to the chapters in which you are weak, read them, and try out more programs relating to those topics. If you've prepared well, you should be able to pass the actual OCPJP 8 exam.

Step 5: Register for the exam and take the exam based on your performance in the mock tests. The day before taking the exam, read the summary sections given at the end of each chapter.

On Coding Examples in This Book

All the programs in this book are self-contained programs (with necessary import statements). We've tested the coding examples in this book using Oracle's Java compiler in JDK 8. It is important that you use a Java compiler and a JVM that supports Java 8 for trying out the programs in this book.

Java is a platform-independent language, but there are certain features that are better explained with a specific platform. Since Windows is the most widely used OS today, some of the programming examples (especially the ones in the NIO.2 chapter) are written with the Windows OS in mind. You may require minor modifications to those programs to get them working under other OSs (Linux, MAC OS, etc.).

Contact Us

In case of any queries, suggestions, or corrections, please feel free to contact us at sgganesh@gmail.com, gharikir@gmail.com, and tusharsharma@ieee.org.

CHAPTER 1

■ ■ ■

The OCPJP 8 Exam: FAQ

The acronym OCPJP 8 exam stands for Java SE 8 Programmer II exam (exam number 1Z0-809). In this first chapter, we address the frequently asked questions (FAQs) that may come up when you are preparing for the OCPJP 8 exam.

Overview

FAQ 1. Can you provide details of the Java associate and professional exams for Java 8?

The OCAJP 8 exam (Oracle Certified Associate Java Programmer certification, exam number 1Z0-808) is mainly meant for entry-level Java developers. When you pass this exam, it demonstrates that you have a strong foundation in Java.

The OCPJP 8 exam (Oracle Certified Professional Java Programmer certification, exam number IZ0-809) is meant for professional Java developers. When you pass this exam, it demonstrates that you can use a wide range of core Java features (especially the ones added in Java 8) in your regular work.

FAQ 2. Can you compare the specifications of the exams targeting OCAJP 8 and OCPJP 8 certifications?

Yes, see Table 1-1.

Table 1-1. *Comparison of the Oracle Exams Leading to OCAJP8 and OCPJP8Certifications*

Exam Number	1Z0-808	1Z0-809	1Z0-810	1Z0-813
Expertise Level	Beginner	Intermediate	Intermediate	Intermediate
Exam Name	Java SE 8 Programmer I	Java SE 8 Programmer II	Upgrade Java SE 7 to Java SE 8 OCP Programmer	Upgrade to Java SE 8 OCP (Java SE 6 and all prior versions)
Associated Certification (abbreviation)	Oracle Certified Associate, Java SE 8 Programmer (OCAJP 8)	Oracle Certified Professional, Java SE 8 Programmer (OCPJP 8)	Oracle Certified Professional, Java SE 8 Programmer (upgrade)(OCPJP 8)	Oracle Certified Professional, Java SE 8 Programmer (OCPJP 8)
Prerequisite Certification	None	Java SE 8 Programmer I (OCAJP8)	Java SE 7 Programmer II (OCPJP 7)	Oracle Certified Professional Java SE 6 Programmer and all prior versions (OCPJP 6 and earlier versions)
Exam Duration	2 hrs 30 minutes (150 mins)	2 hrs 30 minutes (150 mins)	2 hrs 30 minutes (150 mins)	2 hrs 10 minutes (130 mins)
Number of Questions	77Questions	85 Questions	81 Questions	60 Questions
Pass Percentage	65%	65%	65%	63%
Cost	~ USD 245	~USD 245	~USD 245	~USD 245
Exam Topics	Java Basics Working With Java Data Types Using Operators and Decision Constructs Creating and Using Arrays Using Loop Constructs Working with Methods and Encapsulation Working with Inheritance Handling Exceptions Working with Selected classes from the Java API	Java Class Design Advanced Java Class Design Generics and Collections Lambda Built-in Functional Interfaces Java Stream API Exceptions and Assertions Use Java SE 8 Date/ Time API Java I/O Fundamentals Java File I/O (NIO.2) Java Concurrency Building Database Applications with JDBC Localization	Lambda Expressions Using Built-in Lambda Types Filtering Collections with Lambdas Collection Operations with Lambda Parallel Streams Lambda Cookbook Method Enhancements Use Java SE 8 Date/ Time API	Language Enhancements Concurrency Localization Java File I/O (NIO.2) Lambda Java Collections Java Streams

Notes

- In the Cost row, the given USD cost of the exams is approximate as actual cost varies with currency of the country in which you take the exam: $245 in US, £155 in UK, Rs. 9604 in India, etc.

- The Exam Topics row lists only the top-level topics. For sub-topics, please check the Oracle's web pages for these exams.

- The details provided here are as on November 1, 2015. Please check the Oracle website for any updates on the exam details.

Details About the Exam

FAQ 3. OCAJP 8 certification is a prerequisite for OCPJP 8 certification. Does that mean that I have to take the OCAJP8 exam before I can take the OCPJP8 exam?

No, requirements for certification may be met in any order. You may take the OCPJP 8 exam before you take the OCAJP 8 exam, but you will not be granted OCPJP 8 certification until you have passed both 1Z0-808and 1Z0-809 exams.

FAQ 4. How does the OCPJP 8 exam differ from the older OCPJP 7 exam?

When compared to the exam topics in OCPJP 7 exam, the OCPJP 8 exam is updated with topics added in the Java SE 8 release: lambda functions, Java built-in functional interfaces, stream API (including parallel streams), and date and time API, and other changes to the Java library.

FAQ 5.Should I take the OCPJP8 exam or earlier versions such as the OCPJP 7 exam?

Although you can still take exams for older certifications such as OCPJP 7, OCPJP 8 is the best professional credential to have because it is validated against the latest Java SE 8 release.

FAQ 6. What kinds of questions are asked in the OCPJP 8exam?

Some questions on the OCPJP 8 exam test your conceptual knowledge without reference to a specific program or code segment. But most of the questions are programming questions of the following types:

- Given a program or code segment, what is the output or expected behavior?

- Which option(s) would compile without errors or give the desired output?

- Which option(s) constitute the correct usage of a given API (in particular, newly introduced ones such as stream and date/time APIs)?

All questions are multiple choice. Most of them present four or five options, but some have six or seven options. Many questions are designed to have a set of multiple correct answers. Such questions clearly mention the number of options you need to select.

Exam questions are not constrained to be exclusively from the topics on the exam syllabus. You might, for example, get questions on Java fundamentals (from OCAJP syllabus) concerning the basics of exception handling and using wrapper types. You might also get questions on topics related to those on the exam syllabus but not specified in it. For example, in the exam, you may get a question on `java.util.function.BinaryOperator` interface though the "Java Built-in Functional Interfaces" exam topic does not explicitly mention this interface.

A given question is not constrained to test only one topic. Some questions are designed to test multiple topics with a single question. For instance, you may find a question on parallel streams that makes use of built-in functional interfaces and lambda expressions.

FAQ 7. What does the OCPJP 8 exam test for?

The OCPJP 8 exam tests your understanding of the Java language features and APIs that are essential for developing real-world programs. The exam focuses on the following areas:

- *Language concepts that are useful for problem solving*: The exam tests not only your knowledge of how language features work, but also covers your grasp of the nitty-gritty and corner cases of language features. For example, you need to understand not only the generics feature in Java but also problems associated with type-erasure, mixing legacy containers with generic containers, and so on.

- *Java APIs*: The exam tests your familiarity with using the Java class library, as well as unusual aspects or corner cases, such as the following:

    - What is the binary equivalent for `java.util.function.Supplier`? (Answer: Since a `Supplier` does not take any arguments, there is no binary equivalent for the `Supplier` interface).

    - What will happen if you try to use a stream more than once? (Answer: Once a terminal operation is called on a stream, it is considered used or closed; any attempt at reusing the stream will result in throwing an `IllegalStateException`.)

- *Underlying concepts*: For example, the exam might test your understanding of how serialization works, the differences between overloading and overriding, how autoboxing and unboxing work in relation to generics, different kinds of liveness problems with threads, how parallel streams internally use the fork/join framework, etc.

Although the exam does not test memory skills, some questions presume rote knowledge of key elements, such as the following:

- The name of the abstract methods provided in the key functional interfaces in `java.util.function` package ("test" method for `Predicate`, "accept" method for `Consumer`, "apply" method for `Function`, and "get" method for `Supplier` interface).

- In the `java.util.stream.Stream` interface and its primitive type versions, you need to remember the name of the commonly used intermediate operations and terminal operations.

FAQ 8. I've been a Java programmer for the last five years. Do I have to prepare for the OCPJP 8 exam?

Short answer: It's good that you have work experience, but you still need to prepare for the OCPJP 8 exam.

Long answer: No matter how much real-world programming experience you might have, there are two reasons you should prepare for this exam to improve your chances of passing it:

- *You may not have been exposed to certain topics on the exam.* Java is vast, and you might not have had occasion to work on every topic covered in the exam. For example, you may not be familiar with localization if you have never dealt with the locale aspects of the applications you were engaged with. Or your work might not have required you to use JDBC. Or you've always worked on single-threaded programs, so multithreaded programming might be new to you. Moreover, OCPJP8 emphasizes Java 8, and you might not have been exposed yet to such Java 8 topics as lambda expressions, sequential and parallel streams, date and time API, and built-in functional interfaces.

- *You may not remember the unusual aspects or corner cases.* No matter how experienced you are, there is always an element of surprise involved when you program. The OCPJP8 exam tests not just your knowledge and skills in respect of regular features, but also your understanding of unusual aspects or corner cases, such as the behavior of multithreaded code and the use of generics when both overloading and overriding are involved. So you have to bone up on pathological cases that you rarely encounter in your work.

FAQ 9. How do I prepare for the OCPJP 8 exam?

Study this book. In addition,

- *Code, code, code!* Write lots and lots of small programs, experiment with them, and learn from your mistakes.

- *Read, read, read!* Read this book and the tutorial and reference resources on Oracle's site, especially

    - *Oracle's free online Java tutorials:* Access the Java tutorial at `http://docs.oracle.com/javase/tutorial/`.

    - Oracle's Java 8 central: You can download the latest Java SDK, gets links to access the Java SE community, read free technical articles on Java 8 from this page:

      `http://www.oracle.com/technetwork/java/javase/overview/`
      `java8-2100321.html`

    - *Java documentation:* The Java API documentation is a mine of information. This documentation is available online (see `http://docs.oracle.com/javase/8/` `docs/api/`) and is shipped as part of the Java SDK. If you don't have immediate Internet access, you may find javac's-Xprint option handy. For example, to print the textual representation of String class, type the fully qualified name, as in

      ```
      javac -Xprint java.lang.String
      ```

This will print the list of members in `String` class on the console.

- *Read, code, read, code!* Cycle back and forth between your reading and coding so that your book knowledge and its practical application are mutually reinforcing. This way, you'll not just know a concept, but you'll also *understand* it.

- *Focus most on the topics you're least comfortable with.* Grade yourself on each of the topics in OCPJP 8 exam on an ascending scale from 1 to 10. Do remedial preparation in all the topics for which you rate yourself 8 or less.

FAQ 10. How do I know when I'm ready to take the OCPJP 8 exam?

Take the mock exam given in Chapter 14 under actual exam conditions: stick to the 2.5-hour time limit; don't take any breaks and don't refer any books or websites. If you score 65% or above (which is the passing score for 1Z0-809 exam), you are likely to pass the actual exam.

Taking the Exam

FAQ 11. What are my options to register for the exam?

You have three registration options for the OCPJP 8 exam:

- Register and pay at the Pearson VUE website.

- Buy an exam voucher from Oracle and then register yourself in Pearson VUE website.

- Register and pay at the Oracle Testing Center (OTC), if you have one in your region.

FAQ 12. How do I register for the exam, schedule a day and time for taking the exam, and appear for the exam?

Option 1: Register and pay on the Pearson VUE website using the following steps:

Step 1. Go to `www.pearsonvue.com/oracle/` (you will be directed here if you click the first option from Oracle Certification page). Click on "Schedule online" in "Schedule an exam" section.

Step 2. Select "Sign In." Click on "proctored" in the "what type of exam you are planning to take" section. Select this exam as `"Information Technology (IT)"` ➤ `"Oracle"` ➤ `"Proctored"`. Then you'll be asked to sign in.

Step 3. Log in to your web account on the Pearson site. If you don't have one, create one; you will get the user name and password by the e-mail you provide. When you log in first time, you need to change your password and set security questions and their answers. When you are done with this, you're ready to schedule your exam.

Step 4. Once logged in, you'll get the list of Oracle exams to select from. Select the following exam:

- 1Z0-809, Java SE 8Programmer II(aka OCPJP 8 exam)

These exams are in English (You can choose another language if you wish and if it is available in the list). This page will also show you the cost of the exam. Click Next.

Step 5. Now you need to select your test location. Choose `Country` ➤ `City` ➤ `State/Province`, and you'll be shown test locations close to you. Each center will have an icon for information: click it for the address and directions. Select up to four centers near your location and click `Next`.

Step 6. Select a test center and select a date and time for appointments. The page will indicate the available dates and time slots; choose the one most convenient for you. If you have an exam voucher or Oracle University coupon or Oracle promotion code, enter it here.

Step 7. Select from the available payment options (the usual way is to pay using your credit card) and pay your exam fees. Make sure that you have selected the right exam, appropriate test center, and date/time before paying the fees.

Step 8. Done! You will get an appointment confirmation payment receipt by e-mail.

Option 2: Buy an exam voucher from Oracle and register on the Pearson VUE website.

You can buy a generic exam voucher from Oracle and use it at the Pearson site. It costs US$245 if you are living in the United States and is denominated in an appropriate currency if you live elsewhere. To buy the voucher from Oracle, select "OU Java, Solaris, and other Sun Technology Exam eVoucher." You will be asked to create an Oracle account if you do not have one. Once the account is created, confirm customer type, customer contact information, and pay. Once you pay the fees, you can use the eVoucher at the Pearson VUE site.

Option 3: Register and pay online to take the exam in person at an Oracle Testing Center (OTC).

You can choose this option if a physical exam session is scheduled in your vicinity. It costs US$245 or the local equivalent.

FAQ 13. What are the key things I need to remember before taking the exam and on the day of exam?

Before the exam day:

- You'll get e-mail from Pearson confirming your appointment and payment. Check the details on what you should bring when you go to the exam center. Note that you'll need at least two photo IDs.

- Before the exam, you'll get a call from the Pearson exam center where you've booked your appointment.

On the exam day:

- Go to the exam center at least 30 minutes before the exam starts. Your exam center will have lockers for storing your belongings.

- Show your exam schedule information and IDs and then complete the exam formalities, such as signing the documents.

- You'll be taken to a computer in the exam room and will log into the exam-taking software.

Taking the exam:

- You will see the following on the exam-taking software screen:
  - A timer ticking in one corner showing the time left
  - The current question number you are attempting
  - A check box to select if you want to review the question later
  - The button (labeled "Review") for going to a review screen where you can revisit the questions before completing the exam.
- Once you start, you'll get questions displayed one by one. You can choose the answers by selecting them in the check box. If you are unsure of an answer, select the Mark button so that you can revisit it at any point during the exam. You can also right-click on an option to strike-through that option (useful for eliminating incorrect options).
- You may not consult any person or print or electronic materials or programs during the exam.

After the exam:

- Once you're done with the exam, you will not be immediately shown the results. You have to log in to Oracle's CertView website (`https://education.oracle.com/certview.html`) to see the exam results.
- Irrespective of passing or failing the exam, *topics* from questions you've answered incorrectly will be supplied with your score.
- If you've passed the OCPJP 8 exam *and* you've also satisfied the applicable prerequisites for certification (e.g., OCAJP 8 certification as the prerequisite of OCPJP 8 certification via the 1Z0-809 exam), a printable certificate will be e-mailed to you.
- If you failed the exam, you may register and pay again to retake it after a 14-day waiting period.

CHAPTER 2

■ ■ ■

Java Class Design

Certification Objectives

Implement encapsulation

Implement inheritance including visibility modifiers and composition

Implement polymorphism

Override hashCode, equals, and toString methods from Object class

Create and use singleton classes and immutable classes

Develop code that uses static keyword on initialize blocks, variables, methods, and classes

Object-Orientation (OO) is the core of the most mainstream programming languages today. To create high-quality designs and software, it is important to get a good grasp of object oriented concepts. This chapter on class design and the next chapter on advanced class design provides you a firm foundation for creating quality designs in Java.

Since OCAJP 8 is a pre-requisite for the OCPJP 8 exam, we assume that you are familiar with basic concepts such as methods, fields, and how to define a constructor. Hence, in this chapter, we start directly discussing OCPJP 8 exam topics. In the first section, we discuss how to enforce encapsulation using access specifiers, and how to implement inheritance and polymorphism. In the next section, we delve into details on overriding methods in the Object class, define singleton and immutable classes, and analyze different ways of using the static keyword.

Encapsulation

Certification Objective

Implement encapsulation

Structured programming *decomposes* the program's functionality into various procedures (*functions*), without much concern about the data each procedure can work with. Functions are free to operate and modify the (usually global and unprotected) data.

In Object Oriented Programming (OOP), data and associated behavior forms a single unit, which is referred to as a *class*. The term *encapsulation* refers to combining data and associated functions as a single unit. For example, in a Circle class, radius and center are defined as *private fields*. Now you can add methods such as draw() and fillColor() along with fields radius and center, since the fields and methods are closely related to each other. All the data (fields) required for the methods in the class are available inside the class itself. In other words, the class *encapsulates* its fields and methods together.

Access Modifiers

Certification Objective

Implement inheritance including visibility modifiers and composition

Access modifiers determine the level of visibility for a Java entity (a class, method, or field). *Access modifiers enable you to enforce effective encapsulation.* If all member variables of a class can be accessed from anywhere, then there is no point putting these variables in a class and no purpose in encapsulating data and behavior together in a class.

The OCPJP 8 exam includes both direct questions on access modifiers and indirect questions that require an underlying knowledge of access modifiers. Hence it is important to understand the various access modifiers supported in Java.

Java supports four types of access modifiers:

- Public

- Private

- Protected

- Default (no access modifier specified)

To illustrate the four types of access modifiers, let's assume that you have the following classes in a drawing application: Shape, Circle, Circles, and Canvas classes. The Canvas class is in appcanvas package and the other three classes are in graphicshape package (see Listing 2-1).

Listing 2-1. Shape.java, Circle.java, Circles.java, and Canvas.java

```java
// Shape.java
package graphicshape;

class Shape {
        protected int color;
}


// Circle.java
package graphicshape;

import graphicshape.Shape;

public class Circle extends Shape {
        private int radius;     // private field
        public void area() {    // public method
                // access to private field radius inside the class:
                System.out.println("area: " + 3.14 * radius * radius);
        }
        // The fillColor method has default access
        void fillColor() {
                //access to protected field, in subclass:
                System.out.println("color: " + color);
        }
}
```

```java
// Circles.java
package graphicshape;

class Circles {
        void getArea() {
                Circle circle = new Circle();
                // call to public method area() within package:
                circle.area();
                // calling fillColor() with default access within package:
                circle.fillColor();
        }
}

// Canvas.java
package appcanvas;
import graphicshape.Circle;

class Canvas {
        void getArea() {
                Circle   circle = new Circle();
                circle.area();   // call to public method area(), outside package
        }
}
```

Public Access Modifier

The public access modifier is the most liberal one. If a class or its members are declared as *public*, they can be accessed from any other class regardless of the package boundary. It is comparable to a public place in the real world, such as a company cafeteria that all employees can use irrespective of their department. As shown in Listing 2-1, the public method area() in Circle class is accessible within the same package, as well as outside of the package (in the Canvas class).

A *public method* in a class is accessible to the outside world only if the class is declared as public. If the class does not specify any access modifier (i.e., it has default access), then the public method is accessible only within the containing package.

Private Access Modifier

The private access modifier is the most stringent access modifier. A private class member cannot be accessed from outside the class; only members of the same class can access these private members. It's comparable to a safe deposit box room in a bank, which can only be accessed by a set of authorized personnel and safe deposit box owners. In Listing 2-1, the private field radius of the Circle class is accessible only inside the Circle class and not in any other class regardless of the enclosing package.

Protected and Default Access Modifiers

Protected and default access modifiers are quite similar to each other. If a member method or field is declared as protected or default, then the method or field can be accessed within the package. Note that there is no explicit keyword to provide default access; in fact, when no access modifier is specified, the member has default access. Also, note that default access is also known as package-protected access. Protected and default accesses are comparable to the situation in an office where a conference room is accessible only to one department.

What is the difference between protected and default access? One significant difference between these two access modifiers arises when we talk about a subclass belonging to another package than its superclass. In this case, protected members are accessible in the subclass, whereas default members are not.

💣☀ A class (or interface) cannot be declared as private or protected. Furthermore, member methods or fields of an interface cannot be declared as private or protected.

In Listing 2-1, the protected field color is accessed in the class Circle and the default method fillColor() is called from the class Circles.

The visibility offered by various access modifiers is summarized in Table 2-1.

Table 2-1. *Access Modifiers and Their Visibility*

Access modifiers/ accessibility	Within the same class	Subclass inside the package	Subclass outside the package	Other class inside the package	Other class outside the package
Public	Yes	Yes	Yes	Yes	Yes
Private	Yes	No	No	No	No
Protected	Yes	Yes	Yes	Yes	No
Default	Yes	Yes	No	Yes	No

Inheritance

Inheritance is a reusability mechanism in object-oriented programming. With inheritance, the common properties of various objects are exploited to form relationships with each other. The abstract and common properties are provided in the *superclass*, which is available to the more specialized *subclasses*. For example, a color printer and a black-and-white printer are kinds of a printer (*single inheritance*); an all-in-one printer is a printer, scanner, and photocopier (*multiple inheritance*).

Why is inheritance a powerful feature? Because it supports modeling classes in a hierarchy, and such hierarchical models are easy to understand. For example, you can logically categorize vehicles as two-wheelers, three-wheelers, four-wheelers, and so on. In the four-wheelers category, there are cars, vans, buses, and trucks. In the cars category, there are hatchbacks, sedans, and SUVs. When you categorize hierarchically, it becomes easy to understand, model, and write programs.

Consider a simple example used in earlier sections: class Shape is a base class and Circle is a derived class. In other words, a Circle is a Shape; similarly, a Square is a Shape. Therefore, an inheritance relationship can be referred to as an *IS-A relationship*.

In the Java library, you can see extensive use of inheritance. Figure 2-1 shows a partial inheritance hierarchy from java.lang library. The Number class abstracts various numerical (reference) types such as Byte, Integer, Float, Double, Short, and BigDecimal.

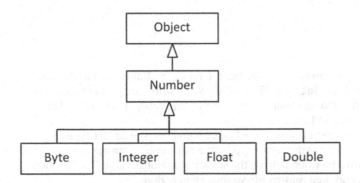

Figure 2-1. *A partial inheritance hierarchy in java.lang package*

The class Number has many common methods that are inherited by the derived classes. The derived classes do not have to implement the common methods implemented by the Number class. Also, you can supply a derived type where the base type is expected. For instance, a Byte is a Number, which means you can provide an object of Byte where an object of Number is expected. You can write general-purpose methods (or algorithms) when you write methods for the base type. Listing 2-2 shows a simple example.

Listing 2-2. TestNumber.java

```java
// Illustrates how abstracting different kinds of numbers in a Number hierarchy
// becomes useful in practice
public class TestNumber {
        // take an array of numbers and sum them up
        public static double sum(Number []nums) {
                double sum = 0.0;
                for(Number num : nums) {
                        sum += num.doubleValue();
                }
                return sum;
        }

        public static void main(String []s) {
                // create a Number array
                Number []nums = new Number[4];
                // assign derived class objects
                nums[0] = new Byte((byte)10);
                nums[1] = new Integer(10);
                nums[2] = new Float(10.0f);
                nums[3] = new Double(10.0f);
                // pass the Number array to sum and print the result
                System.out.println("The sum of numbers is: " + sum(nums));
        }
}
```

This program prints

```
The sum of numbers is: 40.0
```

In the main() method, you declare nums as a Number[]. A Number reference can hold any of its derived type objects. You are creating objects of type Byte, Integer, Float, and Double with initial value 10; the nums array holds these elements. (Note that you needed an explicit cast in new Byte((byte) 10) instead of plain Byte(10) because Byte takes a byte argument and 10 is an int.)

The sum method takes a Number[] and returns the sum of the Number elements. The double type can hold the largest range of values, so you use double as the return type of the sum method. Number has a doubleValue method and this method returns the value held by the Number as a double value. The for loop traverses the array, adds the double values, and then returns the sum once you're done.

As you can see, the sum() method is a general method that can handle any Number[]. A similar example can be given from the Java standard library where java.util.Arrays class has a static method binarySearch():

```
static int binarySearch(Object[] a, Object key, Comparator c)
```

This method searches a given key (an Object type) in the given array of Objects. Comparator is an interface declaring the equals and compare methods. You can use binarySearch for objects of any class type that implements this Comparator interface. As you can see, inheritance is a powerful and useful feature for writing general-purpose methods.

Polymorphism

Certification Objective

Implement polymorphism

The Greek roots of the term *polymorphism* refer to the "several forms" of an entity. In the real world, every message you communicate has a context. Depending on the context, the meaning of the message may change and so may the response to the message. Similarly in OOP, a message can be interpreted in multiple ways (polymorphism), depending on the object.

Polymorphism can be of two forms: *dynamic* and *static*.

- When different forms of a single entity are resolved during runtime (*late binding*), such polymorphism is called *dynamic polymorphism*. In the previous section on inheritance, we discussed overriding. Overriding is an example of *runtime polymorphism*.

- When different forms of a single entity are resolved at compile time (*early binding*), such polymorphism is called *static polymorphism*. *Function overloading* is an example of static polymorphism, and let us explore it now.

Please note that abstract methods use runtime polymorphism. We discuss abstract methods in interfaces and abstract classes in the next chapter (Chapter 3 – Advanced Class Design).

Runtime Polymorphism

You just learned that a base class reference can refer to a derived class object. You can invoke methods from the base class reference; however, the actual method invocation depends on the dynamic type of the object pointed to by the base class reference. The type of the base class reference is known as the *static type* of the object and the actual object pointed by the reference at runtime is known as the *dynamic type* of the object.

When the compiler sees the invocation of a method from a base class reference and if the method is an overridable method (a nonstatic and nonfinal method), the compiler defers determining the exact method to be called to runtime (late binding). At runtime, based on the actual dynamic type of the object, an appropriate method is invoked. This mechanism is known as *dynamic method resolution* or *dynamic method invocation*.

Runtime Polymorphism: An Example

Consider that you have the area() method in Shape class. Depending on the derived class—Circle or Square, for example—the area() method will be implemented differently, as shown in Listing 2-3.

Listing 2-3. TestShape.java

```java
class Shape {
        public double area() { return 0; } // default implementation
        // other members
}
class Circle extends Shape {
        private int radius;
        public Circle(int r) { radius = r; }
        // other constructors
        public double area() {return Math.PI * radius * radius; }
        // other declarations
}

class Square extends Shape {
        private int side;
        public Square(int a) { side = a; }
        public double area() { return side * side; }
        // other declarations
}

public class TestShape {
        public static void main(String []args) {
                Shape shape1 = new Circle(10);
                System.out.println(shape1.area());
                Shape shape2 = new Square(10);
                System.out.println(shape2.area());
        }
}
```

This program prints

```
314.1592653589793
100.0
```

15

This program illustrates how the area() method is called based on the dynamic type of the Shape. In this code, the statement shape1.area(); calls the Circle's area() method while the statement shape2.area(); calls Square's area() method and hence the result.

Now, let's ask a more fundamental question: Why do you need to override methods? In OOP, the fundamental idea in inheritance is to provide a default or common functionality in the base class; the derived classes are expected to provide more specific functionality. In this Shape base class and the Circle and Square derived classes, the Shape provided the default implementation of the area() method. The derived classes of Circle and Square defined their version of the area() method that overrides the base class area() method. So, depending on the type of the derived object you create, from base class reference, calls to area() method will be resolved to the correct method. Overriding (i.e., runtime polymorphism) is a simple yet powerful idea for extending functionality.

Let us now discuss compile-time polymorphism (overloading). After that, we will immediately return back to this topic of runtime polymorphism to discuss more topics such as how to deal with visibility modifiers when overriding and choosing between composition and inheritance.

Method Overloading

In a class, how many methods can you define with the same name? Many! In Java, you can define multiple methods with the same name, provided the argument lists differ from each other. In other words, if you provide different types of arguments, different numbers of arguments, or both, then you can define multiple methods with the same name. This feature is called *method overloading*. The compiler will resolve the call to a correct method depending on the actual number and/or types of the passed parameters.

Let's implement a method in the Circle class called fillColor() that fills a circle object with different colors. When you specify a color, you need use a coloring scheme, and let us consider two schemes - RGB scheme and HSB scheme.

1. When you represent a color by combining Red, Green, and Blue color components, it is known as RGB scheme. By convention, each of the color values is typically given in the range 0 to 255.

2. When you represent a color by combining Hue, Saturation, and Brightness values, it is known as HSB scheme. By convention, each of the values is typically given in the range 0.0 to 1.0.

Since RGB values are integer values and HSB values are floating point values, how about supporting both these schemes for calling fillColor() method?

```
class Circle {
        // other members
        public void fillColor (int red, int green, int blue) {
                /* color the circle using RGB color values - actual code elided */
        }

        public void fillColor (float hue, float saturation, float brightness) {
                /* color the circle using HSB values - actual code elided */
        }
}
```

As you can see, both fillColor() methods have exactly the same name and both take three arguments; however, the argument types are different. Based on the type of arguments used while calling fillColor() method on Circle, the compiler will decide exactly which method to call. For instance, consider following method calls:

```
Circle c1 = new Circle(10, 20, 10);
c1.fillColor(0, 255, 255);

Circle c2 = new Circle(50, 100, 5);
c2.fillColor(0.5f, 0.5f, 1.0f);
```

In this code, for the c1 object, the call to fillColor() has integer arguments 0, 255, and 255. Hence, the compiler resolves this call to the method fillColor(int red, int green, int blue). For the c2 object, the call to fillColor() has arguments 0.5f, 0.5f, and 1.0f; hence it resolves the call to fillColor(float hue, float saturation, float brightness).

In the above example, method fillColor() is an overloaded method. The method has same name and the same number of arguments, but the types of the arguments differ. It is also possible to overload methods with different numbers of arguments.

Such overloaded methods are useful for avoiding repeating the same code in different functions. Let's look at a simple example in Listing 2-4.

Listing 2-4. HappyBirthday.java

```java
class HappyBirthday {
        // overloaded wish method with String as an argument
        public static void wish(String name) {
                System.out.println("Happy birthday " + name + "!");
        }

        // overloaded wish method with no arguments;
        // this method in turn invokes wish(String) method
        public static void wish() {
                wish("to you");
        }

        public static void main(String []args) {
                wish();
                wish("dear James Gosling");
        }
}
```

It prints:

```
Happy birthday to you!
Happy birthday dear James Gosling!
```

Here, the method wish(String name) is meant for wishing "Happy Birthday" when the name of the person is known. The default method wish() is for wishing "Happy Birthday" to anyone. As you can see, you don't have to write System.out.println again in the wish() method; you can just reuse the wish(String) method definition by passing the default value "to you" as argument to wish(). Such reuse is effective for large and related method definitions since it saves time writing and testing the same code.

Constructor Overloading

A default constructor is useful for creating objects with a default initialization value. When you want to initialize the objects with different values in different instantiations, you can pass them as the arguments to constructors. And yes, you can have multiple constructors in a class, which is *constructor overloading*. In a class, the default constructor can initialize the object with default initial values, while another constructor can accept arguments that need to be used for object instantiation.

Here is an example of Circle class that has overloaded constructors (see Listing 2-5).

Listing 2-5. Circle.java

```java
public class Circle {
        private int xPos;
        private int yPos;
        private int radius;

        // three overloaded constructors for Circle
        public Circle(int x, int y, int r) {
                xPos = x;
                yPos = y;
                radius = r;
        }

        public Circle(int x, int y) {
                xPos = x;
                yPos = y;
                radius = 10; // default radius
        }

        public Circle() {
                xPos = 20; // assume some default values for xPos and yPos
                yPos = 20;
                radius = 10; // default radius
        }

        public String toString() {
                return "center = (" + xPos + "," + yPos + ") and radius = " + radius;
        }

         public static void main(String[]s) {
                System.out.println(new Circle());
                System.out.println(new Circle(50, 100));
                System.out.println(new Circle(25, 50, 5));
        }
}
```

This program prints

```
center = (20,20) and radius = 10
center = (50,100) and radius = 10
center = (25,50) and radius = 5
```

As you can see, the compiler has resolved the constructor calls depending on the number of arguments. The default constructor takes no argument and in this case we have assumed some default values for xPos, yPos, and radius (with values 20, 20, and 10 respectively). The Circle constructor with two arguments (int x and int y) sets the position of xPos and yPos based on the values of the passed arguments and assumes default value of 10 for the radius member. The Circle constructor that takes all the three arguments sets the corresponding fields in the Circle class.

Did you notice that you are duplicating the code inside these three constructors? To avoid that code duplication—and reduce your typing effort—you can invoke one constructor from another constructor. Of the three constructors, the constructor taking x-position, y-position, and radius is the most general constructor. The other two constructors can be rewritten in terms of calling the three argument constructors, like so:

```java
public Circle(int x, int y, int r) {
        xPos = x;
        yPos = y;
        radius = r;
}

public Circle(int x, int y) {
        this(x, y, 10); // passing default radius 10
}

public Circle() {
        this(20, 20, 10);
        // assume some default values for xPos, yPos and radius
}
```

The output is exactly the same as for the previous program, but this program is shorter. In this case, you used the this keyword (which refers to the current object) to call one constructor from another constructor of the same class.

Overload Resolution

When you define overloaded methods, how does the compiler know which method to call? Can you guess the output of the code in Listing 2-6?

Listing 2-6. Overloaded.java

```java
class Overloaded {
        public static void aMethod (int val)    { System.out.println ("int");    }
        public static void aMethod (short val)  { System.out.println ("short");  }
        public static void aMethod (Object val) { System.out.println ("object"); }
        public static void aMethod (String val) { System.out.println ("String"); }

        public static void main(String[] args) {
                byte b = 9;
                aMethod(b);      // first call
                aMethod(9);      // second call
                Integer i = 9;
                aMethod(i);      // third call
                aMethod("9");    // fourth call
        }
}
```

It prints

```
short
int
object
String
```

Here is how the compiler resolved these calls:

1. In the first method call, the statement is aMethod(b) where the variable b is of type byte. There is no aMethod definition that takes byte as an argument. The closest type (in size) is short type and not int, so the compiler resolves the call aMethod(b) to aMethod(short val) definition.

2. In the second method call, the statement is aMethod(9). The constant value 9 is of type int. The closest match is aMethod(int), so the compiler resolves the call aMethod(9) to aMethod(int val) definition.

3. The third method call is aMethod(i), where the variable i is of type Integer. There is no aMethod definition that takes Integer as an argument. The closest match is aMethod(Object val), so it is called. Why not aMethod(int val)? For finding the closest match, the compiler allows implicit upcasts, not downcasts, so aMethod(int val) is not considered.

4. The last method call is aMethod("9"). The argument is a String type. Since there is an exact match, aMethod(String val) is called.

This process of the compiler trying to *resolve* the method call from given overloaded method definitions is called *overload resolution*. For resolving a method call, it first looks for the *exact* match—the method definition with exactly same number of parameters and types of parameters. If it can't find an exact match, it looks for the *closest match* by using upcasts. If the compiler can't find any match, then you'll get a compiler error, as in Listing 2-7.

Listing 2-7. OverloadingError.java

```
class OverloadingError {
        public static void aMethod (byte val ) { System.out.println ("byte");  }
        public static void aMethod (short val ) { System.out.println ("short"); }

        public static void main(String[] args) {
                aMethod(9);
        }
}
```

Here is the compiler error:

```
OverloadingError.java:6: error: no suitable method found for aMethod(int)
            aMethod(9);
            ^
method OverloadingError.aMethod(byte) is not applicable
    (argument mismatch; possible lossy conversion from int to byte)
method OverloadingError.aMethod(short) is not applicable
    (argument mismatch; possible lossy conversion from int to short)
1 error
```

The type of constant 9 is int, so there is no matching definition for aMethod for the call aMethod(9). As you saw earlier with respect to the overload resolution, the compiler can do upcasts (e.g., byte to int) for the closest match, but it does not consider downcasts (e.g., int to byte or int to short, as in this case). Hence, the compiler does not find any matches and throws you an error.

What if the compiler finds two matches? It will also become an error! Listing 2-8 shows an example.

Listing 2-8. AmbiguousOverload.java

```java
class AmbiguousOverload {
        public static void aMethod (long val1, int val2) {
                System.out.println ("long, int");
        }

        public static void aMethod (int val1, long val2) {
                System.out.println ("int, long");
        }

        public static void main(String[] args) {
                aMethod(9, 10);
        }
}
```

Here is the compiler error:

```
AmbiguousOverload.java:11: error: reference to aMethod is ambiguous
                aMethod(9, 10);
                ^
        both method aMethod(long,int) in AmbiguousOverload and method aMethod(int,long) in
AmbiguousOverload match
1 error
```

Why did this call become an "ambiguous" call? The constants 9 and 10 are ints. There are two aMethod definitions: one is aMethod(long, int) and another is aMethod(int, long). So there is no exact match for the call aMethod(int, int). An integer can be implicitly upcasted to both long as well as Integer. Which one will the compiler choose? Since there are two matches, the compiler complains with an error that the call is ambiguous.

 Overload resolution fails (with a compiler error) if there are no matches or ambiguous matches.

Points to Remember

Here are some interesting rules regarding method overloading that will help you in the OCPJP 8 exam:

- Overload resolution takes place entirely at compile time (not at runtime).

- You cannot overload methods with the methods differing in return types alone.

- You cannot overload methods with the methods differing in exception specifications alone.

- For overload resolution to succeed, you need to define methods such that the compiler finds one exact match. If the compiler finds no matches for your call or if the matching is ambiguous, the overload resolution fails and the compiler issues an error.

The *signature* of a method is made up of the method name, number of arguments, and types of arguments. You can overload methods with same name but with different signatures. Since return type and exception specification are not part of the signature, you cannot overload methods based on return type or exception specification alone.

Overriding Methods in Object Class

Certification Objective

Override hashCode, equals, and toString methods from Object class

---

Let us now discuss overriding some of the methods in Object class. You can override clone(), equals(), hashCode(), toString(), and finalize() methods in your classes. Since getClass(), notify(), notifyAll(), and the overloaded versions of wait() method are declared final, you cannot override these methods.

Why should we override methods in the Object class? To answer this question, let's discuss what happens when we don't override the toString() method (Listing 2-9).

Listing 2-9. Point.java

```java
class Point {
        private int xPos, yPos;

        public Point(int x, int y) {
                xPos = x;
                yPos = y;
        }

        public static void main(String []args) {
                // Passing a Point object to println
                // automatically invokes the toString method
                System.out.println(new Point(10, 20));
        }
}
```

It prints

```
Point@19821f (Actual address might differ on your machine, but a similar string will show up)
```

The toString() method is defined in the Object class, which is inherited by all the classes in Java. Here is the overview of the toString() method as defined in the Object class:

```
public String toString()
```

The toString() method takes no arguments and returns the String representation of the object. The default implementation of this method returns ClassName@hex version of the object's hashcode. That is why you get this unreadable output. Note that this hexadecimal value will be different for each instance, so if you try this program, you'll get a different hexadecimal value as output. For example, when we ran this program again, we got this output: Point@affc70. Hence, we need to override the toString method in this Point class.

Overriding toString() Method

When you create new classes, you are expected to override this method to return the desired textual representation of your class. Listing 2-10 shows an improved version of the Point class with the overridden version of the toString() method.

Listing 2-10. Point.java

```java
// improved version of the Point class with overridden toString method
class Point {
        private int xPos, yPos;

        public Point(int x, int y) {
                xPos = x;
                yPos = y;
        }

        // this toString method overrides the default toString method implementation
        // provided in the Object base class
        public String toString() {
                return "x = " + xPos + ", y = " + yPos;
        }

        public static void main(String []args) {
                System.out.println(new Point(10, 20));
        }
}
```

This program now prints

```
x = 10, y = 20
```

This is much cleaner, as you would expect. To make it clear, here is a slightly different version of the main() method in this Point class implementation:

```java
public static void main(String []args) {
        Object obj = new Point(10, 20);
        System.out.println(obj);
}
```

It prints

```
x = 10, y = 20
```

Here, the static type of the obj variable is Object class, and the dynamic type of the object is Point. The println statement invokes the toString() method of the obj variable. Here, the method toString() of the derived class—the Point's toString() method—is invoked due to runtime polymorphism.

Overriding Issues

While overriding, you need to be careful about the access levels, the name of the method, and its signature. Here is the toString() method in the Point class just discussed:

```
public String toString() {
        return "x = " + xPos + ", y = " + yPos;
}
```

How about using the protected access specifier instead of public in this method definition? Will it work?

```
protected String toString() {
        return "x = " + xPos + ", y = " + yPos;
}
```

No, it doesn't. For this change, the compiler complains

```
Point.java:12: error: toString() in Point cannot override toString() in Object
        protected String toString() {
                 ^
attempting to assign weaker access privileges; was public
1 error
```

While overriding, you can provide stronger access privilege, not weaker access; otherwise it will become a compiler error.

Here is another slightly modified version of toString() method. Will it work?

```
public Object toString() {
        return "x = " + xPos + ", y = " + yPos;
}
```

You get the following compiler error:

```
Point.java:12: error: toString() in Point cannot override toString() in Object
public Object toString() {
             ^
return type Object is not compatible with String
1 error
```

In this case, you got a compiler error for mismatch because the return type in the overriding method should be exactly the same as the base class method.

Here is another example:

```
public String ToString() {
        return "x = " + xPos + ", y = " + yPos;
}
```

Now the compiler doesn't complain. But this is a new method named ToString and it has nothing to do with the toString method in Object. Hence, this ToString method *does not* override the toString method. Keep the following points in mind for correct overriding. The overriding method

- Should have the same argument list types (or compatible types) as the base version.

- Should have the same return type.

  - But from Java 5 onwards, the return type can be a subclass–covariant return types (which you'll learn shortly).

- Should *not* have a more restrictive access modifier than the base version.

  - But it may have a less restrictive access modifier.

- Should *not* throw new or broader checked exceptions.

  - But it may throw fewer or narrower checked exceptions, or any unchecked exception.

- And, oh yes, the names should exactly match!

Remember that you cannot override a method if you do not inherit it. Private methods cannot be overridden because they are not inherited.

The signatures of the base method and overriding method should be compatible for overriding to take place. Incorrect overriding is a common source of bugs in Java programs. In questions related to overriding, look out for mistakes or problems in overriding when answering the questions.

COVARIANT RETURN TYPES

You know that the return types of the methods should exactly match when overriding methods. However, with the covariant return types feature introduced in Java 5, you can provide the derived class of the return type in the overriding method. Well, that's great, but why do you need this feature? Check out these overridden methods with the same return type:

```
abstract class Shape {
        // other methods elided
        public abstract Shape copy();
}

class Circle extends Shape {
        // other methods elided
        public Circle(int x, int y, int radius) { /* initialize fields here */ }
        public Shape copy() { /* return a copy of this object */ }
}
```

```
class Test {
        public static void main(String []args) {
                Circle c1 = new Circle(10, 20, 30);
                Circle c2 = c1.copy();
        }
}
```

This code will give a compiler error of "incompatible types: Shape cannot be converted to Circle". This is because of the lack of an explicit downcast from Shape to Circle in the assignment "Circle c2 = c1.copy();".

Since you know clearly that you are going to assign a Circle object returned from Circle's copy method, you can give an explicit cast to fix the compiler error:

```
Circle c2 = (Circle) c1.copy();
```

Since it is tedious to provide such downcasts (which are more or less meaningless), Java provides covariant return types where you can give the derived class of the return type in the overriding method. In other words, you can change the definition of copy method in Circle class as follows:

```
public Circle copy() { /* return a copy of this object */ }
```

Now the assignment in the main method Circle c2 = c1.copy(); is valid and no explicit downcast is needed (which is good).

Overriding equals() Method

Let's now override equals method in the Point class. Before that, here is the signature of the equals() method in the Object class:

```
public boolean equals(Object obj)
```

The equals() method in the Object class is an overridable method that takes the Object type as an argument. It checks if the contents of the current object and the passed obj argument are equal. If so, the equals() returns true; otherwise it returns false.

Now, let us enhance to code in Listing 2-10 and override override the equals() method in a class named Point (see Listing 2-11). Is this a correct implementation?

Listing 2-11. Point.java

```
public class Point {
        private int xPos, yPos;

        public Point(int x, int y) {
                xPos = x;
                yPos = y;
        }
```

```
        // override the equals method to perform
        // "deep" comparison of two Point objects
        public boolean equals(Point other){
                if(other == null)
                        return false;
                // two points are equal only if their x and y positions are equal
                if( (xPos == other.xPos) && (yPos == other.yPos) )
                        return true;
                else
                        return false;
        }

        public static void main(String []args) {
                Point p1 = new Point(10, 20);
                Point p2 = new Point(50, 100);
                Point p3 = new Point(10, 20);
                System.out.println("p1 equals p2 is " + p1.equals(p2));
                System.out.println("p1 equals p3 is " + p1.equals(p3));
        }
}
```

This prints

```
p1 equals p2 is false
p1 equals p3 is true
```

The output is as expected, so is this equals() implementation correct? No! Let's make the following slight modification in the main() method (modifications in this code is highlighted using underline like this):

```
public static void main(String []args) {
        Object p1 = new Point(10, 20);
        Object p2 = new Point(50, 100);
        Object p3 = new Point(10, 20);
        System.out.println("p1 equals p2 is " + p1.equals(p2));
        System.out.println("p1 equals p3 is " + p1.equals(p3));
}
```

Now it prints

```
p1 equals p2 is false
p1 equals p3 is false
```

Why? Both main() methods are equivalent. However, this newer main() method uses the Object type for declaring p1, p2, and p3. The dynamic type of these three variables is Point, so it should call the overridden equals() method. However, the overriding is wrong: The equals() method should have Object as the argument instead of the Point argument! The current implementation of the equals() method in the Point class *hides* (*not* overrides) the equals() method of the Object class. Hence, the main() method calls the base version, which is the default implementation of Point in Object class!

💣 If the name or signature of the base class method and the overriding method don't match, you will cause subtle bugs. So ensure that they are exactly the same.

In order to overcome the subtle problems of overloading, you can use @Override annotation, which was introduced in Java 5. This annotation explicitly expresses to the Java compiler the intention of the programmer to use method overriding. In case the compiler is not satisfied with your overridden method, it will issue a complaint, which is a useful alarm for you. Also, the annotation makes the program more understandable, since the @Override annotation just before a method definition helps you understand that you are overriding a method.

Here is the code with @Override annotation for the equals method:

```
@Override
public boolean equals(Point other) {
        if(other == null)
                return false;
        // two points are equal only if their x and y positions are equal
        if((xPos == other.xPos) && (yPos == other.yPos))
                return true;
        else
                return false;
}
```

You'll get a compiler error now for this code:

```
Point.java:11: error: method does not override or implement a method from a supertype
@Override
^
1 error
```

How can you fix it? You need to pass the Object type to the argument of the equals method. Listing 2-12 shows the program with the fixed equals method.

Listing 2-12. Point.java

```
public class Point {
        private int xPos, yPos;

        public Point(int x, int y) {
                xPos = x;
                yPos = y;
        }

        // override the equals method to perform "deep" comparison of two Point objects
        @Override
        public boolean equals(Object other) {
                if(other == null)
                        return false;
```

```
        // check if the dynamic type of 'other' is Point
        // if 'other' is of any other type than 'Point', the two objects cannot be
        // equal if 'other' is of type Point (or one of its derived classes), then
        // downcast the object to Point type and then compare members for equality
        if(other instanceof Point) {
                Point anotherPoint = (Point) other;
                // two points are equal only if their x and y positions are equal
                if((xPos == anotherPoint.xPos) && (yPos == anotherPoint.yPos))
                        return true;
        }
        return false;
    }

    public static void main(String []args) {
        Object p1 = new Point(10, 20);
        Object p2 = new Point(50, 100);
        Object p3 = new Point(10, 20);
        System.out.println("p1 equals p2 is " + p1.equals(p2));
        System.out.println("p1 equals p3 is " + p1.equals(p3));
    }
}
```

Now this program prints

```
p1 equals p2 is false
p1 equals p3 is true
```

This is the expected output and with the correct implementation of the equals method implementation.

Invoking Superclass Methods

It is often useful to call the base class method inside the overridden method. To do that, you can use the super keyword. In derived class constructors, you can call the base class constructor using the super keyword. Such a call should be the *first statement* in a constructor if it is used. You can use the super keyword for referring to the base class members also. In those cases, it need not be the first statement in the method body. Let's look at an example.

You implemented a Point class that is a 2D-point: it had x and y positions. You can also implement a 3D-point class with x, y, and z positions. For that you do not need to start implementing it from scratch: you can extend the 2D-point and add the z position in the 3D-point class. First, you'll rename the simple implementation of Point class to Point2D. Then you'll create the Point3D class by extending this Point2D (see Listings 2-13 and 2-14).

Listing 2-13. Point2D.java

```
class Point2D {
        private int xPos, yPos;
        public Point2D(int x, int y) {
                xPos = x;
                yPos = y;
        }
```

```
        public String toString() {
                return "x = " + xPos + ", y = " + yPos;
        }

        public static void main(String []args) {
                System.out.println(new Point2D(10, 20));
        }
}
```

Listing 2-14. Point3D.java

```
// Here is how we can create Point3D class by extending Point2D class
public class Point3D extends Point2D {
        private int zPos;

        // provide a public constructors that takes three arguments (x, y, and z values)
        public Point3D(int x, int y, int z) {
                // call the superclass constructor with two arguments
                // i.e., call Point2D(int, int) from Point2D(int, int, int) constructor)
                super(x, y); // note that super is the first statement in the method
                        zPos = z;
        }

        // override toString method as well
        public String toString() {
                return super.toString() + ", z = " + zPos;
        }

        // to test if we extended correctly, call the toString method of a Point3D object
        public static void main(String []args) {
                System.out.println(new Point3D(10, 20, 30));
        }
}
```

This program prints

```
x = 10, y = 20, z = 30
```

In the class Point2D, the class members xPos and yPos are private, so you cannot access them directly to initialize them in the Point3D constructor. However, you can call the superclass constructor using super keyword and pass the arguments. Here, super(x, y); calls the base class constructor Point2D(int, int). This call to the superclass constructor should be the first statement; if you call it after zPos = z;, you'll get a compiler error:

```
public Point3D(int x, int y, int z) {
        zPos = z;
        super(x, y);
}
```

```
Point3D.java:19: call to super must be first statement in constructor
                super(x, y);
```

Similarly, you can invoke the toString() method of the base class Point2D in the toString() implementation of the derived class Point3D using the super keyword.

Overriding the hashCode() Method

Overriding the equals and hashCode methods correctly is important for using with classes such as HashMap and HashSet, which we will discuss further in Chapter 4. Listing 2-15 is a simple Circle class example so you can understand what can go wrong when using collections such as HashSets.

Listing 2-15. TestCircle.java

```java
// This program shows the importance of overriding equals() and hashCode() methods
import java.util.*;

class Circle {
        private int xPos, yPos, radius;
        public Circle(int x, int y, int r) {
                xPos = x;
                yPos = y;
                radius = r;
        }

        public boolean equals(Object arg) {
                if(arg == null) return false;
                if(this == arg) return true;
                if(arg instanceof Circle) {
                        Circle that = (Circle) arg;
                        if( (this.xPos == that.xPos) && (this.yPos == that.yPos)
                                && (this.radius == that.radius )) {
                                return true;
                        }
                }
                return false;
        }
}

class TestCircle {
        public static void main(String []args) {
                Set<Circle> circleList = new HashSet<Circle>();
                circleList.add(new Circle(10, 20, 5));
                System.out.println(circleList.contains(new Circle(10, 20, 5)));
        }
}
```

It prints false (not true)! Why? The Circle class overrides the equals() method, but it doesn't override the hashCode() method. When you use objects of Circle in standard containers, it becomes a problem. For fast lookup, the containers compare hashcode of the objects. If the hashCode() method is not overridden, then—even if an object with same contents is passed—the container will not find that object! So you need to override the hashCode() method.

💣⁎ If you're using an object in containers like HashSet or HashMap, make sure you override the hashCode() and equals() methods correctly. If you don't, you'll get nasty surprises (bugs) while using these containers!

Okay, how do you override the hashCode() method? In the ideal case, the hashCode() method should return unique hash codes for different objects.

The hashCode() method *should* return the same hash value if the equals() method returns true. What if the objects are different (so that the equals() method returns false)? It is better (although not required) for the hashCode() to return different values if the objects are different. The reason is that it is difficult to write a hashCode() method that gives unique value for every different object.

📝 The methods hashCode() and equals() need to be consistent for a class. For practical purposes, ensure that you follow this one rule: the hashCode() method should return the same hash value for two objects if the equals() method returns true for them.

When implementing the hashCode() method, you can use the values of the instance members of the class to create a hash value. Here is a simple implementation of the hashCode() method of the Circle class:

```
public int hashCode() {
        // use bit-manipulation operators such as ^ to generate close to unique
        // hash codes here we are using the magic numbers 7, 11 and 53,
        // but you can use any numbers, preferably primes
        return (7 * xPos) ^ (11 * yPos) ^ (53 * yPos);
}
```

Now if you run the main() method, it prints "true". In this implementation of the hashCode() method, you multiply the values by a prime number as well as bit-wise operation. You can write complex code for hashCode() if you want a better hashing function, but this implementation is sufficient for practical purposes.

You can use bitwise operators for int values. What about other types, like floating-point values or reference types? To give you an example, here is hashCode() implementation of java.awt.Point2D, which has floating point values x and y. The methods getX() and getY() return the x and y values respectively:

```
public int hashCode() {
        long bits = java.lang.Double.doubleToLongBits(getX());
        bits ^= java.lang.Double.doubleToLongBits(getY()) * 31;
        return (((int) bits) ^ ((int) (bits >> 32)));
}
```

This method uses the doubleToLongBits() method, which takes a double value and returns a long value. For floating-point values x and y (returned by the getX and getY methods), you get long values in bits and you use bit-manipulation to get hashCode().

Now, how do you implement the hashCode method if the class has reference type members? For example, consider using an instance of Point class as a member instead of xPos and yPos, which are primitive type fields:

```
class Circle {
        private int radius;
        private Point center;
        // other members elided
}
```

In this case, you can use the hashCode() method of Point to implement Circle's hashCode method:

```
public int hashCode() {
        return center.hashCode() ^ radius;
}
```

Object Composition

Certification Objective

Implement inheritance including visibility modifiers and composition

Individual abstractions offer certain functionalities that need to be combined with other objects to represent a bigger abstraction: a composite object that is made up of other smaller objects. You need to make such composite objects to solve real-life programming problems. In such cases, the composite object shares HAS-A relationships with the containing objects, and the underlying concept is referred to as *object composition*.

By way of analogy, a computer is a composite object containing other objects such as CPU, memory, and a hard disk. In other words, the computer object shares a HAS-A relationship with other objects. Listing 2-16 defines a Circle class that uses a Point object to define Circle's center.

Listing 2-16. Circle.java

```
// Point is an independent class and here we are using it with Circle class
class Point {
        private int xPos;
        private int yPos;
        public Point(int x, int y) {
                xPos = x;
                yPos = y;
        }
        public String toString() {
                return "(" + xPos + "," + yPos + ")";
        }
}

// Circle.java
public class Circle {
        private Point center;    // Circle "contains" a Point object
        private int radius;
```

33

```
        public Circle(int x, int y, int r) {
                center = new Point(x, y);
                radius = r;
        }
        public String toString() {
                return "center = " + center + " and radius = " + radius;
        }

        public static void main(String []s) {
                System.out.println(new Circle(10, 10, 20));
        }
        // other members (constructors, area method, etc) are elided ...
}
```

In this example, Circle has a Point object. In other words, Circle and Point share a has-a relationship; in other words, Circle is a composite object containing a Point object. This is a better solution than having independent integer members xPos and yPos. Why? You can reuse the functionality provided by the Point class. Notice the toString() method in the Circle class:

```
public String toString() {
        return "center = " + center + " and radius = " + radius;
}
```

Here, the use of the variable center expands to center.toString() and hence the toString method of Point can be reused in the Circle's toString method.

Composition vs. Inheritance

You are now equipped with a knowledge of composition as well as inheritance (which we covered earlier in this chapter). In some situations, it's difficult to choose between the two. It's important to remember that nothing is a silver bullet—you cannot solve all problems with one construct. You need to analyze each situation carefully and decide which construct is best suited for it.

A rule of thumb is to use HAS-A and IS-A phrases for composition and inheritance, respectively. For instance,

- A computer HAS-A CPU.

- A circle IS-A shape.

- A circle HAS-A point.

- A laptop IS-A computer.

- A vector IS-A list.

This rule can be useful for identifying wrong relationships. For instance, the relationship of car IS-A tire is completely wrong, which means you cannot have an inheritance relationship between the classes Car and Tire. However, the car HAS-A tire (meaning car has one or more tires) relationship is correct—you can compose a Car object containing Tire objects.

In real scenarios, the relationship distinctions can be nontrivial. You learned that you can make a base class and put the common functionality of many classes in it. However, many people ignore a big caution sign suspended over this practice—always check whether the IS-A relationship exists between the derived classes and the base class. If the IS-A relationship does not hold, it's better to use composition instead of inheritance.

For example, take a set of classes DynamicDataSet and SnapShotDataSet that require a common functionality—say, sorting. Now, one could derive these data set classes from a sorting implementation, as given in Listing 2-17.

Listing 2-17. Sorting.java

```java
import java.awt.List;

public class Sorting {
        public List sort(List list) {
                // sort implementation
                return list;
        }
}

class DynamicDataSet extends Sorting {
        // DynamicDataSet implementation
}

class SnapshotDataSet extends Sorting {
        // SnapshotDataSet implementation
}
```

Do you think this is a good solution? No, it's not a good solution for the following reasons:

- The rule of thumb does not hold here. DynamicDataSet is not a Sorting type. If you make such mistakes in class design, it can be very costly—and you might not be able to fix them later if a lot of code has accumulated that makes the wrong use of inheritance relationships. For example, Stack extends Vector in the Java library. Yet a stack clearly is not a vector, so it could not only create comprehension problems but also lead to bugs. When you create an object of Stack class provided by the Java library, you can add or delete items from anywhere in the container because the base class is Vector, which allows you to delete from anywhere in the vector.

- What if these two types of data set classes have a genuine base class, DataSet? In that case, either Sorting will be the base class of DataSet or one could put the class Sorting in between DataSet and two types of data sets. Both solutions would be wrong.

- There is another challenging issue: what if one DataSet class wants to use one sorting algorithm (say, MergeSort) and another data set class wants to use a different sorting algorithm (say, QuickSort)? Will you inherit from two classes implementing two different sorting algorithms? First, you cannot directly inherit from multiple classes, since Java does not support multiple class inheritance. Second, even if you were able to somehow inherit from two different sorting classes (MergeSort extends QuickSort, QuickSort extends DataSet), that would be an even worse design.

In this case it is best to use composition—in other words, use a HAS-A relationship instead of an IS-A relationship. The resultant code is given in Listing 2-18.

Listing 2-18. Sorting.java

```java
import java.awt.List;

interface Sorting {
        List sort(List list);
}

class MergeSort implements Sorting {
        public List sort(List list) {
                // sort implementation
                return list;
        }
}

class QuickSort implements Sorting {
        public List sort(List list) {
                // sort implementation
                return list;
        }
}

class DynamicDataSet {
        Sorting sorting;
        public DynamicDataSet() {
                sorting = new MergeSort();
        }
        // DynamicDataSet implementation
}

class SnapshotDataSet {
        Sorting sorting;
        public SnapshotDataSet() {
                sorting = new QuickSort();
        }
        // SnapshotDataSet implementation
}
```

Use inheritance when a subclass specifies a base class, so that you can exploit dynamic polymorphism. In other cases, use composition to get code that is easy to change and loosely coupled. In summary, **favor composition over inheritance**.

Singleton and Immutable Classes

Certification Objective

Create and use singleton classes and immutable classes

There are many situations where you need to create special kinds of classes. In this section let us discuss two such special kinds of classes: singletons and immutable classes.

Creating Singleton Class

There are scenarios in which you want to make sure that only one instance is present for a particular class. For example, assume that you defined a class that modifies a registry, or you implemented a class that manages printer spooling, or you implemented a thread-pool manager class. In all these situations, you might want to avoid hard-to-find bugs by instantiating no more than one object of such classes. In these situations, you could create a *singleton* class.

A singleton class ensures that only one instance of that class is created. To ensure point of access, the class controls instantiation of its object. Singleton classes are found in many places in Java Development Kit (JDK), such as `java.lang.Runtime`.

Figure 2-2 shows the class diagram of a singleton class. It comprises a single class, the class that you want to make as a singleton. It has a private constructor and a static method to get the singleton object.

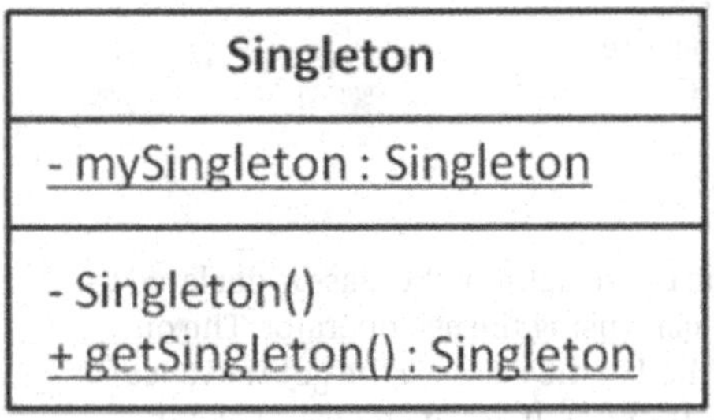

Singleton
- mySingleton : Singleton
- Singleton() + getSingleton() : Singleton

Figure 2-2. UML class diagram of a singleton class

The singleton class offers two things: one and only one instance of the class, and a global single point of access to that object.

Assume that you want to implement a class for logging application details for tracing the application execution for debugging. For this objective, you may want to ensure that only one instance of `Logger` class exists in your application, and hence you can make `Logger` class a singleton class (see Listing 2-19).

Listing 2-19. Logger.java

```java
// Logger class must be instantiated only once in the application; it is to ensure that the
// whole of the application makes use of that same logger instance
public class Logger {
        // declare the constructor private to prevent clients
        // from instantiating an object of this class directly
        private Logger() {     }

        // by default, this field is initialized to null
        // the static method to be used by clients to get the instance of the Logger class
        private static Logger myInstance;

        public static Logger getInstance() {
                if(myInstance == null) {
                        // this is the first time this method is called,
                        // and that's why myInstance is null
                        myInstance = new Logger();
                }
                // return the same object reference any time and
                // every time getInstance is called
                return myInstance;
        }
        public void log(String s) {
                // a trivial implementation of log where
                // we pass the string to be logged to console
                System.err.println(s);
        }
}
```

Look at the singleton implementation of the Logger class. The constructor of the class is declared as private, so you cannot simply create a new instance of the Logger class using the new operator. The only way to get an instance of this class is to call the static member method of the class via the getInstance() method. This method checks whether a Logger object already exists or not. If not, it creates a Logger instance and assigns it to the static member variable. In this way, whenever you call the getInstance() method, it will always return the same object of the Logger class.

Ensuring That Your Singleton Is Indeed a Singleton

It is really important (as well as difficult) to ensure that your singleton implementation allows only instance of the class. For instance, the implementation provided in Listing 2-19 works only if your application is single threaded. In the case of multiple threads, trying to get a singleton object may result in creation of multiple objects, which of course defeats the purpose of implementing a singleton. Listing 2-20 shows a version of the Logger class that implements the singleton design pattern in a multi-threaded environment.

Listing 2-20. Logger.java

```java
public class Logger {
        private Logger() {
                // private constructor to prevent direct instantiation
        }
```

```java
        private static Logger myInstance;
        public static synchronized Logger getInstance() {
                if(myInstance == null)
                        myInstance = new Logger();
                return myInstance;
        }
        public void log(String s){
                // log implementation
                System.err.println(s);
        }
}
```

Note the use of the keyword synchronized in this implementation. This keyword is a Java concurrency mechanism to allow only one thread at a time into the synchronized scope. You will learn more about this keyword in Chapter 11 on concurrency.

So, you made the whole method synchronized in order to make it accessible by only a thread at a time. This makes it a correct solution, but there is a problem: poor performance. You wanted to make this method synchronized only at the first time the method is called, but since you declared the whole method as synchronized, all subsequent calls to this method make it a performance bottleneck.

Listing 2-21 shows another implementation of the Logger class that is based on the "initialization on demand holder" idiom. This idiom uses inner classes and does not use any synchronization construct (we discuss inner classes in Chapter 3). It exploits the fact that inner classes are not loaded until they are referenced.

Listing 2-21. Logger.java

```java
public class Logger {
        private Logger() {
                // private constructor
        }
        public static class LoggerHolder {
                public static Logger logger = new Logger();
        }
        public static Logger getInstance() {
                return LoggerHolder.logger;
        }
        public void log(String s) {
                // log implementation
                System.err.println(s);
        }
}
```

This is an efficient working solution for singletons that works well for multi-threaded applications as well. However, before we close this discussion on singletons, two parting words of caution. First, use singletons wherever it is appropriate, but do not overuse it. Second, make sure that your singleton implementation ensures the creation of only one instance even if your code is multi-threaded.

Immutable Classes

What is an immutable object? Once an object is created and initialized, it cannot be modified. We can call accessor methods (i.e., getter methods), copy the objects, or pass the objects around—but no method should allow modifying the state of the object. Wrapper classes (such as Integer and Float) and String class are well-known examples of classes that are immutable.

Let us now discuss String class. String is immutable: once you create a String object, you cannot modify it. How about methods such as trim that removes leading and trailing whitespace characters–do such methods modify the state of the String object? No. If there are any leading or trailing whitespace characters, the trim method removes them and returns a new String object instead of modifying that String object.

There are many advantages with creating immutable objects. Let us discuss some of these advantages in the context of String class:

- Immutable objects are safer to use than mutable objects. Once you check its value, you can be sure that it remains the same and is not modified behind your back (by some other code). So, it is less error-prone when we use immutable objects. For instance, if you have a reference to a string and found that it has the characters "contents", if you retain that reference and use it later, you can be sure that it still has the characters "contents" in it (because no code can modify it).

- Immutable objects are thread-safe. For instance, a thread can access a String object without worrying if any other thread would change it when it is accessing the object–it cannot happen because a String object is immutable.

- Immutable objects that have same state can save space by sharing the state internally. For example, when the contents are same, String objects share the same contents (known as "string interning"). You can use the intern() method to ascertain that:

```
String str1 = new String("contents");
String str2 = new String("contents");
System.out.println("str1 == str2 is " + (str1 == str2));
System.out.println("str1.intern() == str2.intern() is "
    + (str1.intern() == str2.intern()));

// this code prints:
str1 == str2 is false
str1.intern() == str2.intern() is true
```

Because of the benefits of using immutable objects, Joshua Bloch in his book Effective Java strongly encourages the use of immutable classes: *"Classes should be immutable unless there's a very good reason to make them mutable... If a class cannot be made immutable, you should still limit its mutability as much as possible."*

Defining Immutable Classes

Keep the following aspects in mind for creating your own immutable objects:

- Make the fields final and initialize them in the constructor. For primitive types, the field values are final, there is no possibility of changing the state after it got initialized. For reference types, you cannot change the reference.

- For reference types that are mutable, you need to take of some more aspects to ensure immutability. Why? Even if you make the mutable reference type final it is possible that the members may refer to objects created outside the class or may be referred by others. In this case,

  - Make sure that the methods don't change the contents inside those mutable objects.

  - Don't share the references outside the classes–for example, as a return value from methods in that class. If the references to fields that are mutable are accessible from code outside the class, they can end up modifying the contents of the object.

  - If you must return a reference, return the deep copy of the object (so that the original contents remain intact even if the contents inside the returned object is changed).

- Provide only accessor methods (i.e., getter methods) but don't provide mutator methods (i.e., setter methods)

  - In case changes must be made to the contents of the object, create a new immutable object with the necessary changes and return that reference.

- Declare the class final. Why? If the class is inheritable, methods in its derived class can override them and modify the fields.

Because the final keyword is mentioned as an exam topic under the title "Advanced Class Design", we cover it in the next chapter (Chapter 3); please review that section if you are not familiar with using final keyword.

Let us now review the String class to understand how these aspects of taken care in its implementation:

- All its fields are made private. The String constructors initialize the fields.

- There are methods such as trim, concat, and substring that need to change the contents of the String object. To ensure immutability, such methods return new String objects with modified contents.

- The String class is final, so you cannot extend it and override its methods.

Here is a circle class that is immutable. For brevity, this example shows only the relevant methods for illustrating how to define an immutable class (Listing 2-22).

Listing 2-22. ImmutableCircle.java

```java
// Point is a mutable class
class Point {
    private int xPos, yPos;

    public Point(int x, int y) {
        xPos = x;
        yPos = y;
    }

    public String toString() {
        return "x = " + xPos + ", y = " + yPos;
    }
}
```

```
        int getX() { return xPos; }
        int getY() { return yPos; }
}

// ImmutableCircle is an immutable class - the state of its objects
// cannot be modified once the object is created

public final class ImmutableCircle {
        private final Point center;
        private final int radius;
        public ImmutableCircle(int x, int y, int r) {
                center = new Point(x, y);
                radius = r;
        }
        public String toString() {
                return "center: " + center + " and radius = " + radius;
        }
        public int getRadius() {
                return radius;
        }
        public Point getCenter() {
                // return a copy of the object to avoid
                // the value of center changed from code outside the class
                return new Point(center.getX(), center.getY());
        }
        public static void main(String []s) {
                System.out.println(new ImmutableCircle(10, 10, 20));
        }
        // other members are elided ...
}
```

This program prints

```
center: x = 10, y = 10 and radius = 20
```

Note the following aspects in the definition of the ImmutableCircle class:

- The class is declared final to prevent inheritance and overriding of its methods

- The class has only final data members and they are private

- Because center is a mutable field, the getter method getCenter() returns a copy of the Point object

Immutable objects also have certain drawbacks. To ensure immutability, methods in immutable classes may end-up creating numerous copies of the objects. For instance, every time getCenter() is called on the ImmutableCircle class, this method creates a copy of the Point object and returns it. For this reason, we may need to define a mutable version of the class as well, for example, a mutable Circle class.

The String class is useful in most scenarios, if we call methods such as trim, concat, or substring in a loop, these methods are likely to create numerous (temporary) String objects. Fortunately, Java provides StringBuffer and StringBuilder classes that are not mutable. They provide functionality similar to String, but you can mutate the contents within the objects. Hence, depending on the context, we can choose to use String class or one of StringBuffer or StringBuilder classes.

Using the "static" Keyword

Certification Objective

Develop code that uses static keyword on initialize blocks, variables, methods, and classes

Now let us discuss how you can use static keyword in different ways in Java. Suppose you wanted a write a simple class that counts the number of objects of its class type created so far. Will the program in Listing 2-23 work?

Listing 2-23. Counter.java

```java
// Counter class should count the number of instances created from that class
public class Counter {
        private int count; // variable to store the number of objects created
        // for every Counter object created, the default constructor will be called;
        // so, update the counter value inside the default constructor
        public Counter() {
                count++;
        }
        public void printCount() { // method to print the counter value so far
                System.out.println("Number of instances created so far is: " + count);
        }
        public static void main(String []args) {
                Counter anInstance = new Counter();
                anInstance.printCount();
                Counter anotherInstance = new Counter();
                anotherInstance.printCount();
        }
}
```

The output of the program is

```
Number of instances created so far is: 1
Number of instances created so far is: 1
```

Oops! From the output, it is clear that the class does not keep track of the number of objects created. What happened?

You've used an *instance variable* count to keep track of the number of objects created from that class. Since every instance of the class has the value count, it always prints 1! What you need is a variable that can be shared across all its instances. This can be achieved by declaring a variable static. A static variable is associated with its class rather than its object or instance; hence they are known as *class variables*. A static variable is initialized only once when execution of the program starts. A static variable shares its state with all instances of the class. You access a static variable using its class name (instead of an instance). Listing 2-24 shows the correct implementation of the Counter class with both the count variable and the printCount method declared static.

Listing 2-24. Counter.java

```java
// Counter class should count the number of instances created from that class
public class Counter {
        private static int count; // variable to store the number of objects created
        // for every Counter object created, the default constructor will be called;
        // so, update the counter value inside the default constructor
        public Counter() {
                count++;
        }
        public static void printCount() { // method to print the counter value so far
                System.out.println("Number of instances created so far is: " + count);
        }
        public static void main(String []args) {
                Counter anInstance = new Counter();
                // note we call printCount using the class name
                // instead of instance variable name
                Counter.printCount();
                Counter anotherInstance = new Counter();
                Counter.printCount();
        }
}
```

This program prints

```
Number of instances created so far is: 1
Number of instances created so far is: 2
```

Here, the static variable count is initialized when the execution started. At the time of first object creation, the count is incremented to one. Similarly, when the second object got created, the value of the count became 2. As the output of the program shows, both objects updated the same copy of the count variable.

Note how we changed the call to printCount() to use class name Counter, as in Counter. printCount(). The compiler will accept the previous two calls of anInstance.printCount() and anotherInstance.printCount() as there is no semantic difference between calling a static method using a class name or instance variable name. However, to use instance variables to call static methods is not recommended. It is conventional practice to call instance methods using instance variables and to call static methods using class names.

A static method can only access static variables and can call only static methods. In contrast, an instance method (nonstatic) may call a static method or access a static variable.

Static Block

Apart from static variables and methods, you can also define a *static block* in your class definition. This static block will be executed by JVM when it loads the class into memory. For instance, in the previous example, you can define a static block to initialize the count variable to default 1 instead of the default value 0, as shown in Listing 2-25.

Listing 2-25. Counter.java

```java
public class Counter {
        private static int count;
        static {
                // code in this static block will be executed when
                // the JVM loads the class into memory
                count = 1;
        }
        public Counter() {
                count++;
        }
        public static void printCount() {
                System.out.println("Number of instances created so far is: " + count);
        }
        public static void main(String []args) {
                Counter anInstance = new Counter();
                Counter.printCount();
                Counter anotherInstance = new Counter();
                Counter.printCount();
        }
}
```

This program prints

```
Number of instances created so far is: 2
Number of instances created so far is: 3
```

Do not confuse a static block with a constructor. A constructor will be invoked when an instance of the class is created, while the static block will be invoked when the JVM loads the corresponding class.

Points to Remember

- The main() method, where the main execution of the program starts, is always declared static. Why? If it were an instance method, it would be impossible to invoke it. You'd have to start the program to be able to create an instance and then call the method, right?

- You cannot override a static method provided in a base class. Why? Based on the instance type, the method call is resolved with runtime polymorphism. Since static methods are associated with a class (and not with an instance), you cannot override static methods, and runtime polymorphism is not possible with static methods.

- A static method cannot use the this keyword in its body. Why? Remember that static methods are associated with a class and not an instance. Only instance methods have an implicit reference associated with them; hence class methods do not have a this reference associated with them.

- A static method cannot use the super keyword in its body. Why? You use the super keyword for invoking the base class method from the overriding method in the derived class. Since you cannot override static methods, you cannot use the super keyword in its body.

- Since static methods cannot access instance variables (nonstatic variables), they are most suited for utility functions. That's why there are many utility methods in Java. For example, all methods in the `java.lang.Math` library are static.

- Calling a static method is considered to be slightly more efficient compared to calling an instance method. This is because the complier need not pass the implicit `this` object reference while calling a static method, unlike an instance method.

Summary

Let us briefly review the key points from each certification objective in this chapter. Please read it before appearing for the exam.

Implement encapsulation

- *Encapsulation*: Combining data and the functions operating on it as a single unit.

- You cannot access the *private* methods of the base class in the derived class.

- You can access the *protected* method either from a class in the same package (just like package private or default) as well as from a derived class.

- You can also access a method with a *default access modifier* if it is in the same package.

- You can access *public* methods of a class from any other class.

Implement inheritance including visibility modifiers and composition

- *Inheritance*: Creating hierarchical relationships between related classes. Inheritance is also called an *"IS-A" relationship*.

- You use the `super` keyword to call base class methods.

- Inheritance implies IS-A and composition implies HAS-A relationship.

- Favor composition over inheritance.

Implement polymorphism

- *Polymorphism*: Interpreting the same message (i.e., method call) with different meanings depending on the context.

- Resolving a method call based on the dynamic type of the object is referred to as *runtime polymorphism*.

- Overloading is an example of *static polymorphism* (*early binding*) while overriding is an example of *dynamic polymorphism* (*late binding*).

- *Method overloading*: Creating methods with same name but different types and/or numbers of parameters.

- You can have *overloaded constructors*. You can call a constructor of the same class in another constructor using the `this` keyword.

- *Overload resolution* is the process by which the compiler looks to resolve a call when overloaded definitions of a method are available.

- In *overriding*, the name of the method, number of arguments, types of arguments, and return type should match exactly.

- In *covariant return types*, you can provide the derived class of the return type in the overriding method.

Override hashCode, equals, and toString methods from Object class

- You can override clone(), equals(), hashCode(), toString() and finalize() methods in your classes. Since getClass(), notify(), notifyAll(), and the overloaded versions of wait() method are declared final, you cannot override these methods.

- If you're using an object in containers like HashSet or HashMap, make sure you override the hashCode() and equals() methods correctly. For instance, ensure that the hashCode() method returns the same hash value for two objects if the equals() method returns true for them.

Create and use singleton classes and immutable classes

- A singleton ensures that only one object of its class is created.

- Making sure that an intended singleton implementation is indeed singleton is a nontrivial task, especially in a multi-threaded environment.

- Once an immutable object is created and initialized, it cannot be modified.

- Immutable objects are safer to use than mutable objects; further, immutable objects are thread safe; further, immutable objects that have same state can save space by sharing the state internally.

- To define an immutable class, make it final. Make all its fields private and final. Provide only accessor methods (i.e., getter methods) but don't provide mutator methods. For fields that are mutable reference types, or methods that need to mutate the state, create a deep copy of the object if needed.

Develop code that uses static keyword on initialize blocks, variables, methods, and classes

- There are two types of member variables: class variables and instance variables. All variables that require an instance (object) of the class to access them are known as *instance variables*. All variables that are shared among all instances and are associated with a class rather than an object are referred to as *class variables* (declared using the static keyword).

- All static members do not require an instance to call/access them. You can directly call/access them using the class name.

- A static member can call/access only a static member of the same class.

QUESTION TIME

1. What will be the output of this program?

```java
class Color {
    int red, green, blue;

    void Color() {
        red = 10;
        green = 10;
        blue = 10;
    }

    void printColor() {
        System.out.println("red: " + red + " green: " + green + " blue: " +
        blue);
    }

    public static void main(String [] args) {
        Color color = new Color();
        color.printColor();
    }
}
```

A. Compiler error: no constructor provided for the class

B. Compiles fine, and when run, it prints the following: red: 0 green: 0 blue: 0

C. Compiles fine, and when run, it prints the following: red: 10 green: 10 blue: 10

D. Compiles fine, and when run, crashes by throwing NullPointerException

2. Consider the following program and predict the behavior of this program:

```java
class Base {
    public void print() {
        System.out.println("Base:print");
    }
}

abstract class Test extends Base { //#1
    public static void main(String[] args) {
        Base obj = new Base();
        obj.print(); //#2
    }
}
```

A. Compiler error "an abstract class cannot extend from a concrete class" at statement marked with comment #1

B. Compiler error "cannot resolve call to print method" at statement marked with comment #2

C.   The program prints the following: `Base:print`

D.   The program will throw a runtime exception of
     `AbstractClassInstantiationException`

3.   Consider the following program:

```java
class Base {}
class DeriOne extends Base {}
class DeriTwo extends Base {}

class ArrayStore {
    public static void main(String []args) {
        Base [] baseArr = new DeriOne[3];
        baseArr[0] = new DeriOne();
        baseArr[2] = new DeriTwo();
        System.out.println(baseArr.length);
    }
}
```

Which one of the following options correctly describes the behavior of this program?

A.   This program prints the following: 3

B.   This program prints the following: 2

C.   This program throws an `ArrayStoreException`

D.   This program throws an `ArrayIndexOutOfBoundsException`

4.   Determine the output of this program:

```java
class Color {
    int red, green, blue;

    Color() {
        Color(10, 10, 10);
    }

    Color(int r, int g, int b) {
        red = r;
        green = g;
        blue = b;
    }

    void printColor() {
        System.out.println("red: " + red + " green: " + green + " blue: " +
        blue);
    }

    public static void main(String [] args) {
        Color color = new Color();
        color.printColor();
    }
}
```

A. Compiler error: cannot find symbol

B. Compiles without errors, and when run, it prints: red: 0 green: 0 blue: 0

C. Compiles without errors, and when run, it prints: red: 10 green: 10 blue: 10

D. Compiles without errors, and when run, crashes by throwing
    `NullPointerException`

5. Choose the correct option based on this code segment:

```
class Rectangle { }
class ColoredRectangle extends Rectangle { }
class RoundedRectangle extends Rectangle { }
class ColoredRoundedRectangle extends ColoredRectangle, RoundedRectangle { }
```

Choose an appropriate option:

A. Compiler error: '{' expected cannot extend two classes

B. Compiles fine, and when run, crashes with the exception
    `MultipleClassInheritanceException`

C. Compiler error: class definition cannot be empty

D. Compiles fine, and when run, crashes with the exception
    `EmptyClassDefinitionError`

6. Consider the following program and determine the output:

```
class Test {
    public void print(Integer i) {
            System.out.println("Integer");
    }
    public void print(int i) {
            System.out.println("int");
    }
    public void print(long i) {
            System.out.println("long");
    }
    public static void main(String args[]) {
            Test test = new Test();
                test.print(10);
    }
}
```

A. The program results in a compiler error ("ambiguous overload")

B. `long`

C. `Integer`

D. `int`

7. Consider the following code and choose the right option for the word <access-modifier>:

```
// Shape.java
public class Shape {
    protected void display() {
        System.out.println("Display-base");
    }
}

// Circle.java
public class Circle extends Shape {
    <access-modifier> void display(){
        System.out.println("Display-derived");
    }
}
```

   A. Only protected can be used

   B. Public and protected both can be used

   C. Public, protected, and private can be used

   D. Only public can be used

8. Which of the following method(s) from Object class can be overridden? (Select all that apply.)

   A. finalize() method

   B. clone() method

   C. getClass() method

   D. notify() method

   E. E.wait() method

9. Choose the correct option based on the following program:

```
class Color {
    int red, green, blue;

    Color() {
        this(10, 10, 10);
    }

    Color(int r, int g, int b) {
        red = r;
        green = g;
        blue = b;
    }

    public String toString() {
        return "The color is: " + red + green + blue;
    }
```

```
        public static void main(String [] args) {
                System.out.println(new Color());
        }
}
```

A. Compiler error: incompatible types

B. Compiles fine, and when run, it prints the following: The color is: 30

C. Compiles fine, and when run, it prints the following: The color is: 101010

D. Compiles fine, and when run, it prints the following: The color is:
    red green blue

10. Choose the best option based on the following program:

```
class Color {
    int red, green, blue;

    Color() {
            this(10, 10, 10);
    }

    Color(int r, int g, int b) {
            red = r;
            green = g;
            blue = b;
      }

      String toString() {
          return "The color is: " + " red = " + red + " green = " + green + "
          blue = " + blue;
      }

      public static void main(String [] args) {
          // implicitly invoke toString method
          System.out.println(new Color());
      }
}
```

A. Compiler error: attempting to assign weaker access privileges; toString was
    public in Object

B. Compiles fine, and when run, it prints the following: The color is: red = 10
    green = 10 blue = 10

C. Compiles fine, and when run, it prints the following: The color is: red = 0
    green = 0 blue = 0

D. Compiles fine, and when run, it throws ClassCastException

Answers:

1. B. Compiles fine, and when run, it prints the following: red: 0 green: 0 blue: 0

    Remember that a constructor does not have a return type; if a return type is provided, it is treated as a method in that class. In this case, since Color had void return type, it became a method named Color() in the Color class, with the default Color constructor provided by the compiler. By default, data values are initialized to zero, hence the output.

2. C. The program prints the following: Base:print

    It is possible for an abstract class to extend a concrete class, though such inheritance often doesn't make much sense. Also, an abstract class can have static methods. Since you don't need to create an object of a class to invoke a static method in that class, you can invoke the main() method defined in an abstract class.

3. C. This program throws an ArrayStoreException

    The variable baseArr is of type Base[], and it points to an array of type DeriOne. However, in the statement baseArr[2] = new DeriTwo(), an object of type DeriTwo is assigned to the type DeriOne, which does not share a parent-child inheritance relationship-they only have a common parent, which is Base. Hence, this assignment results in an ArrayStoreException.

4. A. Compiler error: cannot find symbol

    The compiler looks for the method Color() when it reaches this statement: Color(10, 10, 10);. The right way to call another constructor is to use the this keyword as follows: this(10, 10, 10);.

5. A. Compiler error: '{' expected – cannot extend two classes

    Java does not support multiple class inheritance. Since ColoredRectangle and RoundedRectangle are classes, it results in a compiler error when ColoredRoundedRectangle class attempts to extend these two classes. Note that it is acceptable for a class to be empty.

6. D. int

    If Integer and long types are specified, a literal will match to int. So, the program prints int.

7. B. Public and protected both can be used

    You can provide only a less restrictive or same-access modifier when overriding a method.

8. A. finalize() method and B. clone() method

    The methods finalize() and clone() can be overridden. The methods getClass(), notify(), and wait() are final methods and so cannot be overridden.

9. C. Compiles fine, and when run, it prints the following: The color is: 101010

The `toString()` implementation has the expression "The color is:" + red + blue + green. Since the first entry is String, the + operation becomes the string concatenation operator with resulting string "The color is: 10". Following that, again there is a concatenation operator + and so on until finally it prints "The color is: 101010".

10. A. Compiler error: attempting to assign weaker access privileges; `toString` was public in `Object`

No access modifier is specified for the `toString()` method. `Object`'s `toString()` method has a public access modifier; you cannot reduce the visibility of the method. Hence, it will result in a compiler error.

CHAPTER 3

Advanced Class Design

You learned the basic concepts of OOP and used them to build Java programs in the preceding chapter. In this chapter, you will learn advanced class design concepts. You will also learn about the key functional programming feature introduced in Java 8: lambda expressions.

Certification Objectives

Develop code that uses abstract classes and methods

Develop code that uses final keyword

Create inner classes including static inner class, local class, nested class, and anonymous inner class

Use enumerated types including methods and constructors in an enum type

Develop code that declares, implements, and/or extends interfaces and use the atOverride annotation

Create and use Lambda expressions

You learned the basic concepts of OOP and used them to build Java programs in the preceding chapter. In this chapter, you will learn advanced class design concepts. You will also learn about the key functional programming feature introduced in Java 8: lambda expressions.

A significant chunk of questions in the OCPJP exam is related to changes introduced in the Java language and the library in Java 8. This chapter covers lambda expressions, which form the foundation for understanding Stream API and the facilities available in the `java.util.function` package. Hence, ensure that you read the interfaces section and the last section on lambda expressions in this chapter.

Abstract Classes

Certification Objective

Develop code that uses abstract classes and methods

In many programming situations, you want to specify an abstraction without specifying implementation-level details. In such cases, you can use either *abstract classes* or *interfaces*. Abstract classes are used when you want to define an abstraction with some common functionality.

Consider Shape class that provides an abstraction of the different shapes you can draw in a drawing application.

```
abstract class Shape {
    public double area() { return 0; } // default implementation
    // other members
}
```

You prefix the abstract keyword before the class definition to declare the class as an abstract class. You can create objects of Shapes such as Square and Circle, but does it make sense to create an object of Shape class itself directly? No, there is no real-world object named Shape.

If you try to create an instance of a Shape class, the compiler will give an error because abstract classes cannot be instantiated.

In the Shape class definition, there is a method named area() that returns the area of a particular shape. This method is applicable for all shapes, and that's why it's in this base class Shape. However, what should the implementation of the area() method in the Shape class be? You cannot provide a default implementation; implementing this method as return 0; is a bad solution, although the compiler would happily accept it. A better solution is to declare it as an abstract method, like so:

```
public abstract double area(); // note: no implementation (i.e., no method body definition)
```

Similar to declaring a class abstract, you declare the method area() as abstract by prefixing the method with the abstract keyword. The main difference between a normal method and an abstract method is that you don't provide a body for an abstract method. If you provide a body, it will become an error, like so:

```
public abstract double area() { return 0; } // compiler error!
```

You get a compiler error for this definition: "abstract methods cannot have a body". An abstract method declaration forces all the subclasses to provide a definition of that abstract method and that is why it cannot be defined in the abstract class itself. If a derived class does not implement all the abstract methods defined in the base class, then that derived class should be declared as an abstract class, as in the following example:

```
abstract class Shape {
    public abstract double area(); // no implementation
    // other members
}

class Rectangle extends Shape { }
```

This snippet results in a compiler error of "Rectangle is not abstract and does not override abstract method area() in Shape". To fix this, you need to declare the derived class abstract or provide a definition of the area() method in the derived class. It does not make sense to declare Rectangle as abstract; so you can define the area() method like so:

```
class Rectangle extends Shape {
    private int length, height;
    public double area() { return length * height; }
        // other members ...
}
```

Points to Remember

Review the following points about abstract classes and abstract methods for the OCPJP 8 exam:

- The abstract keyword can be applied to a class or a non-static method.

- An abstract class may have methods or fields declared static. However, the abstract keyword cannot be applied to fields or static methods.

- An abstract class can extend another abstract class or can implement an interface.

- An abstract class can be derived from a concrete class! Although the language allows it, it is not a good idea to do so.

- An abstract class need not declare an abstract method, which means it is not necessary for an abstract class to have any methods declared as abstract. However, if a class has an abstract method, it should be declared as an abstract class.

- A subclass of an abstract class needs to provide implementation of all the abstract methods; otherwise you need to declare that subclass as an abstract class.

Using the "final" Keyword

Certification Objective

Develop code that uses final keyword

The final keyword can be applied for classes, methods, and variables. You cannot extend a final class, you cannot override a final method, and you cannot change the value of a final variable once it is initialized.

Final Classes

A final class is a *non-inheritable class*—that is to say, if you declare a class as final, you cannot subclass it. Two important reasons you may not want to allow a class to be subclassed are:

1. *To prevent a behavior change by subclassing.* In some cases, you may think that the implementation of the class is complete and should not change. If overriding is allowed, then the behavior of methods might be changed. You know that a derived object can be used where a base class object is required, and you may not prefer it in some cases. By making a class final, the users of the class are assured the unchanged behavior.

2. *Improved performance.* All method calls of a final class can be resolved at compile time itself. As there is no possibility of overriding the methods, it is not necessary to resolve the actual call at runtime for final classes, which translates to improved performance. For the same reason, final classes encourage the inlining of methods. With inlining, a method body can be expanded as part of the calling code itself, thereby avoiding the overhead of making a function call. If the calls are to be resolved at runtime, they cannot be inlined.

In the Java library, many classes are declared as final; for example, the String (java.lang.String) and System (java.lang.System) classes. These classes are used extensively in Java programs. If these two classes are not declared final, it is possible for someone to change the behavior of these classes by subclassing and then the whole program can start behaving differently. To avoid such a problem, widely used classes like these and wrapper classes such as Number and Integer are made final in the Java library.

The performance gain from making a class final is modest; the focus should be on using final where it is appropriate. The OCPJP 8 exam will mainly check whether you know how to correctly use the final keyword. You don't have to worry about efficiency details.

Final Methods and Variables

In a class, you may declare a method final. The final method cannot be overridden. Therefore, if you have declared a method as final in a non-final class, then you can extend the class but you cannot override the final method. However, other non-final methods in the base class can be overridden in the derived class implementation.

Consider the methods setParentShape() and getParentShape() in Shape class (Listing 3-1).

Listing 3-1. Shape.java

```java
public abstract class Shape {
    // other class members elided
    final public void setParentShape(Shape shape) {
        // method body
    }
    public Shape getParentShape() {
        // method body
    }
}
```

In this case, the Circle class (subclass of Shape) can override only getParentShape(); if you try to override the final method, you will get following error: "Cannot override the final method from Shape".

Final variables are like CD-ROMs: once you write something on them, you cannot write again. In programming, constants such as PI can be declared as final since you don't want anyone to modify their values. If you try to change a final variable after initialization, you will get a compiler error.

Points to Remember

Review the following points, as they may come up in the OCPJP 8 exam:

- The final modifier can be applied to a class, method, or variable. All methods of a final class are implicitly final (hence non-overridable).

- A final variable can be assigned only once. If a variable declaration defines a variable as final but did not initialize it, then it is referred to as blank final. You need to initialize a blank final in all the constructors you have defined in the class or in an initialization block.

- The keyword final can be applied to parameters. The value of a final parameter cannot be changed once assigned.

Flavors of Nested Classes

Certification Objective

Create inner classes including static inner class, local class, nested class, and anonymous inner class

Classes defined within the body of another class (or interface) are known as *nested classes*. Typically you define a class, which is a top-level class directly belonging to a package. In contrast, nested classes are classes contained within another class or interface.

What is the benefit of creating classes inside another class or interface? There are several benefits. First, you can put related classes together as a single logical group. Second, nested classes can access all class members of the enclosing class, which might be useful in certain cases. Third, nested classes simplify code. For example, anonymous inner classes are useful for writing simpler event-handling code with AWT/Swing.

There are four types or *flavors* of nested classes in Java:

- Static nested class

- Inner class

- Local inner class

- Anonymous inner class

The distinctions among these four flavors are not evident at first sight. Figure 3-1 helps clarify the differences between them. A *local class* is defined within a code block (whether a method, constructor, or initialization block), whereas a *non-local class* is defined inside a class. A *static class* is qualified using the static keyword, whereas a *non-static class* does not use the static keyword with the class definition. In an *anonymous class*, you don't provide the name of the class; you just define its body.

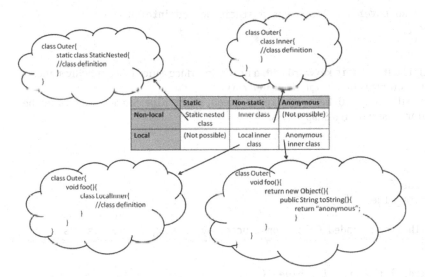

Figure 3-1. *Types of nested classes with examples*

As you can observe in Figure 3-1, *static nested classes* are static and non-local, whereas *inner classes* are non-static and non-local. A non-static and local nested class is a *local inner class*, and a local and anonymous nested class is an *anonymous inner class*.

Now, let's discuss each of these four flavors in more detail.

Static Nested Classes (or Interfaces)

You can define a class (or an interface) as a static member inside another class (or interface). Since the outer type can be a class or an interface and the inner ones can also be a class or interface, there are four combinations. The following are examples of these four types so that you can see their syntax:

```
class Outer {              // an outer class has a static nested class
    static class Inner {}
}

interface Outer {          // an outer interface has a static nested class
    static class Inner {}
}

class Outer {              // an outer class has a static nested interface
    static interface Inner {}
}

interface Outer {          // an outer interface has a static nested interface
    static interface Inner {}
}
```

You don't have to explicitly use the static keyword with a nested interface, since it is implicitly static. Now, let's look at an example that creates and uses static nested classes.

Consider the Color class (Listing 3-2) with fields of m_red, m_green, and m_blue. Since all shapes can be colored, you can define the Color class within a Shape class.

Listing 3-2. TestColor.java

```
abstract class Shape {
    public static class Color {
        int m_red, m_green, m_blue;
        public Color() {
            // call the other overloaded Color constructor by passing default values
            this(0, 0, 0);
        }
        public Color(int red, int green, int blue) {
            m_red = red; m_green = green; m_blue = blue;
        }
        public String toString() {
            return " red = " + m_red + " green = " + m_green + " blue = " + m_blue;
        }
        // other color members elided
    }
    // other Shape members elided
}
```

```
public class TestColor {
    public static void main(String []args) {
        // since Color is a static nested class,
        // we access it using the name of the outer class, as in Shape.Color
        // note that we do not (and cannot) instantiate Shape class for using Color class
        Shape.Color white = new Shape.Color(255, 255, 255);
        System.out.println("White color has values:" + white);
    }
}
```

It prints

```
White color has:  red = 255 green = 255 blue = 255
```

In this code, the Shape class is declared abstract. You can see the Color class defined as a public static class defined within the Shape class. The TestColor class uses the syntax Shape.Color to refer to this class. Other than this minor difference, the Color class looks no different from defining the Color class outside the Shape class. Hence, a static nested class is as good as a class defined as an outer class with one difference—it is physically defined inside another class!

Points to Remember

Here are some notable aspects of static nested classes (and interfaces) that will help you on the OCPJP 8 exam:

- The accessibility (public, protected, etc.) of the static nested class is defined by the outer class.

- The name of the static nested class is expressed with OuterClassName.NestedClassName syntax.

- When you define an inner nested class (or interface) inside an interface, the nested class is declared implicitly public and static. This point is easy to remember: any field in an interface is implicitly declared public and static, and static nested classes have this same behavior.

- Static nested classes can be declared abstract or final.

- Static nested classes can extend another class or they can be used as base classes.

- Static nested classes can have static members. (As you'll see shortly, this statement does not apply to other kinds of nested classes.)

- Static nested classes can access the members of the outer class (only static members, obviously).

- The outer class can also access the members (even private members) of the nested class through an object of a nested class. If you don't declare an instance of the nested class, the outer class cannot access nested class elements directly.

Inner Classes

You can define a class (or an interface) as a non-static member inside another class. How about declaring a class or an interface inside an interface? As you just saw in the third bullet above about static inner classes, when you define a class or an interface inside an interface, it is implicitly static. So, it is not possible to declare a non-static inner interface! That leaves two possibilities:

```
class Outer {            // an outer class has an inner class
     class Inner {}
}

class Outer {            // an outer class has an inner interface
     interface Inner {}
}
```

Let's create a Point class to implement the center of a Circle. Since you want to associate each Circle with a center Point, it is a good idea to make Point an inner class of Circle (Listing 3-3).

Listing 3-3. Circle.java

```java
public class Circle {
    // define Point as an inner class within Circle class
    class Point {
        private int xPos;
        private int yPos;
        // you can provide constructor for an inner class like this
        public Point(int x, int y) {
            xPos = x;
            yPos = y;
        }
        // the inner class is like any other class - you can override methods here
        public String toString() {
            return "(" + xPos + "," + yPos + ")";
        }
    }

    // make use of the inner class for declaring a field
    private Point center;
    private int radius;
    public Circle(int x, int y, int r) {
        // note how to make use of the inner class to instantiate it
        center = this.new Point(x, y);
        radius = r;
    }

    public String toString() {
        return "mid point = " + center + " and radius = " + radius;
    }
```

```
    public static void main(String []s) {
        System.out.println(new Circle(10, 10, 20));
    }
    // other methods such as area are elided
}
```

In this implementation, you have defined Point as a private member of Circle. Notice how you are instantiating the inner class:

```
center = this.new Point(x, y);
```

You might be wondering why you cannot use the usual new statement:

```
center = new Point(x, y);
```

You need to prefix the object reference of the outer class to create an instance of the inner class. In this case, it is a this reference, so you are prefixing it with this before the new operator.

✎ Every inner class is associated with an instance of the outer class. In other words, an inner class is always associated with an enclosing object.

The outer and inner classes share a special relationship, like friends or members of same family. Member accesses are valid irrespective of the access specifiers such as private. However, there is subtle difference. You can access members of an outer class within an inner class without creating an instance; but this is not the case with an outer class. You need to create an instance of inner class in order to access the members (*any* members, including private members) of the inner class.

One limitation of inner classes is that you cannot declare static members in an inner class, like this:

```
class Outer {
    class Inner {
        static int i = 10;
    }
}
```

If you try to do so, you'll get the following compiler error:

```
Outer.java:3: inner classes cannot have static declarations
            static int i = 10;
```

Points to Remember

Here are some important rules about inner classes and interfaces that might prove useful in the OCPJP 8 exam:

- The accessibility (public, protected, etc.) of the inner class is defined by the outer class.

- Just like top-level classes, an inner class can extend a class or can implement interfaces. Similarly, other classes can extend an inner class, and other classes or interfaces can extend or implement an inner interface.

- An inner class can be declared final or abstract.

- Inner classes can have inner classes, but you'll have a hard time reading or understanding such complex nesting of classes. (Meaning: Avoid them!)

Local Inner Classes

A *local inner class* is defined in a code block (say, in a method, constructor, or initialization block). Unlike static nested classes and inner classes, local inner classes are not members of an outer class; they are just local to the method or code in which they are defined.

Here is an example of the general syntax of a local class:

```
class SomeClass {
        void someFunction() {
                class Local { }
        }
}
```

As you can see in this code, Local is a class defined within someFunction. It is not available outside of someFunction, not even to the members of the SomeClass. Since you cannot declare a local variable static, you also cannot declare a local class static.

Since you cannot define methods in interfaces, you cannot have local classes or interfaces inside an interface. Nor can you create local interfaces. In other words, you cannot define interfaces inside methods, constructors, and initialization blocks.

Now that you understand the syntax, let's jump into a practical example. Earlier, you implemented the Color class as a static nested class (Listing 3-2). Here is the code you saw in that discussion:

```
abstract class Shape {
        public static class Color {
                int m_red, m_green, m_blue;
                public Color() {
                        this(0, 0, 0);
                }
                public Color(int red, int green, int blue) {
                        m_red = red; m_green = green; m_blue = blue;
                }
                public String toString() {
                        return " red = " + m_red + " green = " + m_green + " blue = " +
                        m_blue;
                }
                // other color members elided
        }
        // other Shape members elided
}
```

Now, this toString() method displays a string representation of Color. Assume that you want to display the Color string in the following format: "You selected a color with RGB values red = 0 green = 0 blue = 0". For that, you must define a method named getDescriptiveColor() in the class StatusReporter. In getDescriptiveColor(), you must create a derived class of Shape.Color in which the toString method returns this descriptive message. Listing 3-4 is an implementation using local classes.

Listing 3-4. StatusReporter.java

```java
class StatusReporter {
    // important to note that the argument "color" is declared final
    static Shape.Color getDescriptiveColor(final Shape.Color color) {
        // local class DescriptiveColor that extends Shape.Color class
        class DescriptiveColor extends Shape.Color {
            public String toString() {
                return "You selected a color with RGB values" + color;
            }
        }
        return new DescriptiveColor();
    }

    public static void main(String []args) {
        Shape.Color descriptiveColor =
                        StatusReporter.getDescriptiveColor(new Shape.Color(0, 0, 0));
        System.out.println(descriptiveColor);
    }
}
```

The main method checks if the StatusReporter works fine. This program prints

You selected a color with RGB values red = 0 green = 0 blue = 0

Let's see how the local class was defined. The getDescriptiveColor() method takes the plain Shape.Color class object and returns a Shape.Color object. Inside the getDescriptiveColor() method, you have defined the class DescriptiveColor, which is local to this method. This DescriptiveColor is a derived class of Shape.Color. Inside the DescriptiveColor class, the only method defined is the toString() method, which overrides the base class Shape.Color toString() method. After the definition of the DescriptiveColor class, the getDescriptiveColor class creates an object of the DescriptiveColor class and returns it.

In the Test class, you can see a main() method that just calls the StatusReporter.getDescriptiveColor() method and stores the result in a Shape.Color reference. You will notice that the getDescriptiveColor() method returns a DescriptiveColor object, which derives from Shape.Color, so the descriptiveColor variable initialization works fine. In the println, the dynamic type of descriptiveColor is a DescriptiveColor object, and hence the detailed description of the color object is printed.

Did you notice another feature in the getDescriptiveColor() method? Its argument is declared final. Even if you don't provide the final keyword, the compiler will treat is as *effectively final*—what it means is you cannot assign to the variable that you are accessing in the local class. If you do so, you will get a compiler error, as in:

```java
static Shape.Color getDescriptiveColor(Shape.Color color) {
    // local class DescriptiveColor that extends Shape.Color class
    class DescriptiveColor extends Shape.Color {
        public String toString() {
                return "You selected a color with RGB values" + color;
        }
    }
    color = null; // note this assignment - will NOT compile
    return new DescriptiveColor();
}
```

You'll get the following compiler error:

```
StatusReporter.java:8: error: local variables referenced from an inner class must be final
or effectively final
return "You selected a color with RGB values" + color;
        ^
1 error
```

Because of the assignment to the color variable, it is not final anymore and hence the compiler gives an error when the local inner class tries to access that variable.

✎ You can pass only **final** variables to a local inner class. If you don't declare a variable that a local inner class accesses, the compiler will treat it as *effectively final*.

Points to Remember

The following points about local classes may come up in the OCPJP 8 exam:

- You can create a non-static local class inside a body of code. Interfaces cannot have local classes, and you cannot create local interfaces.

- Local classes are accessible only from the body of the code in which the class is defined. The local classes are completely inaccessible outside the body of the code in which the class is defined.

- You can extend a class or implement interfaces while defining a local class.

- A local class can access all the variables available in the body of the code in which it is defined. Variables accessed by local inner classes are considered effectively final.

Anonymous Inner Classes

As the name implies, an *anonymous inner class* does not have a name. The declaration of the class automatically derives from the instance-creation expression. They are also referred to simply as *anonymous classes*.

An anonymous class is useful in almost all situations where you can use a local inner class. A local inner class has a name, whereas an anonymous inner class does not—and that's the main difference. An additional difference is that an anonymous inner class cannot have any explicit constructors. A constructor is named after the name of the class, and since an anonymous class has no name, it follows that you cannot define a constructor!

(A note here before we proceed: there are no such things as "anonymous interfaces.")

Here is an example to understand the syntax of a local class:

```
class SomeClass {
    void someFunction() {
        new Object() { };
    }
}
```

This code looks cryptic, doesn't it? What is going on here? In the statement new Object() { };, you are declaring a derived class of Object directly using the new keyword. It doesn't define any code and returns an instance of that derived object. The created object is not used anywhere, so it is ignored. The new expression invokes the default constructor here; you could choose to invoke a multiple argument constructor of the base class by passing arguments in the new expression.

Let us now look at a more practical example. In the earlier example (Listing 3-4), you saw the DescriptiveColor class defined inside the getDescriptiveColor method in the StatusReporter class. You can simplify the code by converting the local class into an anonymous class, as shown in Listing 3-5.

Listing 3-5. StatusReporter.java

```java
class StatusReporter {
    static Shape.Color getDescriptiveColor(final Shape.Color color) {

        // note the use of anonymous inner classes here
        // -- specifically, there is no name for the class and we construct
        // and use the class "on the fly" in the return statement!

        return new Shape.Color() {
            public String toString() {
                return "You selected a color with RGB values" + color;
            }
        };
    }
    public static void main(String []args) {
        Shape.Color descriptiveColor =
                        StatusReporter.getDescriptiveColor(new Shape.Color(0, 0, 0));
        System.out.println(descriptiveColor);
    }
}
```

It prints

```
You selected a color with RGB values red = 0 green = 0 blue = 0
```

That's nice. The rest of the program, including the main() method, remains the same and the getDescriptiveColor() method became simpler! You did not explicitly create a class with a name (which was DescriptiveColor); instead you just created a derived class of Shape.Color "on the fly" in the return statement. Note that the keyword class is also not needed.

Points to Remember

Note these points about anonymous classes that may be useful for the OPCJP 8 exam:

- Anonymous classes are defined in the new expression itself.

- You cannot explicitly extend a class or explicitly implement interfaces when defining an anonymous class.

Enum Data Type

Certification Objective

Use enumerated types including methods, and constructors in an enum type

Consider that you want the user to choose from a set of constants defining several printer types:

```
public static final int DOTMATRIX = 1;
public static final int INKJET = 2;
public static final int LASER= 3;
```

The solution works. In this case, however, you could pass any other integer (say 10), and the compiler would happily take it. Therefore, this solution is not a *typesafe solution*. Java 5 introduced the data type *enum* to help you in such situations.

Listing 3-6 defines an enum class (yes, enums are special classes) for the above example.

Listing 3-6. EnumTest.java

```
// define an enum for classifying printer types
enum PrinterType {
    DOTMATRIX, INKJET, LASER
}

// test the enum now
public class EnumTest {
    PrinterType printerType;

    public EnumTest(PrinterType pType) {
        printerType = pType;
    }

    public void feature() {
        // switch based on the printer type passed in the constructor
        switch(printerType){
        case DOTMATRIX:
                System.out.println("Dot-matrix printers are economical and almost
                obsolete");
                break;
        case INKJET:
                System.out.println("Inkjet printers provide decent quality prints");
                break;
        case LASER:
                System.out.println("Laser printers provide best quality prints");
                break;
        }
    }
}
```

```
    public static void main(String[] args) {
        EnumTest enumTest = new EnumTest(PrinterType.LASER);
        enumTest.feature();
    }
}
```

It prints

```
Laser printers provide best quality prints
```

Let's review the Listing 3-6 in more detail.

- In a switch-case statement, you do not need to provide the fully qualified name for enum elements. This is because switch takes an instance of the enum type, and hence switch-case understands the context (type) in which you are specifying enum elements.

- We have provided the value PrinterType.LASER when creating the enum object EnumTest. If we provide any other values other than enumeration values, you will get a compiler error. In other words, enumerations are typesafe.

Note that you can declare an enum (PrinterType in this case) in a separate file, just like you can declare any other normal Java class.

Let us now look at a more detailed example in which you define member attributes and methods in an enum data type (Listing 3-7).

Listing 3-7. EnumTest.java

```
enum PrinterType {
    DOTMATRIX(5), INKJET(10), LASER(50);

    private int pagePrintCapacity;

    private PrinterType(int pagePrintCapacity) {
        this.pagePrintCapacity = pagePrintCapacity;
    }

    public int getPrintPageCapacity() {
        return pagePrintCapacity;
    }
}

public class EnumTest {
    PrinterType printerType;

    public EnumTest(PrinterType pType) {
        printerType = pType;
    }

    public void feature() {
        switch (printerType) {
        case DOTMATRIX:
                System.out.println("Dot-matrix printers are economical");
                break;
```

```
            case INKJET:
                    System.out.println("Inkjet printers provide decent quality prints");
                    break;
            case LASER:
                    System.out.println("Laser printers provide the best quality prints");
                    break;
            }
            System.out.println("Print page capacity per minute: " +
                            printerType.getPrintPageCapacity());
    }

    public static void main(String[] args) {
        EnumTest enumTest1 = new EnumTest(PrinterType.LASER);
        enumTest1.feature();
        EnumTest enumTest2 = new EnumTest(PrinterType.INKJET);
        enumTest2.feature();
    }
}
```

The output of the above program is given below:

```
Laser printers provide the best quality prints
Print page capacity per minute: 50
Inkjet printers provide decent quality prints
Print page capacity per minute: 10
```

In this program, you defined a new attribute, a new constructor, and a new method for the enum class. The attribute pagePrintCapacity is set by the initial values specified with enum elements (such as LASER(50)), which calls the constructor of the enum class. However, the enum class cannot have a public constructor, or the compiler will complain with following message: "Illegal modifier for the enum constructor; only private is permitted".

 A constructor in an enum class can only be specified as private.

Points to Remember

- Enums are implicitly declared public, static, and final, which means you cannot extend them.

- When you define an enumeration, it implicitly inherits from java.lang.Enum. Internally, enumerations are converted to classes. Further, enumeration constants are instances of the enumeration class for which the constant is declared as a member.

- You can apply the valueOf() and name() methods to the enum element to return the name of the enum element.

- If you declare an enum within a class, then it is by default static.

- You cannot use the new operator on enum data types, even inside the enum class.

- You can compare two enumerations for equality using == operator.

- If enumeration constants are from two different enumerations, the equals() method does not return true.

- When an enumeration constant's toString() method is invoked, it prints the name of the enumeration constant.

- The static values() method in the Enum class returns an array of the enumeration constants when called on an enumeration type.

- Enumeration constants cannot be cloned. An attempt to do so will result in a CloneNotSupportedException.

Enum avoids magic numbers, which improves readability and understandability of the source code. Also, enums are typesafe constructs. Therefore, use enums wherever you need a set of related constants.

Interfaces

Develop code that declares, implements, and/or extends interfaces and use the atOverride annotation

---

An interface is a set of abstract methods that defines a protocol (i.e., a contract for conduct). Classes that implement an interface must implement the methods specified in the interface. An interface defines a protocol, and a class implementing the interface honors the protocol. In other words, an interface promises certain functionality to its clients by defining an abstraction. All the classes implementing the interface provide their own implementations for the promised functionality.

Declaring and Implementing Interfaces

Now it's time to implement your own interface for shape objects. Some circular shaped objects (such as Circle and Ellipse) can be *rolled* to a given degree. You can create a Rollable interface and declare a method named roll():

```
interface Rollable {
    void roll(float degree);
}
```

As you can see, you define an interface using the interface keyword that declares a method named roll(). The method takes one argument: the degree for rolling. Now let us implement this interface in a Circle class (see Listing 3-8).

Listing 3-8. Circle.java

```java
// Shape is the base class for all shape objects; shape objects that are associated with
// a parent shape object is remembered in the parentShape field
abstract class Shape {
    abstract double area();
    private Shape parentShape;
    public void setParentShape(Shape shape) {
        parentShape = shape;
    }
    public Shape getParentShape() {
        return parentShape;
    }
}

// Rollable interface can be implemented by circular shapes such as Circle
interface Rollable {
    void roll(float degree);
}

abstract class CircularShape extends Shape implements Rollable { }

// Circle is a concrete class that is-a subtype of CircularShape;
// you can roll it and hence implements Rollable through CircularShape base class
public class Circle extends CircularShape {
    private int xPos, yPos, radius;
    public Circle(int x, int y, int r) {
        xPos = x;
        yPos = y;
        radius = r;
    }
    public double area() { return Math.PI * radius * radius; }
    @Override
    public void roll(float degree) {
        // implement rolling functionality here...
        // for now, just print the rolling degree to console
        System.out.printf("rolling circle by %f degrees", degree);
    }
    public static void main(String[] s) {
        Circle circle = new Circle(10,10,20);
        circle.roll(45);
    }
}
```

In this case, CircularShape implements the Rollable interface and extends the Shape abstract class. Now a concrete class such as Circle can extend this abstract class and define the roll() method. Few important points to observe in this example are:

- The abstract class CircularShape implements the Rollable interface but does not need to define the roll() method. The concrete class Circle that extends CircularShape defines this method later.

- You use the `implements` keyword for implementing an interface. Note that the method name, its argument, and the return type in the class definition should exactly match the one given in the interface; if they don't match, the class is not considered to implement that interface.

- Optionally, you can use the `@Override` annotation to indicate that a method is overriding a method from its base type(s). In this case, the roll method is overridden in the `Circle` class and makes use of the `@Override` annotation.

A class can also implement multiple interfaces at the same time—both directly and indirectly through its base classes. For example, the `Circle` class can also implement the standard `Cloneable` interface (for creating copies of the `Circle` object) and the `Serializable` interface (for storing the object in files to recreate the object later, etc.), like so:

```
class Circle extends CircularShape implements Cloneable, Serializable {
        /* definition of methods such as clone here */
}
```

Points to Remember

Here are some key points about interfaces that will help you in the OCPJP 8 exam:

- An interface cannot be instantiated. A reference to an interface can refer to an object of any of its derived types implementing it.

- An interface can extend another interface. Use the `extends` (and not the `implements`) keyword for extending another interface.

- Interfaces cannot contain instance variables. If you declare a data member in an interface, it should be initialized, and all such data members are implicitly treated as "`public static final`" members.

- An interface can have three kinds of methods: abstract methods, default methods, and static methods.

- An interface can be declared with empty body (i.e., an interface without any members). For example, `java.util` defines the interface `EventListener` without a body.

- An interface can be declared within another interface or class; such interfaces are known as nested interfaces.

- Unlike top-level interfaces that can have only `public` or `default` access, a nested interface can be declared `public`, `protected`, or `private`.

- If you are implementing an interface in an abstract class, the abstract class does not need to define the method. But, ultimately a concrete class has to define the abstract method declared in the interface.

- You can use the `@Override` annotation for a method to indicate that it is overriding a method from its base type(s).

Abstract Classes vs. Interfaces

Abstract classes and interfaces have a lot in common. For example, both can declare methods that all the deriving classes should define. They are also similar in the respect that you can create instances neither of an abstract class nor of an interface. So, what are the differences between abstract classes and interfaces? Table 3-1 lists some of the important differences.

Table 3-1. *Abstract Classes v.s Interfaces*

	Abstract Classes	Interfaces
Keyword(s) used	Use the `abstract` and `class` keywords to define a class.	Use the `interface` keyword to define an interface.
Keyword used by the implementing class	Use the `extends` keyword to inherit from an abstract class.	Use the `implements` keyword to implement an interface.
Fields	An abstract class can have static and non-static fields.	You cannot have non-static fields (instance variables) in an interface; all fields are public static final by default (i.e., constants as discussed in next item)
Constants	An abstract class can have both static and non-static constants.	Interfaces can have only static constants. If you declare a field, it must be initialized. All fields are implicitly considered to be `public static` and `final`.
Constructors	You can define a constructor in an abstract class (which is useful for initializing fields, for example).	You cannot declare/define a constructor in an interface.
Access specifiers	You can have private and protected members in an abstract class.	You cannot have any private or protected members in an interface; all members are public by default.
Single vs. multiple inheritance	A class can inherit only one class (which can be either an abstract or a concrete class).	A class can implement any number of interfaces.
Purpose	An abstract base class provides a protocol; in addition, it serves as a base class in an is-a relationship.	An interface provides only a protocol. It specifies functionality that must be provided by the classes implementing it.

Abstract, default and static methods

The `Rollable` example you saw has only one method—`roll()`. However, it is common for interfaces to have multiple methods. For example, `java.util` defines the `Iterator` interface as follows:

```
public interface Iterator<E> {
        boolean hasNext();

        E next();
```

```
    default void remove() {
        throw new UnsupportedOperationException("remove");
    }

    default void forEachRemaining(Consumer<? super E> action) {
        Objects.requireNonNull(action);
        while (hasNext())
            action.accept(next());
    }
}
```

This interface is meant for traversing a collection. (Don't worry about the "<E>" in Iterator<E>. It refers to the element type and falls under *generics*, which we cover in detail in the next chapter). It declares two methods hasNext() and next()—the classes that implement this interface must define these two methods. There is no need to use the abstract keyword (but if you want, you can provide the abstract keyword) because methods without a body are implicitly considered to be abstract.

The interface also has method definitions for remove() and forEachRemaining(). These methods are known as *default methods* and they are qualified using the default keyword. The classes that implement the Iterator interface inherit these two methods and can choose to override them.

An interface can also contain static methods. For example, the java.util.stream.Stream has static methods builder, empty, of, iterate, generate, and concat.

Prior to Java 8, interfaces can only declare methods (i.e., they can provide only abstract methods). To support lambda functions, Java 8 has introduced a big change to interfaces: you can now define default methods and static methods inside interfaces.

Default methods

In interfaces, default methods are methods defined with a method body using the default keyword. Default methods are instance methods. Inside the default methods, this keyword refers to the declaring interface. Default methods can call methods from the interfaces they are enclosed in.

Why did Java 8 add default methods to interfaces? Short answer: for supporting lambda expressions (we will discuss lambdas in the next section). Default methods make it easy to evolve interfaces. How? Prior to Java 8, you cannot define methods—you can only declare them. Hence, if you add a new method in an existing interface, such an addition would break the classes implementing the interface since they will not have defined that method. But in Java 8, with default methods, it is possible to evolve interfaces more easily.

Consider the java.lang.Iterable interface for example. Prior to Java 8, it had only one method:

```
Iterator<T> iterator();
```

With Java 8, the Iterable interface has been extended with two more methods: forEach and spliterator methods. To avoid breaking classes that implement this interface, these methods are defined as default methods. So all the classes that implement the Iterable interface (such as ArrayList class) now have these two methods as well. Here is the definition of Iterable interface without documentation comments.

```java
public interface Iterable<T> {
        Iterator<T> iterator();

        default void forEach(Consumer<? super T> action) {
                Objects.requireNonNull(action);
                for (T t : this) {
                        action.accept(t);
                }
        }

        default Spliterator<T> spliterator() {
                return Spliterators.spliteratorUnknownSize(iterator(), 0);
        }
}
```

The addition of forEach and spliterator methods in this interface does not break the existing classes that implement the Iterator interface because they are default methods. In this way, default methods aid in evolution of interfaces. Default methods also simplify your life because concrete definitions can now be provided within interfaces—so you don't need to override them.

Many of the classes in the existing library (especially Collections) have been added with default methods in Java 8. For example, the List interface in Java has these three methods that were added in Java 8:

```java
default void     sort(Comparator<? super E> c)
default Spliterator<E>  spliterator()
default void     replaceAll(UnaryOperator<E> operator)
```

Points to Remember

Here are some key points about abstract, default, and static methods that will help you in the OCPJP 8 exam:

- You cannot declare members as protected or private. Only public access is allowed for members of an interface. Since all methods are public by default, you can omit the public keyword.

- All methods declared in an interface (i.e., without a method body) are implicitly considered to be abstract. If you want, you can explicitly use the abstract qualifier for the method.

- Default methods must have a method body. Default methods must be qualified using the default keyword. The classes implementing the interface inherit the default method definitions and they can be overridden.

- A default method can be overridden in a derived class as an abstract method; for such overriding, the @Override annotation can also be used.

- You cannot qualify default methods as synchronized or final.

- Static methods must have a method body and they are qualified using the static keyword.

- You cannot provide `abstract` keyword for static methods: Remember that you cannot override static methods in derived classes, so it's conceptually not possible to leave static methods abstract by not providing a method body.

- You cannot use `default` keyword for static methods because all default methods are instance methods.

The Diamond Problem

In Java, an interface or class can extend multiple interfaces. For example, here is a class hierarchy from `java.nio.channels` package (Figure 3-2). The base interface is `Channel`. Two interfaces, `ReadableByteChannel` and `WriteableByteChannel`, extend this base interface. Finally, `ByteChannel` interface extends `ReadableByteChannel` and `WriteableByteChannel`. Notice that the resulting shape of the inheritance hierarchy looks like a "diamond."

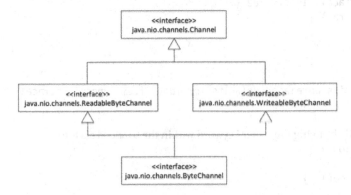

Figure 3-2. *Diamond hierarchy in java.nio.channels package*

In this case, the base interface `Channel` does not have any methods. The `ReadableByteChannel` interface declares read method and the `WriteableByteChannel` interface declares write method; the `ByteChannel` interface inherits both read and write methods from these base types. Since these two methods are different, we don't have a conflict and hence this hierarchy is fine.

But what if we have two method definitions in the base types that have the same signature; which method would the `ByteChannel` interface inherit? When this problem occurs it is known as "diamond problem."

Before we discuss a working example of dealing with the diamond problem, let us first get a clear understanding of when and how the diamond problem occurs in Java.

- In Java, you cannot extend multiple classes; hence the diamond problem cannot occur because of extending two base classes. However, the diamond problem can occur in the derived class when an abstract class and an interface define a method with same signature.

- When two base interfaces have abstract methods with the same signature, it does not really cause the "diamond problem" because they are method declarations and not definitions (as in the case prior to Java 8).

- Interfaces can only define methods and not fields (they can only contain constants). Hence, the diamond problem does not occur for fields in interfaces; it occurs only for method definitions.

Fortunately, rules are available to resolve methods when a derived type inherits method definitions with the same name from different base types. Let us discuss two important scenarios here.

Scenario 1: If two super interfaces define methods with the same signature, the compiler will issue an error. We have to resolve the conflict manually (Listing 3-9).

Listing 3-9. Diamond.java

```java
interface Interface1 {
    default public void foo() { System.out.println("Interface1's foo"); }
}

interface Interface2 {
    default public void foo() { System.out.println("Interface2's foo"); }
}

public class Diamond implements Interface1, Interface2 {
    public static void main(String []args) {
        new Diamond().foo();
    }
}
```

```
Error:(9, 8) java: class Diamond inherits unrelated defaults for foo() from types Interface1
and Interface2
```

In this case, resolve the conflict manually by using the super keyword within the Diamond class to explicitly mention which method definition to use:

```java
public void foo() { Interface1.super.foo(); }
```

After this method definition is added in the Diamond class and executed, this program prints:

```
Interface1's foo
```

Scenario 2: If a base class and a base interface define methods with the same signature, the method definition in the class is used and the interface definition is ignored (Listing 3-10).

Listing 3-10. Diamond.java

```java
class BaseClass {
    public void foo() { System.out.println("BaseClass's foo"); }
}

interface BaseInterface {
    default public void foo() { System.out.println("BaseInterface's foo"); }
}

public class Diamond extends BaseClass implements BaseInterface {
    public static void main(String []args) {
        new Diamond().foo();
    }
}
```

No compiler error in this case: the compiler resolves to the definition in the class and the interface definition is ignored. This program prints "Base foo". This can be considered as "class wins" rule. This rule helps maintain compatibility with versions prior to Java 8. How? When a new default method is added in an interface, it may happen to have the same signature as a method defined in a base class. By resolving the conflict by "class wins" rule, the method from the base class will always be selected.

Functional Interfaces

There are numerous interfaces in Java library that declare a single abstract method; few such interfaces are:

```
// in java.lang package
interface Runnable { void run(); }

// in java.util package
interface Comparator<T> { boolean compare(T x, T y); }

// java.awt.event package:
interface ActionListener { void actionPerformed(ActionEvent e); }

// java.io package
interface FileFilter { boolean accept(File pathName); }
```

Java 8 has introduced the concept of "functional interfaces" that formalizes this idea. A functional interface specifies only one abstract method. Since functional interfaces specify only one abstract method, they are sometimes known as Single Abstract Method (SAM) type or interface.

Note: Functional interfaces can take generic parameters, as in the Comparator<T> and Callable<T> interfaces in the above examples. We cover generics in the next chapter (Chapter 4).

A declaration of a functional interface results in a "functional interface type" that can be used with lambda expressions. Further, functional interfaces are extensively used in java.util.function and java.util.stream packages that were introduced in Java 8. Given the importance of this topic, you can expect many questions related to functional interfaces in your OCPJP 8 exam.

For an interface to be treated as a functional interface, it should have only one abstract method. However, it may have any number of default or static methods defined in it. Let us see a couple of examples from the Java library to understand this.

Here is the definition of java.util.function.IntConsumer interface (without annotations and javadoc comments):

```
public interface IntConsumer {
    void accept(int value);
    default IntConsumer andThen(IntConsumer after) {
        Objects.requireNonNull(after);
        return (int t) -> { accept(t); after.accept(t); };
    }
}
```

Though this interface has two members, andThen method is a default method and only accept method is an abstract method. Hence, IntConsumer interface is a functional interface.

To give another example, java.util.function.Predicate is a functional interface because it has only one abstract method:

```
boolean test(T t)
```

But it is important to note that Predicate also has the following default method definitions:

```
default Predicate<T> and(Predicate<? super T> other)
default Predicate<T> negate()
default Predicate<T> or(Predicate<? super T> other)
```

Further, it also has the definition of a static method isEqual:

```
static <T> Predicate<T> isEqual(Object targetRef)
```

Given all these method definitions, Predicate is still a functional interface because it has only one abstract method test.

@FunctionalInterface annotation

The Java compiler infers any interface with a single abstract method to be a functional interface. However, you can tag functional interface with @FunctionalInterface annotation to affirm that. It is a recommended practice to provide @FunctionalInterface to functional interfaces because the compiler can give better errors/warnings when you have this annotation.

Here is an example of using @FunctionalInterface that has one abstract method, so it will compile cleanly:

```
@FunctionalInterface
public abstract class AnnotationTest {
        abstract int foo();
}
```

How about this one?

```
@FunctionalInterface
public interface AnnotationTest {
        default int foo() {};
}
```

It results in a compiler error "no abstract method found in interface" because it only has a default method provided but does not have any abstract methods. How about this one?

```
@FunctionalInterface
public interface AnnotationTest { /* no methods provided */ }
```

This interface does not have any methods. Since it lacks an abstract method, but is annotated with @FunctionalInterface, it results in a compiler error.

Here is another variation:

```
@FunctionalInterface
public interface AnnotationTest {
        int foo();
        int bar();
}
```

This code also results in a compiler error "multiple non-overriding abstract methods found" because it has more than one abstract method when a functional interface requires providing exactly one abstract method.

METHODS FROM OBJECT CLASS IN FUNCTIONAL INTERFACES

According to Java Language Specification (version 8.0), "interfaces do not inherit from Object, but rather implicitly declare many of the same methods as Object." If you provide an abstract method from Object class in the interface, it still remains a functional interface.

For example, consider the Comparator interface that declares two abstract methods:

```
@FunctionalInterface
public interface Comparator<T> {
        int compare(T o1, T o2);
        boolean equals(Object obj);
        // other methods are default methods or static methods and are elided
}
```

This interface is a functional interface though it declares two abstract methods: compare() and equals() methods. How is it a functional interface when it has two abstract methods? Because equals() method signature matches from Object, and the compare() method is the only remaining abstract method, and hence the Comparator interface is a functional interface.

How about this interface definition?

```
@FunctionalInterface
interface EqualsInterface {
        boolean equals(Object obj);
}
```

The compiler gives the error: "EqualsInterface is not a functional interface: no abstract method found in interface EqualsInterface". Why? Since the method equals is from Object, it is not considered as a functional interface.

Points to Remember

Here are some key points about functional interfaces that will help you in the OCPJP 8 exam:

- Annotate functional interfaces with @FunctionalInterface. Without that, if the functional interface is improper (e.g., it has two abstract methods), the compiler will not issue any errors.

- You can use the @FunctionalInterface annotation only for interfaces and not for classes, enums, and so on.

- A derived interface can be a functional interface if it has only one abstract method or inherits only one abstract method.

- For a functional interface, declaring methods from Object class in an interface does not count as an abstract method.

Lambda Functions

Certification Objectives

Create and use Lambda expressions

One of the major new language features in Java 8 is lambda function. In fact, it is one of the biggest changes since Java 1 release. Lambdas are widely used in the programming language world including the languages that compile to the Java platform. For instance, Groovy language compiles to the Java platform and has a very good support for lambda functions (also known as closures). Oracle decided to bring lambdas to the mainstream language on the JVM—the Java language itself—with Java 8.

LAMBDA FUNCTION RELATED CHANGES IN JAVA 8

Introduction of lambdas required coordinated changes in the language, library, and the VM implementation:

- The arrow operator ("->") for defining lambda functions, the double colon operator ("::") used for method references, and the default keyword

- The streams library and the integration of the collections library with streams

- Lambda functions are implemented using the invokedynamic instruction introduced in Java 7

To support introduction of lambdas into the language, the type inference has also been strengthened in Java 8. Lambdas enabled library writers to create parallel algorithms in the library to exploit inherent parallelism in the modern hardware (i.e., multi cores).

In Java 8, java.util has been considerably enhanced using lambda functions, which we discuss in the next chapter (Chapter 4). Java 8 has added two new packages java.util.function and java.util.streams. We will discuss types in java.util.function in Chapter 5 and java.util.streams (known as Stream API) in Chapter 6.

Lambdas can significantly change the way you design and write code. Why? *Lambdas support functional* programming *paradigm*—that means learning and using lambdas would mean a paradigm shift to you. But you don't need to worry about making a major shift—Java seamlessly integrates functional capabilities with the existing object oriented features and you can gradually shift to using more and more functional features in your programs.

In functional programming paradigm, lambda functions can be stored in variables, passed as arguments to other functions, or returned from other functions just like primitive types and reference variables. Since "lambda functions" are pieces of code that can be passed around, you can consider that the functional paradigm supports "code-as-data." The ability to pass around "executable code segments" enhances the expressive power of Java.

Lambda Functions: Syntax

A lambda function consistss of optional parameters, the arrow token, and the body:

```
LambdaParameters -> LambdaBody
```

- `LambdaParameters` are parameters to the lambda function are passed within opening parenthesis "(" and closing parenthesis ")". When more than one parameter is passed, they are separated by commas.

- The arrow operator. To support lambdas, Java has introduced a new operator "->", also known as lambda operator or arrow operator. This arrow operator is required because we need to syntactically separate the parameter from the body.

- `LambdaBody` can be an expression or a block. The body could consist of single statement (in that case no explicit curly braces defining a block are required); such a lambda body is known as "expression lambda." If there are many statements in a lambda body, they need to be in a block of code; such a lambda body is known as "block lambda."

Compiler performs type inference for lambda expressions:

- The compiler infers the type of the parameters if you do not specify the type parameters in a lambda function definition. When you specify the type of parameters, you need to specify all or none; or else you will get a compiler error.

- You can omit the parenthesis if there is only one parameter. But in this case, you cannot provide the type explicitly. You should leave it to the compiler to infer the type of that single parameter.

- The return type of the lambda function is inferred from the body. If any of the code in the lambda returns a value, then all the paths should return a value; or else you will get a compiler error.

Some examples of valid lambda expressions (assuming that relevant functional interfaces are available):

- `(int x) -> x + x`
- `x -> x % x`
- `() -> 7`
- `(int arg1, int arg2) -> (arg1 + arg2) / (arg1 - arg2)`

Examples of invalid lambda expressions:

- -> 7

    // if no parameters, then empty parenthesis () must be provided

- (arg1, int arg2) -> arg1 / arg2

    // if argument types are provided, then it should be should be provided
    // for all the arguments, or none of them

Lambda Function—An Example

Let us get started with a simple "hello world" example for lambda functions (Listing 3-11).

Listing 3-11. FirstLambda.java

```
interface LambdaFunction {
    void call();
}

class FirstLambda {
    public static void main(String []args) {
        LambdaFunction lambdaFunction = () -> System.out.println("Hello world");
        lambdaFunction.call();
    }
}
```

When executed, this program prints

```
Hello world
```

In this program, the interface LambdaFunction declares an abstract method named call(); hence it is a functional interface. Inside the main method in FirstLambda class, a lambda function is assigned to a variable of the functional interface type LambdaFunction.

```
LambdaFunction lambdaFunction = () -> System.out.println("Hello world");
```

Here, the expression () -> System.out.println("Hello world") is a lambda expression:

- The syntax () indicates no parameters.

- The arrow operator "->" separates method parameters from the lambda body.

- The statement System.out.println("Hello world") is the body of the lambda expression.

How does the lambda expression relate to the functional interface LambdaFunction? It is through the single abstract method inside the LambdaFunction interface: void call(). The signature of this abstract method and the lambda expression must match:

- The lambda expression has () indicating it has no parameters—it matches with the call method that takes no parameters.

- The statement System.out.println("Hello world") is the body of the lambda expression. This body serves as an implementation of the lambda function.

- There is no return statement in this lambda expression body and hence the compiler infers the return type of this expression as void type—that matches with the return type of the call method.

The next statement lambdaFunction.call(); invokes the lambda function. As a result of this function call, "Hello world" is printed on the console.

Why should the function type of the lambda function match that of the abstract method in the given functional interface? It is for type checking. If the types don't match, you will get a compiler error, as in:

```
LambdaFunction lambdaFunction = (int i) -> System.out.println("Hello world");
```

Because this lambda expression has an integer argument but the call() method in LambdaFunction does not take any arguments, the compiler gives an error: "incompatible types: incompatible parameter types in lambda expression".

Block Lambdas

A block lambda is enclosed within a code block within "{" and "}", as in:

```
LambdaFunction lambdaFunction = (int i) -> { System.out.println("Hello world"); }
```

Block lambdas are useful when you want to provide more than one statement in the lambda body (in a lambda expression, you can have only one statement). Further, in a block lambda, you can provide an explicit return statement (see Listing 3-12).

Listing 3-12. BlockLambda.java

```
class BlockLambda {
    interface LambdaFunction {
        String intKind(int a);
    }
    public static void main(String []args) {
        LambdaFunction lambdaFunction =
                (int i) -> {
                        if((i % 2)  == 0) return "even";
                        else return "odd";
                };
        System.out.println(lambdaFunction.intKind(10));
    }
}
```

It prints:

even

In this code, we have defined a block lambda. We are returning a String from this lambda block and we are using explicit return statements. When defining block lambdas, we should ensure that return statements are provided for all the paths, as in this case (otherwise, you will get a compiler error). The return statements should match with the return type for the abstract method defined in the corresponding functional interface (in this case, it is String return type for intKind function in the LambdaFunction interface).

Anonymous Inner Classes vs. Lambda Expressions

Prior to Java 8, as Java programmers we are used to writing anonymous inner classes. Listing 3-13 is equivalent to the earlier program (Listing 3-11) except that it uses anonymous inner classes instead of lambda functions.

Listing 3-13. AnonymousInnerClass.java

```java
interface Function {
    void call();
}

class AnonymousInnerClass {
    public static void main(String []args) {
        Function function = new Function() {
            public void call() {
                System.out.println("Hello world");
            }
        };
        function.call();
    }
}
```

The functionality is the same in Listing 3-11 and Listing 3-12, but using anonymous inner classes results in verbose code whereas lambda expressions are concise.

One way to think about lambdas is "anonymous function" or "unnamed function": they are functions without a name and are not associated with any class. Specifically, they are NOT static or instance members of the class in which they are defined. If you use this keyword inside a lambda function, it refers to the object in the scope in which the lambda is defined.

Effectively Final Variables

Lambda functions can refer to local variables from the enclosing scope. The variable needs to be explicitly declared final or that variable will be treated as *effectively final*. Effectively final means that the compiler treats the variable as a final variable and will issue an error if we try to modify it within the lambda function or in the rest of the function. This behavior of lambdas is similar to accessing variables in outer scope from local and anonymous classes. The variables they access are also considered effectively final (as we discussed earlier).

Here is an example. Have you heard of "Pig Latin"? It is a game that children play by changing the words or adding suffixes to create words to create strange sounding words. In this example, let us simply add the suffix "ay" to a word (Listing 3-14).

Listing 3-14. PigLatin.java

```java
interface SuffixFunction {
    void call();
}

class PigLatin {
    public static void main(String []args) {
        String word = "hello";
        SuffixFunction suffixFunc = () -> System.out.println(word + "ay");
        suffixFunc.call();
    }
}
```

This program prints:

```
helloay
```

Inside the lambda expression, we are using the local variable word. Because it is used in a lambda expression, this variable is considered to be final (though it is not explicitly declared final). Try this code that has an additional statement that assigns to suffix (even before calling the lambda function):

```java
String word = "hello";
SuffixFunction suffixFunc = () -> System.out.println(word + "ay");
word = "e";
suffixFunc.call();
```

The compiler issues an error for this code segment:

```
PigLatin.java:11: error: local variables referenced from a lambda expression must be final
or effectively final
        SuffixFunction suffixFunc = () -> System.out.println(word + "ay");
                                                             ^
1 error
```

This is because suffix is assigned to "e" after it is initialized and hence the compiler cannot treat it as a final variable.

Why is that local variables are considered effectively final when they are accessed in lambda expressions? The reason is that such mutation is not thread safe.

Note that this restriction does not apply to data members and class members. Hence you may be at risk when multiple threads concurrently modify variables within a lambda expression. Further, effectively final applies only to the references and not to the values pointed by the references. Hence, you can mutate the values inside a local array from a lambda function—it is unsafe but possible.

Points to Remember

Here are some key points about lambda functions that will help you in the OCPJP 8 exam:

- Lambda expressions can occur only in the contexts where assignment, function calls, or casts can occur.

- A lambda function is treated as a nested block. Hence, just like a nested block, we cannot declare a variable with the same name as a local variable in the enclosing block.

- Lambda functions must return values from all the branches—otherwise it will result in a compiler error.

- When argument types are declared, the lambda is known as "explicitly typed"; if they are inferred, it is "implicitly typed."

- What happens if a lambda expression throws an exception? If it is a checked exception, then the method in the functional interface should declare that; otherwise it will result in a compiler error.

Summary

Let us briefly review the key points for each certification objective in this chapter. Please read it before appearing for the exam.

Develop code that uses abstract classes and methods

- An abstraction specifying functionality supported without disclosing finer level details.

- You cannot create instances of an abstract class.

- Abstract classes enable runtime polymorphism, and runtime polymorphism in turn enables loose coupling.

Develop code that uses a final keyword

- A final class is a non-inheritable class (i.e., you cannot inherit from a final class).

- A final method is a non-overridable method (i.e., subclasses cannot override a final method).

- All methods of a final class are implicitly final (i.e., non-overridable).

- A final variable can be assigned only once.

Create inner classes including static inner class, local class, nested class, and anonymous inner class

- Java supports four types of nested classes: static nested classes, inner classes, local inner classes, and anonymous inner classes.

- Static nested classes may have static members, whereas the other flavors of nested classes can't.

- Static nested classes and inner classes can access members of an outer class (even private members). However, static nested classes can access only static members of outer classes.

- Local classes (both local inner classes and anonymous inner classes) can access all variables declared in the outer scope (whether a method, constructor, or a statement block).

Use enumerated types including methods, and constructors in an enum type

- Enums are a typesafe way to achieve restricted input from users.

- You cannot use new with enums, even inside the enum definition.

- Enum classes are by default final classes.

- All enum classes are implicitly derived from java.lang.Enum.

Develop code that declares, implements, and/or extends interfaces and use the atOverride annotation

- An interface can have three kinds of methods: abstract methods, default methods, and static methods.

- The "diamond problem" occurs when a derived type inherits two method definitions in the base types that have the same signature.

  - If two super interfaces have the same method name and one of them has a definition, the compiler will issue an error; this conflict has to be resolved manually.

  - If a base class and a base interface define methods with the same signature, the method definition in the class is used and the interface definition is ignored.

- A functional interface consists of exactly one abstract method but can contain any number of default or static methods.

- A declaration of a functional interface results in a "functional interface type" that can be used with lambda expressions.

- For a functional interface, declaring methods from Object class in an interface does not count as an abstract method.

Create and use Lambda expressions

- In a lambda expression, the left side of the -> provides the parameters; the right side, the body. The arrow operator ("->") helps in concise expressions of lambda functions.

- You can create a reference to a functional interface and assign a lambda expression to it. If you invoke the abstract method from that interface, it will call the assigned lambda expression.

- Compiler can perform type inferences of lambda parameters if omitted. When declared, parameters can have modifiers such as final.

- Variables accessed by a lambda function are considered to be *effectively final*.

QUESTION TIME

1. Which ONE of the following statements is TRUE?

   A. You cannot extend a concrete class and declare that derived class abstract

   B. You cannot extend an abstract class from another abstract class

   C. An abstract class must declare at least one abstract method in it

   D. You can create an instance of a concrete subclass of an abstract class but cannot create an instance of an abstract class itself

2. Choose the correct answer based on the following class definition:

   ```
   public abstract final class Shape { }
   ```

   A. Compiler error: a class must not be empty

   B. Compiler error: illegal combination of modifiers abstract and final

   C. Compiler error: an abstract class must declare at least one abstract method

   D. No compiler error: this class definition is fine and will compile successfully

3. Choose the best option based on this program:

   ```
   class Shape {
       public Shape() {
           System.out.println("Shape constructor");
       }
       public class Color {
           public Color() {
               System.out.println("Color constructor");
           }
       }
   }

   class TestColor {
       public static void main(String []args) {
           Shape.Color black = new Shape().Color(); // #1
       }
   }
   ```

   A. Compiler error: the method Color() is undefined for the type Shape

   B. Compiler error: invalid inner class

   C. Works fine: Shape constructor, Color constructor

   D. Works fine: Color constructor, Shape constructor

4. Choose the best option based on this program:

```
class Shape {
    private boolean isDisplayed;
    protected int canvasID;
    public Shape() {
        isDisplayed = false;
        canvasID = 0;
    }
    public class Color {
        public void display() {
            System.out.println("isDisplayed: "+isDisplayed);
            System.out.println("canvasID: "+canvasID);
        }
    }
}

class TestColor {
    public static void main(String []args) {
        Shape.Color black = new Shape().new Color();
        black.display();
    }
}
```

A. Compiler error: an inner class can only access public members of the outer class

B. Compiler error: an inner class cannot access private members of the outer class

C. Runs and prints this output:

D. isDisplayed: false

E. canvasID: 0

F. Compiles fine but crashes with a runtime exception

5. Determine the behavior of this program:

```
public class EnumTest {
    PrinterType printerType;

    enum PrinterType {INKJET, DOTMATRIX, LASER};
    public EnumTest(PrinterType pType) {
        printerType = pType;
    }

    public static void main(String[] args) {
        PrinterType pType = new PrinterType();
        EnumTest enumTest = new EnumTest(PrinterType.LASER);
    }
}
```

A. Prints the output printerType:LASER

B. Compiler error: enums must be declared static

C. Compiler error: cannot instantiate the type EnumTest.PrinterType

D. This program will compile fine, and when run, will crash and throw a runtime exception

6. Is the enum definition given below correct?

```java
public enum PrinterType {
    private int pagePrintCapacity;          // #1
    DOTMATRIX(5), INKJET(10), LASER(50);    // #2

    private PrinterType(int pagePrintCapacity) {
        this.pagePrintCapacity = pagePrintCapacity;
    }

    public int getPrintPageCapacity() {
        return pagePrintCapacity;
    }
}
```

A. Yes, this enum definition is correct and will compile cleanly without any warnings or errors

B. No, this enum definition is incorrect and will result in compile error(s)

C. No, this enum definition will result in runtime exception(s)

Yes, this enum definition is correct but will compile with warnings.

7. Determine the behavior of this program:

```java
interface DoNothing {
    default void doNothing() { System.out.println("doNothing"); }
}

@FunctionalInterface
interface DontDoAnything extends DoNothing {
    @Override
    abstract void doNothing();
}

class LambdaTest {
    public static void main(String []args) {
        DontDoAnything beIdle = () -> System.out.println("be idle");
        beIdle.doNothing();
    }
}
```

    A.   This program results in a compiler error for DontDoAnything interface: cannot override default method to be an abstract method

    B.   This program results in a compiler error: DontDoAnything is not a functional interface

    C.   This program prints: doNothing

    D.   This program prints: be idle

8.   Determine the behavior of this program:

```java
public class EnumTest {
    public EnumTest() {
        System.out.println("In EnumTest constructor ");
    }
    public void printType() {
        enum PrinterType { DOTMATRIX, INKJET, LASER }
    }
}
```

    A.   This code will compile cleanly without any compiler warnings or errors, and when used, will run without any problems

    B.   This code will compile cleanly without any compiler warnings or errors, and when used, will generate a runtime exception

    C.   This code will produce a compiler error: enum types must not be local

    D.   This code will give compile-time warnings but not any compiler errors

9.   Determine the behavior of this program:

```java
interface BaseInterface {
    default void foo() { System.out.println("BaseInterface's foo"); }
}

interface DerivedInterface extends BaseInterface {
    default void foo() { System.out.println("DerivedInterface's foo"); }
}

interface AnotherInterface {
    public static void foo() { System.out.println("AnotherInterface's foo"); }
}

public class MultipleInheritance implements DerivedInterface, AnotherInterface {
    public static void main(String []args) {
        new MultipleInheritance().foo();
    }
}
```

A. This program will result in a compiler error: Redundant method definition for function foo

B. This program will result in a compiler error in MultipleInheritance class: Ambiguous call to function foo

C. The program prints: DerivedInterface's foo

D. The program prints: AnotherInterface's foo

10. Determine the behavior of this program:

```
class LambdaFunctionTest {
    @FunctionalInterface
    interface LambdaFunction {
        int apply(int j);
        boolean equals(java.lang.Object arg0);
    }

    public static void main(String []args) {
        LambdaFunction lambdaFunction = i -> i * i;     // #1
        System.out.println(lambdaFunction.apply(10));
    }
}
```

A. This program results in a compiler error: interfaces cannot be defined inside classes

B. This program results in a compiler error: @FunctionalInterface used for LambdaFunction that defines two abstract methods

C. This program results in a compiler error in code marked with #1: syntax error

D. This program compiles without errors, and when run, it prints 100 in console

Answers:

1. D. You can create an instance of a concrete subclass of an abstract class but cannot create an instance of an abstract class itself

2. B. Compiler error: illegal combination of modifiers abstract and final

    You cannot declare an abstract class final since an abstract class must to be extended. Class can be empty in Java, including abstract classes. An abstract class can declare zero or more abstract methods.

3. A. Compiler error: The method Color() is undefined for the type Shape

    You need to create an instance of outer class Shape in order to create an inner class instance, as in `new Shape().new Color();`.

4. C. Runs and prints this output:

    isDisplayed: false

    canvasID: 0

An inner class can access all members of an outer class, including the private members of the outer class.

5. C. Compiler error: cannot instantiate the type EnumTest.PrinterType

You cannot instantiate an enum type using new.

6. B. No, this enum definition is incorrect and will result in compile error(s)

You need to define enum elements first before any other attribute in an enum class. In other words, this enum definition will compile cleanly if you interchange the statements marked with "#1" and "#2" within comments in this code.

7. D. This program prints: be idle

A default method can be overridden in a derived interface and can be made abstract. DoNothing is a functional interface because it has an abstract method. The call beIdle. doNothing() calls the System.out.println given inside the lambda expression and hence it prints "be idle" on the console.

8. C. It will produce a compiler error: enum types must not be local

An enum can only be defined inside of a top-level class or interface and not within a method.

9. C. The program prints: DerivedInterface's foo

A default method can be overridden. Since DerivedInterface extends BaseInterface, the default method definition for foo is overridden in the DerivedInterface. Static methods do not cause conflicting definition of foo since they are not overridden, and they are accessed using the interface name, as in AnotherInterface.foo. Hence, the program compiles without errors. In the main method within MultipleInheritance class, the overridden foo method is invoked and hence the call resolves to foo method defined in DerivedInterface.

10. D. This program compiles without errors, and when run, it prints 100 in console

An interface can be defined inside a class. The signature of the equals method matches that of the equal method in Object class; hence it is not counted as an abstract method in the functional interface. It is acceptable to omit the parameter type when there is only one parameter and the parameter and return type are inferred from the LambdaFunction abstract method declaration int apply(int j). Since the lambda function is passed with the value 10, the returned value is 10 * 10, and hence 100 is printed in console.

CHAPTER 4

■ ■ ■

Generics and Collections

Certification Objectives

Create and use a generic class

Create and use ArrayList, TreeSet, TreeMap, and ArrayDeque objects

Use java.util.Comparator and java.lang.Comparable interfaces

Collections Streams and Filters

Iterate using forEach methods of Streams and List

Describe Stream interface and Stream pipeline

Filter a collection by using lambda expressions

Use method references with Streams

Every non-trivial Java application makes use of data structures and algorithms. The Java collection's framework provides a large set of readily usable general-purpose data structures and algorithms. These data structures and algorithms can be used with any suitable data type in a type-safe manner; this is achieved through the use of a language feature known as generics.

Collections in Java implement data structures and algorithms are implemented using generics and lambda functions. Hence, these topics are combined together as a single topic in the 1Z0-809 exam syllabus. In this chapter, we start with discussing generics. Since our experience shows that it is often tricky to correctly answer questions on generics, we cover generics in detail. Following that we discuss important collections and also discuss java.lang.Comparator and java.lang.Comparable interfaces. Finally we cover in detail how lambda functions and streams can be used within the Java collections framework. You can expect numerous questions in your OCPJP 8 exam on generics, collections, and streams, so this chapter provides detailed coverage of the exam topics.

Creating and Using Generic Classes

Certification Objective

Create and use a generic class

Generics are a language feature introduced to Java in version 1.5. Before generics were introduced in Java, the Object base class was used as an alternative to generics. With generics, you write code for one type (say T) that is applicable for all types, instead of writing separate classes for each type. Let us start with a simple example.

Assume that you want to print the object's value within square brackets. For example, to print an Integer object with value 10, instead of printing "10" to the console, you want to print the value inside a "box" like this: "[10]". Listing 4-1 contains a generic version of the BoxPrinter class.

Listing 4-1. BoxPrinterTest.java

```java
// This program shows container implementation using generics
class BoxPrinter<T> {
    private T val;
    public BoxPrinter(T arg) {
        val = arg;
    }
    public String toString() {
        return "[" + val + "]";
    }
}

class BoxPrinterTest {
    public static void main(String []args) {
        BoxPrinter<Integer> value1 = new BoxPrinter<Integer>(new Integer(10));
        System.out.println(value1);

        BoxPrinter<String> value2 = new BoxPrinter<String>("Hello world");
        System.out.println(value2);
    }
}
```

It prints the following:

```
[10]
[Hello world]
```

There are many things you need to note here.

1. See the declaration of BoxPrinter:

        class BoxPrinter<T>

You gave the BoxPrinter class a *type placeholder* <T>—the type name T within angle brackets "<" and ">" following the class name. You can use this type name inside the class to indicate that it is a placeholder for the actual type to be provided later.

2. Inside the class you first use T in field declaration:

        private T val;

You are declaring val of the *generic type*—the actual type will be specified later when you use BoxPrinter. In main(), you declare a variable of type BoxPrinter for an Integer like this:

BoxPrinter<Integer> value1

Here, you are specifying that T is of type Integer—identifier T (a placeholder) is replaced with the type Integer. So, the val inside BoxPrinter becomes Integer because T gets replaced with Integer.

CHAPTER 4 ■ GENERICS AND COLLECTIONS

3. Now, here is another place where you use T:

```
public BoxPrinter(T arg) {
        val = arg;
}
```

Similar to the declaration of val with type T, you are saying that the argument for BoxPrinter constructor is of type T. Later in the main() method, when the constructor is called in new, you specify that T is of type Integer:

```
new BoxPrinter<Integer>(new Integer(10));
```

Now, inside the BoxPrinter constructor, arg and val *should be of the same type* since both are of type T. For example, if you change the constructor as follows:

```
new BoxPrinter<String>(new Integer(10));
```

The BoxPrinter is of type String, and the argument passed is of type Integer, so you'll get a compiler error for type mismatch in using the generics (which is good because you'll find the problem earlier).

Let us consider another example. Here is a Pair generic class that can hold objects of two different types, T1 and T2 (Listing 4-2).

Listing 4-2. PairTest.java

```
// It demonstrates the usage of generics in defining classes
class Pair<T1, T2> {
        T1 object1;
        T2 object2;
        Pair(T1 one, T2 two) {
            object1 = one;
            object2 = two;
        }
        public T1 getFirst() {
            return object1;
        }
        public T2 getSecond() {
            return object2;
        }
}

class PairTest {
    public static void main(String []args) {
        Pair<Integer, String> worldCup = new Pair<Integer, String>(2018, "Russia");
        System.out.println("World cup " + worldCup.getFirst() +
                        " in " + worldCup.getSecond());
    }
}
```

This program prints the following:

```
World cup 2018 in Russia
```

Here T1 and T2 are type holders. You give these type placeholders inside angle brackets: <T1, T2>. When using the Pair class, you must specify which specific types you are going to use in place of T1 and T2. For example, you use Integer and String for Pair, as in Pair<Integer, String> in the main() method. Now, think of the Pair class as if it has this body:

```
// how Pair<Integer, String> can be treated internally
class Pair {
    Integer object1;
    String object2;
    Pair(Integer one, String two) {
        object1 = one;
        object2 = two;
    }

    public Integer getFirst() {
        return object1;
    }

    public String getSecond() {
        return object2;
    }
}
```

In other words, try manually doing a find-and-replace for the type placeholders and replace them with actual types in the code. This will help you understand how generics actually work. With this, you can understand how the getFirst() and getSecond() methods return Integer and String values in the main() method.

In the statement

```
Pair<Integer, String> worldCup = new Pair<Integer, String>(2018, "Russia");
```

note that the types match exactly. If you try

```
Pair<Integer, String> worldCup = new Pair<String, String>(2018, "Russia");
```

you'll get the following compiler error:

```
TestPair.java:20: cannot find symbol
symbol  : constructor Pair(int,java.lang.String)
location: class Pair<java.lang.String,java.lang.String>
```

Now, how about trying this statement?

```
Pair<Integer, String> worldCup = new Pair<Number, String>(2018, "Russia");
```

You'll get another compiler error because of the type mismatch in the declared type of worldCup and the type given in the initialization expression:

```
TestPair.java:20: incompatible types
found    : Pair<java.lang.Number,java.lang.String>
required: Pair<java.lang.Integer,java.lang.String>
```

Now modify the generic Pair class. Pair<T1, T2> stores objects of type T1 and T2. How about a generic pair class that takes a type T and stores two objects of that type T? Obviously, one way to do that is to instantiate Pair<T1, T2> with same type, say Pair<String, String>, but it is not a good solution. Why? There is no way to ensure that you are instantiating the Pair with the same types! Listing 4-3 is a modified version of Pair—let's call it PairOfT—that takes one's type placeholder T.

Listing 4-3. PairOfT.java

```java
// This program shows how to use generics in your programs
class PairOfT<T> {
    T object1;
    T object2;

    PairOfT(T one, T two) {
        object1 = one;
        object2 = two;
    }

    public T getFirst() {
        return object1;
    }

    public T getSecond() {
        return object2;
    }
}
```

Now, will this statement work?

```java
PairOfT<Integer, String> worldCup = new PairOfT<Integer, String>(2018, "Russia");
```

No, because PairOfT takes one type parameter and you have given two type parameters here. So, you'll get a compiler error. So, how about this statement?

```java
PairOfT<String> worldCup = new PairOfT<String>(2018, "Russia");
```

No, you still get a compiler error:

```
TestPair.java:20: cannot find symbol
symbol  : constructor PairOfT(int,java.lang.String)
location: class PairOfT<java.lang.String>
        PairOfT<String> worldCup = new PairOfT<String>(2018, "Russia");
```

The reason is that 2018—when boxed—is an Integer and you should give a String as argument. How about this statement?

```java
PairOfT<String> worldCup = new PairOfT<String>("2018", "Russia");
```

Yes, it compiles and will work fine.

Diamond Syntax

In the previous section, we discussed how to create generic type instances, as in the following statement:

```
Pair<Integer, String> worldCup = new Pair<Integer, String>(2018, "Russia");
```

We also discussed how a compiler error would result if these types don't match, as in the following statement, which would not compile:

```
Pair<Integer, String> worldCup = new Pair<String, String>(2018, "Russia");
```

See how tedious it is to ensure that you provide same-type parameters in both the declaration type (Pair<Integer, String> in this case) and the new object creation expression (new Pair<String, String>() in this case)?

To simplify your life, Java 1.7 introduced the *diamond* syntax, in which the type parameters may be omitted: you can just leave it to the compiler to infer the types from the type declaration. So, the declaration can be simplified as

```
Pair<Integer, String> worldCup = new Pair<>(2018, "Russia");
```

To make it clear, Listing 4-4 contains the full program making use of this diamond syntax.

Listing 4-4. TestPair.java

```java
// This program shows the usage of the diamond syntax when using generics
class Pair<T1, T2> {
    T1 object1;
    T2 object2;

    Pair(T1 one, T2 two) {
        object1 = one;
        object2 = two;
    }

    public T1 getFirst() {
        return object1;
    }

    public T2 getSecond() {
        return object2;
    }
}

class TestPair {
    public static void main(String []args) {
        Pair<Integer, String> worldCup = new Pair<>(2018, "Russia");
        System.out.println("World cup " + worldCup.getFirst() +
                        " in " + worldCup.getSecond());
    }
}
```

This program will compile cleanly and print the following statement:

```
World cup 2018 in Russia
```

Note that it is a common mistake to forget the diamond operator < > in the initialization expression, as in

```
Pair<Integer, String> worldCup = new Pair(2018, "Russia");
```

Here are the warnings you will get from the compiler (when you pass the command line option -Xlint:unchecked to javac):

```
Pair.java:19: warning: [unchecked] unchecked call to Pair(T1,T2) as a member of the
raw type Pair
Pair<Integer, String> worldCup = new Pair(2018, "Russia");
                                 ^
  where T1,T2 are type-variables:
    T1 extends Object declared in class Pair
    T2 extends Object declared in class Pair

Pair.java:19: warning: [unchecked] unchecked conversion
Pair<Integer, String> worldCup = new Pair(2018, "Russia");
                                 ^
  required: Pair<Integer,String>
  found:    Pair
2 warnings
```

Since Pair is a generic type and you forgot to use the <> or provide the type parameters explicitly, the compiler treats it as a raw type with Pair taking two Object type parameters. Though this behavior did not cause any problem in this particular code segment, it is dangerous and can cause bugs, as the next section shows.

Interoperability of Raw Types and Generic Types

A generic type can be used without specifying its associated type. In that case, the type is referred to as *raw type*. For instance, List<T> should be used along with an associated type, i.e., List<String>; however, it can be used without specifying the accompanied type, i.e., just List. In the latter case, the List is referred to as raw type.

When you use a raw type, you lose the advantage of type safety afforded by generics. For instance, the type Vector is a raw type. Raw types bypass the type checking at compile time; however, they might throw runtime exceptions (for instance, ClassCastException). Therefore, it is not recommended to use raw types in new code.

Okay, now you understand that you should not use raw types. But, you may ask, why doesn't the compiler itself throw errors for such type declarations? The answer is *backward compatibility*. Java generics were introduced in Java 1.5. Java supports raw types in order to make the generics-based code compatible with legacy code. However, it is strongly recommended that you should not use raw types in your code.

Why? What will happen if you use raw types along with generics? Let's use both types in Listing 4-5 and examine the effect.

Listing 4-5. RawTest1.java

```java
import java.util.List;
import java.util.LinkedList;
import java.util.Iterator;

class RawTest1 {
    public static void main(String []args) {
        List list = new LinkedList();
        list.add("First");
        list.add("Second");
        List<String> strList = list;  //#1
        for(Iterator<String> itemItr = strList.iterator(); itemItr.hasNext();)
            System.out.println("Item: " + itemItr.next());

        List<String> strList2 = new LinkedList<>();
        strList2.add("First");
        strList2.add("Second");
        List list2 = strList2; //#2
        for(Iterator<String> itemItr = list2.iterator(); itemItr.hasNext();)
            System.out.println("Item: " + itemItr.next());
    }
}
```

What you expect from the above program? Do you think it will compile/execute properly? Well, yes—it will compile (with warnings) and execute without any problem. It prints the following:

```
Item: First
Item: Second
Item: First
Item: Second
```

Listing 4-6 introduces a couple of changes; observe the output.

Listing 4-6. RawTest2.java

```java
import java.util.List;
import java.util.LinkedList;
import java.util.Iterator;

class RawTest2 {
    public static void main(String []args) {
        List list = new LinkedList();
        list.add("First");
        list.add("Second");
        List<String> strList = list;
        strList.add(10);          // #1: generates compiler error
        for(Iterator<String> itemItr = strList.iterator(); itemItr.hasNext();)
            System.out.println("Item : " + itemItr.next());
```

```
        List<String> strList2 = new LinkedList<>();
        strList2.add("First");
        strList2.add("Second");
        List list2 = strList2;
        list2.add(10); // #2: compiles fine, results in runtime exception
        for(Iterator<String> itemItr = list2.iterator(); itemItr.hasNext();)
            System.out.println("Item : " + itemItr.next());
    }
}
```

In the above example, you added two statements. The first statement is as follows:

```
strList.add(10);     // #1: generates compiler error
```

You are trying to add an integer item in a List<String> type list, so you get a compile-time error "no suitable method found for add(int)". As discussed earlier, this type of checking at the compiler level is good, as without it, a runtime exception might have resulted later on. Here is the second statement you added:

```
list2.add(10);     // #2: compiles fine, results in runtime exception
```

Here, the list2 linked-list (raw type) is initialized with a generic type List<String>. After the initialization, you added an integer in the list raw type. This is allowed since list2 is a raw type. However, it will result in a ClassCastException.

The lesson we learned from this example is to avoid mixing raw types and generic types in our programs, since it might result in erroneous behavior at runtime. If you need to use both in a program, make sure you add a single type of item in the containers and retrieve using the same type.

 Avoid mixing raw types with generic types.

Generic Methods

Similar to generic classes, you can create generic methods—that is, methods that take generic parameter types. Generic methods are useful for writing methods that are applicable to a wide range of types while the functionality remains the same. For example, there are numerous generic methods in the java.util.Collections class.

Let's implement a simple method named fill(). Given a container, the fill() method fills all the container elements with value val. Listing 4-7 contains the implementation of the fill() method in the Utilities class.

Listing 4-7. UtilitiesTest.java

```
// This program demonstrates generic methods
import java.util.List;
import java.util.ArrayList;
```

```
class Utilities {
    public static <T> void fill(List<T> list, T val) {
        for(int i = 0; i < list.size(); i++)
            list.set(i, val);
    }
}

class UtilitiesTest {
    public static void main(String []args) {
        List<Integer> intList = new ArrayList<Integer>();
        intList.add(10);
        intList.add(20);
        System.out.println("The original list is: " + intList);
        Utilities.fill(intList, 100);
        System.out.println("The list after calling Utilities.fill() is: " + intList);
    }
}
```

It prints the following

```
The original list is: [10, 20]
The list after calling Utilities.fill() is: [100, 100]
```

Let's look step-by-step at this code:

1. You create a method named fill() in the Utilities class with this declaration:

    ```
    public static <T> void fill(List<T> list, T val)
    ```

You declare the generic type parameter T in this method. After the qualifiers public and static, you put <T> and then followed it by return type, method name, and its parameters. This declaration is different from generic classes—you give the generic type parameters after the class name in generic classes.

2. In the body, you write the code as if it's a normal method.

    ```
    for(int i = 0; i < list.size(); i++)
        list.set(i, val);
    ```

You loop over the list from 0 until its size and set each of the elements to value val in each iteration. You use the set() method in List, which takes the index position in the container as the first argument and the actual value to be set as the second argument.

3. In the main() method in the UtilitiesTest class, this is how you call the fill() method:

    ```
    Utilities.fill(intList, 100);
    ```

Note that you didn't give the generic type parameter value explicitly. Since intList is of type Integer and 100 is boxed to type Integer, the compiler inferred that the type T in the fill() method is of type Integer.

Generics and Subtyping

You can assign a derived type object to its base type reference; this is what you mean by *subtyping*. However, for generics, the type parameters should match exactly; otherwise you'll get a compiler error. In other words, *subtyping does not work for generic parameters*. Yes, this is a difficult rule to remember, so let's discuss in more detail why subtyping doesn't work for generic type parameters.

Subtyping works for class types: you can assign a derived type object to its base type reference. However, subtyping does not work for generic type parameters: you cannot assign a derived generic type parameter to a base type parameter.

Let's look at what can go wrong if you assume that you can use subtyping for generic type parameters.

```
// illegal code - assume that the following intialization is allowed
List<Number> intList = new ArrayList<Integer>();
intList.add(new Integer(10)); // okay
intList.add(new Float(10.0f)); // oops!
```

The intList of List<Number> type is supposed to hold an ArrayList<Number> object. However, you are storing an ArrayList<Integer>. This looks reasonable since List extends ArrayList and Integer extends Number. However, you can end up inserting a Float value in the intList! Recall that the dynamic type of intList is the ArrayList<Integer> type—so you are violating type safety here (and thus will get the compiler error of incompatible types). Since generics are designed to avoid type-safety mistakes like this, you cannot assign a derived generic type parameter to a base type parameter.

As you can see, subtyping for generic parameter types is not allowed because it is unsafe—but still it is an inconvenient limitation. Fortunately, Java supports *wildcard parameter types* in which you can use subtyping. We'll explore that capability now.

Type parameters for generics have a limitation: generic type parameters should match exactly for assignments. To overcome this subtyping problem, you can use wildcard types.

Wildcard Parameters

You saw in the preceding section that subtyping doesn't work for generic type parameters. So,

```
List<Number> intList = new ArrayList<Integer>();
```

gives the compiler error

```
WildCardUse.java:6: incompatible types
found   : java.util.ArrayList<java.lang.Integer>
required: java.util.List<java.lang.Number>
            List<Number> numList = new ArrayList<Integer>();
```

If you slightly change the statement to use wildcard parameter, it will compile

```
List<?> wildCardList = new ArrayList<Integer>();
```

What does a *wildcard* mean? Just like the wildcard you use for substituting for any card in a card game (ah, it's so fun to play card games!), you can use a wildcard to indicate that it can match for any type. With List<?>, you mean that it is a List of any type—in other words, you can say it is a "list of unknowns!"

But wait a minute…when you want a type indicating "any type," you use the Object class, don't you? How about the same statement, but using the Object type parameter?

```
List<Object> numList = new ArrayList<Integer>();
```

No luck—you get the same error you got above using List<Number>!

```
WildCardUse.java:6: incompatible types
found    : java.util.ArrayList<java.lang.Integer>
required: java.util.List<java.lang.Object>
                List<Object> numList = new ArrayList<Integer>();
```

In other words, you are still trying to use subtyping for generic parameters—and it still doesn't work. As you can see, List<Object> is not the same as List<?>. In fact, List<?> is a supertype of any List type, which means you can pass List<Integer>, or List<String>, or even List<Object> where List<?> is expected.

Let's use the wildcard in an example and see whether it'll work (see Listing 4-8).

Listing 4-8. WildCardUse.java

```
// This program demonstrates the usage of wild card parameters

import java.util.List;
import java.util.ArrayList;

class WildCardUse {
    static void printList(List<?> list){
    for(Object element: list)
        System.out.println("[" + element + "]");
    }

    public static void main(String []args) {
        List<Integer> list = new ArrayList<>();
        list.add(10);
        list.add(100);
        printList(list);
        List<String> strList = new ArrayList<>();
        strList.add("10");
        strList.add("100");
        printList(strList);
    }
}
```

This program prints the following:

```
[10]
[100]
[10]
[100]
```

Well, it works, and the list using wildcard can be passed list of integers as well as list of strings. This happens because of the parameter type of printList() method—List<?>. That's great!

Limitations of Wildcards

Let's consider the following snippet, which tries to add an element and print the list:

```
List<?> wildCardList = new ArrayList<Integer>();
wildCardList.add(new Integer(10));
System.out.println(wildCardList);
```

You get the following compiler error:

```
WildCardUse.java:7: cannot find symbol
symbol  : method add(java.lang.Integer)
location: interface java.util.List<capture#145 of ? extends java.lang.Number>
                wildCardList.add(new Integer(10));
```

Why? You are absolutely sure that the add() method exists in the List interface. Then why doesn't the compiler find the method?

The problem requires some detailed explanation. When you use wildcard type <?>, you say to the compiler that you are *ignoring* the type information, so <?> stands for unknown type. Every time you try to pass arguments to a generic type, the java compiler tries to infer the type of the passed argument as well as the type of the generics and to justify the type safety. Now, you are trying to use the add() method to insert an element in the list. Since wildCardList doesn't know which type of objects it holds, it is risky to add elements to it. You might end up adding a string—"hello", for example—instead of an integer value. To avoid this problem (remember, generics was introduced in the language to ensure type safety!), the compiler doesn't allow you to call methods that modify the object. Since the add method modifies the object, you get an error! The error message also looks confusing, as in <capture#145 of ? extends java.lang.Number>.

💣 In general, when you use wildcard parameters, you cannot call methods that modify the object. If you try to modify, the compiler will give you confusing error messages. However, you can call methods that access the object.

Points to Remember

Here are some pointers that might prove valuable in your OCPJP 8 exam:

- It's possible to define or declare generic methods in an interface or a class even if the class or the interface itself is not generic.

- A generic class used without type arguments is known as a *raw type*. Of course, raw types are not type safe. Java supports raw types so that it is possible to use the generic type in code that is older than Java 5 (note that generics were introduced in Java 5). The compiler generates a warning when you use raw types in your code. You may use @SuppressWarnings({ "unchecked" }) to suppress the warning associated with raw types.

- List<?> is a supertype of any List type, which means you can pass List<Integer>, or List<String>, or even List<Object> where List<?> is expected.

- Implementation of generics is static in nature, which means that the Java compiler interprets the generics specified in the source code and replaces the generic code with concrete types. This is referred to as *type erasure*. After compilation, the code looks similar to what a developer would have written with concrete types. Essentially, the use of generics offers two advantages: first, it introduces an abstraction, which enables you to write generic implementation; second, it allows you to write generic implementation with type safety.

- There are many limitations of generic types due to type erasure. A few important ones are as follows:

  - You cannot instantiate a generic type using a new operator. For example, assuming mem is a field, the following statement will result in a compiler error:

    ```
    T mem = new T();  // wrong usage - compiler error
    ```

  - You cannot instantiate an array of a generic type. For example, assuming mem is a field, the following statement will result in a compiler error:

    ```
    T[] amem = new T[100]; // wrong usage - compiler error
    ```

  - You can declare instance fields of type T, but not of static fields of type T. For example,

    ```
    class X<T> {
        T instanceMem;  // okay
        static T statMem;      // wrong usage - compiler error
    }
    ```

- It is not possible to have generic exception classes; as a result, the following will not compile:

  ```
  class GenericException<T> extends Throwable { } // wrong usage - compiler error
  ```

- You cannot instantiate a generic type with primitive types—in other words, List<int> cannot be instantiated. However, you can use boxed primitive types.

Create and Use Collection Classes

Certification Objective

Create and use ArrayList, TreeSet, TreeMap, and ArrayDeque objects

The Java library has a collections framework that makes extensive use of generics and provides a set of containers and algorithms. In this section, we will focus on how to use the collections framework. Specifically, we will discuss important collection classes including ArrayList, TreeSet, TreeMap, and ArrayDeque objects.

The term *collection(s)* is a generic term, while Collection and Collections are the specific APIs of the java.util package. Collections—as in java.util.Collections—is a utility class that contains only static methods. The general term *collection(s)* refers to a container such as map, set, stack, and queue. We'll use the term *container(s)* when referring to these *collection(s)* in this chapter to avoid confusion.

Abstract Classes and Interfaces

The type hierarchy in the java.util library consists of numerous abstract classes and interfaces that provide generic functionality. Table 4-1 lists a few important types in this hierarchy. We'll cover some of these types in more detail a bit later in this section.

Table 4-1. *Important Abstract Classes and Interfaces in the Collections Framework*

Abstract Class/ Interface	Short Description
Iterable	A class implementing this interface can be used for iterating with a foreach statement.
Collection	Common base interface for classes in the collection hierarchy. When you want to write methods that are very general, you can pass the Collection interface. For example, max() method in java.util.Collections takes a Collection and returns an object.
List	Base interface for containers that store a sequence of elements. You can access the elements using an index, and retrieve the same element later (so that it maintains the insertion order). You can store duplicate elements in a List.
Set, SortedSet, NavigableSet	Interfaces for containers that don't allow duplicate elements. SortedSet maintains the set elements in a sorted order. NavigableSet allows searching the set for the closest matches.
Queue, Deque	Queue is a base interface for containers that holds a sequence of elements for processing. For example, the classes implementing Queue can be LIFO (last in, first out—as in stack data structure) or FIFO (first in, first out—as in queue data structure). In a Deque you can insert or remove elements from *both* the ends.
Map, SortedMap, NavigableMap	Interfaces for containers that map keys to values. In SortedMap, the keys are in a sorted order. A NavigableMap allows you to search and return the closest match for given search criteria. Note that Map hierarchy does *not* extend the Collection interface.
Iterator, ListIterator	You can traverse over the container in the forward direction if a class implements the Iterator interface. You can traverse in both forward and reverse directions if a class implements the ListIterator interface.

Those are quite a few base types, but don't get overwhelmed by them. You'll see specific concrete classes and use some of these base types. We'll only cover the `Collection` interface and then move on to cover specific concrete classes that are part of this collection hierarchy and mentioned in exam topics.

The Collection Interface

The `Collection` interface provides methods such as `add()` and `remove()` that are common to all containers. Table 4-2 lists the most important methods in this interface. Take a look at them before you use them.

Table 4-2. *Important Methods in the Collection Interface*

Method	Short description
`boolean add(Element elem)`	Adds elem into the underlying container.
`void clear()`	Removes all elements from the container.
`boolean isEmpty()`	Checks whether the container has any elements or not.
`Iterator<Element> iterator()`	Returns an `Iterator<Element>` object for iterating over the container.
`boolean remove(Object obj)`	Removes the element if `obj` is present in the container.
`int size()`	Returns the number of elements in the container.
`Object[] toArray()`	Returns an array that has all elements in the container.

Methods such as `add()` and `remove()` can fail depending on the underlying container. For example, if the container is read-only, you will not be able to add or remove elements. Apart from these methods, there are many methods in the `Collection` interface that apply to multiple elements in the container (Table 4-3).

Table 4-3. *Methods in the Collection Interface That Apply to Multiple Elements*

Method	Short Description
`boolean addAll(Collection<? extends Element> coll)`	Adds all the elements in `coll` into the underlying container.
`boolean containsAll(Collection<?> coll)`	Checks if all elements given in `coll` are present in the underlying container.
`boolean removeAll(Collection<?> coll)`	Removes all elements from the underlying container that are also present in `coll`.
`boolean retainAll(Collection<?> coll)`	Retains elements in the underlying container only if they are also present in `coll`; it removes all other elements.

Concrete Classes

Numerous interfaces and abstract classes in the `Collection` hierarchy provide the common methods that specific concrete classes implement/extend. The concrete classes provide the actual functionality, and you'll have to learn only a handful of them to be properly prepared for the OCPJP 8 exam. Table 4-4 summarizes the features of the classes you should know.

Table 4-4. Important Concrete Classes in Collection Framework

Concrete Class	Short Description
ArrayList	Internally implemented as a resizable array. This is one of the most widely used concrete classes. Fast to search, but slow to insert or delete. Allows duplicates.
LinkedList	Internally implements a doubly linked list data structure. Fast to insert or delete elements, but slow for searching elements. Additionally, LinkedList can be used when you need a stack (LIFO) or queue (FIFO) data structure. Allows duplicates.
HashSet	Internally implemented as a hash-table data structure. Used for storing a set of elements—it does not allow storing duplicate elements. Fast for searching and retrieving elements. It does *not* maintain any order for stored elements.
TreeSet	Internally implements a red-black tree data structure. Like HashSet, TreeSet does not allow storing duplicates. However, unlike HashSet, it stores the elements in a sorted order. It uses a tree data structure to decide where to store or search the elements, and the position is decided by the sorting order.
HashMap	Internally implemented as a hash-table data structure. Stores key and value pairs. Uses hashing for finding a place to search or store a pair. Searching or inserting is very fast. It does *not* store the elements in any order.
TreeMap	Internally implemented using a red-black tree data structure. Unlike HashMap, TreeMap stores the elements in a sorted order. It uses a tree data structure to decide where to store or search for keys, and the position is decided by the sorting order.
PriorityQueue	Internally implemented using heap data structure. A PriorityQueue is for retrieving elements based on priority. Irrespective of the order in which you insert, when you remove the elements, the highest priority element will be retrieved first.

There are many old java.util classes (now known as legacy collection types) that were superceded by new collection classes. Some of them are (with newer types in parentheses): Enumeration (Iterator), Vector (ArrayList), Dictionary (Map), and Hashtable (HashMap). In addition, Stack and Properties are legacy classes that do not have direct replacements.

ArrayList Class

Lists are used for storing a sequence of elements. You can insert an element of the container in a specific position using an index, and retrieve the same element later (i.e., it maintains the insertion order). You can store duplicate elements in a list. There are two concrete classes that you need to know: ArrayList and LinkedList.

ArrayList implements a resizable array. When you create a native array (say, new String[10];), the size of the array is known (fixed) at the time of creation. However, ArrayList is a *dynamic array*: it can grow in size as required. Internally, an ArrayList allocates a block of memory and grows it as required. So, accessing array elements is very fast in an ArrayList. However, when you add or remove elements, internally the rest of the elements are copied; so addition/deletion of elements is a costly operation.

Here's a simple example to visit elements in an ArrayList. You take an ArrayList and use the for-each construct for traversing a collection:

```
ArrayList<String> languageList = new ArrayList<>();
languageList.add("C");
languageList.add("C++");
languageList.add("Java");
for(String language : languageList) {
    System.out.println(language);
}
```

It prints the following:

```
C
C++
Java
```

This for-each is equivalent to the following code, which explicitly uses an Iterator:

```
for(Iterator<String> languageIter = languageList.iterator(); languageIter.hasNext();) {
        String language = languageIter.next();
        System.out.println(language);
}
```

This code segment will also print the same output as the previous for-each loop code. Here is a step-by-step description of how this for loop works:

1. You use the iterator() method to get the iterator for that container. Since languageList is an ArrayList of type <String>, you should create Iterator with String. Name it languageIter.

2. Before entering the loop, you check if there are any elements to visit. You call the hasNext() method for checking that. If it returns true, there are more elements to visit; if it returns false, the iteration is over and you exit the loop.

3. Once you enter the body of the loop, the first thing you have to do is call next() and move the iterator. The next() method returns the iterated value. You capture that return value in the language variable.

4. You print the language value, and then the loop continues.

This *iteration idiom*—the way you call iterator(), hasNext(), and next() methods—is important to learn; we'll be using either the for-each loop or this idiom extensively in our examples.

Note that you create ArrayList<String> and Iterator<String> instead of just using ArrayList or Iterator (i.e., you provide type information along with these classes). The Collection classes are generic classes; therefore you need to specify the type parameters to use them. Here you are storing/iterating a list of strings, so you use <String>.

You can remove elements while traversing a container using iterators. Let's create an object of ArrayList<Integer> type with ten elements. You'll iterate over the elements and remove all of them (instead of using the removeAll() method in ArrayList). Listing 4-9 shows the code. Will it work?

Listing 4-9. TestIterator.java

```
// This program shows the usage of Iterator

import java.util.ArrayList;
import java.util.Iterator;

class TestIterator {
    public static void main(String []args) {
        ArrayList<Integer> nums = new ArrayList<Integer>();
        for(int i = 1; i < 10; i++)
            nums.add(i);
        System.out.println("Original list " + nums);
        Iterator<Integer> numsIter = nums.iterator();
        while(numsIter.hasNext()) {
            numsIter.remove();
        }

        System.out.println("List after removing all elements" + nums);
    }
}
```

It prints the following:

```
Original list [1, 2, 3, 4, 5, 6, 7, 8, 9]
Exception in thread "main" java.lang.IllegalStateException
        at java.util.AbstractList$Itr.remove(AbstractList.java:356)
        at TestIterator.main(Main.java:12)
```

Oops! What happened? The problem is that you haven't called next() before calling remove(). Checking hasNext() in the while loop condition, moving to the element using next(), and calling remove() is the correct idiom for removing an element. If you don't follow it correctly, you can get into trouble (i.e., you'll get IllegalStateException). Similarly, if you call remove() twice without sandwiching a next() between the statements, you'll get this exception.

Let's fix this program by calling next() before calling remove(). Here is the relevant part of the code:

```
Iterator<Integer> numsIter = nums.iterator();
while(numsIter.hasNext()) {
    numsIter.next();
    numsIter.remove();
}
System.out.println("List after removing all elements " + nums);
```

It prints the list with no elements, as expected:

```
List after removing all elements []
```

Remember that `next()` needs to be called before calling `remove()` in an `Iterator`; otherwise, you'll get an `IllegalStateException`. Similarly, calling `remove()` in subsequent statements without calling `next()` between these statements will also result in this exception. In short, any modifications to the underlying container while an iterator is traversing through the container will result in this exception.

Using Arrays.asList()

The `java.util.Arrays` class has a useful method named `asList()` method that returns a fixed-size list. Here is an interesting aspect about the returned `List` object: you cannot add or remove elements but you can modify the object returned by the `asList()` method! Also, the modifications you make through the `List` are reflected in the original array (see Listing 4-10).

Listing 4-10. ArrayAsList.java

```
import java.util.List;
import java.util.Arrays;

class ArrayAsList {
    public static void main(String []args) {
        Double [] temperatureArray = {31.1, 30.0, 32.5, 34.9, 33.7, 27.8};
        System.out.println("The original array is: " +
                        Arrays.toString(temperatureArray));
        List<Double> temperatureList = Arrays.asList(temperatureArray);
        temperatureList.set(0, 35.2);
        System.out.println("The modified array is: " +
        Arrays.toString(temperatureArray));
    }
}
```

It prints the following:

```
The original array is: [31.1, 30.0, 32.5, 34.9, 33.7, 27.8]
The modified array is: [35.2, 30.0, 32.5, 34.9, 33.7, 27.8]
```

The `Arrays` class provides only limited functionality and you will often want to use methods in the `Collections` class. To achieve that, calling the `Arrays.asList()` method is a useful technique.

The TreeSet Class

Set, as we studied in our math classes in high school, contains no duplicates. Unlike `List`, a `Set` doesn't remember where you inserted the element (i.e., it doesn't remember the insertion order).

There are two important concrete classes for Set: HashSet and TreeSet. A HashSet is for quickly inserting and retrieving elements; it does *not* maintain any sorting order for the elements it holds. A TreeSet stores the elements in a sorted order (and it implements the SortedSet interface).

Given a sentence, how can you sort the letters used in that sentence into alphabetical order? A TreeSet puts the values in a sorted order, so you can use a TreeSet container for solving this problem (see Listing 4-11).

Listing 4-11. TreeSetTest.java

```java
// This program demonstrates the usage of TreeSet class

import java.util.Set;
import java.util.TreeSet;

class TreeSetTest {
    public static void main(String []args) {
        String pangram = "the quick brown fox jumps over the lazy dog";
        Set<Character> aToZee = new TreeSet<Character>();
        for(char gram : pangram.toCharArray())
            aToZee.add(gram);
        System.out.println("The pangram is: " + pangram);
        System.out.print("Sorted pangram characters are: " + aToZee);
    }
}
```

It prints the following:

```
The pangram is: the quick brown fox jumps over the lazy dog
Sorted pangram characters are: [ , a, b, c, d, e, f, g, h, i, j, k, l, m, n, o, p, q, r, s,
t, u, v, w, x, y, z]
```

A *pangram* is a sentence that uses all letters in the alphabet at least once. You want to store characters of a pangram in the set. Since you need to use reference types for containers, you've created a TreeSet of Characters.

Now, how to get the characters from a String? Remember that array indexing doesn't work for Strings. For example, to get the first character "t", if you use pangram[0] in the program, you'll get a compiler error. Fortunately, String has a method called toCharArray() that returns a char[]. So, you use this method for traversing over the string and get all the characters. As you add the characters into the TreeSet, the characters are stored in a sorted order. So, you get all the lowercase letters when you print the set.

Note in the output that there is one leading comma. Why? The pangram string has many whitespace characters. One whitespace also gets stored in the set, so it also gets printed!

The Map Interface

A Map stores key and value pairs. The Map interface does *not* extend the Collection interface. However, there are methods in the Map interface that you can use to get the objects classes that implement the Collection interface to work around this problem. Also, the method names in Map are very similar to the methods in Collection, so it is easy to understand and use Map. There are two important concrete classes of Map: HashMap and TreeMap.

- A HashMap uses a hash table data structure internally. In HashMap, searching (or looking up elements) is a fast operation. However, HashMap neither remembers the order in which you inserted elements nor keeps elements in any sorted order.

- A TreeMap uses a red-black tree data structure internally. Unlike HashMap, TreeMap keeps the elements in sorted order (i.e., sorted by its keys). So, searching or inserting is somewhat slower than the HashMap.

The NavigableMap Interface and TreeMap Class

The NavigableMap interface extends the SortedMap interface. The TreeMap class is the widely used class that implements NavigableMap. As the name indicates, with NavigableMap, you can navigate the Map easily. It has many methods that make Map navigation easy. You can get the nearest value matching the given key, all values less than the given key, all values greater than the given key, and so on. Let's look at an example: Lennon, McCartney, Harrison, and Starr have taken an online exam. In that exam, the maximum they can score is 100, with a passing score of 40. If you want to find details such as who passed the exam, and sort the exam scores in ascending or descending order, NavigableMap (and TreeMap) is very convenient (see Listing 4-12).

Listing 4-12. NavigableMapTest.java

```
// This program demonstrates the usage of navigable tree interface and TreeMap class

import java.util.NavigableMap;
import java.util.TreeMap;

public class NavigableMapTest {
    public static void main(String []args) {
        NavigableMap<Integer, String> examScores = new TreeMap<Integer, String>();

        examScores.put(90, "Sophia");
        examScores.put(20, "Isabella");
        examScores.put(10, "Emma");
        examScores.put(50, "Olivea");

        System.out.println("The data in the map is: " + examScores);
        System.out.println("The data descending order is: " + examScores.descendingMap());
        System.out.println("Details of those who passed the exam: " + examScores.tailMap(40));
        System.out.println("The lowest mark is: " + examScores.firstEntry());
    }
}
```

It prints the following:

```
The data in the map is: {10=Emma, 20=Isabella, 50=Olivea, 90=Sophia}
The data descending order is: {90=Sophia, 50=Olivea, 20=Isabella, 10=Emma}
Details of those who passed the exam: {50=Olivea, 90=Sophia}
The lowest mark is: 10=Emma
```

In this program, you have a NavigableMap<Integer, String> that maps the exam score and the name of the person. You create a TreeMap<Integer, String> to actually store the exam scores. By default, a TreeMap stores data in ascending order. If you want the data in descending order, it's easy: you just have to use the descendingMap() method (or descendingKeySet() if you are only interested in the keys).

Given that the passing score is 40, you might want to get the map with data of those who failed in the exam. For that, you can use the headMap() method with the key value 40 (since the data is in ascending order, you want to get the "head" part of the map from the given position). Similarly, to get the data of those who passed the exam, you can use the tailMap() method.

If you want the immediate ones above and below the passing score, you can use the higherEntry() and lowerEntry() methods, respectively. The firstEntry() and lastEntry() methods give the entries with lowest and highest key values. So, when you use the firstEntry() method on examScores, you get Emma with 10 marks. If you use lastEntry(), you get Sophia, who has score 90.

The Deque Interface and ArrayDeque class

Deque (Doubly ended queue) is a data structure that allows you to insert and remove elements from both the ends. The Deque interface was introduced in Java 6 in java.util.collection package. The Deque interface extends the Queue interface. Hence, all methods provided by Queue are also available in the Deque interface.

There are three concrete implementations of the Deque interface: LinkedList, ArrayDeque, and LinkedBlockingDeque. Let's use ArrayDeque to understand the features of the Deque interface.

Consider implementing a special queue (say, to pay a utility bill) where a customer can be added only at the end of the queue and can be removed either at the front of the queue (when the customer paid the bill) or from the end of the queue (when the customer gets frustrated from the long line and leaves the queue himself). Listing 4-13 shows how to do this.

Listing 4-13. SplQueueTest.java

```java
// This program shows the usage of Deque interface

import java.util.ArrayDeque;
import java.util.Deque;

class SplQueue {
    private Deque<String> splQ = new ArrayDeque<>();
    void addInQueue(String customer){
        splQ.addLast(customer);
    }

    void removeFront(){
        splQ.removeFirst();
    }

    void removeBack(){
        splQ.removeLast();
    }

    void printQueue(){
        System.out.println("Special queue contains: " + splQ);
    }
}

class SplQueueTest {
    public static void main(String []args) {
        SplQueue splQ = new SplQueue();
        splQ.addInQueue("Harrison");
        splQ.addInQueue("McCartney");
        splQ.addInQueue("Starr");
        splQ.addInQueue("Lennon");

        splQ.printQueue();
        splQ.removeFront();
        splQ.removeBack();
        splQ.printQueue();
    }
}
```

It prints the following:

```
Special queue contains: [Harrison, McCartney, Starr, Lennon]
Special queue contains: [McCartney, Starr]
```

You first define a class—SplQueue—that defines a container splQ of type ArrayDeque with basic four operations. The method addInQueue() adds a customer at the end of the queue, the method removeBack() removes a customer from the end of the queue, the method removeFront() removes a customer from the front of the queue, and the method printQueue() simply prints all elements of the queue. You simply use the addLast(), removeFirst(), and removeLast() methods from the Deque interface to realize the methods of the SplQueue class. In your main() method, you instantiate the SplQueue and called the addInQueue() method of the SplQueue class. After it, you remove one customer from the front and one from the end, and print the contents of the queue before and after this removal. Well, it is working as you expected.

The difference between an ArrayList and ArrayDeque is that you can add an element anywhere in an array list using an index; however, you can add an element only either at the front or end of the array deque. That makes insertion in array deque more efficient than array list; however, navigation in an array deque becomes more expensive than in an array list.

Comparable and Comparator Interfaces

Certification Objectives

Use java.util.Comparator and java.lang.Comparable interfaces

As their names suggest, Comparable and Comparator interfaces are used to compare similar objects (for example, while performing searching or sorting). Assume that you have a container containing a list of Person object. Now, how do you compare two Person objects? There are many comparable attributes, such as SSN, name, driver's license number, and so on. Two objects can be compared on SSN as well as person's name; this depends on the context. Hence, the criterion to compare the Person objects cannot be predefined; a developer has to define this criterion. Java defines Comparable and Comparator interfaces to achieve the same.

The Comparable interface has only one method compareTo(), which is declared as follows:

```
int compareTo(Element that)
```

Since you are implementing the compareTo() method in a class, you have this reference available. You can compare the current element with the passed Element and return an int value. What should the int value be? Well, here are the rules for returning the integer value:

```
return 1 if current object > passed object
return 0 if current object == passed object
return -1 if current object < passed object
```

Now, an important question: what does >, < or == mean for an Element? Hmm, it is left to you to decide how to compare two objects! But the meaning of comparison should be a natural one; in other words, the comparison should mean *natural ordering*. For example, you saw how Integers are compared with each other, based on a *numeric order*, which is the natural order for Integer types. Similarly, you compare Strings using *lexicographic comparison*, which is the natural order for Strings. For user-defined classes, you need to find the natural order in which you can compare the objects. For example, for a Student class, StudentId might be the natural order for comparing Student objects. Listing 4-14 implements a simple Student class now.

Listing 4-14. ComparatorTest1.java

```java
// This program shows the usage of Comparable interface

import java.util.Arrays;

class Student implements Comparable<Student> {
    String id;
    String name;
    Double cgpa;

    public Student(String studentId, String studentName, double studentCGPA) {
        id = studentId;
        name = studentName;
        cgpa = studentCGPA;
    }

    public String toString() {
        return " \n " + id + "  \t  " + name + "  \t  " + cgpa;
    }

    public int compareTo(Student that) {
        return this.id.compareTo(that.id);
    }
}

class ComparatorTest1 {
    public static void main(String []args) {
        Student []students = {  new Student("cs011", "Lennon   ", 3.1),
                    new Student("cs021", "McCartney", 3.4),
                    new Student("cs012", "Harrison ", 2.7),
                    new Student("cs022", "Starr ", 3.7) };

        System.out.println("Before sorting by student ID");
        System.out.println("Student-ID \t  Name \t  CGPA (for 4.0) ");
        System.out.println(Arrays.toString(students));

        Arrays.sort(students);

        System.out.println("After sorting by student ID");
        System.out.println("Student-ID \t  Name \t  CGPA (for 4.0) ");
        System.out.println(Arrays.toString(students));
    }
}
```

It prints the following:

```
Before sorting by student ID
Student-ID        Name    CGPA (for 4.0)
[
 cs011            Lennon        3.1,
 cs021            McCartney     3.4,
 cs012            Harrison      2.7,
 cs022            Starr         3.7]
After sorting by student ID
Student-ID        Name    CGPA (for 4.0)
[
 cs011            Lennon        3.1,
 cs012            Harrison      2.7,
 cs021            McCartney     3.4,
 cs022            Starr         3.7]
```

You have implemented the Comparable<Student> interface. When you call the sort() method, it calls the compareTo() method to compare Student objects by their IDs. Since Student IDs are unique, it is a natural comparison order that works well.

Now, you may need to arrange students based on the cumulative grade point average (CGPA) they got. You may even need to compare Students based on their names. If you need to implement two or more alternative ways to compare two similar objects, then you may implement the Comparator interface. Listing 4-15 is an implementation (there is no change in the Student class, so we are not producing it here again).

Listing 4-15. ComparatorTest2.java

```java
// This program shows the implementation of Comparator interface

import java.util.Arrays;
import java.util.Comparator;

class CGPAComparator implements Comparator<Student> {
    public int compare(Student s1, Student s2) {
        return (s1.cgpa.compareTo(s2.cgpa));
    }
}

class ComparatorTest2 {
    public static void main(String []args) {
        Student []students = {  new Student("cs011", "Lennon   ", 3.1),
                        new Student("cs021", "McCartney", 3.4),
                        new Student("cs012", "Harrison ", 2.7),
                        new Student("cs022", "Starr ", 3.7) };

        System.out.println("Before sorting by CGPA ");
        System.out.println("Student-ID \t  Name \t  CGPA (for 4.0) ");
        System.out.println(Arrays.toString(students));

        Arrays.sort(students, new CGPAComparator());
```

```
        System.out.println("After sorting by CGPA");
        System.out.println("Student-ID \t  Name \t  CGPA (for 4.0) ");
        System.out.println(Arrays.toString(students));
    }
}
```

It prints the following:

```
Before sorting by CGPA
Student-ID       Name     CGPA (for 4.0)
[
  cs011          Lennon        3.1,
  cs021          McCartney     3.4,
  cs012          Harrison      2.7,
  cs022          Starr         3.7]
After sorting by CGPA
Student-ID       Name     CGPA (for 4.0)
[
  cs012          Harrison      2.7,
  cs011          Lennon        3.1,
  cs021          McCartney     3.4,
  cs022          Starr         3.7]
```

Yes, the program prints the Student data sorted by their CGPA. You didn't change the Student class, the class still implements the Comparable<String> interface and defines the compareTo() method, but you don't use the compareTo() method in your program. You create a separate class named CGPAComparator and implement the Comparator<Student> interface. You define the compare() method, which takes two Student objects as arguments. You compare the CGPA of the arguments s1 and s2 by (re)using the compareTo() method from the Double class. You didn't change anything in the main() method except for the way you call the sort() method. You create a new CGPAComparator() object and pass as the second argument to the sort() method. By default sort() uses the compareTo() method; since you are passing a Comparator object explicitly, it now uses the compare() method defined in the CGPAComparator. So, the Student objects are now compared and sorted based on their CGPA.

📝 Most classes have a natural order for comparing objects, so use Comparable interface in those cases. If you want to compare the objects other than the natural order or if there is no natural ordering present for your class type, then use the Comparator interface.

Collection Streams and Filters

Certification Objective

Collections Streams and Filters

The new stream API is provided in the java.util.stream package introduced in Java 8. The main type in this package is Stream<T> interface, which is the stream of object references. IntStream, LongStream, and DoubleStream are streams for primitive types int, long and double types respectively.

The Collection interface has been added with the methods stream() and parallelStream() in Java 8. A stream is a sequence of elements. You can perform sequential operations when you obtain a stream using the stream() method, and parallel operations with parallelStream() method. (We discuss parallel streams in Chapter 11.) Since interfaces such as List, Set, Deque, and Queue extend the Collection interface, you can get a stream or a parallel stream from the collection classes that implement these interfaces. For instance, you can get a stream from an ArrayList object.

Streams provide pipelining capability—you can filter, map, and search data. In other words, stream operations can be "chained" together to form a pipeline known as "stream pipeline". We introduce stream pipelines later in this section and cover them in detail in the chapter dedicated to streams (Chapter 6 on Java Stream API).

The most common source of streams is collection objects such as sets, maps, and lists. However, note that we can use the streams API independent of the collections. In the rest of this chapter, we will discuss how collections are used with streams.

Iterate Using forEach

Certification Objectives

Iterate using forEach methods of Streams and List

As Java programmers, we are used to performing external iteration on collections. Consider this list of strings for example:

```
List<String> strings = Arrays.asList("eeny", "meeny", "miny", "mo");
```

When we traverse such a collection using a for loop, we are using external iteration, as in:

```
for(String string : strings) {
System.out.println(string);
}
```

Internal iteration leaves the iteration to the library code. The same code can be converted to the following equivalent code that makes use of lambda expressions (Listing 4-16):

Listing 4-16. InternalIteration.java

```
import java.util.Arrays;
import java.util.List;

public class InternalIteration {
    public static void main(String []args) {
        List<String> strings = Arrays.asList("eeny", "meeny", "miny", "mo");
        strings.forEach(string -> System.out.println(string));
    }
}
```

This program prints:

```
eeny
meeny
miny
mo
```

Note that he List interface extends Iterable interface that has a default forEach method (this method was added in Java 8). Hence, we were able to perform internal iteration by calling the forEach method on strings object and pass a lambda expression to it as the parameter.

Though this example is simple, it illustrates a *major* change with the Java 8 approach: we are moving from external iteration to internal iteration. In fact, the whole of Stream API (Chapter 6) is based on the concept of internal iteration.

Before we discuss the Stream interface and the stream pipeline, let us discuss an important topic related to lambda functions that we use in the discussion on streams: method references.

Method References with Streams

Certification Objective

Use method references with Streams

In Listing 4-16, we used this lambda expression:

```
strings.forEach(string -> System.out.println(string));
```

This code is somewhat verbose because we are taking the string parameter and just passing it to System.out.println. Fortunately, Java 8 has introduced a feature known as "method references". Method references use the "::" operator. Here is a simplified expression using method references:

```
strings.forEach(System.out::println);
```

Method references route the given parameters. In this case, System.out::println is equivalent to using the lambda expression string -> System.out.println(string).

How about simplifying the following statement to use method references?

```
strings.forEach(string -> System.out.println(string.toUpperCase()));
```

The lambda expression in this code calls toUpperCase() method on the given String object. Since method references just route the parameters, so you cannot use them directly for simplifying this lambda expression. An alternative is to put this code inside a method and use the reference of that method (Listing 4-17).

Listing 4-17. MethodReference.java

```java
import java.util.Arrays;
import java.util.List;

class MethodReference {
    public static void printUpperCaseString(String string) {
        System.out.println(string.toUpperCase());
    }

    public static void main(String []args) {
        List<String> strings = Arrays.asList("eeny", "meeny", "miny", "mo");
        strings.forEach(MethodReference::printUpperCaseString);
    }
}
```

This program prints:

```
EENY
MEENY
MINY
MO
```

In this case, we have introduced a static method inside MethodReference class. The printUpperCaseString calls the toUpperCase() method on the passed String argument and prints the resulting string.

To summarize, there are two key benefits of method references:

- Method references serve as a way to route the parameters, and hence it is often convenient (results in more concise code) to use them than the equivalent lambda expressions. For instance, we saw how System.out::println can be used as an equivalent to arg -> System.out.println(arg) given in Listing 4-16.

The method reference syntax makes it easier to use a method as a lambda expression (as in Listing 4-17).

Understanding the Stream Interface

Certification Objective

Describe Stream interface and Stream pipeline

The Stream interface is the most important interface provided in the java.util.stream package. The classes IntStream, LongStream, and DoubleStream are Stream specializations for int, long, and double respectively. Figure 4-1 shows the inheritance hierarchy of these streams.

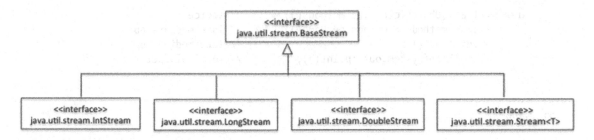

Figure 4-1. *Some important interfaces in java.util.stream package*

The Stream Pipeline

Stream operations can be "chained" together to form a "stream pipeline". There are three parts in the stream pipeline (see Figure 4-2):

- *Source*: Create a stream (from a collection or an array or using `Stream` methods such as `of()` and `generate()`).

- *Intermediate operations*: Optional operations that can be chained together (such as `map()`, `filter()`, `distinct()`, and `sorted()` methods in the `Stream` interface).

- *Terminal operations*: Produce a result (such as `sum()`, `collect()`, `forEach()`, and `reduce()` methods in the `Stream` interface).

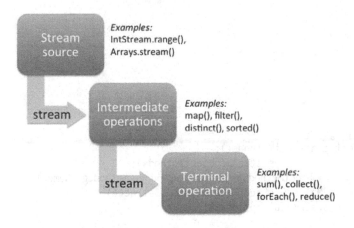

Figure 4-2. *The stream pipeline with examples*

Here is an example for a stream pipeline (Listing 4-18).

Listing 4-18. StreamPipelineExample.java

```java
import java.util.Arrays;

class StreamPipelineExample {
    public static void main(String []args) {
```

127

```
        Arrays.stream(Object.class.getMethods())      // source
                .map(method -> method.getName())      // intermediate op
                .distinct()                           // intermediate op
                .forEach(System.out::println);        // terminal operation
    }
}
```

This code prints

```
wait
equals
toString
hashCode
getClass
notify
notifyAll
```

The `Object.class.getMethods()` results in an array of `Method` objects in the `Object` class. The operation `map(method -> method.getName())` returns the names of the methods as an array (as part of a `Stream`). Note that the `wait()` method in `Object` class is an overloaded method. To get unique method names, we can use the `distinct()` operation to remove the duplicate entries in the array. Finally, the `forEach()` terminal operation prints the names of the methods.

One way to understand the stream pipeline is to break the components of the pipeline into separate statements. Listing 4-18 breaks the parts into separate components and is the equivalent code for Listing 4-19.

Listing 4-19. StreamPipelineComponents.java

```java
import java.util.Arrays;
import java.util.stream.Stream;
import java.lang.reflect.Method;

class StreamPipelineComponents {
    public static void main(String []args) {
        Method[] objectMethods = Object.class.getMethods();
        Stream<Method> objectMethodStream = Arrays.stream(objectMethods);
        Stream<String> objectMethodNames = objectMethodStream.map(method -> method.getName());
        Stream<String> uniqueObjectMethodNames = objectMethodNames.distinct();
        uniqueObjectMethodNames.forEach(System.out::println);
    }
}
```

In this case, we get a stream by calling `Arrays.stream()` method on the result of `Object.class.getMethod()`—this is the source of the stream. Both `map()` and `distinct()` methods take a stream as input and return a (modified) stream as the output. Finally, the `forEach()` method on the stream is the terminal operation in the pipeline.

Don't confuse `map` in streams with `java.util.Map` interface. The `map()` method is an intermediate operation that takes in elements from an incoming stream, applies the operation, and generates a stream of elements as output; the `Map` interface holds key value pairs.

Stream Sources

There are many sources for a stream, including generator methods in stream interfaces, collections, and arrays. Let us consider the simple task of getting a stream of integers values 1 to 5.

1. You can use range or iterate factory methods in the IntStream interface.

```
IntStream.range(1, 6)
```

The range() method takes two arguments: it starts from the start value (given as the first argument) and goes on adding 1 to result in stream elements till it reaches the end value (given as the second argument and is excluding that value itself). In this case, we have passed the values 1 and 6, so the reduce() method generates the stream of integer values starting from 1, adds the value 1 and results in values 2, 3, 4, and 5, and stops there because it hit the end value 6.

```
IntStream.iterate(1, i -> i + 1).limit(5)
```

The iterate() method takes two arguments: the initial value (as the first argument) and iteratively calls the given function (as second argument) by using the initial value as the seed. In this case, the first argument is 1, and it iteratively calls i + 1, generating the integer values 2, 3, 4, 5, ... This is an *infinite stream*. We limit the stream to the first five values by calling limit(5) over this infinite stream of integer values.

2. You can use the stream() method in java.util.Arrays class to create a stream from a given array, as in:

```
Arrays.stream(new int[] {1, 2, 3, 4, 5})
Arrays.stream(new Integer[] {1, 2, 3, 4, 5})
```

The stream() method was added in the Arrays class in Java 8:

```
// in Arrays class
public static IntStream stream(int[] array) { /* returns a stream of integers */ }
public static <T> Stream<T> stream(T[] array) { /* returns a stream of T objects */ }
```

Overloaded versions of stream() method takes long[], double[], and T[]. Since we are passing an int[] and the Integer[], the calls stream() method resolve to stream(int []) and stream(T[]) respectively and a integer stream is returned.

3. We can also create streams using factories and builders. The of() method is a factory method in the Stream interface:

```
Stream.of(1, 2, 3, 4, 5)
Stream.of(new Integer[]{1, 2, 3, 4, 5})
```

The overloaded of() method in Stream interface takes variable argument list or an element of type T. Also, you can use the builder() method and build the Stream object by adding each element, as in:

```
Stream.builder().add(1).add(2).add(3).add(4).add(5).build()
```

This is not an exhaustive list of ways that you can use to generate an integer stream—this is just to give you an idea that there are many ways to get a stream. As mentioned earlier, the Collection interface has been added with the methods stream() and parallelStream(). Hence, any Collection object is a source of a stream—you just need to call the stream() or parallelStream() method on it. For example:

```
List<String> strings = Arrays.asList("eeny", "meeny", "miny", "mo");
strings.stream().forEach(string -> System.out.println(string));
```

In this case, we are getting a stream from a List<String> object by calling the stream() method. There are numerous other types in the Java library that return a stream, such as:

- The lines() method in java.nio.file.Files class

- The splitAsStream() method in java.util.regex.Pattern class

- The ints() method in java.util.Random class

- The chars() method in java.lang.String class

Here are some quick one-liners on how to use them.

1. The java.nio.file.Files class has lines() method that returns a Stream<String>. This code prints the contents of the file "FileRead.java" in the current directory.

   ```
   Files.lines(Paths.get("./FileRead.java")).forEach(System.out::println);
   ```

2. The java.util.Pattern class has splitAsStream() method that returns a Stream<String>. This code splits the input string "java 8 streams" based on whitespace and hence prints the strings "java", "8", and "streams" on the console.

   ```
   Pattern.compile(" ").splitAsStream("java 8 streams").forEach
   (System.out::println);
   ```

3. The java.util.Random class has ints() method that returns an IntStream. It generates an infinite stream of random integers; so to restrict the number of integers to 5 integers, we call limit(5) on that stream.

   ```
   new Random().ints().limit(5).forEach(System.out::println);
   ```

4. The String class has chars() method (newly introduced in Java 8 in CharSequence—an interface that String class implements). This method returns an IntStream (why IntStream? Remember that there is no equivalent char specialization for Streams). This code calls sorted() method on this stream, so the stream elements get sorted in ascending order. Because it is a stream of integers, this code uses "%c" to explicitly force the conversion from int to char.

   ```
   "hello".chars().sorted().forEach(ch -> System.out.printf("%c ", ch));
   // prints e h l l o
   ```

In these examples we have already used intermediate operations such as limit() and sorted(). Let us discuss such intermediate operations in more detail now.

Intermediate Operations

Intermediate operations transform elements in a stream. Table 4-5 lists some of the important intermediate operations in Stream<T>. We discuss other intermediate operations such as flatMap() and its variants in Chapter 6 on Streams API.

Table 4-5. *Important Intermediate Operations in the Stream Interface*

Method	Short description
Stream<T> filter(Predicate<? super T> check)	Removes the elements for which the check predicate returns false.
<R> Stream<R> map(Function<? super T,? extends R> transform)	Applies the transform() function for each of the elements in the stream.
Stream<T> distinct()	Removes duplicate elements in the stream; it uses the equals() method to determine if an element is repeated in the stream.
Stream<T> sorted() Stream<T> sorted(Comparator<? super T> compare)	Sorts the elements in its natural order. The overloaded version takes a Comparator—you can pass a lambda function for that.
Stream<T> peek(Consumer<? super T> consume)	Returns the same elements in the stream, but also executes the passed consume lambda expression on the elements.
Stream<T> limit(long size)	Removes the elements if there are more elements than the given size in the stream.

Observe that all the intermediate operations in this table return a Stream<T> as the result.

Intermediate operations are optional; there need not be any intermediate operations in a stream pipeline. Here is a simple example:

```
Stream.of(1, 2, 3, 4, 5).count();
```

This code returns the value 5. In this case, Stream.of() method is the stream source, and the count() method is a terminal operation. The count() method returns the number of elements in the stream.

Let us introduce an intermediate operation in this stream pipeline:

```
Stream.of(1, 2, 3, 4, 5).map(i -> i * i).count();
```

The map() operation applies the given function passed as its argument on the elements of the stream. In this case, it squares the elements in the stream. This code also returns the value 5. You can you the check result of applying the map() method in this code? You can use peek() method for that:

```
Stream.of(1, 2, 3, 4, 5).map(i -> i * i).peek(i -> System.out.printf("%d ", i)).count();
```

This code prints

```
1 4 9 16 25
```

This example also illustrates how the intermediate operations can be chained together. This is made possible because intermediate operations return streams.

Now, let us add a peek() method before calling the map() method to understand how it works:

```
Stream.of(1, 2, 3, 4, 5)
            .peek(i -> System.out.printf("%d ", i))
            .map(i -> i * i)
            .peek(i -> System.out.printf("%d ", i))
            .count();
```

This code prints

```
1 1 2 4 3 9 4 16 5 25
```

As you can observe from this output, the stream pipeline is processing the elements one by one. Each element is mapped to its square value. The peek() method helps us understand how the stream is processing the elements.

The peek() method is meant primarily for debugging purposes. It helps us understand how the elements are transformed in the pipeline. Do *not* use it in production code.

Filtering a Collection

Certification Objective

Filter a collection by using lambda expressions

The filter() method in the Stream interface is used for removing the elements that do not match the given condition. Here is a simple example that uses Stream's filter() method for removing odd integers (Listing 4-20).

Listing 4-20. EvenNumbers.java

```
import java.util.stream.IntStream;

class EvenNumbers {
    public static void main(String []args) {
        IntStream.rangeClosed(0, 10)
                .filter(i -> (i % 2) == 0)
                .forEach(System.out::println);
    }
}
```

This program prints

```
0
2
4
6
8
10
```

In this example, we are using IntStream class—one of the specializations of Stream for ints. The rangeClosed(startValue, endValueInclusiveOfEnd) method generates a sequence of integers starting with startValue till (and inclusive of) endValueInclusiveOfEnd. Here, the rangeClosed(0, 10) results in integer values 0, 1, 2, ... , 9, 10 (note the value 10). There is also a similar method range(startValue, endValueExclusiveOfEnd) that generates a sequence of integers starting with startValue till (without including) endValueExclusiveOfEnd.

From the result of this rangeClosed() method, we apply filter() method on it. Here is the signature of the filter() method:

```
IntStream filter(IntPredicate predicate)
```

The filter() method applies the given predicate to determine if the element should be included as part of the returned stream or eliminated (i.e., filter). The java.util.function.IntPredicate functional interface has the function with the following signature:

```
boolean test(int value);
```

Here we pass a lambda function i -> (i % 2) == 0 to match the IntPredicate functional interface that returns a boolean value. If the element currently being processed returns true (i.e., in this case, it is even), then it is part of the stream or it is eliminated.

Alternatively, you can define a function with the function type of IntPredicate functional interface and pass it to filter.

```
// you can define this static function within EvenNumbers class
public static boolean isEven(int i) {
    return (i % 2) == 0;
}
```

Now, instead of passing the lambda function to filter() method, you can pass a method reference instead, as in filter(EvenNumbers::isEven).

Often map() and filter() methods are used together. For example, the following program prints the squares of the even numbers (Listing 4-21).

Listing 4-21. EvenSquares.java

```
import java.util.stream.IntStream;

class EvenSquares {
    public static void main(String []args) {
        IntStream.rangeClosed(0, 10)
                .map(i -> i * i)
                .filter(i -> (i % 2) == 0)
                .forEach(System.out::println);
    }
}
```

This program prints

```
0
4
16
36
64
100
```

However, this code unnecessarily computes the squares of odd numbers (squares of odd numbers are always odd). So, we can change the order of map and filter operations to eliminate those unnecessary computations:

```
IntStream.rangeClosed(0, 10)
        .filter(i -> (i % 2) == 0)
        .map(i -> i * i)        // call map AFTER calling filter
        .forEach(System.out::println);
```

This output is the same. This simple example shows how you can sometimes change the order of intermediate operations without changing the behavior.

Terminal Operations

You need to provide a terminal operation at the end of a pipeline. This terminal operation typically produces a result, such as calling the methods sum(), min(), max(), or average() on an IntStream. A terminal operation can also perform other actions such as accumulating the elements with reduce(), collect() methods or just perform an action as in calling the forEach() method. Table 4-6 lists some of the important terminal operations in Stream<T>.

Table 4-6. *Important Terminal Operations in the Stream Interface*

Method	Short description
void forEach(Consumer<? super T> action)	Calls the action for every element in the stream.
Object[] toArray()	Returns an Object array that has the elements in the stream.
Optional<T> min(Comparator<? super T> compare)	Returns the minimum value in the stream (compares the objects using the given compare function).
Optional<T> max(Comparator<? super T> compare)	Returns the maximum value in the stream (compares the objects using the given compare function).
long count()	Returns the number of elements in the stream.

There are many important terminal operations such as reduce(), collect(), findFirst(), findAny(), anyMatch(), allMatch(), **and** noneMatch() methods. We discuss these methods (and also the Optional<T> mentioned in this table) later in Chapter 6 on Stream API. Further, the IntStream, LongStream, and DoubleStream have methods such as sum(), min(), max(), and average() that operate on the stream of ints, longs, and doubles respectively.

Here is an example that uses toArray() method in the Stream interface:

```
Object [] words = Pattern.compile(" ").splitAsStream("1 2 3 4 5").toArray();
System.out.println(Arrays.stream(words).mapToInt(str -> Integer.valueOf((String)str)).sum());
```

This program prints:

15

In this program, we have a string "1 2 3 4 5" and splitAsStream() returns a stream of Strings. We have converted that stream of Strings into an Object array named words; we then convert the array back to streams using Arrays.stream(words) (just for illustrating how you can convert a stream to an array and back!). Now, we map each Object entry into a String and then to an integer value. Finally, we call the terminal operation sum() to get the sum of the integers as 15.

Once a terminal operation is complete, the stream on which it operated on is considered "consumed". If you attempt to "use" the stream again, you will get an IllegalStateException (Listing 4-22).

Listing 4-22. StreamReuse.java

```
import java.util.stream.IntStream;

public class StreamReuse {
    public static void main(String []args) {
    IntStream chars =  "bookkeep".chars();
        System.out.println(chars.count());
        chars.distinct().sorted().forEach(ch -> System.out.printf("%c ", ch));
    }
}
```

The variable chars points to the stream created from the string "bookkeep". When we get chars.count(), the stream is "consumed". Why? Because count() method is a terminal operation. Because we try to use the stream again in the next statement, this program crashes by throwing IllegalStateException.

Summary

Let us briefly review the key points for each certification objective in this chapter. Please read it before appearing for the exam.

Create and use a generic class

- Generics will ensure that any attempts to add elements of types other than the specified type(s) will be caught at compile time itself. Hence, generics offer generic implementation with type safety.

- Java 7 introduced *diamond* syntax where the type parameters (after new operator and class name) can be omitted. The compiler will infer the types from the type declaration.

- Generics are not covariant. That is, subtyping doesn't work with generics; you cannot assign a derived generic type parameter to a base type parameter.

- Avoid mixing raw types with generic types. In other cases, make sure of the type safety manually.

- The `<?>` specifies an unknown type in generics and is known as a wildcard. For example, `List<?>` refers to a list of unknowns.

Create and use ArrayList, TreeSet, TreeMap, and ArrayDeque objects

- The terms Collection, Collections, and collection are different. `Collection`—`java.util.Collection<E>`—is the root interface in the collection hierarchy. `Collections`—`java.util.Collections`—is a utility class that contains only static methods. The general term *collection(s)* refers to containers like map, stack, and queue.

- Remember that you cannot add or remove elements to the `List` returned by the `Arrays.asList()` method. But, you can make changes to the elements in the returned `List`, and the changes made to that `List` are reflected back in the array.

- A `HashSet` is for quickly inserting and retrieving elements; it does *not* maintain any sorting order for the elements it holds. A `TreeSet` stores the elements in a sorted order (and it implements the `SortedSet` interface).

- A `HashMap` uses a hash table data structure internally. In `HashMap`, searching (or looking up elements) is a fast operation. However, `HashMap` neither remembers the order in which you inserted elements nor keeps elements in any sorted order. Unlike `HashMap`, `TreeMap` keeps the elements in sorted order (i.e., sorted by its keys). So, searching or inserting is somewhat slower than the `HashMap`.

- Deque (Doubly ended queue) is a data structure that allows you to insert and remove elements from both ends. There are three concrete implementations of the Deque interface: `LinkedList`, `ArrayDeque`, and `LinkedBlockingDeque`.

- The difference between an `ArrayList` and `ArrayDeque` is that you can add an element anywhere in an array list using an index; however, you can add an element only either at the front or end of the array deque.

Use java.util.Comparator and java.lang.Comparable interfaces

- Implement the `Comparable` interface for your classes where a natural order is possible. If you want to compare the objects other than the natural order or if there is no natural ordering present for your class type, then create separate classes implementing the `Comparator` interface. Also, if you have multiple alternative ways to decide the order, then go for the `Comparator` interface.

Collections Streams and Filters

- The new stream API is provided in the `java.util.stream` package introduced in Java 8. The main type in this package is `Stream<T>` interface, which is the stream of object references. `IntStream`, `LongStream`, and `DoubleStream` are streams for primitive types `int`, `long`, and `double` types respectively.

- A stream is a sequence of elements. In Java 8, the `Collection` interface has been added with the methods `stream()` and `parallelStream()` from which you can respectively get sequential and parallel streams.

Iterate using forEach methods of Streams and List

- In Java 8, we are moving from external iteration to internal iteration. It is a *major* change with Java 8 approach of functional programming.

- The interfaces Stream and Iterable define forEach() method. The forEach() method supports internal iteration.

Describe Stream interface and Stream pipeline

- Stream operations can be "chained" together to form a pipeline known as "stream pipeline".

- A stream pipeline has a beginning, middle, and an end: *source* (that creates a stream), *intermediate operations* (that consist of optional operations that can be chained together), and *terminal operations* (that produce a result).

- The terminal operation can produce a result, accumulate the stream elements, or just perform an action.

- You can use a stream only once. Any attempt at reusing the stream (for example, by calling intermediate or terminal operations) will result in throwing an IllegalStateException.

Filter a collection by using lambda expressions

- The filter() method in the Stream interface is used for removing the elements that do not match the given condition.

Use method references with Streams

- When lambda expressions just route the given parameters, you can use method references instead.

- Since method references serve as a way to route the parameters, it is often convenient (as it results in more concise code) to use them than their equivalent lambda expressions.

QUESTION TIME

1. Choose the correct option based on this program:

```java
import java.util.*;

class UtilitiesTest {
    public static void main(String []args) {
        List<int> intList = new ArrayList<>();
        intList.add(10);
        intList.add(20);
        System.out.println("The list is: " + intList);
    }
}
```

    A.   It prints the following: The list is: [10, 20]

    B.   It prints the following: The list is: [20, 10]

    C.   It results in a compiler error

    D.   It results in a runtime exception

2.   Choose the correct option based on this program:

```java
import java.util.*;

class UtilitiesTest {
    public static void main(String []args) {
        List<Integer> intList = new LinkedList<>();
        List<Double> dblList = new LinkedList<>();
        System.out.println("First type: " + intList.getClass());
        System.out.println("Second type:" + dblList.getClass());
    }
}
```

    A.   It prints the following:

        First type: class java.util.LinkedList

        Second type:class java.util.LinkedList

    B.   It prints the following:

        First type: class java.util.LinkedList<Integer>

        Second type:class java.util.LinkedList<Double>

    C.   It results in a compiler error

    D.   It results in a runtime exception

3.   Choose the correct option based on this program:

```java
import java.util.Arrays;

class DefaultSorter {
    public static void main(String[] args) {
        String[] brics = {"Brazil", "Russia", "India", "China"};
        Arrays.sort(brics, null);    // LINE A
        for(String country : brics) {
            System.out.print(country + " ");
        }
    }
}
```

A. This program will result in a compiler error in line marked with comment LINE A

B. When executed, the program prints the following: Brazil Russia India China

C. When executed, the program prints the following: Brazil China India Russia

D. When executed, the program prints the following: Russia India China Brazil

E. When executed, the program throws a runtime exception of
NullPointerException when executing the line marked with comment LINE A

F. When executed, the program throws a runtime exception of
InvalidComparatorException when executing the line marked with
comment LINE A

4. Choose the correct option based on this code segment:

```
"abracadabra".chars().distinct().peek(ch -> System.out.printf("%c ", ch)).
sorted();
```

A. It prints: "a b c d r"

B. It prints: "a b r c d"

C. It crashes by throwing a java.util.IllegalFormatConversionException

D. This program terminates normally without printing any output in the console

5. Choose the correct option based on this code segment:

```
IntStream.rangeClosed(1, 1).forEach(System.out::println);
```

A. It prints: 1

B. It crashes by throwing a java.lang.UnsupportedOperationException

C. It crashes by throwing a java.lang.StackOverflowError

D. It crashes by throwing a java.lang.IllegalArgumentException

E. This program terminates normally without printing any output in the console

6. Choose the correct option based on this program:

```
import java.util.stream.DoubleStream;

public class DoubleUse {
    public static void main(String []args) {
        DoubleStream nums = DoubleStream.of(1.0, 2.0, 3.0).map(i -> -i); // #1
        System.out.printf("count = %d, sum = %f", nums.count(), nums.sum());
    }
}
```

A. This program results in a compiler error in the line marked with comment #1

B. This program prints: "count = 3, sum = -6.000000"

C. This program crashes by throwing a java.util.IllegalFormatConversionException

D. This program crashes by throwing a java.lang.IllegalStateException

7. Choose the correct option based on this program:

```java
class Consonants {
    private static boolean removeVowels(int c) {
        switch(c) {
        case 'a': case 'e': case 'i': case 'o': case 'u': return true;
        }
        return false;
    }
    public static void main(String []args) {
        "avada kedavra".chars()
                .filter(Consonants::removeVovels)
                .forEach(ch -> System.out.printf("%c", ch));
    }
}
```

A. This program results in a compiler error

B. This program prints: "aaaeaa"

C. This program prints: "vd kdvr"

D. This program prints: "avada kedavra"

E. This program crashes by throwing a java.util.IllegalFormatConversionException

F. This program crashes by throwing a java.lang.IllegalStateException

8. Choose the correct option based on this program:

```java
import java.util.*;

class DequeTest {
    public static void main(String []args) {
        Deque<Integer> deque = new ArrayDeque<>();
        deque.addAll(Arrays.asList(1, 2, 3, 4, 5));
        System.out.println("The removed element is: " + deque.remove());
        // ERROR?
    }
}
```

A. When executed, this program prints the following: "The removed element is: 5"

B. When executed, this program prints the following: "The removed element is: 1"

C. When compiled, the program results in a compiler error of "`remove()` returns void" for the line marked with the comment `ERROR`.

D. When executed, this program throws `InvalidOperationException`.

9. Determine the behavior of this program:

```java
import java.io.*;

class LastError<T> {
    private T lastError;
    void setError(T t){
        lastError = t;
        System.out.println("LastError: setError");
    }
}

class StrLastError<S extends CharSequence> extends LastError<String>{
    public StrLastError(S s) {
    }
    void setError(S s){
        System.out.println("StrLastError: setError");
    }
}

class Test {
    public static void main(String []args) {
        StrLastError<String> err = new StrLastError<String>("Error");
        err.setError("Last error");
    }
}
```

A. It prints the following: `StrLastError: setError`

B. It prints the following: `LastError: setError`

C. It results in a compilation error

D. It results in a runtime exception

Answers:

1. C. It results in a compiler error

    You cannot specify primitive types along with generics, so List<int> needs to be changed to List<Integer>.

2. A. It prints the following:

    First type: class java.util.LinkedList

    Second type:class java.util.LinkedList

    Due to type erasure, after compilation both types are treated as same LinkedList type.

3. C. When executed, the program prints the following: Brazil China India Russia

    When null is passed as a second argument to the Arrays.sort() method, it means that the default Comparable (i.e., natural ordering for the elements) should be used. The default Comparator results in sorting the elements in ascending order. The program does not result in a NullPointerException or any other exceptions or a compiler error.

4. D. This program terminates normally without printing any output in the console

    A stream pipeline is lazily evaluated. Since there is no terminal operation provided (such as count, forEach, reduce, or collect), this pipeline is not evaluated and hence the peek does not print any output to the console.

5. A. It prints: 1

    The rangeClosed(startValue, endValueInclusiveOfEnd) method generates a sequence of integers starting with startValue till (and inclusive of) endValueInclusiveOfEnd. Hence the call IntStream.rangeClosed(1, 1) results in a stream with only one element and the forEach() method prints that value.

6. D. This program crashes by throwing a java.lang.IllegalStateException

    A stream is considered "consumed" when a terminal operation is called on that stream. The methods count() and sum() are terminal operations in DoubleStream. When this code calls nums.count(), the underlying stream is already "consumed". When the printf calls nums.sum(), this program results in throwing java.lang. IllegalStateException due to the attempt to use a consumed stream.

7. B. This program prints: "aaaeaa"

    Because the Consonants::removeVowels returns true when there is a vowel passed, only those characters are retained in the stream by the filter method. Hence, this program prints "aaaeaa".

8. B. When executed, this program prints the following: "The removed element is: 1".

    The remove() method is equivalent to the removeFirst() method, which removes the first element (head of the queue) of the Deque object.

9. C. It results in a compilation error

It looks like the `setError()` method in `StrLastError` is overriding `setError()` in the `LastError` class. However, it is not the case. At the time of compilation, the knowledge of type `S` is not available. Therefore, the compiler records the signatures of these two methods as `setError(String)` in superclass and `setError(S_extends_CharSequence)` in subclass—treating them as overloaded methods (not overridden). In this case, when the call to `setError()` is found, the compiler finds both the overloaded methods matching, resulting in the ambiguous method call error. Here is the error message

```
Test.java:22: error: reference to setError is ambiguous, both method setError(T)
in LastError and method setError(S) in StrLastError match
               err.setError("Last error");
                  ^
```

where T and S are type-variables:

T extends `Object` declared in class `LastError`. S extends `CharSequence` declared in class `StrLastError`.

■ ■ ■

CHAPTER 5

Lambda Built-in Functional Interfaces

Certification Objectives

Use the built-in interfaces included in the java.util.function package such as Predicate, Consumer, Function, and Supplier

Develop code that uses primitive versions of functional interfaces

Develop code that uses binary versions of functional interfaces

Develop code that uses the UnaryOperator interface

The java.util.function has numerous built-in interfaces. Other packages in the Java library (notably java.util.stream package) make use of the interfaces defined in this package. For OCPJP 8 exam, you should be familiar with using key interfaces provided in this package.

As we discussed earlier (in Chapter 3), a functional interface declares a single abstract method (but in addition it can have any number of default or static methods). Functional interfaces are useful for creating lambda expressions. The entire java.util.function package consists of functional interfaces.

Before defining your own functional interfaces, consider using readily available functional interfaces defined in the java.util.function package based on your need. If the signature of the lambda function you are looking for is not available in any of the functional interfaces provided in this library, you can define your own functional interfaces.

Using Built-in Functional Interfaces

Certification Objective

Use the built-in interfaces included in the java.util.function package such as Predicate, Consumer, Function, and Supplier

In this section, let us discuss four important built-in interfaces included in the java.util.function package: Predicate, Consumer, Function, and Supplier. See Table 5-1 and Figure 5-1 to get an overview of these functional interfaces.

Table 5-1. *Key Functional Interfaces in java.util.function Package*

Functional Interface	Brief Description	Common Use
Predicate<T>	Checks a condition and returns a boolean value as result	In filter() method in java.util.stream.Stream which is used to remove elements in the stream that don't match the given condition (i.e., predicate) as argument.
Consumer<T>	Operation that takes an argument but returns nothing	In forEach() method in collections and in java.util.stream.Stream; this method is used for traversing all the elements in the collection or stream.
Function<T, R>	Functions that take an argument and return a result	In map() method in java.util.stream.Stream to transform or operate on the passed value and return a result.
Supplier<T>	Operation that returns a value to the caller (the returned value could be same or different values)	In generate() method in java.util.stream.Stream to create an infinite stream of elements.

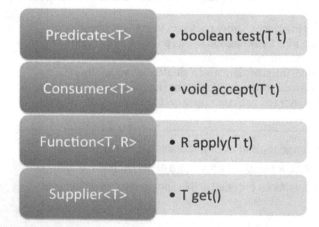

Figure 5-1. *Abstract method declarations in key functional interfaces in java.util.function package*

The Predicate Interface

In code, we often need to use functions that check a condition and return a boolean value. Consider the following code segment:

```
Stream.of("hello", "world")
    .filter(str -> str.startsWith("h"))
    .forEach(System.out::println);
```

This code segment just prints "hello" on the console. The filter() method returns true only if the passed string starts with "h", and hence it "filters out" the string "world" from the stream because the string does not start with "h". In this code, the filter() method takes a Predicate as an argument. Here is the Predicate functional interface:

```
@FunctionalInterface
public interface Predicate<T> {
    boolean test(T t);
    // other methods elided
}
```

The abstract method named test() that takes an argument and returns true or false (Figure 5-2).

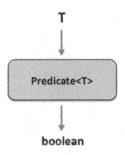

Figure 5-2. A Predicate<T> takes an argument of type T and returns a boolean value as the result

---

📋 A Predicate<T> "affirms" something as true or false: it takes an argument of type T, and returns a boolean value. You can call test() method on a Predicate object.

This functional interface also defines default methods named and() and or() that take a Predicate and return a Predicate. These methods have behavior similar to && and || operators. The method negate() returns a Predicate, and its behavior is similar to the ! operator. How are they useful? Here is a program that illustrates the use of and() method in Predicate interface (Listing 5-1).

Listing 5-1. PredicateTest.java

```
import java.util.function.Predicate;

public class PredicateTest {
    public static void main(String []args) {
        Predicate<String> nullCheck = arg -> arg != null;
        Predicate<String> emptyCheck = arg -> arg.length() > 0;
        Predicate<String> nullAndEmptyCheck = nullCheck.and(emptyCheck);
        String helloStr = "hello";
        System.out.println(nullAndEmptyCheck.test(helloStr));

        String nullStr = null;
        System.out.println(nullAndEmptyCheck.test(nullStr));
    }
}
```

This program prints:

```
true
false
```

In this program, the object nullCheck is a Predicate that returns true if the given String argument is not null. The emptyCheck predicate returns true if the given string is not empty. The nullAndEmptyCheck predicate combines nullCheck and emptyCheck predicates by making use of the default method named and() provided in Predicate. Since helloStr points to the string "hello" in the first call nullAndEmptyCheck. test(helloStr), and the string is not empty, it returns true. However, in the next call, nullStr is null, and hence the call nullAndEmptyCheck.test(nullStr) returns false.

To give another example for using Predicates, here is a code segment that makes use of the removeIf() method added in the Collection interface in Java 8 (Listing 5-2).

Listing 5-2. RemoveIfMethod.java

```java
import java.util.List;
import java.util.ArrayList;

public class RemoveIfMethod {
    public static void main(String []args) {
        List<String> greeting = new ArrayList<>();
        greeting.add("hello");
        greeting.add("world");

        greeting.removeIf(str -> !str.startsWith("h"));
        greeting.forEach(System.out::println);
    }
}
```

It prints "hello" in the console. The default method removeIf() defined in the Collection interface (a super interface of ArrayList) takes a Predicate as an argument:

```
default boolean removeIf(Predicate<? super E> filter)
```

In the call to removeIf() method, we are passing a lambda expression that matches the abstract method boolean test(T t) declared in the Predicate interface:

```
greeting.removeIf(str -> !str.startsWith("h"));
```

As a result, the string "world" from the ArrayList object greeting is removed and hence only "hello" is printed in the console. In this code we have used the ! operator. Instead of that, how about using the equivalent negate() method defined in Predicate? Yes, it is possible, and here is the changed code:

```
greeting.removeIf(((Predicate<String>) str -> str.startsWith("h")).negate());
```

When you execute the program in Listing 5.2 with this change, the program prints "hello". Note how we have performed explicit typecast (to Predicate<String>) in this expression. Without this explicit type cast–as in ((str -> str.startsWith("h")).negate())–the compiler cannot perform type inference to determine the matching functional interface and hence will report an error.

The Consumer Interface

There are many methods that take one argument, perform some operations based on the argument but do not return anything to their callers–they are consumer methods. Consider the following code segment:

```
Stream.of("hello", "world")
    .forEach(System.out::println);
```

This code segment prints the words "hello" and "world" that are part of the stream by using the forEach() method defined in the Stream interface. This method is declared in java.util.stream.Stream interface as follows:

```
void forEach(Consumer<? super T> action);
```

The forEach() takes an instance of Consumer as the argument. The Consumer functional interface declares an abstract method named accept() (Figure 5-3):

```
@FunctionalInterface
public interface Consumer<T> {
    void accept(T t);
        // the default andThen method elided
}
```

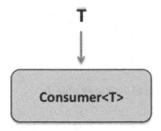

Figure 5-3. *A Consumer<T> takes an argument of type T and returns nothing*

The accept() method "consumes" an object and returns nothing (void).

📝 A Consumer<T> "consumes" something: it takes an argument (of generic type T) and returns nothing (void). You can call accept() method on a Consumer object.

Here is an example that uses the Consumer interface:

```
Consumer<String> printUpperCase = str -> System.out.println(str.toUpperCase());
printUpperCase.accept("hello");
// prints: HELLO
```

In this code, the lambda expression takes the given string, converts to upper case, and prints it to the console. We are passing the actual argument "hello" to the accept() method.

Now, let us come back to the discussion on forEach(): how does the call forEach(System.out::println) work?

The System class has a static variable named out that is of type PrintStream. The PrintStream class defines overloaded println methods; one of the overloaded methods has the signature void println(String). In the call forEach(System.out::println), we are passing the method reference for println, i.e., System.out::println. This method reference matches the signature of the abstract method in the Consumer interface, i.e., void accept(T). Hence, the method reference System.out::println serves to implement the functional interface Consumer and the code prints the strings "hello" and "world" to console. Listing 5-3 breaks the code Stream.of("hello", "world").forEach(System.out::println); into three different statements just to show how it works.

Listing 5-3. ConsumerUse.java

```java
import java.util.stream.Stream;
import java.util.function.Consumer;

class ConsumerUse {
    public static void main(String []args) {
        Stream<String> strings = Stream.of("hello", "world");
        Consumer<String> printString = System.out::println;
        strings.forEach(printString);
    }
}
```

This program prints:

```
hello
world
```

Consumer also has a default method named andThen(); it allows chaining calls to Consumer objects.

The Function Interface

Consider this example that makes use of map() method in java.util.stream.Stream interface (Listing 5-4):

Listing 5-4. FunctionUse.java

```java
import java.util.Arrays;

public class FunctionUse {
    public static void main(String []args) {
        Arrays.stream("4, -9, 16".split(", "))
                .map(Integer::parseInt)
                .map(i -> (i < 0) ? -i : i)
                .forEach(System.out::println);
    }
}
```

This program prints:

```
4
9
16
```

This program creates a stream of Strings by splitting the string "4, -9, 16". The method reference Integer::parseInt is passed to map() method–this call returns an Integer object for each element in the stream. In the second call to map() method in the stream, we have used the lambda function (i -> (i < 0) ? -i : i) to produce a list of non-negative integers (alternatively, we could have used Math::abs method). The map() method we have used here takes a Function as an argument (this example is to illustrate where a Function interface is useful). Finally, the resulting integers are printed using the forEach() method.

The Function interface defines a single abstract method named apply() that takes an argument of generic type T and returns an object of generic type R (Figure 5-4):

```
@FunctionalInterface
public interface Function<T, R> {
    R apply(T t);
    // other methods elided
}
```

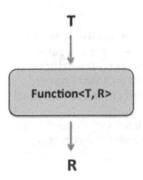

Figure 5-4. *A Function<T, R> takes an argument of type T and returns a value of type R*

The Function interface also has default methods such as compose(), andThen(), and identity().

🖉 A Function<T, R> "operates" on something and returns something: it takes one argument (of generic type T) and returns an object (of generic type R). You can call apply() method on a Function object.

Here is a simple example that uses a Function:

```
Function<String, Integer> strLength = str -> str.length();
System.out.println(strLength.apply("supercalifragilisticexpialidocious"));
// prints: 34
```

This code takes a string and returns its length. For the call, strLength.apply, we pass the string "supercalifragilisticexpialidocious". As a result of making the call apply(), we get the length of this string 34 as the result.

Let us change our earlier program in Listing 5-4 to use andThen() method (Listing 5-5).

Listing 5-5. CombineFunctions.java

```java
import java.util.Arrays;
import java.util.function.Function;

public class CombineFunctions {
    public static void main(String []args) {
        Function<String, Integer> parseInt = Integer::parseInt;
        Function<Integer, Integer> absInt = Math::abs;
        Function<String, Integer> parseAndAbsInt = parseInt.andThen(absInt);

        Arrays.stream("4, -9, 16".split(", "))
                .map(parseAndAbsInt)
                .forEach(System.out::println);
    }

}
```

This program prints 4, 9, and 16 in separate lines: the same output as Listing 5-4, but makes a single call to map() method in Stream. Because the Integer::parseInt() takes a String as an argument, parses it to return an Integer, we declare parseInt() method of type Function<String, Integer>. The Math::abs method takes an integer and returns an integer, and hence we declare it to be of type Function<Integer, Integer>. Since the parseAndAbsInt takes a String as argument and returns an integer as result, we declare it to be of type Function<String, Integer>.

What is the difference between andThen() and compose() methods in Function interface? The andThen() method applies the passed argument *after* calling the current Function (as in this example). The compose() method calls the argument *before* calling the current Function, as in:

```java
Function<String, Integer> parseAndAbsInt = absInt.compose(parseInt);
```

The identity() function in Function just returns the passed argument without doing anything! Then what is its use? It is sometimes used for testing – when you write a piece of code that takes a Function and want to check if it works, you can call identity() because it doesn't do anything. Here is an example:

```java
Arrays.stream("4, -9, 16".split(", "))
                .map(Function.identity())
                .forEach(System.out::println);
```

In this code, the map(Function.identity()) does nothing; it just passes along the elements in the stream to the call forEach(System.out::println). Hence the code prints the elements as they are, i.e., the values 4, -9, and 16 in separate lines.

The Supplier Interface

In programs, often we need to use a method that does not take any input but returns some output. Consider the following program that generates Boolean values (Listing 5-6):

Listing 5-6. GenerateBooleans.java

```java
import java.util.stream.Stream;
import java.util.Random;

class GenerateBooleans {
    public static void main(String []args) {
        Random random = new Random();
        Stream.generate(random::nextBoolean)
                .limit(2)
                .forEach(System.out::println);
    }
}
```

This program randomly prints two boolean values, for example, "true" and "false". The generate() method in Stream interface is a static member that takes a Supplier as the argument:

```java
static <T> Stream<T> generate(Supplier<T> s)
```

Here, you are passing the method reference for nextBoolean defined in java.util.Random class. It returns a boolean value chosen randomly:

```java
boolean          nextBoolean()
```

You can pass the method reference for nextBoolean to Stream's generate() method because it matches the abstract method in the Supplier interface, i.e., T get() Figure 5-5).

```java
@FunctionalInterface
public interface Supplier<T> {
    T get();
    // no other methods in this interface
}
```

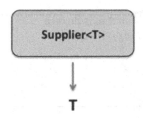

Figure 5-5. *A Supplier<T > takes no arguments and returns a value of type T*

🗒️ A Supplier<T> "supplies" takes nothing but returns something: it has no arguments and returns an object (of generic type T). You can call get() method on a Supplier object.

153

Here is a simple example that returns a value without taking anything as input:

```
Supplier<String> currentDateTime = () -> LocalDateTime.now().toString();
System.out.println(currentDateTime.get());
```

We have invoked the now() method on java.time.LocalDateTime (we discuss the java date and time API in Chapter 8). When we executed it, it printed: 2015-10-16T12:40:55.164. Of course, if you try this code, you will get a different output. Here we are using a Supplier<String>. The lambda expression does not take any output but returns the current date/time as a String format. We are invoking the lambda when we call the get() method on currentDateTime variable.

Constructor References

Consider the following code:

```
Supplier<String> newString = String::new;
System.out.println(newString.get());
// prints an empty string (nothing) to the console and then a newline character
```

This code makes use of constructor references. This code is equivalent to:

```
Supplier<String> newString = () -> new String();
System.out.println(newString.get());
```

With a method reference using ::new, this lambda expression gets simplified, as in String::new. How to use constructors that take arguments? For example, consider the constructor Integer(String): this Integer constructor takes a String as an argument and creates an Integer object with the value given in that string. Here is how you can use that constructor:

```
Function<String, Integer> anotherInteger = Integer::new;
System.out.println(anotherInteger.apply("100"));
// this code prints: 100
```

We cannot use a Supplier here because Suppliers do not take any arguments. Functions do take arguments and the return type here is Integer, and hence we can use Function<String, Integer>.

Primitive Versions of Functional Interfaces

Certification Objective

Develop code that uses primitive versions of functional interfaces

The built-in interfaces Predicate, Consumer, Function, and Supplier operate on reference type objects. For primitive types there are specializations available for int, long and double types for these functional interfaces. Consider Predicate that operates on objects of type T, i.e., it is Predicate<T>. The specializations for int, long, and double for Predicate are IntPredicate, LongPredicate, and DoublePredicate respectively.

Due to limitations in generics, you cannot use primitive type values with functional interfaces Predicate, Consumer, Function, and Supplier. But you can use wrapper types such as Integer and Double with these functional interfaces. When you try to use primitive types with these functional interfaces, it results in implicit autoboxing and unboxing, for example, an int value gets converted to an Integer object and vice versa. In fact, you often won't even realize that you are using the wrapper types with these functional interfaces. However, performance can suffer when we use wrapper types: think of boxing and unboxing a few million integers in a stream. To avoid this performance problem, you can instead use relevant primitive versions of these functional interfaces.

Primitive Versions of Predicate Interface

Consider this example:

```
IntStream.range(1, 10).filter(i -> (i % 2) == 0).forEach(System.out::println);
```

Here the filter() method takes an IntPredicate as the argument since the underlying stream is an IntStream. Here is the equivalent code that explicitly uses an IntPredicate:

```
IntPredicate evenNums = i -> (i % 2) == 0;
IntStream.range(1, 10).filter(evenNums).forEach(System.out::println);
```

Table 5-2 lists primitive versions of Predicate interface provided in java.util.function package.

Table 5-2. *Primitive Versions of Predicate Interface*

Functional Interface	Abstract Method	Brief Description
IntPredicate	boolean test(int value)	Evaluates the condition passed as int and returns a boolean value as result
LongPredicate	boolean test(long value)	Evaluates the condition passed as long and returns a boolean value as result
DoublePredicate	boolean test(double value)	Evaluates the condition passed as double and returns a boolean value as result

Primitive Versions of Function Interface

Here is an example that uses a Stream with the primitive type integers:

```
AtomicInteger ints = new AtomicInteger(0);
Stream.generate(ints::incrementAndGet).limit(10).forEach(System.out::println);
// prints integers from 1 to 10 on the console
```

This code calls the int incrementAndGet() method defined in the class java.util.concurrent. atomic.AtomicInteger. Note that this method returns an int and not an Integer. Still, we can use it with Stream because of implicit autoboxing and unboxing to and from int's wrapper type Integer. This boxing and unboxing is simply unnecessary. Instead you can use the IntStream interface; its generator() method takes an IntSupplier as an argument. With this change, here is the equivalent code:

```
AtomicInteger ints = new AtomicInteger(0);
IntStream.generate(ints::incrementAndGet).limit(10).forEach(System.out::println);
// prints integers from 1 to 10 on the console
```

Because his code uses IntStream and the generate() method takes an IntSupplier, there is no implicit boxing and unboxing; hence this code performs faster as it does not generate unnecessary temporary Integer objects.

To give another example, here is a segment of code we saw earlier on using the Math.abs() method:

```
Function<Integer, Integer> absInt = Math::abs;
```

You can replace it with its equivalent using int specialization for Function, known as IntFunction:

```
IntFunction absInt = Math::abs;
```

Depending on the kind of arguments and return types, there are numerous versions of primitive types for Function interface (see Table 5-3).

Table 5-3. *Primitive Versions of Function Interface*

Functional Interface	Abstract Method	Brief Description
IntFunction<R>	R apply(int value)	Operates on the passed int argument and returns value of generic type R
LongFunction<R>	R apply(long value)	Operates on the passed long argument and returns value of generic type R
DoubleFunction<R>	R apply(double value)	Operates on the passed double argument and returns value of generic type R
ToIntFunction<T>	int applyAsInt(T value)	Operates on the passed generic type argument T and returns an int value
ToLongFunction<T>	long applyAsLong(T value)	Operates on the passed generic type argument T and returns a long value
ToDoubleFunction<T>	double applyAsDouble(T value)	Operates on the passed generic type argument T and returns an double value
IntToLongFunction	long applyAsLong(int value)	Operates on the passed int type argument and returns a long value
IntToDoubleFunction	double applyAsDouble(int value)	Operates on the passed int type argument and returns a double value
LongToIntFunction	int applyAsInt(long value)	Operates on the passed long type argument and returns an int value
LongToDoubleFunction	double applyAsLong(long value)	Operates on the passed long type argument and returns a double value
DoubleToIntFunction	int applyAsInt(double value)	Operates on the passed double type argument and returns an int value
DoubleToLongFunction	long applyAsLong(double value)	Operates on the passed double type argument and returns a long value

Primitive Versions of Consumer Interface

Depending on the kind of arguments, there are numerous versions of primitive types for Consumer interface available (see Table 5-4).

Table 5-4. *Primitive Versions of Consumer Interface*

Functional Interface	Abstract Method	Brief Description
IntConsumer	void accept(int value)	Operates on the given int argument and returns nothing
LongConsumer	void accept(long value)	Operates on the given long argument and returns nothing
DoubleConsumer	void accept(double value)	Operates on the given double argument and returns nothing
ObjIntConsumer<T>	void accept(T t, int value)	Operates on the given generic type argument T and int arguments and returns nothing
ObjLongConsumer<T>	void accept(T t, long value)	Operates on the given generic type argument T and long arguments and returns nothing
ObjDoubleConsumer<T>	void accept(T t, double value)	Operates on the given generic type argument T and double arguments and returns nothing

Primitive Versions of Supplier Interface

The primitive versions of Supplier are BooleanSupplier, IntSupplier, LongSupplier, and DoubleSupplier that return boolean, int, long, and double respectively (see Table 5-5).

Table 5-5. *Primitive Versions of Supplier Interface*

Functional Interface	Abstract Method	Brief Description
BooleanSupplier	boolean getAsBoolean()	Takes no arguments and returns a boolean value
IntSupplier	int getAsInt()	Takes no arguments and returns an int value
LongSupplier	long getAsLong()	Takes no arguments and returns a long value
DoubleSupplier	double getAsDouble()	Takes no arguments and returns a double value

The primitive versions of the functional interfaces are available only for int, long, and double (and boolean type in addition to these three types for Supplier). What if you need a functional interface that takes or returns other primitive types char, byte, or short? You have to use implicit conversions to relevant int specializations. Similarly, when you can use specialization for double type when you are using float.

Binary Versions of Functional Interfaces

Certification Objective

Develop code that uses binary versions of functional interfaces

The functional interfaces Predicate, Consumer, and Function have abstract methods that take one argument. For instance, consider the Function interface:

```
@FunctionalInterface
public interface Function<T, R> {
    R apply(T t);
    // other methods elided
}
```

The abstract method apply() takes one argument (generic type T). Here is the binary version of the Function interface:

```
@FunctionalInterface
public interface BiFunction<T, U, R> {
    R apply(T t, U u);
    // other methods elided
}
```

📋 A BiFunction is similar to Function, but the difference is that it takes two arguments: it takes arguments of generic types T and U and returns an object of generic type R. You can call apply() method on a BiFunction object.

The prefix "Bi" indicates the version that takes "two" arguments. Along the same line as BiFunction for Function, there is BiPredicate for Predicate and BiConsumer for Consumer that takes two arguments (see Table 5-6). How about Supplier? Since the abstract method in Supplier does not take any argument, there is no equivalent BiSupplier available.

Table 5-6. *Binary Versions of Functional Interfaces*

Functional Interface	Abstract Method	Brief Description
BiPredicate<T, U>	boolean test(T t, U u)	Checks if the arguments match the condition and returns a boolean value as result
BiConsumer<T, U>	void accept(T t, U u)	Operation that consumes two arguments but returns nothing
BiFunction<T, U, R>	R apply(T t, U u)	Function that takes two argument and returns a result

The BiFunction Interface

Here is an example of using BiFunction interface:

```
BiFunction<String, String, String> concatStr = (x, y) -> x + y;
System.out.println(concatStr.apply("hello ", "world"));
// prints: hello world
```

In this example, the arguments and return type are same type, but they can be different, as in:

```
BiFunction<Double, Double, Integer> compareDoubles = Double::compare;
System.out.println(compareDoubles.apply(10.0, 10.0));
// prints: 0
```

In this case, the argument types are of type double, and the return type is integer. When the passed double values are equal, the compare method in Double class returns 0, and hence we get the output 0 for this code segment.

Finding a suitable function interface for a given context can be tricky given that there are a large number of functional interfaces available in the java.util.function package. For instance, in our earlier example, we used BiFunction<Double, Double, Integer>. Instead of that, we could use the functional interface ToIntBiFunction because it returns an int.

The BiPredicate Interface

Consider the following code segment:

```
BiPredicate<List<Integer>, Integer> listContains = List::contains;
List aList = Arrays.asList(10, 20, 30);
System.out.println(listContains.test(aList, 20));
// prints: true
```

This code shows how to use BiPredicate. The contains() method in List takes an element as an argument and checks if the underlying list contains the element. Because it takes an argument and returns an Integer, we can use a BiPredicate. Why not use BiFunction<T, U, Boolean>? Yes, the code will work, but a better choice is the equivalent BiPredicate<T, U> because the BiPredicate returns a boolean value.

The BiConsumer Interface

Consider this code segment:

```
BiConsumer<List<Integer>, Integer> listAddElement = List::add;
List aList = new ArrayList();
listAddElement.accept(aList, 10);
System.out.println(aList);
// prints: [10]
```

This code segment shows how to use BiConsumer. Similar to using List::contains method reference in the previous example for BiPredicate, this example shows how to use BiConsumer to call add() method in List using this interface.

The UnaryOperator Interface

Certification Objective

Develop code that uses the UnaryOperator interface

Consider the following example.

```
List<Integer> ell = Arrays.asList(-11, 22, 33, -44, 55);
System.out.println("Before: " + ell);
ell.replaceAll(Math::abs);
    System.out.println("After: " + ell);
```

This code prints:

```
Before: [-11, 22, 33, -44, 55]
After: [11, 22, 33, 44, 55]
```

This code uses `replaceAll()` method introduced in Java 8 that replaces the elements in the given `List`. The `replaceAll()` method takes a `UnaryOperator` as the sole argument:

```
void replaceAll(UnaryOperator<T> operator)
```

The `replaceAll()` method is passed with `Math::abs` method to it.
Math has four overloaded methods for `abs()` method:

```
abs(int)
abs(long)
abs(double)
abs(float)
```

Because the type is `Integer`, the overloaded method `abs(int)` is selected through type inference.
`UnaryOperator` is a functional interface and it extends `Function` interface, and you can use the `apply()` method declared in the `Function` interface; further, it inherits the default functions `compose()` and `andThen()` from the `Function` interface. Similar to `UnaryOperator` that extends `Function` interface, there is a `BinaryOperator` that extends `BiFunction` interface.
Primitive types versions of `UnaryOperator` interface `IntUnaryOperator`, `LongUnaryOperator`, and `DoubleUnaryOperator` are also provided as part of the `java.util.function` package.

The java.util.function package consists of only functional interfaces. There are only four core interfaces in this package: `Predicate`, `Consumer`, `Function`, and `Supplier`. The rest of the interfaces are primitive versions, binary versions, and derived interfaces such as `UnaryOperator` interface. These interfaces differ mainly on the signature of the abstract methods they declare. You need to choose the suitable functional interface based on the context and your need.

Summary

Let us briefly review the key points from each certification objective in this chapter. Please read it before appearing for the exam.

Use the built-in interfaces included in the java.util.function package such as Predicate, Consumer, Function, and Supplier

- Built-in functional interfaces Predicate, Consumer, Function, and Supplier differ mainly based on the signature of the abstract method they declare.

- A Predicate tests the given condition and returns true or false; hence it has an abstract method named "test" that takes a parameter of generic type T and returns boolean type.

- A Consumer "consumes" an object and returns nothing; hence it has an abstract method named "accept" that takes an argument of generic type T and has return type void.

- A Function "operates" on the argument and returns a result; hence it has an abstract method named "apply" that takes an argument of generic type T and has generic return type R.

- A Supplier "supplies" takes nothing but returns something; hence it has an abstract method named "get" that takes no arguments and returns a generic type T.

- The forEach() method defined in Iterable (implemented by collection classes) method accepts a Consumer<T>.

Develop code that uses primitive versions of functional interfaces

- The built-in interfaces Predicate, Consumer, Function, and Supplier operate on reference type objects. For primitive types, there are specializations available for int, long, and double types for these functional interfaces.

- When the Stream interface is used with primitive types, it results in unnecessary boxing and unboxing of the primitive types to their wrapper types. This results in slower code as well as wastes memory because the unnecessary wrapper objects get created. Hence, whenever possible, prefer using the primitive type specializations of the functional interfaces Predicate, Consumer, Function, and Supplier.

- The primitive versions of the functional interfaces Predicate, Consumer, Function, and Supplier are available only for int, long and double types (and boolean type in addition to these three types for Supplier). You have to use implicit conversions to relevant int version when you need to use char, byte, or short types; similarly, you can use the version for double type when you need to use float.

Develop code that uses binary versions of functional interfaces

- The functional interfaces BiPredicate, BiConsumer, and BiFunction are binary versions of Predicate, Consumer, and Function respectively. There is no binary equivalent for Supplier since it does not take any arguments. The prefix "Bi" indicates the version that takes "two" arguments.

Develop code that uses the UnaryOperator interface

- UnaryOperator is a functional interface and it extends Function interface.

- The primitive type specializations of UnaryOperator are IntUnaryOperator, LongUnaryOperator, and DoubleUnaryOperator for int, long, and double types respectively.

QUESTION TIME

1. Which of the following are functional interfaces? (Select ALL that apply)

   A. java.util.stream.Stream<T>

   B. java.util.function.Consumer<T>

   C. java.util.function.Supplier<T>

   D. java.util.function.Predicate<T>

   E. java.util.function.Function<T, R>

2. Choose the correct option based on this program:

   ```
   import java.util.function.Predicate;

   public class PredicateTest {
       public static void main(String []args) {
           Predicate<String> notNull =
                   ((Predicate<String>)(arg -> arg == null)).negate(); // #1
           System.out.println(notNull.test(null));
       }
   }
   ```

   A. This program results in a compiler error in line marked with the comment #1

   B. This program prints: true

   C. This program prints: false

   D. This program crashes by throwing NullPointerException

3. Choose the correct option based on this program:

   ```
   import java.util.function.Function;

   public class AndThen {
       public static void main(String []args) {
           Function<Integer, Integer> negate = (i -> -i), square = (i -> i * i),
                       negateSquare = negate.compose(square);

           System.out.println(negateSquare.apply(10));
       }
   }
   ```

A. This program results in a compiler error

B. This program prints: -100

C. This program prints: 100

D. This program prints: -10

E. This program prints: 10

4. Which one of the following functional interfaces can you assign the method reference Integer::parseInt? Note that the static method parseInt() in Integer class takes a String and returns an int, as in: int parseInt(String s)

A. BiPredicate<String, Integer>

B. Function<Integer, String>

C. Function<String, Integer>

D. Predicate<String>

E. Consumer<Integer, String>

F. Consumer<String, Integer>

5. Choose the correct option based on this program:

```
import java.util.function.BiFunction;

public class StringCompare {
    public static void main(String args[]){
        BiFunction<String, String, Boolean> compareString = (x, y) ->
            x.equals(y);
        System.out.println(compareString.apply("Java8","Java8")); // #1
    }
}
```

A. This program results in a compiler error in line marked with #1

B. This program prints: true

C. This program prints: false

D. This program prints: (x, y) -> x.equals(y)

E. This program prints: ("Java8", "Java8") -> "Java8".equals("Java8")

6. Which one of the following abstract methods does not take any argument but returns a value?

A. The accept() method in java.util.function.Consumer<T> interface

B. The get() method in java.util.function.Supplier<T> interface

C. The test() method in java.util.function.Predicate<T> interface

D. The apply() method in java.util.function.Function<T, R> interface

7. Choose the correct option based on this program:

```java
import java.util.function.Predicate;

public class PredUse {
    public static void main(String args[]){
        Predicate<String> predContains = "I am going to write OCP8
        exam"::contains;
        checkString(predContains, "OCPJP");
    }
    static void checkString(Predicate<String> predicate, String str) {
        System.out.println(predicate.test(str) ? "contains" : "doesn't contain");
    }
}
```

A. This program results in a compiler error for code within `main()` method

B. This program results in a compiler error for code within `checkString()` method

C. This program prints: contains

D. This program prints: doesn't contain

8. Choose the correct option based on this program:

```java
import java.util.function.ObjIntConsumer;

class ConsumerUse {
    public static void main(String []args) {
        ObjIntConsumer<String> charAt = (str, i) -> str.charAt(i); // #1
        System.out.println(charAt.accept("java", 2));              // #2
    }
}
```

A. This program results in a compiler error for the line marked with comment #1

B. This program results in a compiler error for the line marked with comment #2

C. This program prints: a

D. This program prints: v

E. This program prints: 2

Answers:

1. B, C, D, and E

   The interface `java.util.stream.Stream<T>` is not a functional interface—it has numerous abstract methods. The other four options are functional interfaces.

   The functional interface `java.util.function.Consumer<T>` has an abstract method with the signature `void accept(T t);`

The functional interface `java.util.function.Supplier<T>` has an abstract method with the signature `T get();`

The functional interface `java.util.function.Predicate<T>` has an abstract method with the signature `boolean test(T t);`

The functional interface `java.util.function.Function<T, R>` has an abstract method with the signature `R apply(T t);`

2. **C. This program prints: false**

    The expression `((Predicate<String>)(arg -> arg == null))` is a valid cast to the type `(Predicate<String>)` for the lambda expression `(arg -> arg == null)`. Hence, it does not result in a compiler error. The `negate` function in `Predicate` interface turns `true` to `false` and `false` to `true`. Hence, given `null`, the `notNull.test(null)` results in returning the value `false`.

3. **B. This program prints: -100**

    The `negate.compose(square)` calls square before calling negate. Hence, for the given value 10, square results in 100, and when negated, it becomes -100.

4. **C. Function<String, Integer>**

    The `parseInt()` method takes a `String` and returns a value, hence we need to use the `Function` interface because it matches the signature of the abstract method `R apply(T t)`. In `Function<T, R>`, the first type argument is the argument type and the second one is the return type. Given that `parseInt` takes a `String` as the argument and returns an `int` (that can be wrapped in an `Integer`), we can assign it to `Function<String, Integer>`.

5. **B. This program prints: true**

    The `BiFunction` interface takes two type arguments—they are of types `String` in this program. The return type is `Boolean`. `BiFunction` functional interface has abstract method named `apply()`. Since the signature of `String`'s `equals()` method matches that of the signature of the abstract method `apply()`, this program compiles fine. When executed, the strings "Java8" and "Java8" are equal; hence, the evaluation returns true that is printed on the console.

6. **B. The get() method in java.util.function.Supplier<T> interface**

    The signature of `get()` method in `java.util.function.Supplier<T>` interface is: `T get()`.

7. **D. This program prints: doesn't contain**

    You can create method references for object as well, so the code within `main()` compiles without errors. The code within `checkString()` method is also correct and hence it also compiles without errors. The string "OCPJP" is not present in the string "I am going to write OCP8 exam" and hence this program prints "doesn't contain" on the console.

8. D. This program results in a compiler error for the line marked with comment #2

    `ObjIntConsumer` operates on the given `String` argument `str` and `int` argument `i` and returns nothing. Though the `charAt` method is declared to return the `char` at given index `i`, the `accept` method in `ObjIntConsumer` has return type `void`. Since `System.out.println` expects an argument to be passed, the call `charAt.accept("java", 2)` results in a compiler error because `accept()` method returns void.

CHAPTER 6

■ ■ ■

Java Stream API

Certification Objectives

Develop code to extract data from an object using peek() and map() methods including primitive versions of the map() method

Search for data by using search methods of the Stream classes including findFirst, findAny, anyMatch, allMatch, noneMatch

Develop code that uses the Optional class

Develop code that uses Stream data methods and calculation methods

Sort a collection using Stream API

Save results to a collection using the collect method and group/partition data using the Collectors class

Use flatMap() methods in the Stream API

In this chapter, we discuss the most important addition to the Java library in Java 8: the stream API. The stream API is part of the java.util.stream package. The focus of this chapter is on the key interface in this package: the Stream<T> interface (and its primitive type versions). We also discuss classes such as Optional and Collectors in this chapter.

We have already introduced the stream API in Chapter 4 (Generics and Collections). The stream API makes extensive use of built-in functional interfaces that are part of the java.util.function package that we discussed in the previous chapter (Chapter 5). So, we assume that you have already read these two chapters before reading this chapter.

Extract Data from a Stream

Certification Objective

Develop code to extract data from an object using peek() and map() methods including primitive versions of the map() method

Let us start with a simple example:

```
long count = Stream.of(1, 2, 3, 4, 5).map(i -> i * i).count();
System.out.printf("The stream has %d elements", count);
```

This code segment prints:

```
The stream has 5 elements
```

The map() operation in this stream applies the given lambda function passed as its argument on the elements of the stream. In this case, it squares the elements in the stream. The count() method returns the value 5 – you capture it in a variable and print it on the console. But how can you check the result of applying the intermediate operation map() in this code? For that you can use the peek() method:

```
long count = Stream.of(1, 2, 3, 4, 5)
                .map(i -> i * i)
                .peek(i -> System.out.printf("%d ", i))
                .count();
System.out.printf("%nThe stream has %d elements", count);
```

This code prints

```
1 4 9 16 25
The stream has 5 elements
```

This example also illustrates how the intermediate operations can be chained together. This is possible because intermediate operations return streams.

Now, let us add another peek() method before calling the map() method to understand how it works:

```
Stream.of(1, 2, 3, 4, 5)
                .peek(i -> System.out.printf("%d ", i))
                .map(i -> i * i)
                .peek(i -> System.out.printf("%d ", i))
                .count();
```

This code prints

```
1 1 2 4 3 9 4 16 5 25
```

As you can observe from this output, the stream pipeline is processing the elements one by one. Each element is mapped to its square. The peek() method helps us understand what is being processed in the stream without distributing it.

The peek() method is meant primarily for debugging purposes. It helps us understand how the elements are transformed in the pipeline. Do not use it in production code.

You can use map() and peek() methods in primitive versions of Stream<T>; then following code snippet uses a DoubleStream:

```
DoubleStream.of(1.0, 4.0, 9.0)
        .map(Math::sqrt)
        .peek(System.out::println)
        .sum();
```

This code prints 1.0, 2.0, and 3.0 in separate lines on the console. Figure 6-1 visually shows the source, intermediate operations and the terminal operations in this stream pipeline.

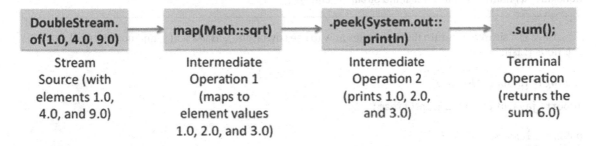

DoubleStream.of(1.0, 4.0, 9.0)	map(Math::sqrt)	.peek(System.out::println)	.sum();
Stream Source (with elements 1.0, 4.0, and 9.0)	Intermediate Operation 1 (maps to element values 1.0, 2.0, and 3.0)	Intermediate Operation 2 (prints 1.0, 2.0, and 3.0)	Terminal Operation (returns the sum 6.0)

Figure 6-1. *A stream pipeline with source, intermediate operations and terminal operation*

Search Data from a Stream

Certification Objective

Search for data by using search methods of the Stream classes including findFirst, findAny, anyMatch, allMatch, noneMatch

Methods ending with the word "Match" and methods starting with the word "find" in the Stream interface are useful for searching data from the stream (Table 6-1). You can use matching operations such as anyMatch(), allMatch(), and noneMatch() if you are looking for elements in the stream that matches the given condition. These methods return a boolean value. For searching operations findFirst() and findAny(), matching elements may not be present in the Stream, so they return Optional<T> (we discuss Optional<T> in the next section).

Table 6-1. *Important Match and Find Methods in the Stream Interface*

Method Name	Short Description
boolean anyMatch(Predicate<? super T> check)	Returns true if there is any elements in the stream that matches the given predicate. Returns false if the stream is empty or if there are no matching elements.
boolean allMatch(Predicate<? super T> check)	Returns true only if *all* elements in the stream matches the given predicate. Returns true if the stream is empty without evaluating the predicate!
boolean noneMatch(Predicate<? super T> check)	Returns true only if *none* of the elements in the stream matches the given predicate. Returns true if the stream is empty without evaluating the predicate!
Optional<T> findFirst()	Returns the first element from the stream; if there is no element present in the stream, it returns an empty Optional<T> object.
Optional<T> findAny()	Returns one of the elements from the stream; if there is no element present in the stream, it returns an empty Optional<T> object.

⬤ Unlike the anyMatch() method that returns false when the stream is empty, the allMatch() and noneMatch() methods return true if the stream is empty!

Here is a simple program that illustrates how to use anyMatch(), allMatch(), and noneMatch() methods (Listing 6-1).

Listing 6-1. MatchUse.java

```java
import java.util.stream.IntStream;

public class MatchUse {
    public static void main(String []args) {
        // Average temperatures in Concordia, Antarctica in a week in October 2015
        boolean anyMatch
                = IntStream.of(-56, -57, -55, -52, -48, -51, -49).anyMatch(temp -> temp > 0);
        System.out.println("anyMatch(temp -> temp > 0): " + anyMatch);

        boolean allMatch
                = IntStream.of(-56, -57, -55, -52, -48, -51, -49).allMatch(temp -> temp > 0);
        System.out.println("allMatch(temp -> temp > 0): " + allMatch);

        boolean noneMatch
                = IntStream.of(-56, -57, -55, -52, -48, -51, -49).noneMatch(temp -> temp > 0);
        System.out.println("noneMatch(temp -> temp > 0): " + noneMatch);

    }
}
```

This program prints:

```
anyMatch(temp -> temp > 0): false
allMatch(temp -> temp > 0): false
noneMatch(temp -> temp > 0): true
```

Because all the given temperatures are negative, the anyMatch() and allMatch() methods return false whereas noneMatch() returns true.

The findFirst() and findAny() methods are useful for searching elements in streams. Here is a program that uses findFirst() method (Listing 6-2).

Listing 6-2. FindFirstUse1.java

```java
import java.lang.reflect.Method;
import java.util.Arrays;
import java.util.Optional;
import java.util.stream.Stream;
```

```java
public class FindFirstUse1 {
    public static void main(String []args) {
        Method[] methods = Stream.class.getMethods();
        Optional<String> methodName = Arrays.stream(methods)
                .map(method -> method.getName())
                .filter(name -> name.endsWith("Match"))
                .sorted()
                .findFirst();
        System.out.println("Result: " + methodName.orElse("No suitable method found"));
    }
}
```

This program prints:

```
Result: allMatch
```

In this program, we get the list of methods in the Stream itself using reflection. Then, using map() method, we get the list of method names and check if the names end with the string "Match", sort those methods, and return the first found method. If we are looking for any method name that ends with "Match", then we could use findAny() method instead.

___

Why does the java.util.function package have both findFirst() and findAny() methods? In parallel streams, findAny() is faster to use than findFirst() (we discuss parallel streams in Chapter 11).

___

Listing 6-3 has a stream with many temperature values given as double values. Using findFirst(), we are looking for any temperature that is greater than 0. What will the program print?

Listing 6-3. FindFirstUse2.java

```java
import java.util.OptionalDouble;
import java.util.stream.DoubleStream;

public class FindFirstUse2 {
    public static void main(String []args) {
        OptionalDouble temperature = DoubleStream.of(-10.1, -5.4, 6.0, -3.4, 8.9, 2.2)
                .filter(temp -> temp > 0)
                .findFirst();
        System.out.println("First matching temperature > 0 is " + temperature.getAsDouble());
    }
}
```

This program prints:

```
First matching temperature > 0 is 6.0
```

In this stream of double values, the `filter()` method filters the elements, 10.1 and -5.4 because the condition `temp > 0` is false. For the element 6.0, the `filter()` method evaluates the condition to true and `findFirst()` returns that element. Notice that the remaining elements get ignored in this stream pipeline: the elements 8.9 and 2.2 also satisfy the condition `temp > 0`, but the stream pipeline is closed as the `findFirst()` method already returned the value 6.0. In other words, searching methods such as `findFirst()` are short-circuiting. Once the result is determined, the rest of the elements in the stream are not processed.

The "match" and "find" methods for searching elements are "short-circuiting" in nature. What is short-circuiting? The evaluation stops once the result is found (and the rest is not evaluated). You are already familiar with the "short-circuiting" name of the operators && and ||. For example, in the expression ((s != null) && (s.length() > 0)), if the String s is null, the condition (s != null) evaluates to false; hence false is the result of the expression. The remaining expression (s.length() > 0) is not evaluated in this case.

In Listings 6-2 and 6-3, we have used `Optional` and `OptionalDouble` classes; let us discuss these two classes now.

The Optional class

Develop code that uses the Optional class

The class `java.util.Optional` is a holder for value that can be `null`. There are numerous methods in classes in `java.util.stream` package that return `Optional` values. Let us see an example now.
Consider this method:

```
public static void selectHighestTemperature(Stream<Double> temperatures) {
    System.out.println(temperatures.max(Double::compareTo));
}
```

Here is a call to this method:

```
selectHighestTemperature(Stream.of(24.5, 23.6, 27.9, 21.1, 23.5, 25.5, 28.3));
```

This code prints:

```
Optional[28.3]
```

The `max()` method in `Stream` takes a `Comparator` as an argument and returns an `Optional<T>`:

```
Optional<T> max(Comparator<? super T> comparator);
```

Why Optional<T> instead of return type T? It is because max() method may fail to find the maximum value – think about an empty stream, for example:

```
selectHighestTemperature(Stream.of());
```

Now, this code prints:

```
Optional.empty
```

To get the value from Optional, you can use isPresent() and get() methods, as in:

```
public static void selectHighestTemperature(Stream<Double> temperatures) {
    Optional<Double> max = temperatures.max(Double::compareTo);
    if(max.isPresent()) {
        System.out.println(max.get());
    }
}
```

Writing an if condition is tedious (and is not functional style), so you can use ifPresent method to write simplified code:

```
max.ifPresent(System.out::println);
```

This ifPresent() method in Optional takes a Consumer<T> as the argument. You can also use methods such as orElse() and orElseThrow() that we will discuss a bit later after discussing how to create Optional objects.

Creating Optional Objects

There are many ways to create Optional objects. One way to create Optional objects is to use factory methods in Optional class, as in:

```
Optional<String> empty = Optional.empty();
```

You can also use of() in Optional class:

```
Optional<String> nonEmptyOptional = Optional.of("abracadabra");
```

However, you cannot pass null to Optional.of() method, as in:

```
Optional<String> nullStr = Optional.of(null);
System.out.println(nullStr);
// crashes with a NullPointerException
```

This will result in throwing a NullPointerException. If you want to create an Optional object that has null value, then you can instead use ofNullable() method:

```
Optional<String> nullableStr = Optional.ofNullable(null);
System.out.println(nullableStr);
// prints: Optional.empty
```

Figure 6-2 visualizes the representation of the Optional<String> objects pointed by nonEmptyOptional, nullStr, and nullableStr.

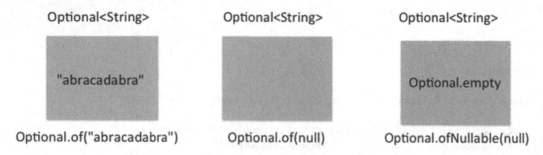

Figure 6-2. *Representation of three Optional<String> objects*

Optional Stream

You can also consider Optional as a stream that can have zero elements or one element. So you can apply methods such as map(), filter(), and flatMap() operations on this stream! How is it useful? Here is an example (Listing 6-4):

Listing 6-4. OptionalStream.java

```java
import java.util.Optional;

public class OptionalStream {
    public static void main(String []args) {
        Optional<String> string = Optional.of("  abracadabra  ");
        string.map(String::trim).ifPresent(System.out::println);
    }
}
```

This program prints:

```
abracadabra
```

You can use orElse() or orElseThrow() methods, when these operations fail (i.e., the underlying Optional has a null value), as in:

```java
Optional<String> string = Optional.ofNullable(null);
System.out.println(string.map(String::length).orElse(-1));
```

This code prints -1 because the variable string is an Optional variable that holds null and hence the orElse() method executes and returns -1. Alternatively, you can throw an exception using the orElseThrow() method:

```java
Optional<String> string = Optional.ofNullable(null);
    System.out.println(string.map(String::length).orElseThrow(IllegalArgumentException::new));
```

This code segments throws an IllegalArgumentException. Calling methods such as map(), flatMap(), or filter() on an Optional object is useful when you are dealing with Optional object returned from a function where you don't know what the Optional object contains.

Primitive Versions of Optional<T>

In the code we discussed earlier, we used both Stream<Double> and Optional<Double> types:

```
public static void selectHighestTemperature(Stream<Double> temperatures) {
    Optional<Double> max = temperatures.max(Double::compareTo);
    if(max.isPresent()) {
        System.out.println(max.get());
    }
}
```

It is better to use DoubleStream and OptionalDouble, which are primitive type versions for double for Stream<T> and Optional<T> respectively. (The other two primitive type versions available are for int and long, named as OptionalInt and OptionalLong respectively.) So, this code can be rewritten as:

```
public static void selectHighestTemperature(DoubleStream temperatures) {
    OptionalDouble max = temperatures.max();
    max.ifPresent(System.out::println);
}
```

When invoked with the following call,

```
selectHighestTemperature(DoubleStream.of(24.5, 23.6, 27.9, 21.1, 23.5, 25.5, 28.3));
```

We get the maximum value correctly printed on the console:

28.3

Similar to the max() method Stream<T> that returns Optional<T>, the max() method in DoubleStream returns an OptionalDouble.

Stream Data Methods and Calculation Methods

Certification Objective

Develop code that uses Stream data methods and calculation methods

The Stream<T> interface has data and calculation methods count(), min() and max(). The min() and max() methods take a Comparator object as the argument and return an Optional<T>. Here is an example of using these methods (Listing 6-5).

Listing 6-5. WordsCalculation.java

```java
import java.util.Arrays;

public class WordsCalculation {
    public static void main(String []args) {
        String[] string = "you never know what you have until you clean your room".split(" ");
        System.out.println(Arrays.stream(string).min(String::compareTo).get());
    }
}
```

This program prints:

```
clean
```

Since `min()` method requires a way to compare the elements in the stream, we are passing the `String::compareTo` method reference in this program. Since `min()` returns an `Optional<T>`, we have used the `get()` method to get the resulting string. Since the `String::compareTo` compares two strings lexicographically, we get the word "clean" as the result.

Here is the modified code snippet that compares the strings not lexicographically but based on the length of the string:

```java
Comparator<String> lengthCompare = (str1, str2) -> str1.length() - str2.length();
System.out.println(Arrays.stream(string).min(lengthCompare).get());
```

With this change, the program prints "you" because it is the smallest word by length in the given `string`.

There are additional data and calculation methods such as `sum()` and `average()` provided in the primitive versions of `Stream<T>` interface. Table 6-2 lists the important methods in `IntStream` interface that we discuss in this section.

Table 6-2. *Important Data and Calculation Methods in `IntStream` Interface*

Method	Short Description
`int sum()`	Returns the sum of elements in the stream; 0 in case the stream is empty.
`long count()`	Returns the number of elements in the stream; 0 if the stream is empty.
`OptionalDouble average()`	Returns the average value of the elements in the stream; an empty `OptionalDouble` value in case the stream is empty.
`OptionalInt min()`	Returns the minimum integer value in the stream; an empty `OptionalInt` value in case the stream is empty.
`OptionalInt max()`	Returns the maximum integer value in the stream; an empty `OptionalInt` value in case the stream is empty.
`IntSummaryStatistics summaryStatistics()`	Returns an `IntSummaryStatistics` object that has sum, count, average, min, and max values.

The `LongStream` and `DoubleStream` interfaces have methods similar to ones listed for `IntStream` in this table (Table 6-2). Here is a simple program that uses them (Listing 6-6).

Listing 6-6. WordStatistics.java

```java
import java.util.IntSummaryStatistics;
import java.util.regex.Pattern;

public class WordStatistics {
    public static void main(String []args) {
        String limerick = "There was a young lady named Bright " +
                          "who traveled much faster than light " +
                          "She set out one day " +
                          "in a relative way " +
                          "and came back the previous night ";

        IntSummaryStatistics wordStatistics =
                Pattern.compile(" ")
                .splitAsStream(limerick)
                .mapToInt(word -> word.length())
                .summaryStatistics();

        System.out.printf(" Number of words = %d \n Sum of the length of the words = %d \n" +
                        " Minimum word size = %d \n Maximum word size %d \n " +
                        " Average word size = %f \n", wordStatistics.getCount(),
                        wordStatistics.getSum(), wordStatistics.getMin(),
                        wordStatistics.getMax(), wordStatistics.getAverage());
    }
}
```

This program prints:

```
Number of words = 28
Sum of the length of the words = 115
Minimum word size = 1
Maximum word size 8
Average word size = 4.107143
```

After splitting the words as a stream using splitAsStream() method in the Pattern class, this program calls mapToInt() method to transform the word into their lengths. Why mapToInt() instead of map() method? The map() method returns a Stream but we want to perform calculations on the underlying elements in the stream. The Stream interface does not have methods that perform calculations but its primitive type versions have data and calculation methods. Hence, we call the mapToInt() method that returns an IntStream: IntStream has many useful data and calculation methods (listed in Table 6-2). We have called summaryStatistics() method on the IntStream. Finally, we have called various methods such as sum() and average() on the returned IntSummaryStatistics object to summarize the calculation on words used in the given limerick.

You can also directly call methods such as sum() and average() provided in IntStream, as in:

```java
IntStream.of(10, 20, 30, 40).sum();
```

These methods are more concise than their equivalent using the reduce() method:

```java
IntStream.of(10, 20, 30, 40).reduce(0, ((sum, val) -> sum + val));
```

Why does stream API provide reduce() method when we can use methods such as sum() that are more concise, convenient to use, and also easy to read?

The answer is that reduce() is a generalized method: you can use it when you want to perform repeated operations on stream elements to compute a result. Consider the factorial of 10. We don't have a method like sum() in IntStream that can help us multiply all the values. Hence, we can use reduce() method in this case:

```
// factorial of 5
System.out.println(IntStream.rangeClosed(1, 5).reduce((x, y) -> (x * y)).getAsInt());
// prints: 120
```

In fact, the sum() method of IntStream is internally implemented by calling reduce() method (in IntPipeline class):

```
@Override
public final int sum() {
    return reduce(0, Integer::sum);
}
```

In this case, the sum() method is implemented by passing the method reference Integer::sum as the second argument to the reduce() method.

Reduction operations (aka "reducers") could be implicit or explicit. Methods such as sum(), min(), and max() in IntStream are examples of implicit reducers. When we use reduce() method directly in our code, we are using explicit reducers. We can convert implicit reducers to their equivalent explicit reducers.

Sort a Collection Using Stream API

Certification Objectives

Sort a collection using Stream API

In Chapter 4 (on Generics and Collections), we discussed how to sort a collection using Comparator and Comparable interfaces. Streams simplify the task of sorting a collection. Here is a program that sorts strings with lexicographical comparison (Listing 6-7).

Listing 6-7. SortingCollection.java

```
import java.util.Arrays;
import java.util.List;

public class SortingCollection {
    public static void main(String []args) {
        List words =
                Arrays.asList("follow your heart but take your brain with you".split(" "));
        words.stream().distinct().sorted().forEach(System.out::println);
    }
}
```

This program prints:

```
brain
but
follow
heart
take
with
you
your
```

In this code, words is a collection of type List. We first get a stream from that list using the stream() method and then call the distinct() method to remove duplicates (the word "your" is repeated in the collection). After that, we call the sorted() method.

The sorted() method sorts the elements in their "natural order"; the sorted() method requires that the elements in the stream implement the Comparable interface. How to sort the elements in some other order? For that you can invoke the overloaded sorted method that takes a Comparator as the argument:

```
Stream<T> sorted(Comparator<? super T> comparator)
```

Here (Listing 6-8) is the modified version of the earlier program (in Listing 6-7) that sorts the elements based on the length of the strings.

Listing 6-8. SortByLength.java

```
import java.util.Arrays;
import java.util.List;
import java.util.Comparator;

public class SortByLength {
    public static void main(String []args) {
        List words =
                Arrays.asList("follow your heart but take your brain with you".split(" "));
        Comparator<String> lengthCompare = (str1, str2) -> str1.length() - str2.length();
        words.stream().distinct().sorted(lengthCompare).forEach(System.out::println);
    }
}
```

This program prints:

```
but
you
your
take
with
heart
brain
follow
```

179

In this output, the words are sorted based on the length of the words. The word "heart" appears before "brain" though they are of same length. So, what if we want to first sort the words by length and then sort the words of same length by natural order? For that you can use thenComparing() default method provided in the Comparator interface (Listing 6-9).

Listing 6-9. SortByLengthThenNatural.java

```java
import java.util.Arrays;
import java.util.Comparator;
import java.util.List;

public class SortByLengthThenNatural {
    public static void main(String []args) {
        List words =
                Arrays.asList("follow your heart but take your brain with you".split(" "));
        Comparator<String> lengthCompare = (str1, str2) -> str1.length() - str2.length();
        words.stream()
                .distinct()
                .sorted(lengthCompare.thenComparing(String::compareTo))
                .forEach(System.out::println);
    }
}
```

This program prints:

```
but
you
take
with
your
brain
heart
follow
```

What if we want to reverse this order? Fortunately, the Comparator interface has been enhanced with many useful default and static methods in Java 8. One such method added is reversed() and you can make use of that (Listing 6-10).

Listing 6-10. SortByLengthThenNaturalReversed.java

```java
import java.util.Arrays;
import java.util.Comparator;
import java.util.List;

public class SortByLengthThenNaturalReversed {
    public static void main(String []args) {
        List words =
                Arrays.asList("follow your heart but take your brain with you".split(" "));
                Comparator<String> lengthCompare = (str1, str2) -> str1.length() - str2.length();
```

```
        words.stream()
          .distinct()
          .sorted(lengthCompare.thenComparing(String::compareTo).reversed())
          .forEach(System.out::println);
    }
}
```

This program prints:

```
follow
heart
brain
your
with
take
you
but
```

Save Results to a Collection

Certification Objectives

Save results to a collection using the collect method and group/partition data using the Collectors class

The Collectors class has methods that support the task of collecting elements to a collection. You can use methods such as toList(), toSet(), toMap(), and toCollection() to create a collection from a stream. Here is a simple example that creates a List from a stream and returns it (Listing 6-11). This code uses collect() method of Stream and the toList() method of the Collectors class.

Listing 6-11. CollectorsToList.java

```
import java.util.stream.Collectors;
import java.util.regex.Pattern;
import java.util.List;

public class CollectorsToList {
    public static void main(String []args) {
        String frenchCounting = "un:deux:trois:quatre";
        List gmailList = Pattern.compile(":")
                .splitAsStream(frenchCounting)
                .collect(Collectors.toList());
        gmailList.forEach(System.out::println);
    }
}
```

The collect() method in Stream takes a Collector as an argument:

```
<R, A> R collect(Collector<? super T, A, R> collector);
```

In this code, we have used toList() method in Collectors class to collect the elements from the stream into a List.

Here is an example that uses Collectors.toSet() method (Listing 6-12):

Listing 6-12. CollectorsToSet.java

```java
import java.util.Arrays;
import java.util.Set;
import java.util.stream.Collectors;

public class CollectorsToSet {
    public static void main(String []args) {
        String []roseQuote = "a rose is a rose is a rose".split(" ");
        Set words = Arrays.stream(roseQuote).collect(Collectors.toSet());
        words.forEach(System.out::println);
    }
}
```

This program prints:

```
a
rose
is
```

This code converts the given sentence in a string into a stream of words. The Collectors.toSet() method called within the collect() method collects the words into a Set. Since a Set removes duplicates, this program prints only the words "a", "rose" and "is" to the console.

Just like Lists and Sets, you can also create Maps from a stream. Here is a program that creates a Map from a stream of strings (Listing 6-13).

Listing 6-13. CollectorsToMap.java

```java
import java.util.Map;
import java.util.stream.Collectors;
import java.util.stream.Stream;

public class CollectorsToMap {
    public static void main(String []args) {
        Map<String, Integer> nameLength = Stream.of("Arnold", "Alois", "Schwarzenegger")
                .collect(Collectors.toMap(name -> name, name -> name.length()));
        nameLength.forEach((name, len) -> System.out.printf("%s - %d \n", name, len));
    }
}
```

This program prints:

```
Alois - 5
Schwarzenegger - 14
Arnold - 6
```

The `Collectors.toMap()` method takes two arguments – the first one for keys and the second one for values. Here, we have used the elements in the stream itself as the key and the length of the string as the value. Did you notice that the order of strings "Arnold", "Alois", and "Schwarzenegger" in the stream is not retained? It is because `Map` does not maintain the insertion order of the elements.

In this code, note that we have used `name -> name`:

```
Collectors.toMap(name -> name, name -> name.length())
```

We can simplify it by passing `Function.identity()` instead, as in:

```
Collectors.toMap(Function.identity(), name -> name.length())
```

Recall that `identity()` method in `Function` interface returns the argument it receives (discussed in Chapter 5).

What if you want to use a specific collection–say `TreeSet`–to aggregate elements from the `collect()` method? For that you can use `Collections.toCollection()` method and pass the constructor reference of `TreeSet` as the argument (Listing 6-14).

Listing 6-14. CollectorsToTreeSet.java

```java
import java.util.Arrays;
import java.util.Set;
import java.util.TreeSet;
import java.util.stream.Collectors;

public class CollectorsToTreeSet {
    public static void main(String []args) {
        String []roseQuote = "a rose is a rose is a rose".split(" ");
        Set words = Arrays.stream(roseQuote).collect(Collectors.toCollection(TreeSet::new));
        words.forEach(System.out::println);
    }
}
```

This program prints:

```
a
is
rose
```

Remember that a `TreeSet` orders the elements and hence the output is in sorted order.

You can also group the elements in a stream based on certain criteria (Listing 6-15).

Listing 6-15. GroupStringsByLength.java

```java
import java.util.Arrays;
import java.util.List;
import java.util.Map;
import java.util.stream.Collectors;
import java.util.stream.Stream;
```

```
public class GroupStringsByLength {
    public static void main(String []args) {
        String []string= "you never know what you have until you clean your room".split(" ");
        Stream<String> distinctWords = Arrays.stream(string).distinct();
        Map<Integer, List<String>> wordGroups =
                            distinctWords.collect(Collectors.groupingBy(String::length));
        wordGroups.forEach(
                (count, words) -> {
                        System.out.printf("word(s) of length %d %n", count);
                            words.forEach(System.out::println);
                });
    }
}
```

This program prints:

```
word(s) of length 3
you
word(s) of length 4
know
what
have
your
room
word(s) of length 5
never
until
clean
```

The groupingBy() method in Collectors class takes a Function as an argument. It uses the result of the function to return a Map. The Map object consists of the values returned by the Function and the List of elements that matched.

What if you want to separate longer words from smaller words? For that you can use partitioningBy() method in Collectors class (Listing 6-16). The partition method takes a Predicate as an argument.

Listing 6-16. PartitionStrings.java

```
import java.util.Arrays;
import java.util.List;
import java.util.Map;
import java.util.stream.Collectors;
import java.util.stream.Stream;

public class PartitionStrings {
    public static void main(String []args) {
        String []string= "you never know what you have until you clean your room".split(" ");
        Stream<String> distinctWords = Arrays.stream(string).distinct();
        Map<Boolean, List<String>> wordBlocks =
                distinctWords.collect(Collectors.partitioningBy(str -> str.length() > 4));
```

```
        System.out.println("Short words (len <= 4): " + wordBlocks.get(false));
        System.out.println("Long words (len > 4): " + wordBlocks.get(true));
    }
}
```

This program prints:

```
Short words (len <= 4): [you, know, what, have, your, room]
Long words (len > 4): [never, until, clean]
```

In the partitioningBy() method, we have given the condition str -> str.length() > 4. Now, the result will be divided into two parts: a part with elements that evaluated to true for this condition and another part that evaluated to false. In this case, we have used partitioningBy() method to divide the words into small words (with words of length <= 4) and long words (with words of length > 4).

🖉 How are the methods groupingBy() and partitioningBy() different? The groupingBy() method takes a classification function (of type Function) and returns the input elements and their matching entries based on the classification function (and organizes the results in a Map<K, List<T>>). The partitioningBy() method takes a Predicate as the argument and classifies the entries as true and false based on the given Predicate (and organizes the results in a Map<Boolean, List<T>>).

Using flatMap Method in Stream

Certification Objective

Use flatMap() methods in the Stream API

In the earlier program, we found distinct words in a string after calling split() method:

```
String []string= "you never know what you have until you clean your room".split(" ");
Stream<String> distinctWords = Arrays.stream(string).distinct();
```

What if we want to find distinct (unique) characters in the sentence? How about this code, does it work?

```
String []string= "you never know what you have until you clean your room".split(" ");
Arrays.stream(string)
    .map(word -> word.split(""))
    .distinct()
    .forEach(System.out::print);
```

This code prints gibberish like this:

```
Ljava.lang.String;@5f184fc6[Ljava.lang.String;@3feba861[Ljava.lang.String;@5b480cf9[
```

Why? Because the word.split() returns a String[] and distinct() removes duplicate references. Since the elements in the stream are of type String[], the forEach() prints calls the default toString() implementation that prints something that is not human-readable.

One way to solve this problem is to use Arrays.stream() again on word.split(""), and convert the resulting streams into individual entries (i.e., "flatten" the streams) as in: flatMap(word -> Arrays.stream(word.split(""))). With this change, here is the program (Listing 6-17) that prints unique characters in a sentence.

Listing 6-17. UniqueCharacters.java

```java
import java.util.Arrays;

public class UniqueCharacters {
    public static void main(String []args) {
        String []string= "you never know what you have until you clean your room".split(" ");
        Arrays.stream(string)
                .flatMap(word -> Arrays.stream(word.split("")))
                .distinct()
                .forEach(System.out::print);
    }
}
```

This program correctly prints:

younevrkwhatilcm

Let us discuss an example that clearly illustrates the difference between map() and flatMap() methods (Listings 6-18 and 6-19).

Listing 6-18. UsingMap.java

```java
import java.util.Arrays;
import java.util.List;

public class UsingMap {
    public static void main(String []args) {
        List<Integer> integers = Arrays.asList(1, 2, 3, 4, 5);
        integers.stream()
                .map(i -> i * i)
                .forEach(System.out::println);
    }
}
```

This program prints:

1
4
9
16
25

In this program, we have a List<Integer> with values 1 to 5. Since we have Integer elements, we can directly call map() method and transform the elements to their square values (see Figure 6-3).

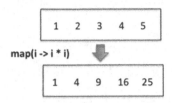

Figure 6-3. *The map() method transforms elements in a stream*

Now, things become difficult if we have a List of List<Integer>, as in Listing 6-19.

Listing 6-19. UsingFlatMap.java

```java
import java.util.Arrays;
import java.util.List;

public class UsingFlatMap {
    public static void main(String []args) {
        List<List<Integer>> intsOfInts = Arrays.asList(
                                        Arrays.asList(1, 3, 5),
                                        Arrays.asList(2, 4));
        intsOfInts.stream()
                .flatMap(ints -> ints.stream())
                    .sorted()
                    .map(i -> i * i)
                    .forEach(System.out::println);
    }
}
```

The output of this program is same as the previous program (Listing 6-18). It also prints the squares of the values 1 to 5.

In this program, we have a variable intsOfInts that is a List of List<Integer>. When you call the stream() method on intsOfInts, what will be the type of elements? It will be List<Integer>. How do we process the elements within the List<Integer>? For that, one way is to call stream() method on each of its elements. To convert those streams into Integer elements, we call the flatMap() method. After the call to flatMap(), we have a stream of Integers. We can now perform operations such as sorted(), and map() to process or transform those elements. Figure 6-4 visually shows the difference between map() and flatMap() methods in a Stream.

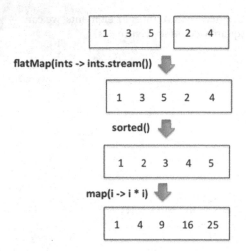

Figure 6-4. *The flatMap() method flattens the streams*

The `flatMap()` method operates on elements just like `map()` method. However, `flatMap()` flattens the streams that result from mapping each of its elements into one flat stream.

Summary

Let us briefly review the key points for each certification objective in this chapter. Please read it before appearing for the exam.

Develop code to extract data from an object using peek() and map() methods including primitive versions of the map() method

- The `peek()` method is useful for debugging: it helps us understand how the elements are transformed in the pipeline.

- You can transform (or just extract) elements in a stream using `map()` method

Search for data by using search methods of the Stream classes including findFirst, findAny, anyMatch, allMatch, noneMatch

- You can match for a given predicate in a stream using the `allMatch()`, `noneMatch()`, and `anyMatch()` methods. Unlike the `anyMatch()` method that returns false when the stream is empty, the `allMatch()` and `noneMatch()` methods return true if the stream is empty.

- You can look for elements in a stream using the `findFirst()` and `findAny()` methods. The `findAny()` method is faster to use than the `findFirst()` method in case of parallel streams.

- The "`match`" and "`find`" methods "short-circuit": the evaluation stops once the result is found and the rest of the stream is not evaluated.

Develop code that uses the Optional class

- When there are no entries in a stream and operations such as max are called, then instead of returning null or throwing an exception, the (better) approach taken in Java 8 is to return Optional values.

- Primitive type versions of Optional<T> for int, long, and double are OptionalInteger, OptionalLong, and OptionalDouble respectively.

Develop code that uses Stream data methods and calculation methods

- The Stream<T> interface has data and calculation methods count(), min() and max(); you need to pass a Comparator object as the parameter when invoking these min() and max() methods.

- The primitive type versions of Stream interface have the following data and calculation methods: count(), sum(), average(), min(), and max().

- The summaryStatistics() method in IntStream, LongStream, and DoubleStream have methods for calculating count, sum, average, minimum, and maximum values of elements in the stream.

Sort a collection using Stream API

- One way to sort a collection is to get a stream from the collection and call sorted() method on that stream. The sorted() method sorts the elements in the stream in natural order (it requires that the stream elements implements the Comparable interface).

- When you want to sort elements in the stream other than the natural order, you can pass a Comparator object to the sorted() method.

- The Comparator interface has been enhanced with many useful static or default methods in Java 8 such as thenComparing() and reversed() methods.

Save results to a collection using the collect method and group/partition data using the Collectors class

- The collect() method of the Collectors class has methods that support the task of collecting elements to a collection.

- The Collectors class provides methods such as toList(), toSet(), toMap(), and toCollection() to create a collection from a stream.

- You can group the elements in a stream using the Collectors.groupingBy() method and pass the criteria for grouping (given as a Function) as the argument.

- You can separate the elements in a stream based on a condition (given as a Predicate) using the partition() method in the Collectors class. .

Use flatMap() method of the Stream API

- The flatMap() method in Stream flattens the streams that result from mapping each element into one flat stream.

QUESTION TIME

1. Choose the best option based on this code segment:

    ```
    "abracadabra".chars().distinct().peek(ch ->
    System.out.printf("%c ", ch)).sorted();
    ```

    A. It prints: "a b c d r"

    B. It prints: "a b r c d"

    C. It crashes by throwing a `java.util.IllegalFormatConversionException`

    D. This code segment terminates normally without printing any output in the console

2. Choose the best option based on this program:

    ```java
    import java.util.function.IntPredicate;
    import java.util.stream.IntStream;

    public class MatchUse {
        public static void main(String []args) {
            IntStream temperatures = IntStream.of(-5, -6, -7, -5, 2, -8, -9);
            IntPredicate positiveTemperature = temp -> temp > 0;    // #1

            if(temperatures.anyMatch(positiveTemperature)) {        // #2
                int temp = temperatures
                                .filter(positiveTemperature)
                                .findAny()
                                .getAsInt();                        // #3
                System.out.println(temp);
            }
        }
    }
    ```

    A. This program results in a compiler error in line marked with comment #1

    B. This program results in a compiler error in line marked with comment #2

    C. This program results in a compiler error in line marked with comment #3

    D. This program prints: 2

    E. This program crashes by throwing `java.lang.IllegalStateException`

3. Choose the best option based on this program:

```
import java.util.stream.Stream;

public class AllMatch {
    public static void main(String []args) {
        boolean result = Stream.of("do", "re", "mi", "fa", "so", "la", "ti")
                .filter(str -> str.length() > 5)        // #1
                .peek(System.out::println)              // #2
                .allMatch(str -> str.length() > 5);     // #3
        System.out.println(result);
    }
}
```

A. This program results in a compiler error in line marked with comment #1

B. This program results in a compiler error in line marked with comment #2

C. This program results in a compiler error in line marked with comment #3

D. This program prints: false

E. This program prints the strings "do", "re", "mi", "fa", "so", "la", "ti", and "false" in separate lines

F. This program prints: true

4. Choose the best option based on this program:

```
import java.util.*;

class Sort {
    public static void main(String []args) {
        List<String> strings = Arrays.asList("eeny ", "meeny ", "miny ", "mo ");
        Collections.sort(strings, (str1, str2) -> str2.compareTo(str1));
        strings.forEach(string -> System.out.print(string));
    }
}
```

A. Compiler error: improper lambda function definition

B. This program prints: eeny meeny miny mo

C. This program prints: mo miny meeny eeny

D. This program will compile fine, and when run, will crash by throwing a runtime exception.

5. Choose the best option based on this program:

```java
import java.util.regex.Pattern;
import java.util.stream.Stream;

public class SumUse {
    public static void main(String []args) {
        Stream<String> words = Pattern.compile(" ").splitAsStream("a bb ccc");
        System.out.println(words.map(word -> word.length()).sum());
    }
}
```

A.   Compiler error: Cannot find symbol "sum" in interface Stream<Integer>

B.   This program prints: 3

C.   This program prints: 5

D.   This program prints: 6

E.   This program crashes by throwing `java.lang.IllegalStateException`

6. Choose the best option based on this program:

```java
import java.util.OptionalInt;
import java.util.stream.IntStream;

public class FindMax {
    public static void main(String args[]) {
        maxMarks(IntStream.of(52,60,99,80,76));          // #1
    }
    public static void maxMarks(IntStream marks) {
            OptionalInt max = marks.max();               // #2
        if(max.ifPresent()) {                            // #3
                System.out.print(max.getAsInt());
        }
    }
}
```

A.   This program results in a compiler error in line marked with comment #1

B.   This program results in a compiler error in line marked with comment #2

C.   This program results in a compiler error in line marked with comment #3

D.   This program prints: 99

7. Choose the best option based on this program:

```
import java.util.Optional;
import java.util.stream.Stream;

public class StringToUpper {
    public static void main(String args[]){
        Stream.of("eeny ","meeny ",null).forEach(StringToUpper::toUpper);
    }
    private static void toUpper(String str) {
        Optional <String> string = Optional.ofNullable(str);
        System.out.print(string.map(String::toUpperCase).orElse("dummy"));
    }
}
```

A. This program prints: EENY MEENY dummy

B. This program prints: EENY MEENY DUMMY

C. This program prints: EENY MEENY null

D. This program prints: Optional[EENY] Optional[MEENY] Optional[dummy]

E. This program prints: Optional[EENY] Optional[MEENY] Optional[DUMMY]

Answers:

1. D. This code segment terminates normally without printing any output in the console.

    A stream pipeline is lazily evaluated. Since there is no terminal operation provided (such as count(), forEach(), reduce(), or collect()), this pipeline is not evaluated and hence the peek() method does not print any output to the console.

2. E. This program crashes by throwing java.lang.IllegalStateException

    A stream once used–i.e., once "consumed"–cannot be used again. In this program, anyMatch() is a terminal operation. Hence, once anyMatch() is called, the stream in temperatures is considered "used" or "consumed". Hence, calling findAny() terminal operation on temperatures results in the program throwing java.lang. IllegalStateException.

3. F. This program prints: true

    The predicate str -> str.length() > 5 returns false for all the elements because the length of each string is 2. Hence, the filter() method results in an empty stream and the peek() method does not print anything. The allMatch() method returns true for an empty stream and does not evalute the given predicate. Hence this program prints true.

4. C. This program prints: mo miny meeny eeny

   This is a proper definition of a lambda expression. Since the second argument of `Collections.sort()` method takes the functional interface `Comparator` and a matching lambda expression is passed in this code. Note that second argument is compared with the first argument in the lambda expression `(str1, str2) -> str2.compareTo(str1)`. For this reason, the comparison is performed in descending order.

5. A. Compiler error: Cannot find symbol "sum" in interface `Stream<Integer>`

   Data and calculation methods such as `sum()` and `average()` are not available in the `Stream<T>` interface; they are available only in the primitive type versions `IntStream`, `LongStream`, and `DoubleStream`. To create an `IntStream`, one solution is to use `mapToInt()` method instead of `map()` method in this program. If `mapToInt()` were used, this program would compile without errors, and when executed, it will print 6 to the console.

6. C. This program results in a compiler error in line marked with comment #3

   The `ifPresent()` method in `Optional` takes a `Consumer<T>` as the argument. This program uses `ifPresent()` without passing an argument and hence it results in a compiler error. If the method `isPresent()` were used instead of `ifPresent()` in this program, it will compile cleanly and print 99 on the console.

7. A. This program prints: EENY MEENY dummy

   Note that the variable `string` points to `Optional.ofNullable(str)`. When the element null is encountered in the stream, it cannot be converted to uppercase and hence the `orElse()` method executes to return the string "dummy". In this program, if `Optional.of(str)` were used instead of `Optional.ofNullable(str)` the program would have resulted in throwing a `NullPointerException`.

CHAPTER 7

■ ■ ■

Exceptions and Assertions

Certification Objectives

Use try-catch and throw statements

Use catch, multi-catch, and finally clauses

Use Autoclose resources with a try-with-resources statement

Create custom exceptions and Auto-closeable resources

Test invariants by using assertions

In this chapter, you'll learn about Java's support for exception handling in detail. The OCAJP 8 exam (which is a pre-requisite for OCPJP 8 exam) covers fundamentals of exception handling as an exam topic. Hence, we assume that you are already familiar with the basic syntax used for exception handling and types of exceptions. In this chapter, you'll learn how to provide try, catch, multi-catch, and finally block. You'll also learn about the recently added language features such as try-with-resources and multi-catch statements. Following that, you'll learn how to define your own exception classes (custom exceptions). Finally, we'll discuss the related topic of assertions and teach you how to use them in your programs. Many programming examples in this chapter make use of I/O functions (Chapters 9 and 10) to illustrate the concepts of exception handling.

Throwable and its Subclasses

In Java the thrown object should be an instance of the class Throwable or one of its subclasses (Throwable is the apex class of the exception hierarchy in Java). Exception handling constructs such as the throw statement, throws clause, and catch clause deal only with Throwable and its subclasses. There are three important subclasses of Throwable that you need to learn in detail: the Error, Exception, and RuntimeException classes. Figure 7-1 provides a high-level overview of these classes.

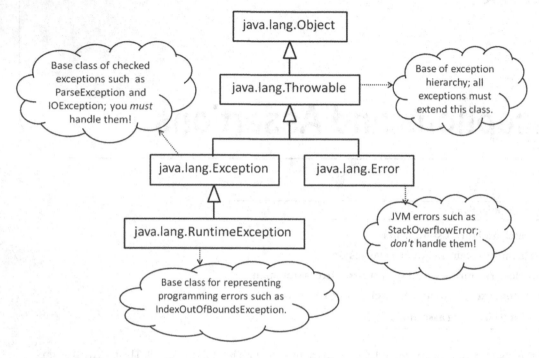

Figure 7-1. *Java's exception hierarchy*

Here is a brief description of the three important classes that extends the Throwable class:

- Exceptions of type Exception are known as *checked exceptions*. If code can throw an Exception, you must handle it using a catch block or declare that the method throws that exception, forcing the caller of that method to handle that exception.

- RuntimeException is a derived class of the Exception class. The exceptions deriving from this class are known as *unchecked exceptions*. It is optional to handle unchecked exceptions. If a code segment you write in a method can throw an unchecked exception, it is not mandatory to catch that exception or declare that exception in the throws clause of that method.

- When the JVM detects a serious abnormal condition in the program, it raises an exception of type Error. Exceptions of type Error indicate an abnormal condition in the program. There is no point in catching this exception and trying to continue execution and pretending nothing has happened. It is a *really* bad practice to do so!

Now, let us start discussing how to throw and catch exceptions.

Throwing Exceptions

Certification Objective

Use try-catch and throw statements

Listing 7-1 is a very simple programming example in which you want to echo the text typed as command-line arguments back to the user. Assume that the user must type some text as command-line arguments to echo, or else you need to inform the user about the "error condition."

Listing 7-1. Echo.java

```
// A simple program without exception handling code
class Echo {
    public static void main(String []args) {
        if(args.length == 0) {
            // no arguments passed - display an error to the user
            System.out.println("Error: No input passed to echo command... ");
            System.exit(-1);
        }
        else {
            for(String str : args) {
                // command-line arguments are separated and passed as an array
                // print them by adding a space between the array elements
                System.out.print(str + " ");
            }
        }
    }
}
```

In this case, you print the error in the console using a `println()` statement. This is a trivial program and the error occurred in the `main()` method, so the error handling is easy. In this case, you can terminate the program after printing the error message to the console. However, if you are deep within the function calls in a complex application, you need a better way to indicate that an "exceptional condition" has occurred and then inform the caller about that condition. Further, you often need to recover from an error condition instead of terminating the program. So you need to be able to "handle" an exception or "rethrow" that exception further up in the call stack so that a caller can handle that exception. (We'll revisit this topic of rethrowing exceptions later in this chapter.) At present, you'll change the program in Listing 7-1 to throw an exception instead of printing an error message (in a separate program, `Echo1.java`), like so:

```
if(args.length == 0) {
    // no arguments passed - throw an exception
    throw new IllegalArgumentException("No input passed to echo command");
}
```

This block inside the `if` condition for `args.length == 0` is the only part that needs to be changed within this program. Note the syntax for throwing an exception: the `throw` keyword followed by the exception object. Here you make use of `IllegalArgumentException`, which is already defined in the Java library. Later in this chapter, you'll see how to define your own exceptions.

Now, if you run this program without passing any arguments in the command line, the program will throw an `IllegalArgumentException`:

```
Exception in thread "main" java.lang.IllegalArgumentException: No input passed to echo command
        at Echo1.main(Echo1.java:5)
```

Since there was no handler for this exception, this uncaught exception terminated the program. In this case, you explicitly threw an exception. Exceptions can also get thrown when you write some code or call Java APIs. Let's look at an example now.

Unhandled Exceptions

Consider the program in Listing 7-2, which attempts to read an integer value that the user types in the console and prints the read integer back to the console. For reading an integer from the console, you make use of the `nextInt()` method provided in the `java.util.Scanner` class. To instantiate the Scanner class, you pass in `System.in`, which is a reference to the *system input stream*.

Listing 7-2. ScanInt1.java

```java
// A simple progam to accept an integer from user

import java.util.Scanner;

class ScanInt1 {
    public static void main(String [] args) {
        System.out.println("Type an integer in the console: ");
        Scanner consoleScanner = new Scanner(System.in);
        System.out.println("You typed the integer value: " + consoleScanner.nextInt());
    }
}
```

When you run this program and type an integer, say 10, in the console, the program works correctly and prints the integer back to you successfully.

```
D:\> java ScanInt1
Type an integer in the console:
10
You typed the integer value: 10
```

However, what if you (or the user of the program) mistakenly type the string "ten" instead of the integer value "10"? The program will terminate after throwing an exception like this:

```
D:\> java ScanInt1
Type an integer in the console:
ten
Exception in thread "main" java.util.InputMismatchException
        at java.util.Scanner.throwFor(Scanner.java:909)
        at java.util.Scanner.next(Scanner.java:1530)
        at java.util.Scanner.nextInt(Scanner.java:2160)
        at java.util.Scanner.nextInt(Scanner.java:2119)
        at ScanInt.main(ScanInt1.java:7)
```

If you read the documentation of nextInt(), you'll see that this method can throw InputMismatchException - "if the next token does not match the Integer regular expression, or is out of range." In this simple program, you assume that you (or the user) will always type an integer value as expected, and when that assumption fails, an exception gets thrown. If there is an exception thrown from a program, and it is left unhandled, the program will terminate abnormally after throwing a stack trace like the ones shown here.

A *stack trace* shows the list of the method (with the line numbers) that was called before the control reached the statement where the exception was thrown. As a programmer, you'll find it useful to trace the control flow for debugging the program and fix the problem that led to this exception.

So, how do you handle this situation? You need to put this code within try and catch blocks and then handle the exception.

Try and Catch Statements

Certification Objective

Use catch, multi-catch, and finally clauses

Java provides the try and catch keywords to handle any exceptions that can get thrown in the code you write. Listing 7-3 is the improved version of the program from Listing 7-2.

Listing 7-3. ScanInt2.java

```java
// A simple progam to accept an integer from user in normal case,
// otherwise prints an error message

import java.util.Scanner;
import java.util.InputMismatchException;

class ScanInt2 {
    public static void main(String [] args) {
        System.out.println("Type an integer in the console: ");
        Scanner consoleScanner = new Scanner(System.in);
        try {
            System.out.println("You typed the integer value: " + consoleScanner.nextInt());
        } catch(InputMismatchException ime) {
            // nextInt() throws InputMismatchException in case anything
            // other than an integer is typed in the console; so handle it
            System.out.println("Error: You typed some text that is not an integer value...");
        }
    }
}
```

If anything other than a valid integer is typed in the input, this program prints a readable error message to the user.

```
D:\> java ScanInt2
Type an integer in the console:
ten
Error: You typed some text that is not an integer value...
```

Now let's analyze this code. The block followed by the `try` keyword limits the code segment for which you expect that some exceptions could be thrown. If any exception gets thrown from the `try` block, the Java runtime will search for a *matching handler* (which we'll discuss in more detail a bit later). In this case, an exception handler for `InputMismatchException` is present, which is of exactly the same type as the exception that got thrown. This *exactly matching* catch handler is available just outside the try block in the form of a block preceded by the keyword `catch`, and this catch block gets executed. In the catch block you caught the exception, so you're handling the exception here. You are providing a human readable error string rather than throwing a raw stack trace (as you did in the earlier program in Listing 7-2), so you're providing a graceful exit for the program.

Multiple Catch Blocks

In Listing 7-2, you used a `Scanner` object to read an integer from the console. Note that you can use a `Scanner` object to read from a String as well (see Listing 7-4).

Listing 7-4. ScanInt3.java

```java
// A program that scans an integer from a given string

import java.util.Scanner;
import java.util.InputMismatchException;

class ScanInt3 {
    public static void main(String [] args) {
        String integerStr = "100";
        System.out.println("The string to scan integer from it is: " + integerStr);
        Scanner consoleScanner = new Scanner(integerStr);
        try {
            System.out.println("The integer value scanned from string is: " +
                                consoleScanner.nextInt());
        } catch(InputMismatchException ime) {
            // nextInt() throws InputMismatchException in case
            // anything other than an integeris provided in the string
            System.out.println("Error: Cannot scan an integer from the given string");
        }
    }
}
```

This program prints the following:

```
The string to scan integer from it is: 100
The integer value scanned from string is: 100
```

What happens if you modify the program in Listing 7-4 so that the string contains a non-integer value, as in

```java
String integerStr = "hundred";
```

The try block will throw an InputMismatchException, which will be handled in the catch block, and you'll get this output:

```
The string to scan integer from it is: hundred
Error: Cannot scan an integer from the given string
```

Now, what if you modify the program in Listing 7-4 so that the string contains an empty string, as in

```
String integerStr = "";
```

For this, nextInt() will throw a NoSuchElementException, which is not handled in this program, so this program would crash.

```
The string to scan integer from it is:
Exception in thread "main" java.util.NoSuchElementException
        at java.util.Scanner.throwFor(Scanner.java:907)
        at java.util.Scanner.next(Scanner.java:1530)
        at java.util.Scanner.nextInt(Scanner.java:2160)
        at java.util.Scanner.nextInt(Scanner.java:2119)
        at ScanInt3.main(ScanInt.java:11)
```

Further, if you look at the JavaDoc for Scanner.nextInt() method, you'll find that it can also throw an IllegalStateException (this exception is thrown if the nextInt() method is called on a Scanner object that is already closed). So, let's provide catch handlers for InputMismatchException, NoSuchElementException, and IllegalStateException (see Listing 7-5).

Listing 7-5. ScanInt4.java

```java
// A program that scans an integer from a given string

import java.util.Scanner;
import java.util.InputMismatchException;
import java.util.NoSuchElementException;

class ScanInt4 {
    public static void main(String [] args) {
        String integerStr = "";
        System.out.println("The string to scan integer from it is: " + integerStr);
        Scanner consoleScanner = new Scanner(integerStr);
        try {
            System.out.println("The integer value scanned from string is: " +
                consoleScanner.nextInt());
        } catch(InputMismatchException ime) {
            System.out.println("Error: Cannot scan an integer from the given string");
        } catch(NoSuchElementException nsee) {
            System.out.println("Error: Cannot scan an integer from the given string");
        } catch(IllegalStateException ise) {
            System.out.println("Error: nextInt() called on a closed Scanner object");
        }
    }
}
```

Here is the output when you run this program:

```
The string to scan integer from it is:
Error: Cannot scan an integer from the given string
```

As you can see from the output, since the string is empty, NoSuchElementException gets thrown. It is caught in the catch handler for this exception, and the code provided inside the catch block gets executed to result in a graceful exit.

Note how you provided more than one catch handler by stacking them up: you provided specific (i.e., derived type) exception handlers followed by more general (i.e., base type) exception handlers. If you provide a derived exception type after a base exception type, you get a compiler error. You might not already know, but NoSuchElementException is the base class of InputMismatchException! See what happens when you try to reverse the order of catch handlers for InputMismatchException and NoSuchElementException.

```
try {
    System.out.println("The integer value scanned from string is: "
                + consoleScanner.nextInt());
} catch(NoSuchElementException nsee) {
    System.out.println("Error: Cannot scan an integer from the given string");
} catch(InputMismatchException ime) {
    System.out.println("Error: Cannot scan an integer from the given string");
}
```

This code segment will result in this compiler error:

```
ScanInt4.java:14: error: exception InputMismatchException has already been caught

    } catch(InputMismatchException ime) {
      ^
1 error
```

> When providing multiple catch handlers, handle specific exceptions before handling general exceptions. If you provide a derived class exception catch handler *after* a base class exception handler, your code will not compile.

Multi-Catch Blocks

Java provides a feature named *multi-catch blocks* in which you can combine multiple catch handlers. Let's use this feature to combine the catch clauses of NoSuchElementException and IllegalStateException (see Listing 7-6):

Listing 7-6. ScanInt5.java

```
// A program that illustrates multi-catch blocks

import java.util.Scanner;
import java.util.NoSuchElementException;
```

```
class ScanInt5 {
    public static void main(String [] args) {
        String integerStr = "";
        System.out.println("The string to scan integer from it is: " + integerStr);
        Scanner consoleScanner = new Scanner(integerStr);
        try {
            System.out.println("The integer value scanned from string is: " +
              consoleScanner.nextInt());
        } catch(NoSuchElementException | IllegalStateException multie) {
            System.out.println("Error: An error occured while attempting to scan the integer");
        }
    }
}
```

Note how you combine the catch handlers together using the | (OR) operator here (the same operator you use for performing bit-wise OR operation on integral values) for combining the catch clauses of NoSuchElementException and IllegalStateException.

Unlike the combined catch clauses for NoSuchElementException and IllegalStateException, you cannot combine the catch clauses of NoSuchElementException and InputMismatchException. As we've already discussed, NoSuchElementException is the base class of InputMismatchException, and you cannot catch both of them in the multi-catch block. If you try compiling such a multi-catch clause, you'll get this compiler error:

ScanInt5.java:11: error: Alternatives in a multi-catch statement cannot be related by subclassing
        } catch(InputMismatchException | NoSuchElementException exception) {
                                                                ^

So what is the alternative? When you need such a catch handler for the exceptions where one exception is the base class of another exception class, providing the catch handler for the base class alone is sufficient (since that base class catch handler will handle the derived class exception if it occurs).

In a multi-catch block, you cannot combine catch handlers for two exceptions that share a base- and derived-class relationship. You can only combine catch handlers for exceptions that do not share the parent-child relationship between them.

How do you know if it is better to combine exception handling blocks or stack them? It is a design choice where you must consider the following aspects: (a) Do the exceptions get thrown for similar reasons or for different reasons? (b) Is the handling code similar or different? If you answer "similar" for both the questions, it is better to combine them; if you say "different" for either one of these two questions, then it is better to separate them.

How about the specific situation in Listing 7-6? Is it better to combine or separate the handlers for the InputMismatchException and IllegalStateException exceptions? You can see that the exception handling is the same for both of the catch blocks. But the reasons for these two exceptions are considerably different. The InputMismatchException gets thrown invalid input is passed (e.g., "hundred" as we discussed earlier). The IllegalStateException gets thrown because of a programming mistake when you call the nextInt() method after calling the close() method on Scanner. So, in this case, it is a better design choice to separate the handlers for these two exceptions.

General Catch Handlers

Did you notice that many exceptions can get thrown when you use APIs related to I/O operations? We just discussed that in order to call just one method, nextInt() of the Scanner class, you need to handle three exceptions: the InputMismatchException, the NoSuchElementException, and the IllegalStateException. If you keep handling specific exceptions such as this that may or may not actually result in an exceptional condition when you run the program, most of your code will consist of try-catch code blocks! Is there a better way to say "handle all other exceptions"? Yes, you can provide a *general exception handler*.

Here is the code snippet that shows only the try-catch blocks for the class ScanInt3 from Listing 7-4, enhanced with a general exception handler:

```
try {
    System.out.println("You typed the integer value: " + consoleScanner.nextInt());
} catch(InputMismatchException ime) {
    // if something other than integer is typed, we'll get this exception, so handle it
    System.out.println("Error: You typed some text that is not an integer value...");
} catch(Exception e) {
    // catch IllegalStateException here which is unlikely to occur...
    System.out.println("Error: Encountered an exception and could not read an integer from
    the console... ");
}
```

This code provides a catch handler for the base exception of the type Exception. So, if the try block throws any other exception than the InputMismatchException, and if that exception is a derived class of the Exception class, this general catch handler will handle it. It is recommended practice to catch specific exceptions, and then provide a general exception handler to ensure that all other exceptions are handled as well.

Releasing Resources

Do you notice that programs we discussed in Listings 7-2, 7-3, and 7-4 have a *resource leak* (because we opened a Scanner object but did not close it)? The word "resource" refers to any of the classes that acquire some system sources from the underlying operating system, such as network, file, database, and other handles. But how do you know which classes need to be closed? The answer is that if a class implements java.io.Closeable, then you must call the close() method of that class; otherwise, it will result in a resource leak.

●⚞ The Garbage Collector (GC) is responsible for releasing only memory resources. If you are using any class that acquires system resources, it is your responsibility to release them by calling the close() method on that object.

ScanInt6 (Listing 7-7) calls the close() method of the Scanner object in its main() method; you want to shorten the code, so you'll use a general exception handler for handling all exceptions that can be thrown within the try block.

Listing 7-7. ScanInt6.java

```java
import java.util.Scanner;

class ScanInt6 {
    public static void main(String [] args) {
        System.out.println("Type an integer in the console: ");
        Scanner consoleScanner = new Scanner(System.in);
        try {
            System.out.println("You typed the integer value: " + consoleScanner.nextInt());
            System.out.println("Done reading the text... closing the Scanner");
            consoleScanner.close();
        } catch(Exception e) {
            // call all other exceptions here ...
            System.out.println("Error: Encountered an exception and could not read an
            integer from the console... ");
            System.out.println("Exiting the program - restart and try the program again!");
        }
    }
}
```

Let's see if this program works.

```
D:\> java ScanInt6
Type an integer in the console:
10
You typed the integer value: 10
Done reading the text... closing the Scanner
```

Because the program printed "Done reading the text... closing the Scanner", and completed the execution normally, you can assume that the statement consoleScanner.close(); has executed successfully. What happens if an exception gets thrown?

```
D:\> java ScanInt6
Type an integer in the console:
ten
Error: Encountered an exception and could not read an integer from the console...
Exiting the program - restart and try the program again!
```

As you can see from the output, the program did not print "Done reading the text... closing the Scanner", so the statement consoleScanner.close(); has not executed. How can you fix it? One way is to call consoleScanner.close() in the catch block as well, like this:

```java
try {
    System.out.println("You typed the integer value: " + consoleScanner.nextInt());
    System.out.println("Done reading the text... closing the Scanner");
    consoleScanner.close();
} catch(Exception e) {
```

```
    // call all other exceptions here ...
    consoleScanner.close();
    System.out.println("Error: Encountered an exception and could not read an integer from
    the console... ");
    System.out.println("Exiting the program - restart and try the program again!");
}
```

This solution will work but is not elegant. You know you can have multiple catch blocks and you have to provide calls to consoleScanner.close(); in all the catch blocks! Is there a better way to release the resources? Yes, you can use release resources in a finally block (see Listing 7-8).

Listing 7-8. ScanInt7.java

```java
import java.util.Scanner;

class ScanInt7 {
    public static void main(String [] args) {
        System.out.println("Type an integer in the console: ");
        Scanner consoleScanner = new Scanner(System.in);
        try {
            System.out.println("You typed the integer value: " + consoleScanner.nextInt());
        } catch(Exception e) {
            // call all other exceptions here ...
            System.out.println("Error: Encountered an exception and could not read an
            integer from the console... ");
            System.out.println("Exiting the program - restart and try the program again!");
        } finally {
            System.out.println("Done reading the integer... closing the Scanner");
            consoleScanner.close();
        }
    }
}
```

In this case, a finally block is provided after the catch block. This finally block will be executed whether an exception has occurred or not. So, the finally block is a good place to call the close() method on the Scanner object to ensure that this resource is always released.

💣 If you call System.exit() inside a method, it will abnormally terminate the program. So, if the calling method has a finally block, it will not be called and resources may leak. For this reason, it is a bad programming practice to call System.exit() to terminate a program.

Now, let's see if the scanner is closed both in the case when the program completes normally (i.e., without throwing an exception) and when the program terminates after throwing an exception.

```
D:\> java ScanInt7
Type an integer in the console:
10
You typed the integer value: 10
Done reading the integer... closing the Scanner
```

```
D:\> java ScanInt7
Type an integer in the console:
ten
Error: Encountered an exception and could not read an integer from the console...
Exiting the program - restart and try the program again!
Done reading the integer... closing the Scanner
```

Yes, the statement "Done reading the integer... closing the Scanner" is called whether an exception is thrown or not. Note that you can have a finally block directly after a try block without a catch block as well; though this feature is used rarely, it is a useful feature.

A note: the finally block is always executed irrespective of whether the code in the try block throws an exception or not. Consider the following method. Will it return true or false to the caller?

```
boolean returnTest() {
    try {
        return true;
    }
    finally {
        return false;
    }
}
```

This method will always return false because finally is always invoked though it is unintuitive. In fact, if you use the "-Xlint" option, you'll get this compiler warning: "finally clause cannot complete normally." (Note that you can have a try block followed by either catch block or finally block or both blocks.)

The Throws Clause

A method can throw checked exceptions; the clause throw specifies these checked exceptions in the method signature. In the throws clause, you list *checked exceptions* that a method can throw. Why do we need the throws clause? By looking at the throws clause, you can get a clear idea of what exceptions the method can throw. Understanding checked exceptions is a prerequisite for understanding the throws clause. Since we've covered checked exceptions in the previous section on exception types, we'll cover the throws clause now.

Let's try reading an integer stored in a file named integer.txt in the current directory. There is an overloaded constructor of the Scanner class that takes a File object as input, so let's try using it. Listing 7-9 shows the program. Will it work?

Listing 7-9. ThrowsClause1.java

```
import java.io.File;
import java.util.Scanner;

class ThrowsClause1 {
    public static void main(String []args) {
        System.out.println("Reading an integer from the file 'integer.txt': ");
        Scanner consoleScanner = new Scanner(new File("integer.txt"));
        System.out.println("You typed the integer value: " + consoleScanner.nextInt());
    }
}
```

This code will result in a compiler error of "unreported exception FileNotFoundException; must be caught or declared to be thrown". If you look at the declaration of this Scanner method, you'll see a throws clause:

```
public Scanner(File source) throws FileNotFoundException {
```

So, any method that invokes this constructor should either handle this exception or add a throws clause to declare that the method can throw this exception. Add a throws clause to the main() method; see Listing 7-10.

Listing 7-10. ThrowsClause2.java

```java
import java.io.File;
import java.io.FileNotFoundException;
import java.util.Scanner;

class ThrowsClause2 {
    public static void main(String []args) throws FileNotFoundException {
        System.out.println("Reading an integer from the file 'integer.txt': ");
        Scanner consoleScanner = new Scanner(new File("integer.txt"));
        System.out.println("You typed the integer value: " + consoleScanner.nextInt());
    }
}
```

If you run this program and there is no file named integer.txt, the program will crash after throwing this exception:

```
Reading an integer from the file 'integer.txt':
Exception in thread "main" java.io.FileNotFoundException: integer.txt (The system cannot
find the file specified)
        at java.io.FileInputStream.open(Native Method)
        at java.io.FileInputStream.<init>(FileInputStream.java:138)
        at java.util.Scanner.<init>(Scanner.java:656)
        at ThrowsClause2.main(ThrowsClause2.java:7)
```

Let's now extract the code inside the main() method to a new method named readIntFromFile(). You have defined it as an instance method, so you also create an object of the ThrowsClause3 class to invoke this method from the main() method. Since the code inside readIntFromFile() can throw a FileNotFoundException, it has to either introduce a catch handler to handle this exception or declare this exception in its throws clause (see Listing 7-11).

Listing 7-11. ThrowsClause3.java

```java
import java.io.File;
import java.io.FileNotFoundException;
import java.util.Scanner;

class ThrowsClause3 {
    // since this method does not handle FileNotFoundException,
    // the method must declare this exception in the throws clause
```

```
public int readIntFromFile() throws FileNotFoundException {
    Scanner consoleScanner = new Scanner(new File("integer.txt"));
    return consoleScanner.nextInt();
}

// since readIntFromFile() throws FileNotFoundException and main() does not handle
// it, the main() method declares this exception in its throws clause
public static void main(String []args) throws FileNotFoundException {
    System.out.println("Reading an integer from the file 'integer.txt': ");
    System.out.println("You typed the integer value: "
                        + new ThrowsClause3().readIntFromFile());
}
}
```

The behavior of the program remains the same in both Listings 7-10 and 7-11. However, Listing 7-11 shows how the main() method also must still declare to throw the FileNotFoundException in its throws clause (otherwise, the program will not compile).

Method Overriding and the Throws Clause

When an overridable method has a throws clause, there are many things to consider while overriding that method. Consider the program in Listing 7-12, which implements an interface named IntReader. This interface declares a single method named readIntFromFile() with the throws clause listing a FileNotFoundException.

Listing 7-12. ThrowsClause4.java

```
import java.io.File;
import java.io.FileNotFoundException;
import java.io.IOException;
import java.util.Scanner;

// This interface is meant for implemented by classes that would read an integer from a file
interface IntReader {
    int readIntFromFile() throws IOException;
}

class ThrowsClause4 implements IntReader {
    // implement readIntFromFile with the same throws clause
    // or a more specific throws clause
    public int readIntFromFile() throws FileNotFoundException {
        Scanner consoleScanner = new Scanner(new File("integer.txt"));
        return consoleScanner.nextInt();
    }
    // main method elided in this code since the focus here is to understand
    // issues related to overriding when throws clause is present
}
```

In this code, you can observe a few important facts:

- You can declare the throws clause for methods declared in interfaces; in fact, you can provide the throws clause for abstract methods declared in abstract classes as well.

- The method declared in the IntReader interface declares to throw IOException, which is a more general exception than a FileNotFoundException (Figure 7-2). While implementing a method, it is acceptable to either provide the throws clause listing the same exception type as the base method or a more specific type than the base method. In this case, the readIntFromFile() method lists a more specific exception (FileNotFoundException) in its throws clause against the more general exception of IOException listed in the throws clause of the base method declared in the IntReader interface.

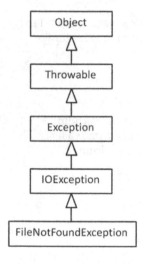

Figure 7-2. *Class hierarchy of FileNotFoundException*

What if you try changing the throws clause? There are many ways to change the throws clause in the overriding method, including the following:

a. Listing more general checked exceptions to throw.

b. Listing more checked exceptions in addition to the given checked exception(s) in the base method.

If you attempt any of these cases, you'll get a compiler error. For example, if you provide a more general exception than specified in the base class will result in a compiler error.

You can choose not to specify any exception using throws clause in the overridden method provided the overridden method does not throw any checked exception or if it does, it provides a try-catch block.

To summarize, the base class method's throws clause is a contract that it provides to the caller of that method: it says that the caller should handle the listed exceptions or declare those exceptions in its throws clause. When overriding the base method, the derived method should also adhere to that contract. The caller of the base method is prepared to handle only the exceptions listed in the base method, so the overriding method cannot throw more general or other than the listed checked exceptions.

However, note that this discussion that the derived class method's throws clause should follow the contract for the base method's throws clause is limited to checked exceptions. Unchecked exceptions can still be added or removed from the contract when compared to the base class method's throws clause. For example, consider the following:

```
public int readIntFromFile() throws IOException, NoSuchElementException {
    Scanner consoleScanner = new Scanner(new File("integer.txt"));
    return consoleScanner.nextInt();
}
```

This is an acceptable throws clause since NoSuchElementException can get thrown from the readIntFromFile() method. This exception is an unchecked exception, and it gets thrown when the nextInt() method could not read an integer from the file. This is a common situation, for example, if you have an empty file named integer.txt; an attempt to read an integer from this file will result in this exception.

@THROWS TAG

It is a good practice to use the @throws JavaDoc tag (or its synonym @exception tag) to document the specific situations or cases in which an (unchecked or checked) exception might be thrown from a method. Here is the format for providing @throws tag with an example:

```
@throws exception-name    description-text
@throws IllegalStateException if this scanner is closed
```

This tag can be used only for methods and constructors.

Here is an example of JavaDoc comment for nextInt() method in Scanner class:

```
/**
 * Scans the next token of the input as an <tt>int</tt>.
 *
 * <p> An invocation of this method of the form
 * <tt>nextInt()</tt> behaves in exactly the same way as the
 * invocation <tt>nextInt(radix)</tt>, where <code>radix</code>
 * is the default radix of this scanner.
 *
 * @return the <tt>int</tt> scanned from the input
 * @throws InputMismatchException
 *            if the next token does not match the <i>Integer</i>
 *            regular expression, or is out of range
 * @throws NoSuchElementException if input is exhausted
 * @throws IllegalStateException if this scanner is closed
 */
public int nextInt() {
    return nextInt(defaultRadix);
}
```

Note the @throws tag for InputMismatchException, NoSuchElementException and IllegalStateException. When a method can throw multiple exceptions, they are listed in alphabetical order by convention (as in this case).

Points to Remember

Here are some noteworthy points about the throws statement that could help you in the OCPJP 8 exam:

- If a method does not have a throws clause, it does *not* mean it cannot throw any exceptions; it just means it cannot throw any *checked* exceptions.

- Static initialization blocks cannot throw any checked exceptions. Why? Remember that static initialization blocks are invoked when the class is loaded, so there is no way to handle the thrown exceptions in the caller. Further, there is no way to declare the checked exceptions in a throws clause (because they are *blocks*, not methods).

- Non-static initialization blocks can throw checked exceptions; however, all the constructors should declare those exceptions in their throws clause. Why? The compiler merges the code for non-static initialization blocks and constructors during its code generation phase, hence the throws clause of the constructor can be used for declaring the checked exceptions that a non-static initialization block can throw.

- An overriding method cannot declare more checked exceptions in the throws clause than the list of exceptions declared in the throws clause of the base method. Why? The callers of the base method see only the list of the exceptions given in the throws clause of that method and will declare or handle these checked exceptions in their code (and not more than that).

- An overriding method can declare more specific exceptions than the exception(s) listed in the throws clause of the base method; in other words, you can declare derived exceptions in the throws clause of the overriding method.

- If a method is declared in two or more interfaces, and if that method declares to throw different exceptions in the throws clause, the method implementation should list all of these exceptions.

Chaining and Rethrowing Exceptions

You can catch exceptions and wrap them into more generic exceptions and throw them higher up in the call stack. When you catch an exception and create a more general exception, you can retain reference to the original exception; this is called *exception chaining*.

```
catch(LowLevelException lle) {
    // wrap the low-level exception to a higher-level exception;
    // also, chain the original exception to the newly thrown exception
    throw new HighLevelException(lle);
}
```

Chaining exceptions is useful for debugging purposes. When you get a general exception, you can check if there is a chained lower-level exception and try to understand why that lower-level exception occurred.

Try-with-Resources

Certification Objective

Use Autoclose resources with a try-with-resources statement

It is a fairly common mistake by Java programmers to forget releasing resources, even in the finally block. Also, if you're dealing with multiple resources, it is tedious to remember to call the `close()` method in the finally block. Try-with-resources feature (introduced in Java 7) will help make your life easier. Listing 7-13 makes use of this feature; it is an improved version of Listing 7-8 which made an explicit call to close, as in, `consoleScanner.close()`.

Listing 7-13. TryWithResources1.java

```java
import java.util.Scanner;

class TryWithResources1 {
    public static void main(String [] args) {
        System.out.println("Type an integer in the console: ");
        try(Scanner consoleScanner = new Scanner(System.in)) {
            System.out.println("You typed the integer value: " + consoleScanner.nextInt());
        } catch(Exception e) {
            // catch all other exceptions here ...
            System.out.println("Error: Encountered an exception and could not read an
            integer from the console... ");
            System.out.println("Exiting the program - restart and try the program again!");
        }
    }
}
```

Make sure you take a closer look at the syntax for try-with-resources block.

```java
try(Scanner consoleScanner = new Scanner(System.in)) {
```

In this statement, you have acquired the resources inside the parenthesis after the `try` keyword, but before the `try` block. Also, in the example, you don't provide the finally block. The Java compiler will internally translate this try-with-resources block into a try-finally block (of course, the compiler will retain the catch blocks you provide). You can acquire multiple resources in the try-with-resources block. Such resource acquisition statements must be separated using semicolons.

Can you provide try-with-resources statements without any explicit catch or finally blocks? Yes! Remember that a try block can be associated with a catch block, finally block, or both. A try-with-resources statement block gets expanded internally into a try-finally block. So, you can provide a try-with-resources statement without explicit catch or finally blocks. Listing 7-14 uses a try-with-resources statement without any explicit catch or finally blocks.

Listing 7-14. TryWithResources2.java

```java
import java.util.Scanner;

class TryWithResources2 {
    public static void main(String [] args) {
        System.out.println("Type an integer in the console: ");
        try(Scanner consoleScanner = new Scanner(System.in)) {
            System.out.println("You typed the integer value: " + consoleScanner.nextInt());
        }
    }
}
```

Although it is possible to create a try-with-resources statement without any explicit catch or finally, it doesn't mean you should do so! For example, since this code does not have a catch block, if you type some invalid input, the program will crash.

```
D:\> java TryWithResources2
Type an integer in the console:
ten
Exception in thread "main" java.util.InputMismatchException
        at java.util.Scanner.throwFor(Scanner.java:864)
        at java.util.Scanner.next(Scanner.java:1485)
        at java.util.Scanner.nextInt(Scanner.java:2117)
        at java.util.Scanner.nextInt(Scanner.java:2076)
        at TryWithResources2.main(TryWithResources2.java:7)
```

So, the benefit of a try-with-resources statement is that it simplifies your life by not having to provide finally blocks explicitly. However, you still need to provide necessary catch blocks.

Note that for a resource to be usable with a try-with-resources statement, the class of that resource must implement the java.lang.AutoCloseable interface. This interface declares one single method named close(). Along with try-with-resources feature, AutoCloseable interface was also introduced in Java 7, and the interface is made of the base interface of the Closeable interface. This is to make sure that the existing resource classes work seamlessly with a try-with-resources statement. In other words, you can use all old stream classes with try-with-resources because they implement the AutoCloseable interface.

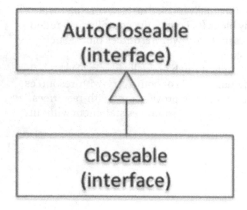

Figure 7-3. *Closeabe Interface extends AutoCloseable Interface*

Closing Multiple Resources

You can use more than one resource in a try-with-resources statement. Here is a code snippet for creating a zip file from a given text file that makes use of a try-with-resources statement:

```
// buffer is the temporary byte buffer used for copying data
// from one stream to another stream
byte [] buffer = new byte[1024];

// these stream constructors can throw FileNotFoundException
try (ZipOutputStream zipFile = new ZipOutputStream(new FileOutputStream(zipFileName));
    FileInputStream fileIn = new FileInputStream(fileName)) {
    zipFile.putNextEntry(new ZipEntry(fileName));           // putNextEntry can throw
                                                            // IOException
    int lenRead = 0; // the variable to keep track of number of bytes sucessfully read
    // copy the contents of the input file into the zip file
    while((lenRead = fileIn.read(buffer)) > 0) {           // read can throw IOException
        zipFile.write(buffer, 0, lenRead);                 // write can throw IOException
    }
    // the streams will be closed automatically because they are within try-with-
    // resources statement
}
```

In this code, the buffer is a byte array. This array is temporary storage useful for copying raw data from one stream to another stream. In the try-with-resources statement, you open two streams: ZipOutputStream for writing to the zip file and FileInputStream for reading in the text file. (Note: API support for zip (and jar) files is available in java.util.zip package.) You want to read the input text file, zip it, and put that entry in the zip file. For putting a file/directory entry into the zip file, the ZipOutputStream class provides a method named putNextEntry(), which takes a ZipEntry object as an argument. The statement zipFile.putNextEntry(new ZipEntry(fileName)); puts a file entry named fileName into the zipFile.

For reading the contents of the text file, you use the read() method in the FileInputStream class. The read() method takes the buffer array as the argument. The amount of data to read per iteration (i.e., "data chunk size" to read) is given by the size of the passed array; it is 1024 bytes in this code. The read() method returns the number of bytes it read, and if there is no more data to read, it returns -1. The while loop checks if read succeeded (using the > 0 condition) before writing it to the zip file.

For writing data to the zip file, you use the write() method in the ZipOutputStream class. The write() method takes three arguments: the first argument is the data buffer; the second argument is start offset in the data buffer (which is 0 because you always read from the start of the buffer); and the third is the number of bytes to be written.

Now we come to the main discussion. Note how you open two resources in the try block and semicolons separate these two resource acquisition statements. You do not have an explicit finally block to release the resources because the compiler will automatically insert calls to the close methods for these two streams in the finally block(s).

Listing 7-15 is the complete program that makes use of this code segment to illustrate the use of try-with-resources statement for auto-closing multiple streams.

Listing 7-15. ZipTextFile.java

```java
import java.util.*;
import java.util.zip.*;
import java.io.*;

// class ZipTextFile takes the name of a text file as input and creates a zip file
// after compressing that text file.

class ZipTextFile {
    public static final int CHUNK = 1024; // to help copy chunks of 1KB
    public static void main(String []args) {
        if(args.length == 0) {
            System.out.println("Pass the name of the file in the current directory to be
            zipped as an argument");
            System.exit(-1);
        }

        String fileName = args[0];
        // name of the zip file is the input file name with the suffix ".zip"
        String zipFileName = fileName + ".zip";

        byte [] buffer = new byte[CHUNK];
        // these constructors can throw FileNotFoundException
        try (ZipOutputStream zipFile = new ZipOutputStream(new FileOutputStream(zipFileName));
                FileInputStream fileIn = new FileInputStream(fileName)) {
            // putNextEntry can throw IOException
            zipFile.putNextEntry(new ZipEntry(fileName));
            int lenRead = 0; // variable to keep track of number of bytes
            // successfully read
            // copy the contents of the input file into the zip file
            while((lenRead = fileIn.read(buffer)) > 0) {
                // both read and write methods can throw IOException
                zipFile.write (buffer, 0, lenRead);
            }
            // the streams will be closed automatically because they are
            // within try-with-resources statement
        }
        // this can result in multiple exceptions thrown from the try block;
        // use "suppressed exceptions" to get the exceptions that were suppressed!
        catch(Exception e) {
            System.out.println("The caught exception is: " + e);
            System.out.print("The suppressed exceptions are: ");
            for(Throwable suppressed : e.getSuppressed()) {
                System.out.println(suppressed);
            }
        }
    }
}
```

We've already discussed try-with-resources block. What we have not discussed is *suppressed exceptions*. In a try-with-resources statement, there might be more than one exception that could get thrown; for example, one within the try block, one within the catch block, and another one within the finally block. However, only one exception can be caught, so the other exception(s) will be listed as suppressed exceptions. From a given exception object, you can use the method getSuppressed() to get the list of suppressed exceptions.

Points to Remember

Here are some interesting points about try-with-resources statement that will help you in the OCPJP 8 exam:

- You cannot assign to the resource variables declared in the try-with-resources within the body of the try-with-resources statement. This is to make sure that the same resources acquired in the try-with-resources header are released in the finally block.

- It is a common mistake to close a resource explicitly inside the try-with-resources statement. Remember that try-with-resources expands to calling the close() method in the finally block, so the expanded code will have a double call to the close() method if you explicitly provide a close() method. Consider the following code:

```
try(Scanner consoleScanner = new Scanner(System.in)) {
    System.out.println("You typed the integer value: " +
    consoleScanner.nextInt());
    consoleScanner.close();
    // explicit call to close() method - remember that try-with-resources
    // statement will also expand to calling close() in finally method;
    // hence this will result in call to close() method in Scanner twice!
}
```

- The documentation of the close() method in the Scanner class says that if the scanner object is already closed, then invoking the method again will have no effect. So, you are safe in this case. However, in general, you cannot expect all the resources to have implemented a close() method that is safe to call twice. So, it is a bad practice to explicitly call the close() method inside a try-with-resource statement.

Custom Exceptions

Certification Objective

Create custom exceptions and Auto-closeable resources

In most situations, it will be sufficient to throw exceptions that are already provided in the Java library. For example, if you're checking for the validity of the arguments passed to a public function, and you find them to be null or out of expected range, you can throw an IllegalArgumentException. However, for most non-trivial applications, it will be necessary for you to develop your own exception classes (custom exceptions) to indicate exceptional conditions.

How do you define a custom exception? There are two options: you can extend either the Exception or RuntimeException class depending on your need.

If you want to force the users of your custom exception to handle the exception, then you can extend your exception class from the Exception class – that will make your custom exception a checked exception.

If you want to give flexibility to the users of your custom exception, and leave it to the users of your exception to decide if they want to handle the exception or not, you can derive your exception from the RuntimeException class.

So you need to make a decision if you want to make your custom exception a checked exception or unchecked exception by extending from either Exception class or RuntimeException class.

How about extending the Throwable or Error class for custom exceptions? The Throwable class is too generic to make it the base class of your exception, so it is not recommended. The Error class is reserved for fatal exceptions that the JVM can throw (such as StackOverflowError), so it is not advisable to make this the base class of your exception.

Custom exceptions should extend either the Exception or RuntimeException class. It is a bad practice to create custom exceptions by extending the Throwable or Error classes.

For extending from a base class, you need to see what methods the base class provides. In this case, you want to create a custom exception by extending the Exception or RuntimeException classes. Since the Exception class is the base class of the RuntimeException class, it is sufficient to know the members of the Exception class. Table 7-1 lists the important methods (including constructors) of the Exception class.

Table 7-1. *Important Methods and Constructors of the Exception Class*

Member	Short description
Exception()	Default constructor of the Exception class with no additional (or detailed) information on the exception.
Exception(String)	Constructor that takes a detailed information string about the constructor as an argument.
Exception(String, Throwable)	In addition to a detailed information string as an argument, this exception constructor takes the cause of the exception (which is another exception) as an argument.
Exception(Throwable)	Constructor that takes the cause of the exception as an argument.
String getMessage()	Returns the detailed message (passed as a string when the exception was created).
Throwable getCause()	Returns the cause of the exception (if any, or else returns null).
Throwable[] getSuppressed()	Returns the list of suppressed exceptions (typically caused when using a try-with-resources statement) as an array.
void printStackTrace()	Prints the stack trace (i.e., the list of method calls with relevant line numbers) to the console (standard error stream). If the cause of an exception (which is another exception object) is available in the exception, then that information will also be printed. Further, if there are any suppressed exceptions, they are also printed.

For illustrating how to create your own exception classes, assume that you want to create a custom exception named InvalidInputException. When you try to read input (read an integer, in this case), and if it fails, you want to throw this InvalidInputException. Listing 7-16 defines this exception class by extending the RuntimeException class.

Listing 7-16. InvalidInputException.java

```
// a custom "unchecked exception" that is meant to be thrown
// when the input provided by the user is invalid
class InvalidInputException extends RuntimeException {
    // default constructor
    public InvalidInputException() {
        super();
    }

    // constructor that takes the String detailed information we pass while
    // raising an exception
    public InvalidInputException(String str) {
        super(str);
    }

    // constructor that remembers the cause of the exception and
    // throws the new exception
    public InvalidInputException(Throwable originalException) {
        super(originalException);
    }

    // first argument takes detailed information string created while
    // raising an exception
    // and the second argument is to remember the cause of the exception
    public InvalidInputException(String str, Throwable originalException) {
        super(str, originalException);
    }
}
```

In this InvalidInputException class, you did not introduce any new fields but you can add any fields if necessary. This is also a simple custom exception where the constructors simply call the base class versions of the same constructor type. The class CustomExceptionTest (see Listing 7-17) shows how to make use of this custom exception.

Listing 7-17. CustomExceptionTest.java

```
import java.util.Scanner;
import java.util.NoSuchElementException;

// class for testing the custom exception InvalidInputException
class CustomExceptionTest {
    public static int readIntFromConsole() {
        Scanner consoleScanner = new Scanner(System.in);
        int typedInt = 0;
```

```
    try {
        typedInt = consoleScanner.nextInt();
    } catch(NoSuchElementException nsee) {
        System.out.println("Wrapping up the exception and throwing it...");
        throw new InvalidInputException("Invalid integer input typed in console", nsee);
    } catch(Exception e) {
        // call all other exceptions here ...
        System.out.println("Error: Encountered an exception and could not read an
        integer from the console... ");
    }
    return typedInt;
}

public static void main(String [] args) {
    System.out.println("Type an integer in the console: ");
    try {
        System.out.println("You typed the integer value: " + readIntFromConsole());
    } catch(InvalidInputException iie) {
        System.out.println("Error: Invalid input in console... ");
        System.out.println("The current caught exception is of type: " + iie);
        System.out.println("The originally caught exception is of type: " +
                                    iie.getCause());
    }
}
}
```

First compile and run this program before reading the discussion of the code.

```
D:\> java CustomExceptionTest
Type an integer in the console:
one
Wrapping up the exception and throwing it...
Error: Invalid input in console...
The current caught exception is of type: InvalidInputException: Invalid integer input typed
in console
The originally caught exception is of type: java.util.InputMismatchException
```

In this code, you use InvalidInputException just like any other exception already defined in the Java library. You are catching the InvalidInputException InputMismatchException (which extends InvalidInputException for which catch handler is provided) thrown from the readIntFromConsole() method in the main() method. The following statement invokes the toString() method of the InvalidInputException:

```
System.out.println("The current caught exception is of type: " + iie);
```

You did not override the toString() method, so the InvalidInputException class inherits the default implementation of the toString() method from the RuntimeException base class. This default toString() method prints the name of the exception thrown (InvalidInputException) and it also includes the detailed information string ("Invalid integer input typed in console") that you passed while creating the exception object. The last statement in the main() method is to get the cause of the exception.

```
System.out.println("The originally caught exception is of type: " + iie.getCause());
```

Since the cause of InvalidInputException is InputMismatchException, this exception name is printed in the console as a fully qualified name, java.util.InputMismatchException. You can think of InputMismatchException *causing* InvalidInputException; these two exceptions are known as *chained exceptions*.

Assertions

Certification Objective

Test invariants by using assertions

When creating application programs, you assume many things. However, often it happens that the assumptions don't hold, resulting in an erroneous condition. The assert statement is used to check or test your assumptions about the program.

The keyword assert provides support for assertions in Java. Each assertion statement contains a Boolean expression. If the result of the Boolean expression is true, it means the assumption is true, so nothing happens. However, if the Boolean result is false, then the assumption you had about the program holds no more, and an AssertionError is thrown. Remember that the Error class and its derived classes indicate serious runtime errors and are not meant to be handled. In the same way, if an AssertionError is thrown, the best course of action is not to catch the exception and to allow the program to terminate. After that, you need to examine why the assumption did not hold true and then fix the program.

There are many reasons you should add assertions to the program. One reason is that it helps find the problems early; when you check your assumptions in the program, and when any of them fail, you immediately know where to look out for the problem and what to fix. Also, when other programmers read your code with assertions, they will be in a better position to understand the code because you are making your assumptions explicit using assertions.

Assert Statement

Assert statements in Java are of two forms:

```
assert booleanExpression;
```

```
assert booleanExpression : "Detailed error message string";
```

It is a compiler error if a non-Boolean expression is used within the assert statement. Listing 7-18 contains the first example for assertions.

Listing 7-18. AssertionExample1.java

```
class AssertionExample1 {
    public static void main(String []args) {
        int i = -10;
        if(i < 0) {
            // if negative value, convert into positive value
            i = -i;
        }
```

```
        System.out.println("the value of i is: " + i);
        // at this point the assumption is that i cannot be negative;
        // assert this condition since its an assumption that will always hold
        assert (i >= 0) : "impossible: i is negative!";
    }
}
```

In this program, you are checking if the value of i is < 0; you are using the expression –i to convert it to a positive value. Once the condition check if(i < 0) is completed, the value of i cannot be negative, or that is your assumption. Such assumptions can be asserted with an assert statement. Here is the assert statement:

```
assert (i >= 0) : "impossible: i is negative!";
```

The program will run fine if the Boolean expression (i >= 0) evaluates to true. However, if it evaluates to false, the program will crash by throwing an AssertionError. Let's check this behavior (you need to use the –ea flag to enable assertions at runtime; we will discuss more about this flag in a moment).

```
D:\>java -ea AssertionExample1
the value of i is: 10
```

Yes, this program executed successfully without throwing any exceptions.

Is there any value of i for which the condition will fail? Yes, there is! If the value of i is a minimum possible value of integer, then it cannot be converted into a positive value. Why? Remember that the range of integers is -2^{31} to $2^{31} - 1$, so the integer values the value of i as -2147483648 to 2147483647. In other words, the positive value 2147483648 is not in the range of integers. So, if the value of i is -2147483648, then the expression -i will *overflow* and again result in the value -2147483648. Thus, your assumption is not true.

In Listing 7-26, change the value of i to the minimum value of an integer, as in the following:

```
int i = Integer.MIN_VALUE;
```

Now, try running this program.

```
D:\> java -ea AssertionExample1
the value of i is: -2147483648
Exception in thread "main" java.lang.AssertionError: impossible: i is negative!
        at AssertionExample1.main(AssertionExample1.java:12)
```

In this output, note how the assertion failed. The application crashes because the program threw the AssertionError, and there is no handler, so the program terminates.

An important point to remember from an exam perspective is that assertions are disabled by default at runtime; to enable assertions at runtime, use an -ea switch (or its longer form of -enableasserts). To disable assertions at runtime, use a -da switch. If assertions are disabled by default at runtime, then what is the use of -da switch? There are many uses. For example, if you want to enable assertions for all classes within a given package and want to disable asserts in a specific class in that package, then a -da switch is useful. Table 7-2 lists the important command-line arguments and their meaning. Note that you need not recompile your programs to enable or disable assertions; just use the command-line arguments when invoking the JVM to enable or disable them.

Table 7-2. *Important Command-Line Arguments for Enabling/Disabling Assertions*

Command-Line Argument	Short Description
-ea	Enables assertions by default (except system classes).
-ea:<class name>	Enables assertions for the given class name.
-ea:<package name>...	Enables assertions in all the members of the given package <package name>.
-ea:...	Enable assertions in the given unnamed package.
-esa	Short for -enablesystemsassertions; enables assertions in system classes. This option is rarely used.
-da	Disable assertions by default (except system classes).
-da:<class name>	Disable assertions for the given class name.
-da:<package name>...	Disables assertions in all the members of the given package <package name>.
-da:...	Disable assertions in the given unnamed package.
-dsa	Short for -disablesystemsassertions; disables assertions in system classes. This option is rarely used.

Summary

Let us briefly review the key points for each certification objective in this chapter. Please read it before appearing for the exam.

Use try-catch and throw statements

- When an exception is thrown from a try block, the JVM looks for a matching catch handler from the list of catch handlers in the method call-chain. If no matching handler is found, that unhandled exception will result in crashing the application.

- While providing multiple exception handlers (stacked catch handlers), specific exception handlers should be provided before general exception handlers.

- You can programmatically access the stack trace using the methods such as printStackTrace() and getStackTrace(), which can be called on any exception object.

Use catch, multi-catch, and finally clauses

- A try block can have multiple catch handlers. If the cause of two or more exceptions is similar, and the handling code is also similar, you can consider combining the handlers and make it into a multi-catch block.

- A catch block should either handle the exception or rethrow it. To *hide* or *swallow* an exception by catching an exception and doing nothing is really a bad practice.

- You can wrap one exception and throw it as another exception. These two exceptions become *chained exceptions*. From the thrown exception, you can get the cause of the exception.

- The code inside a finally block will be executed irrespective of whether a try block has successfully executed or resulted in an exception.

Use autoclose resources with a try-with-resources statement

- Forgetting to release resources by explicitly calling the close() method is a common mistake. You can use a try-with-resources statement to simplify your code and auto-close resources.

- You can auto-close multiple resources within a try-with-resources statement. These resources need to be separated by semicolons in the try-with-resources statement header.

- If a try block throws an exception, and a finally block also throws exception(s), then the exceptions thrown in the finally block will be added as suppressed exceptions to the exception that gets thrown out of the try block to the caller.

Create custom exceptions and auto-closeable resources

- It is recommended that you derive custom exceptions from either the Exception or RuntimeException class.

- A method's throws clause is part of the contract that its overriding methods in derived classes should obey.

- An overriding method can provide the same throw clause as the base method's throws clause or a more specific throws clause than the base method's throws clause.

- The overriding method cannot provide a more general throws clause or declare to throw additional checked exceptions when compared to the base method's throws clause.

- For a resource to be usable in a try-with-resources statement, the class of that resource must implement the java.lang.AutoCloseable interface and define the close() method.

Test invariants by using assertions

- Assertions are condition checks in the program and should be used for explicitly checking the assumptions you make while writing programs.

- The assert statement is of two forms: one that takes a Boolean argument and one that takes an additional string argument.

- If the Boolean condition given in the assert argument fails (i.e., evaluates to false), the program will terminate after throwing an AssertionError. It is not advisable to catch and recover from when an AssertionError is thrown by the program.

- By default, assertions are disabled at runtime. You can use the command-line arguments of -ea (for enabling asserts) and -da (for disabling asserts) and their variants when you invoke the JVM.

QUESTION TIME!

1. Consider the following class hierarchy from the package `java.nio.file` and answer the question.

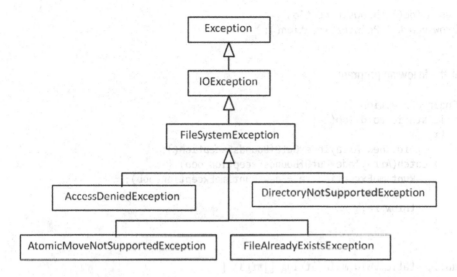

In the following class definitions, the base class `Base` has the method `foo()` that throws a `FileSystemException`; the derived class `Deri` extending the class `Base` overrides the `foo()` definition.

```
class Base {
    public void foo() throws FileSystemException {
        throw new FileSystemException("");
    }
}
class Deri extends Base {
    /* provide foo definition here */
}
```

Which of the following overriding definitions of the `foo()` method in the `Deri` class are compatible with the base class `foo()` method definition? Choose ALL the `foo()` method definitions that could compile without errors when put in the place of the comment: /* provide foo definition here */

A.
```
public void foo() throws IOException {
    super.foo();
}
```

B.
```
public void foo() throws AccessDeniedException {
    throw new AccessDeniedException("");
}
```

```
    C.
    public void foo() throws FileSystemException, RuntimeException {
        throw new NullPointerException();
    }

    D.
    public void foo() throws Exception {
        throw new NullPointerException();
    }
```

2. Consider the following program:

```
class ChainedException {
    public static void foo() {
        try {
            throw new ArrayIndexOutOfBoundsException();
        } catch(ArrayIndexOutOfBoundsException oob) {
            RuntimeException re = new RuntimeException(oob);
            re.initCause(oob);
            throw re;
        }
    }

    public static void main(String []args) {
        try {
            foo();
        } catch(Exception re) {
            System.out.println(re.getClass());
        }
    }
}
```

When executed, this program prints which of the following?

A. class java.lang.RuntimeException

B. class java.lang.IllegalStateException

C. class java.lang.Exception

D. class java.lang.ArrayIndexOutOfBoundsException

3. Consider the following program:

```
class ExceptionTest {
    public static void foo() {
        try {
            throw new ArrayIndexOutOfBoundsException();
        } catch(ArrayIndexOutOfBoundsException oob) {
            throw new Exception(oob);
        }
    }
```

```
        public static void main(String []args) {
            try {
                foo();
            } catch(Exception re) {
                System.out.println(re.getCause());
            }
        }
    }
```

Which one of the following options correctly describes the behavior of this program?

    A.   `java.lang.Exception`

    B.   `java.lang.ArrayIndexOutOfBoundsException`

    C.   `class java.lang.IllegalStateException`

    D.   This program fails with compiler error(s)

4.   Consider the following program:

```
import java.io.FileNotFoundException;
import java.sql.SQLException;

class MultiCatch {
    public static void fooThrower() throws FileNotFoundException {
        throw new FileNotFoundException();
    }
    public static void barThrower() throws SQLException {
        throw new SQLException();
    }
    public static void main(String []args) {
        try {
            fooThrower();
            barThrower();
        } catch(FileNotFoundException || SQLException multie) {
            System.out.println(multie);
        }
    }
}
```

Which one of the following options correctly describes the behavior of this program?

    A.   This program prints the following: `java.io.FileNotFoundException`

    B.   This program prints the following: `java.sql.SQLException`

    C.   This program prints the following: `java.io.FileNotFoundException ||`
       `java.sql.SQLException`

    D.   This program fails with compiler error(s)

5. Consider the following class hierarchy from the package `javax.security.auth.login` and answer the questions.

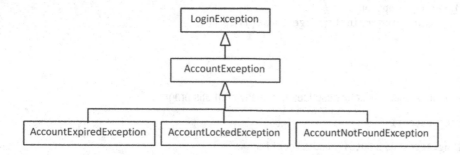

5.1. Which of the following handlers that makes use of multi-catch exception handler feature will compile without errors?

A. `catch (AccountException | LoginException exception)`

B. `catch (AccountException | AccountExpiredException exception)`

C. `catch (AccountExpiredException | AccountNotFoundException exception)`

D. `catch (AccountExpiredException exception1 | AccountNotFoundException exception2)`

5.2. Consider the following code segment, which makes use of this exception hierarchy:

```
try {
    LoginException le = new AccountNotFoundException();
    throw (Exception) le;
}
catch (AccountNotFoundException anfe) {
    System.out.println("In the handler of AccountNotFoundException");
}
catch (AccountException ae) {
    System.out.println("In the handler of AccountException");
}
catch (LoginException le) {
    System.out.println("In the handler of LoginException");
}
catch (Exception e) {
    System.out.println("In the handler of Exception");
}
```

When executed, which of the following statements will this code segment print?

    A.   In the handler of AccountNotFoundException

    B.   In the handler of AccountException

    C.   In the handler of LoginException

    D.   In the handler of Exception

6.   Consider the following program:

```java
import java.sql.SQLException;

class CustomSQLException extends SQLException {}

class BaseClass {
    void foo() throws SQLException {
        throw new SQLException();
    }
}

class DeriClass extends BaseClass {
    public void foo() throws CustomSQLException {          // LINE A
        throw new CustomSQLException();
    }
}

class EHTest {
    public static void main(String []args) {
        try {
            BaseClass base = new DeriClass();
            base.foo();
        } catch(Exception e) {
            System.out.println(e);
        }
    }
}
```

Which one of the following options correctly describes the behavior of this program?

    A.   The program prints the following: SQLException

    B.   The program prints the following: CustomSQLException

    C.   The program prints the following: Exception

    D.   When compiled, the program will result in a compiler error in line marked with comment Line A due to incompatible throws clause in the overridden foo method

7. Consider the following program:

```
class EHBehavior {
    public static void main(String []args) {
        try {
            int i = 10/0; // LINE A
            System.out.print("after throw -> ");
        } catch(ArithmeticException ae) {
            System.out.print("in catch -> ");
            return;
        } finally {
            System.out.print("in finally -> ");
    }

        System.out.print("after everything");
    }
}
```

Which one of the following options best describes the behavior of this program?

A. The program prints the following: in catch -> in finally -> after everything

B. The program prints the following: after throw -> in catch -> in finally -> after everything

C. The program prints the following: in catch -> after everything

D. The program prints the following: in catch -> in finally ->

E. When compiled, the program results in a compiler error in line marked with comment in LINE A for divide-by-zero

8. Consider the following program:

```
import java.util.Scanner;

class AutoCloseableTest {
    public static void main(String []args) {
        try (Scanner consoleScanner = new Scanner(System.in)) {
            consoleScanner.close(); // CLOSE
            consoleScanner.close();
        }
    }
}
```

Which one of the following statements is correct?

A. This program terminates normally without throwing any exceptions

B. This program throws an IllegalStateException

C. This program throws an IOException

D. This program throws an AlreadyClosedException

E. This program results in a compiler error in the line marked with the comment CLOSE

9. Consider the following program:

```
class AssertionFailure {
    public static void main(String []args) {
        try {
            assert false;
        } catch(RuntimeException re) {
            System.out.println("RuntimeException");
        } catch(Exception e) {
            System.out.println("Exception");
        } catch(Error e) {          // LINE A
            System.out.println("Error" + e);
        } catch(Throwable t) {
            System.out.println("Throwable");
        }
    }
}
```

This program is invoked from the command line as follows:

```
java AssertionFailure
```

Choose one of the following options describes the behavior of this program:

A.   Compiler error at line marked with comment LINE A

B.   Prints "RuntimeException" in console

C.   Prints "Exception"

D.   Prints "Error"

E.   Prints "Throwable"

F.   Does not print any output on console

10. Consider the following program:

```
import java.io.*;
class ExceptionTest {
    public static void thrower() throws Exception {
        try {
            throw new IOException();
        } finally {
            throw new FileNotFoundException();
        }
    }

    public static void main(String []args) {
        try {
            thrower();
        } catch(Throwable throwable) {
            System.out.println(throwable);
        }
    }
}
```

When executed, this program prints which one of the following?

   A.   java.io.IOException

   B.   java.io.FileNotFoundException

   C.   java.lang.Exception

   D.   java.lang.Throwable

Answers:

1.   Options B and C

   In option A and D, the throws clause declares to throw exceptions `IOException` and `Exception` respectively, which are more general than the `FileSystemException`, so they are not compatible with the base method definition. In option B, the `foo()` method declares to throw `AccessDeniedException`, which is more specific than `FileSystemException`, so it is compatible with the base definition of the `foo()` method. In option C, the throws clause declares to throw `FileSystemException`, which is the same as in the base definition of the `foo()` method. Additionally it declares to throw `RuntimeException`, which is not a checked exception, so the definition of the `foo()` method is compatible with the base definition of the `foo()` method.

2.   B. class `java.lang.IllegalStateException`

   In the expression `new RuntimeException(oob);`, the exception object `oob` is already chained to the `RuntimeException` object. The method `initCause()` cannot be called on an exception object that already has an exception object chained during the constructor call. Hence, the call `re.initCause(oob);` results in `initCause()` throwing an `IllegalStateException`.

3.   D. This program fails with compiler error(s)

   The `foo()` method catches `ArrayIndexOutOfBoundsException` and chains it to an `Exception` object. However, since `Exception` is a checked exception, it must be declared in the throws clause of `foo()`. Hence this program results in this compiler error:

```
ExceptionTest.java:6: error: unreported exception Exception; must be caught or
declared to be thrown
        throw new Exception(oob);
     ^
1 error
```

4.   D. This program fails with compiler error(s)

   For multi-catch blocks, the single pipe (|) symbol needs to be used and not double pipe (||), as provided in this program. Hence this program will fail with compiler error(s).

5.1.   C. catch (`AccountExpiredException | AccountNotFoundException` exception)

   For A and B, the base type handler is provided with the derived type handler, hence the multi-catch is incorrect. For D, the exception name exception1 is redundant and will result in a syntax error. C is the correct option and this will compile fine without errors.

5.2. A. In the handler of `AccountNotFoundException`

In this code, the created type of the exception is `AccountNotFoundException`. Though the exception object is stored in the variable of type `LoginException` and then type-casted to `Exception`, the dynamic type of the exception remains the same, which is `AccountNotFoundException`. When looking for a catch handler, the Java runtime looks for the exact handler based on the dynamic type of the object. Since it is available immediately as the first handler, this exactly matching catch handler got executed.

6. B. The program prints the following: `CustomSQLException`

The exception thrown is `CustomSQLException` object from the overridden `foo` method in `DeriClass`. Note that `SQLException` is a checked exception since it extends the Exception class. Inside the `BaseClass`, the `foo` method lists `SQLException` in its throws clause. In the `DeriClass`, the overridden `foo` method lists `CustomSQLException` in its throws clause: it is acceptable to have a more restrictive exception throws clause in a derived class. Hence, the given program compiles successfully and prints `CustomSQLException`.

7. D. The program prints the following: in catch -> in finally ->

The statement `println("after throw -> ");` will never be executed since the line marked with the comment LINE A throws an exception. The catch handles `ArithmeticException`, so `println("in catch -> ");` will be executed. Following that, there is a return statement, so the function returns. But before the function returns, the finally statement should be called, hence the statement `println("in finally -> ");` will get executed. So, the statement `println("after everything");` will never get executed.

8. A. This program terminates normally without throwing any exceptions

The try-with-resources statement internally expands to call the `close()` method in the finally block. If the resource is explicitly closed in the try block, then calling `close()` again does not have any effect. From the description of the `close()` method in the `AutoCloseable` interface: "Closes this stream and releases any system resources associated with it. If the stream is already closed, then invoking this method has no effect."

9. F. Does not print any output on the console

By default, assertions are disabled. If -ea (or the -enableassertions option to enable assertions), then the program would have printed "`Error`" since the exception thrown in the case of assertion failure is `java.lang.AssertionError`, which is derived from the `Error` class.

10. B. `java.io.FileNotFoundException`

If both the try block and finally block throw exceptions, the exception thrown from the try block will be ignored. Hence, the method `thrower()` throws a `FileNotFoundException`. The dynamic type of the variable throwable is `FileNotFoundException`, so the program prints that type name.

CHAPTER 8

■ ■ ■

Using the Java SE 8 Date/Time API

Certification Objectives

Create and manage date-based and time-based events including a combination of date and time into a single object using LocalDate, LocalTime, LocalDateTime, Instant, Period, and Duration

Work with dates and times across timezones and manage changes resulting from daylight savings including format date and times values

Define and create and manage date-based and time-based events using Instant, Period, Duration, and TemporalUnit

---

The new Java date and time API is provided in the java.time package. This new API in Java 8 replaces the older classes supporting date- and time-related functionality such as the Date, Calendar, and TimeZone classes provided as part of the java.util package.

Why did Java 8 introduce a new date and time API when it already had classes such as Date and Calendar from the early days of Java? The main reason was *inconvenient API design*. For example, the Date class has both date and time components; if you only want time information and not date-related information, you have to set the date-related values to zero. Some aspects of the classes are unintuitive as well. For example, in the Date constructor, the range of date values is 1 to 31 but the range of month values is 0 to 11 (not 1 to 12)! Further, there are many concurrency-related issues with java.util.Date and SimpleDateFormatter because they are not thread-safe.

Java 8 provides very good support for date- and time-related functionality in the newly introduced java.time package. Most of the classes in this package are immutable and thread-safe. This chapter explains how to use important classes and interfaces in this package, including LocalDate, LocalTime, LocalDateTime, Instant, Period, Duration, and TemporalUnit. You also learn how to work with time zones and daylight savings and how to format date and times values.

The java.time API incorporates the concept of *fluent interfaces*: it is designed in such a way that the code is more readable and easier to use. For this reason, classes in this package have numerous static methods (many of them factory methods). In addition, the methods in the classes follow a common naming convention (for example, they use the prefixes plus and minus to add or subtract date or time values).

Understanding Important Classes in java.time

Certification Objectives

Create and manage date-based and time-based events including a combination of date and time into a single object using LocalDate, LocalTime, LocalDateTime, Instant, Period, and Duration

Define and create and manage date-based and time-based events using Instant, Period, Duration, and TemporalUnit

The java.time package consists of four subpackages:

- java.time.temporal—Accesses date/time fields and units
- java.time.format—Formats the input and output of date/time objects
- java.time.zone—Handles time zones
- java.time.chrono—Supports calendar systems such as Japanese and Thai calendars

This chapter focuses only on date/time topics covered by the exam objectives. Let's get started by learning to use the LocalDate, LocalTime, LocalDateTime, Instant, Period, and Duration classes.

Using the LocalDate class

java.time.LocalDate represents a date without time or time zone. LocalDate is represented in the ISO-8601 calendar system in a year-month-day format (YYYY-MM-DD): for example, 2015-10-26.

The Java 8 date and time API uses ISO 8601 as the default calendar format. In this internationally accepted format, the date and time values are sorted from the largest to the smallest unit of time: year, month/week, day, hour, minute, second, and millisecond/nanosecond.

Here's an example that uses LocalDate:

```
LocalDate today = LocalDate.now();
System.out.println("Today's date is: " + today);
```

This code printed the following when we ran it:

```
Today's date is: 2015-10-26
```

The LocalDate.now() method gets the current date using the system clock, based on the default time zone. You can get a LocalDate object by explicitly specifying the day, month, and year components:

```
LocalDate newYear2016 = LocalDate.of(2016, 1, 1);
System.out.println("New year 2016: " + newYear2016);
```

This code prints the following:

```
New year 2016: 2016-01-01
```

How about this code?

```
LocalDate valentinesDay = LocalDate.of(2016, 14, 2);
System.out.println("Valentine's day is on: " + valentinesDay);
```

It throws an exception:

```
Exception in thread "main" java.time.DateTimeException: Invalid value for MonthOfYear
(valid values 1 - 12): 14
```

In this case, the month and dayOfMonth argument values are interchanged. The of() method of LocalDate is declared as follows:

```
LocalDate of(int year, int month, int dayOfMonth)
```

To avoid making this mistake, you can use the overloaded version LocalDate.of(int year, Month month, int day). The second argument, java.time.Month, is an enumeration that represents the 12 months of the year. If you interchange the day and month arguments, you get a compiler error. Here is the improved version that uses this enumeration:

```
LocalDate valentinesDay = LocalDate.of(2016, Month.FEBRUARY, 14);
System.out.println("Valentine's day is on: " + valentinesDay);
```

This code prints

```
Valentine's day is on: 2016-02-14
```

The LocalDate class has methods with which you can add or subtract days, weeks, months, or years to or from the current LocalDate object. For example, suppose your visa expires 180 days from now. Here is a code segment that shows the expiry date (assuming today's date is 2015-10-26):

```
long visaValidityDays = 180L;
LocalDate currDate = LocalDate.now();
System.out.println("My Visa expires on: " + currDate.plusDays(visaValidityDays));
```

This code segment prints the following:

```
My Visa expires on: 2016-04-23
```

In addition to the plusDays() method, LocalDate also provides plusWeeks(), plusMonths(), and plusYears() methods, as well as methods for subtracting: minusDays(), minusWeeks(), minusMonths(), and minusYears(). Table 8-1 lists a few more methods in the LocalDate class that you need to know (this table mentions classes such as ZoneId—they're discussed later in this chapter).

Table 8-1. *Important Methods in the* `LocalDate` *Class*

Method	Short Description	Example Code

`LocalDate now(Clock clock)`
`LocalDate now(ZoneId zone)`
	Returns a `LocalDate` object with the current date using the passed clock or zone argument	`// assume today's date is 26 Oct 2015`
		
		`LocalDate.now(Clock.systemDefaultZone());`
		`// returns current date as 2015-10-26`
		
		`LocalDate.now(ZoneId.of("Asia/Kolkata"));`
		`// returns current date as 2015-10-26`
		
		`LocalDate.now(ZoneId.of("Asia/Tokyo"));`
		`// returns current date as 2015-10-27`

`LocalDate ofYearDay(int year, int dayOfYear)`	Returns the `LocalDate` from the year and dayOfYear passed as arguments	`LocalDate.ofYearDay(2016,100);` `// returns date as 2016-04-09`

`LocalDate parse(CharSequence dateString)`	Returns the `LocalDate` from the dateString passed as the argument	`LocalDate.parse("2015-10-26");`
		`// returns a LocalDate corresponding`
		`// to the passed string argument;`
		hence it
		`// returns date as 2015-10-26`

`LocalDate ofEpochDay(Long epochDay)`	Returns the `LocalDate` by adding the number of days to the epoch starting day (the epoch starts in 1970)	`LocalDate.ofEpochDay(10);` `// returns 1970-01-11;`

Using the LocalTime Class

The `java.time.LocalTime` class is similar to `LocalDate` except that `LocalTime` represents time without dates or time zones. The time is in the ISO-8601 calendar system format: `HH:MM:SS.nanosecond`. Both `LocalTime` and `LocalDate` use the system clock and the default time zone.

Here is an example that uses `LocalTime`:

```
LocalTime currTime = LocalTime.now();
System.out.println("Current time is: " + currTime);
```

When we executed it, it printed the following:

```
Current time is: 12:23:05.072
```

As mentioned, `LocalTime` uses the system clock and its default time zone. To create different time objects based on specific time values, you can use the overloaded of() method of the `LocalTime` class:

```
System.out.println(LocalTime.of(18,30));
// prints: 18:30
```

LocalTime provides many useful methods with which you can add or subtract hours, minutes, seconds, and nanoseconds. For example, assume that you have a meeting 6.5 hours from now, and you want to find the exact meeting time. Here is a code segment for that:

```
long hours = 6;
long minutes = 30;
LocalTime currTime = LocalTime.now();
System.out.println("Current time is: " + currTime);
System.out.println("My meeting is at: " + currTime.plusHours(hours).plusMinutes(minutes));
```

This code segment prints the following:

```
Current time is: 12:29:13.624
My meeting is at: 18:59:13.624
```

In addition to plusHours(), LocalTime supports plusMinutes(), plusSeconds(), and plusNanos() methods; also, for subtracting, it supports minusHours(), minusMinutes(), minusNanos(), and minusSeconds(). Table 8-2 lists some of the important methods in the LocalTime class.

Table 8-2. *Important Methods in the LocalTime Class*

Method	Short Description	Example Code

LocalTime now(Clock clock)
LocalTime now(ZoneId zone)
	Returns a LocalTime object with the current time using the passed clock or zone argument	LocalTime.now(Clock.systemDefaultZone())
		// returns current time as 18:30:35.744
		
		LocalDate.now(ZoneId.of("Asia/Tokyo"));
		// returns current time as 22:00:35.193

LocalTime ofSecondOfDay(long daySeconds)	Returns the LocalTime from daySeconds passed as the argument (note that a 24-hour day has 86,400 seconds)	LocalTime.ofSecondOfDay(66620); // returns 18:30:20 because // 66620 seconds have elapsed

LocalTime parse(CharSequence timeString)	Returns the LocalTime from the dateString passed as the argument	LocalTime.parse("18:30:05");
		// returns a LocalTime object
		// corresponding to the given String
		// hence it prints: 18:30:05

Using the LocalDateTime Class

The class java.time.LocalDateTime represents both date and time without time zones. You can think of LocalDateTime as a logical combination of the LocalTime and LocalDate classes. The date and time formats use the ISO-8601 calendar system: YYYY-MM-DD HH:MM:SS.nanosecond.

Here is a simple example that prints today's date and the current time:

```
LocalDateTime currDateTime = LocalDateTime.now();
System.out.println("Today's date and current time is: " + currDateTime);
```

When we ran this code, it printed the following:

```
Today's date and current time is: 2015-10-29T21:04:36.376
```

In this output, note that the character *T* stands for *time*, and it separates the date and time components. Using LocalDateTime.now() gets the current date and time using the system clock and its default time zone.

Many classes in the java.time package, including LocalDate, LocalTime, and LocalDateTime, support isAfter() and isBefore() methods for comparison:

```
LocalDateTime christmas = LocalDateTime.of(2015, 12, 25, 0, 0);
LocalDateTime newYear = LocalDateTime.of(2016, 1, 1, 0, 0);
System.out.println("New Year 2016 comes after Christmas 2015? "+newYear.isAfter(christmas));
```

This code prints the following:

```
New Year 2016 comes after Christmas 2015? true
```

You can use the toLocalDate() and toLocalTime() methods, respectively, to get LocalDate and LocalTime objects from a given LocalDateTime object:

```
LocalDateTime dateTime = LocalDateTime.now();
System.out.println("Today's date and current time: " + dateTime);
System.out.println("The date component is:  " + dateTime.toLocalDate());
System.out.println("The time component is: " + dateTime.toLocalTime());
```

When we executed this code, it printed

```
Today's date and current time: 2015-11-04T13:19:10.497
The date component is:  2015-11-04
The time component is: 13:19:10.497
```

Similar to the methods listed in Tables 8-1 and 8-2, LocalDateTime has methods such as now(), of(), and parse(). Again, similar to LocalDate and LocalTime, this class also provides methods to add or subtract years, months, days, hours, minutes, seconds, and nanoseconds. To avoid repetition, these methods are not listed again here.

Using the Instant Class

Suppose you want to trace the execution of a Java application or store the application events in a file. For these purposes, you need to get timestamp values, and you can do so using the java.time.Instant class. The instant values began on January 1, 1970, at 00:00:00 hours (known as the *Unix epoch*).

The Instant class internally uses a long variable that holds the number of seconds since the start of the Unix epoch: 1970-01-01T00:00:00Z (values that occur before this epoch are treated as negative values). In addition, Instant uses an integer variable to store the number of nanoseconds elapsed for each second. The program in Listing 8-1 uses the Instant class.

Listing 8-1. UsingInstant.java

```java
import java.time.Instant;

public class UsingInstant {
    public static void main(String args[]){
        // prints the current timestamp with UTC as time zone
        Instant currTimeStamp = Instant.now();
        System.out.println("Instant timestamp is: "+ currTimeStamp);

        // prints the number of seconds as Unix timestamp from epoch time
        System.out.println("Number of seconds elapsed: " + currTimeStamp.getEpochSecond());

        // prints the Unix timestamp in milliseconds
        System.out.println("Number of milliseconds elapsed: " + currTimeStamp.toEpochMilli());
    }
}
```

When executed, it prints the following:

```
Instant timestamp is: 2015-11-02T03:16:04.502Z
Number of seconds elapsed: 1446434164
Number of milliseconds elapsed: 1446434164502
```

What is the difference between LocalDateTime and Instant? Here is an example that illustrates:

```java
LocalDateTime localDateTime = LocalDateTime.now();
Instant instant = Instant.now();
System.out.println("LocalDateTime is: " + localDateTime + " \nInstant is: " + instant);
```

When we executed this, it printed the following:

```
LocalDateTime is: 2015-11-02T17:21:11.402
Instant is: 2015-11-02T11:51:11.404Z
```

As you can see, the time value printed by LocalDateTime is different from the result of Instant. Why? Because we live in the Asia/Kolkata time zone, which is +05:30 hours from Greenwich time. LocalDateTime uses the default time zone, but Instant doesn't.

Using the Period Class

The java.time.Period class is used to measure an amount of time in terms of years, months, and days. Assume that you have bought some expensive medicine and want to use it before it expires. Here is how you can find out when it will expire:

```java
LocalDate manufacturingDate = LocalDate.of(2016, Month.JANUARY, 1);
LocalDate expiryDate = LocalDate.of(2018, Month.JULY, 18);

Period expiry = Period.between(manufacturingDate, expiryDate);
System.out.printf("Medicine will expire in: %d years, %d months, and %d days (%s)\n",
                expiry.getYears(), expiry.getMonths(), expiry.getDays(), expiry);
```

This code segment prints the following:

```
Medicine will expire in: 2 years, 6 months, and 17 days (P2Y6M17D)
```

This example uses the Period.between() method, which takes two LocalDate values as arguments and returns a Period. This program uses the methods getYears(), getMonths(), and getDays() (these three methods return an int value), which respectively return the number of years, months, and days in the given period. The toString() method of Period prints the value P2Y6M17D. In this string, the characters P, Y, M, and D, respectively, stand for *period*, *years*, *months*, and *days*.

From a Period, you can add or subtract years, months, and days using the methods plusYears(), plusMonths(), plusDays(), minusYears(), minusMonths(), and minusDays(). Table 8-3 lists other important methods in this class.

Table 8-3. *Important Methods in the* Period *Class*

Method	Short Description	Example Code
Period of(int years, int months, int days)	Returns a Period object based on the given arguments	LocalDate christmas = LocalDate.of(2015, 12, 25); System.out.println(Period.between(LocalDate.now(), christmas)); // prints P1M23D as of 2015-11-02

Period ofWeeks(int unit)
 	
Period ofDays(int unit)
 	
Period ofMonths(int unit)
 	
Period ofYears (int unit)
	Returns a Period object based on the unit in the argument	Period.ofWeeks(2)
		// returns P14D
		
		Period.ofDays(15)
		// returns P15D
		
		Period.ofMonths(6)
		// returns P6M
		
		Period.ofYears(4)
		// returns P4Y

Period parse(CharSequence string)	Returns a Period from the string passed as the argument	Period.parse("P4Y6M15D"); // returns P4Y6M15D

✎ The Java 8 date and time API differentiates how humans and computers use date- and time-related information. For example, the Instant class represents a Unix timestamp and internally uses long and int variables. Instant values are not very readable or usable by humans because the class does not support methods related to day, month, hours, and so on (in contrast, the Period class supports such methods).

Using the Duration Class

We discussed the Period class earlier—it represents time in terms of years, months, and days. Duration is the time equivalent of Period. The Duration class represents time in terms of hours, minutes, seconds, and so on. It is suitable for measuring machine time or when working with Instance objects. Similar to the Instance class, the Duration class stores the seconds component as a long value and nanoseconds using an int value.

Say you want to wish your best friend Becky a happy birthday at midnight tonight. Here is how you can find out how many hours to go:

```
LocalDateTime comingMidnight =
        LocalDateTime.of(LocalDate.now().plusDays(1), LocalTime.MIDNIGHT);
LocalDateTime now = LocalDateTime.now();

Duration between = Duration.between(now, comingMidnight);
System.out.println(between);
```

This code prints the following:

```
PT7H13M42.003S
```

This example uses the overloaded version of the of() method in the LocalDateTime class: LocalDateTime of(LocalDate, LocalTime). The LocalDate.now() call returns the current date, but you need to add a day to this value so that you can use LocalTime.MIDNIGHT to refer to the upcoming midnight. The between() method in Duration takes two time values—in this case, two LocalDateTime objects. When we executed this program, the time was 16:46:17; from then to midnight was 7 hours, 13 minutes, and 42 seconds. That is indicated by the toString() output, Period: PT7H13M42.003S. The prefix PT indicates eriod time, H indicates hours, M indicates minutes, and S indicates seconds.

Table 8-4 lists some of the important methods of the Duration class. TemporalUnit and ChronoUnit are discussed later in this chapter.

Table 8-4. *Important Methods in the Duration Class*

Method	Short Description	Example Code
Duration of(long number, TemporalUnit unit)	Returns a Duration object for the given number in the specified format	Duration.of(3600, ChronoUnit. MINUTES) // returns "PT60H"
Duration ofDays(long unit) Duration ofHours(long unit) Duration ofMinutes(long unit) Duration ofSeconds(long unit) Duration ofMillis(long unit) Duration ofNanos(long unit)	Returns Duration based on the unit given in the argument	Duration.ofDays(4) // returns "PT96H" Duration.ofHours(2) // returns "PT2H" Duration.ofMinutes(15) // returns "PT15M" Duration.ofSeconds(30) //returns "PT30S" Duration.ofMillis(120) // returns "PT0.12S" Duration.ofNanos(120) // returns "PT0.00000012S"
Duration parse(CharSequence string)	Returns a Period from the string passed as the argument	Duration.parse("P2DT10H30M") // returns a Duration object // with value PT58H30M

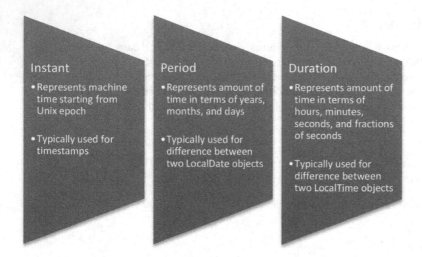

Figure 8-1. *Summary of the* Instant, Period, *and* Duration *classes*

Using the TemporalUnit Interface

The TemporalUnit interface is part of the java.time.temporal package. It represents date or time units such as seconds, hours, days, months, years, and so on. The enumeration java.time.temporal.ChronoUnit implements this interface. Instead of using constant values, it is better to use their equivalent enumeration values. Why? Because using enumeration values in ChronoUnit results in more readable code; further, you are less likely to make mistakes.

Listing 8-2 prints the enumeration values, whether they are date-based or time-based, and the duration.

Listing 8-2. ChronoUnitValues.java

```java
import java.time.temporal.ChronoUnit;

public class ChronoUnitValues {
    public static void main(String []args) {
        System.out.println("ChronoUnit DateBased TimeBased Duration");
        System.out.println("----------------------------------------");
        for(ChronoUnit unit : ChronoUnit.values()) {
            System.out.printf("%10s \t %b \t\t %b \t\t %s %n",
                    unit, unit.isDateBased(), unit.isTimeBased(), unit.getDuration());
        }
    }
}
```

The result is as follows:

```
ChronoUnit      DateBased       TimeBased       Duration
-----------------------------------------   --------------------
      Nanos     false           true          PT0.000000001S
     Micros     false           true          PT0.000001S
     Millis     false           true          PT0.001S
    Seconds     false           true          PT1S
    Minutes     false           true          PT1M
      Hours     false           true          PT1H
   HalfDays     false           true          PT12H
       Days     true            false         PT24H
      Weeks     true            false         PT168H
     Months     true            false         PT730H29M6S
      Years     true            false         PT8765H49M12S
    Decades     true            false         PT87658H12M
  Centuries     true            false         PT876582H
  Millennia     true            false         PT8765820H
       Eras     truc            falsc         PT8765820000000H
    Forever     false           false         PT2562047788015215H30M7.999999999S
```

Numerous methods in the java.time package take TemporalUnit as the argument. For example, consider the of() method in the Duration class:

```
Duration of(long amount, TemporalUnit unit)
```

Because the ChronoUnit enumeration implements the TemporalUnit interface, you can pass a ChronoUnit enumeration value as the second argument in this constructor:

```
System.out.println(Duration.of(1, ChronoUnit.MINUTES).getSeconds());
// prints: 60
System.out.println(Duration.of(1, ChronoUnit.HOURS).getSeconds());
// prints:3600
System.out.println(Duration.of(1, ChronoUnit.DAYS).getSeconds());
// prints: 86400
```

As you can see from this example, ChronoUnit helps you deal with time unit values such as seconds, minutes, and hours and date values such as days, months, and years.

Dealing with Time Zones and Daylight Savings

Certification Objective

Work with dates and times across timezones and manage changes resulting from daylight savings including format date and times values

The previous section discussed some of the important classes in the java.time package. This section discusses how to work with dates and times across time zones, deal with daylight savings, and format date and time values.

Using Time Zone–Related Classes

There are three important classes related to time zones that you need to know in order to work with dates and times across time zones: ZoneId, ZoneOffset, and ZonedDateTime. Let's discuss them now.

Using the ZoneId Class

In the java.time package, the java.time.ZoneId class represents time zones. Time zones are typically identified using an offset from Greenwich Mean Time (GMT, also known as UTC/Greenwich).

For instance, we live in India, and the only time zone in India is Asia/Kolkata (zones are given using this region/city format). This code prints the time zone:

```
System.out.println("My zone id is: " + ZoneId.systemDefault());
```

For our time zone, it printed this:

```
My zone id is: Asia/Kolkata
```

You can get the list of time zones by calling the static method getAvailableZoneIds() in ZoneId, which returns a Set<String>:

```
Set<String> zones = ZoneId.getAvailableZoneIds();
System.out.println("Number of available time zones is: " + zones.size());
zones.forEach(System.out::println);
```

Here is the result:

```
Number of available time zones is: 589
Asia/Aden
America/Cuiaba
// rest of the output elided...
```

You can pass any of these time-zone identifiers to the of() method to create the corresponding ZoneId object, as in

```
ZoneId AsiaKolkataZoneId = ZoneId.of("Asia/Kolkata");
```

Using the ZoneOffset Class

ZoneId identifies a time zone, such as Asia/Kolkata. Another class, ZoneOffset, represents the time-zone offset from UTC/Greenwich. For example, zone ID "Asia/Kolkata" has a zone offset of +05:30 (plus 5 hours and 30 minutes) from UTC/Greenwich. The ZoneOffset class extends the ZoneId class. We discuss an example that uses ZoneOffset in the next section.

Using the ZonedDateTime Class

In Java 8, if you want to deal only with the date, time, or time zone, you can use LocalDate, LocalTime, or ZoneId, respectively. What if you want all three—date, time, and time zone—together? For that, you can use the ZonedDateTime class:

```
LocalDate currentDate = LocalDate.now();
LocalTime currentTime = LocalTime.now();
ZoneId myZone = ZoneId.systemDefault();
ZonedDateTime zonedDateTime = ZonedDateTime.of(currentDate, currentTime, myZone);
System.out.println(zonedDateTime);
```

Here is the result:

```
2015-11-05T11:38:40.647+05:30[Asia/Kolkata]
```

This code segment uses the overloaded static method ZonedDateTime of(LocalDate, LocalTime, ZoneID). Given a LocalDateTime, you can use a ZoneId to get a ZonedDateTime object:

```
LocalDateTime dateTime = LocalDateTime.now();
ZoneId myZone = ZoneId.systemDefault();
ZonedDateTime zonedDateTime = dateTime.atZone(myZone);
```

To illustrate the conversion between these different time zone–related classes, here is a code segment that creates a ZoneId object, adds that zone information to a LocalDateTime object to get a ZonedDateTime object, and finally gets the zone offset from the ZonedDateTime:

```
ZoneId myZone = ZoneId.of("Asia/Kolkata");
LocalDateTime dateTime = LocalDateTime.now();
ZonedDateTime zonedDateTime = dateTime.atZone(myZone);
ZoneOffset zoneOffset = zonedDateTime.getOffset();
System.out.println(zoneOffset);
```

It prints the following:

```
+05:30
```

Assume that you are in Singapore, the date is January 1, 2016, and the time is 6:00 a.m. Before talking to your friend who lives in Auckland (New Zealand), you want to find out the time difference between Singapore and Auckland. Listing 8-3 shows a program that uses the ZoneId, ZonedDateTime, and Duration classes, to illustrate how to use these classes together.

Listing 8-3. TimeDifference.java

```
import java.time.LocalDateTime;
import java.time.Month;
import java.time.ZoneId;
import java.time.ZonedDateTime;
import java.time.Duration;
```

```java
public class TimeDifference {
    public static void main(String[] args) {
        ZoneId singaporeZone = ZoneId.of("Asia/Singapore");
        ZonedDateTime dateTimeInSingapore = ZonedDateTime.of(
        LocalDateTime.of(2016, Month.JANUARY, 1, 6, 0), singaporeZone);

        ZoneId aucklandZone = ZoneId.of("Pacific/Auckland");
        ZonedDateTime sameDateTimeInAuckland =
                    dateTimeInSingapore.withZoneSameInstant(aucklandZone);

        Duration timeDifference = Duration.between(
                            dateTimeInSingapore.toLocalTime(),
                            sameDateTimeInAuckland.toLocalTime());

        System.out.printf("Time difference between %s and %s zones is %d hours",
                    singaporeZone, aucklandZone, timeDifference.toHours());
    }
}
```

Here is the result:

```
Time difference between Asia/Singapore and Pacific/Auckland zones is 5 hours
```

This program creates two ZoneIds: one for Singapore and another for Auckland. After creating a ZonedDateTime object for the Singapore time zone with the given date and time, you get the equivalent ZonedDateTime object for Auckland by calling the withZoneSameInstant() method of the ZonedDateTime class. To find the time difference in hours, you use the Duration.between() method and the toHours() method of Duration.

Dealing with Daylight Savings

The amount of daylight does not remain the same throughout the year, because the seasons change. There is more daylight in summer, for example. With daylight savings time (DST), the clock is set one hour earlier or later to make the best use of the daylight. As the saying goes, "Spring forward, fall back"—the clock is typically set one hour earlier when Spring begins and one hour later at the start of Fall:

```java
ZoneId kolkataZone = ZoneId.of("Asia/Kolkata");
Duration kolkataDST = kolkataZone.getRules().getDaylightSavings(Instant.now());
System.out.printf("Kolkata zone DST is: %d hours %n", kolkataDST.toHours());

ZoneId aucklandZone = ZoneId.of("Pacific/Auckland");
Duration aucklandDST = aucklandZone.getRules().getDaylightSavings(Instant.now());
System.out.printf("Auckland zone DST is: %d hours", aucklandDST.toHours());
```

Here is the result (when executed on November 5, 2015):

```
Kolkata zone DST is: 0 hours
Auckland zone DST is: 1 hours
```

The call `zoneId.getRules().getDaylightSavings(Instant.now());` returns a `Duration` object based on whether DST is in effect at that time. If `Duration.isZero()` is false, DST is in effect in that zone; otherwise, it is not. In this example, the Kolkata time zone does not have DST in effect, but the Auckland time zone has +1 hour of DST.

Formatting Dates and Times

When programming with dates and times, you often have to print them in different formats. Also, you may have to read date/time information given in different formats. To read or print date and time values in various formats, you can use the `DateTimeFormatter` class in the `java.time.format` package.

The `DateTimeFormatter` class provides many predefined constants for formatting date and time values. Here is a list of a few such predefined formatters (with sample output values):

- ISO_DATE (2015-11-05)

- ISO_TIME (11:25:47.624)

- RFC_1123_DATE_TIME (Thu, 5 Nov 2015 11:27:22 +0530)

- ISO_ZONED_DATE_TIME (2015-11-05T11:30:33.49+05:30[Asia/Kolkata])

Here is a simple example that uses the predefined ISO_TIME of type `DateTimeFormatter`:

```
LocalTime wakeupTime = LocalTime.of(6, 0, 0);
System.out.println("Wake up time: " + DateTimeFormatter.ISO_TIME.format(wakeupTime));
```

This printed the following:

```
Wake up time: 06:00:00
```

What if you want to use a custom format instead of any of the predefined formats? To do so, you can use the `ofPattern()` method in the `DateTimeFormatter` class:

```
DateTimeFormatter customFormat = DateTimeFormatter.ofPattern("dd MMM yyyy");
System.out.println(customFormat.format(LocalDate.of(2016, Month.JANUARY, 01)));
```

Here is the result:

```
01 Jan 2016
```

You encode the format of the date or time using letters to form a date or time pattern string. Usually these letters are repeated in the pattern.

Uppercase and lowercase letters can have similar or different meanings when used in format strings for dates and times. Read the Javadoc for these patterns carefully before trying to use these letters. For example, in dd-MM-yy, *MM* refers to *month*; however, in dd-mm-yy, *mm* refers to *minutes*!

The previous code segment gave a simple example of creating a custom date format. Similar letters are available for creating custom date and time pattern strings. Here is the list of important letters and their meanings for creating patterns for dates (with examples):

- G (era: BC, AD)

- y (year of era: 2015, 15)

- Y (week-based year: 2015, 15)

- M (month: 11, Nov, November)

- w (week in year: 13)

- W (week in month: 2)

- E (day name in week: Sun, Sunday)

- D (day of year: 256)

- d (day of month: 13)

The program in Listing 8-4 uses simple and complex pattern strings to create custom date formats.

Listing 8-4. CustomDatePatterns.java

```java
import java.time.LocalDateTime;
import java.time.format.DateTimeFormatter;

public class CustomDatePatterns {
    public static void main(String []args) {
        // patterns from simple to complex ones
        String [] dateTimeFormats = {
                "dd-MM-yyyy", /* d is day (in month), M is month, y is year */
                "d '('E')' MMM, YYYY", /*E is name of the day (in week), Y is year*/
                "w'th week of' YYYY", /* w is the week of the year */
                "EEEE, dd'th' MMMM, YYYY" /*E is day name in the week */
        };
            LocalDateTime now = LocalDateTime.now();
            for(String dateTimeFormat : dateTimeFormats) {
                System.out.printf("Pattern \"%s\" is %s %n", dateTimeFormat,
                        DateTimeFormatter.ofPattern(dateTimeFormat).format(now));
            }
        }
    }
}
```

Here is the result:

```
Pattern "dd-MM-yyyy" is 05-11-2015
Pattern "d '('E')' MMM, YYYY" is 5 (Thu) Nov, 2015
Pattern "w'th week of' YYYY" is 45th week of 2015
Pattern "EEEE, dd'th' MMMM, YYYY" is Thursday, 05th November, 2015
```

As you can see, repeated letters result in a longer form for an entry. For example, when you use E (which is the name of the day in the week), the result is "Thu", whereas using EEEE prints the full form of the day name, which is "Thursday".

Another important thing to notice is how to print text within the given pattern string. For that, you use text separated by single quotes, which is printed as is by DateTimeFormatter. For example, '('E')' prints "(Wed)". If you give an incorrect pattern or forget to use single quotes to separate your text from pattern letters in the pattern string, you get a DateTimeParseException for passing an "Illegal pattern."

Now, let's look at a similar example for creating custom time-pattern strings. Here is the list of important letters for defining a custom time pattern:

a (marker for the text a.m./p.m. marker)

H (hour: value range 0–23)

k (hour: value range 1–24)

K (hour in a.m./p.m.: value range 0–11)

h (hour in a.m./p.m.: value range 1–12)

m (minute

s (second)

S (fraction of a second)

z (time zone: general time-zone format)

For more letters and their descriptions, see the Javadoc for the DateTimeFormatter class. Listing 8-5 shows a program that uses simple and complex pattern strings to create custom time formats.

Listing 8-5. CustomTimePatterns.java

```java
import java.time.LocalTime;
import java.time.format.DateTimeFormatter;

// Using examples, illustrates how to use "pattern strings" for creating custom time formats
class CustomTimePatterns {
    public static void main(String []args) {
        // patterns from simple to complex ones
        String [] timeFormats = {
                "h:mm",          /* h is hour in am/pm (1 12), m is minute */
                "hh 'o''clock'", /* '' is the escape sequence to print a single quote */
                "H:mm a",        /* H is hour in day (0-23), a is am/pm*/
                "hh:mm:ss:SS",   /* s is seconds, S is milliseconds */
                "K:mm:ss a"      /* K is hour in am/pm(0-11) */
        };
        LocalTime now = LocalTime.now();
        for(String timeFormat : timeFormats) {
            System.out.printf("Time in pattern \"%s\" is %s %n", timeFormat,
                    DateTimeFormatter.ofPattern(timeFormat).format(now));
        }
    }
}
```

Here is the result:

```
Time in pattern "h:mm" is 12:27
Time in pattern "hh 'o''clock'" is 12 o'clock
Time in pattern "H:mm a" is 12:27 PM
Time in pattern "hh:mm:ss:SS" is 12:27:10:41
Time in pattern "K:mm:ss a" is 0:27:10 PM
```

Note how the output differs based on the pattern string used.

Flight Travel Example

Let's look at an example that uses many of the classes covered so far. Assume that you need to catch a flight from Singapore on January 1, 2016 at 6:00 a.m. The flight takes 10 hours to reach Auckland, New Zealand. Can you get the arrival time in Auckland? The program in Listing 8-6 solves this problem.

Listing 8-6. FlightTravel.java

```java
import java.time.Month;
import java.time.ZoneId;
import java.time.ZonedDateTime;
import java.time.LocalDateTime;
import java.time.format.DateTimeFormatter;

public class FlightTravel {
    public static void main(String[] args) {
        DateTimeFormatter dateTimeFormatter =
                DateTimeFormatter.ofPattern("dd MMM yyyy hh.mm a");

        // Leaving on 1st Jan 2016, 6:00am from "Singapore"
        ZonedDateTime departure = ZonedDateTime.of(
                LocalDateTime.of(2016, Month.JANUARY, 1, 6, 0),
                ZoneId.of("Asia/Singapore"));

        System.out.println("Departure: " + dateTimeFormatter.format(departure));

        // Arrival on the same day in 10 hours in "Auckland"
        ZonedDateTime arrival =
                departure.withZoneSameInstant(ZoneId.of("Pacific/Auckland"))
                .plusHours(10);

        System.out.println("Arrival: " + dateTimeFormatter.format(arrival));
    }
}
```

Here is the result:

```
Departure: 01 Jan 2016 06.00 AM
Arrival: 01 Jan 2016 09.00 PM
```

Summary

Let's briefly review the key points from each certification objective in this chapter. Please read it before appearing for the exam.

Create and manage date-based and time-based events including a combination of date and time into a single object using LocalDate, LocalTime, LocalDateTime, Instant, Period, and Duration

- The Java 8 date and time API uses ISO 8601 as the default calendar format.

- The java.time.LocalDate class represents a date without time or time zones; the java.time.LocalTime class represents time without dates and time zones; the java.time.LocalDateTime class represents both date and time without time zones.

- The java.time.Instant class represents a Unix timestamp.

- The java.time.Period is used to measure the amount of time in terms of years, months, and days.

- The java.time.Duration class represents time in terms of hours, minutes, seconds, and fraction of seconds.

Work with dates and times across timezones and manage changes resulting from daylight savings including Format date and times values

- ZoneId identifies a time zone; ZoneOffset represents time zone offset from UTC/Greenwich

- ZonedDateTime provides support for all three aspects: date, time, and time zone.

- You have to account for daylight savings time (DST) when working with different time zones.

- The java.time.format.DateTimeFormatter class provides support for reading or printing date and time values in different formats.

- The DateTimeFormatter class provides predefined constants (such as ISO_DATE and ISO_TIME) for formatting date and time values.

- You encode the format of the date or time using case-sensitive letters to form a date or time pattern string with the DateTimeFormatter class.

Define and create and manage date-based and time-based events using Instant, Period, Duration, and TemporalUnit

- The enumeration java.time.temporal.ChronoUnit implements the java.time.temporal.TemporalUnit interface.

- Both TemporalUnit and ChronoUnit deal with time unit values such as seconds, minutes, and hours and date values such as days, months, and years.

QUESTION TIME

1. **Choose the correct option based on this code segment:**

```
LocalDate babyDOB = LocalDate.of(2015, Month.FEBRUARY, 20);
LocalDate now = LocalDate.of(2016, Month.APRIL, 10);
System.out.println(Period.between(now, babyDOB).getYears()); // PERIOD_CALC
```

   A. The code segment results in a compiler error in the line marked with the comment `PERIOD_CALC`

   B. The code segment throws a `DateTimeException`

   C. The code segment prints: `1`

   D. The code segment prints: `-1`

2. **Which one of the following classes is best suited for storing timestamp values of application events in a file?**

   A. `java.time.ZoneId` class

   B. `java.time.ZoneOffset` class

   C. `java.time.Instant` class

   D. `java.time.Duration` class

   E. `java.time.Period` class

3. **Given this code segment**

```
ZoneId zoneId = ZoneId.of("Asia/Singapore");
ZonedDateTime zonedDateTime =
        ZonedDateTime.of(LocalDateTime.now(), zoneId);
System.out.println(zonedDateTime.getOffset());
```

   assume that the time-offset value for the Asia/Singapore time zone from UTC/Greenwich is +08:00. Choose the correct option.

   A. This code segment results in throwing `DateTimeException`

   B. This code segment results in throwing `UnsupportedTemporalTypeException`

   C. The code segment prints: `Asia/Singapore`

   D. The code segment prints: `+08:00`

   E. This code segment prints: `+08:00 [Asia/Singapore]`

4. **Choose the correct option based on this code segment:**

```
DateTimeFormatter dateFormat = DateTimeFormatter.ISO_DATE;       // DEF
LocalDate dateOfBirth = LocalDate.of(2015, Month.FEBRUARY, 31);
System.out.println(dateFormat.format(dateOfBirth));              // USE
```

A. The program gives a compiler error in the line marked with the comment DEF

B. The program gives a compiler error in the line marked with the comment USE

C. The code segment prints: 2015-02-31

D. The code segment prints: 2015-02-03

E. This code segment throws java.time.DateTimeException with the message "Invalid date 'FEBRUARY 31'"

5. **Consider this code segment:**

```
DateTimeFormatter formatter =
        DateTimeFormatter.ofPattern("EEEE", Locale.US);
System.out.println(formatter.format(LocalDateTime.now()));
```

Which of the following outputs matches the string pattern "EEEE" given in this code segment?

A. F

B. Friday

C. Sept

D. September

Answers:

1. The code segment prints: -1

    Here are the arguments to the between() method in the Period class:

    ```
    Period between(LocalDate startDateInclusive, LocalDate
    endDateExclusive)
    ```

    The first argument is the start and the second argument is the end, and hence the call Period.between(now, babyDOB) results in -1 (not +1).

2. C. Instant class

    The Instant class stores the number of seconds elapsed since the start of the Unix epoch (1970-01-01T00:00:00Z). The Instant class is suitable for storing a log of application events in a file as timestamp values.

    The ZoneId and ZoneOffset classes are related to time zones and hence are unrelated to storing timestamp values. The Duration class is for time-based values in terms of quantity of time (such as seconds, minutes, and hours). The Period class is for date-based values such as years, months, and days.

3. D. The code segment prints: +08:00

    Given a ZonedDateTime object, the getOffset() method returns a ZoneOffset object that corresponds to the offset of the time zone from UTC/Greenwich. Given that the time-offset value for the Asia/Singapore zone from UTC/Greenwich is +08:00, the toString() method of ZoneOffset prints the string "+08:00" to the console.

4. E. This code segment throws `java.time.DateTimeException` with the message `"Invalid date 'FEBRUARY 31'"`.

The date value 31 passed in the call `LocalDate.of(2015, 2, 31);` is invalid for the month February, and hence the `of()` method in the `LocalDate` class throws `DateTimeException`.

One of the predefined values in `DateTimeFormatter` is `ISO_DATE`. Hence, it does not result in a compiler error for the statement marked with the comment `DEF`. The statement marked with the comment `USE` compiles without errors because it is the correct way to use the `format()` method in the `DateTimeFormatter` class.

5. B. Friday

`E` is the day name in the week; the pattern `"EEEE"` prints the name of the day in its full format. "Fri" is a short form that would be printed by the pattern `"E"`, but `"EEEE"` prints the day of the week in full form: for example, "Friday". Because the locale is `Locale.US`, the result is printed in English. The output "Sept" or "September" is impossible because `E` refers to the name in the week, not in a month.

CHAPTER 9

■ ■ ■

Java I/O Fundamentals

Certification Objectives

Read and write data from the console

Use BufferedReader, BufferedWriter, File, FileReader, FileWriter, FileInputStream, FileOutputStream, ObjectOutputStream, ObjectInputStream, and PrintWriter in the java.io package

In this chapter, we'll introduce you to the fundamentals of Java I/O programming. We'll cover two topics: how to read and write data from console, and then how to use (file) streams to read and write data.

The support for file manipulation is provided in the java.io and java.nio packages. In the initial part of this chapter, we'll focus only on the java.io package, later, we'll focus on reading and writing data using streams, but none of the other features provided in the java.io package. The java.nio package provides comprehensive support for file I/O, and we cover it in Chapter 10.

Reading from and Writing to Console

Certification Objective

Read and write data from the console

For reading from and writing to console, you can use standard input, output, and error streams or use the Console class. Let us discuss both of these approaches now.

Understanding Standard Streams

The public static fields in, out, and err in java.lang.System class respectively represent the standard input, output and error streams. System.in is of type java.io.InputStream and System.out and System.err are of type java.io.PrintStream.

Here is a programming example that reads and prints an integer from console (Listing 9-1):

Listing 9-1. Read.java

```java
import java.io.IOException;

class Read {
    public static void main(String []args) {
        System.out.print("Type a character: ");
        int val = 0;
        try {
            // the return type of read is int, but it returns a byte value!
            val = System.in.read();
        } catch(IOException ioe) {
            System.err.println("Cannot read input " + ioe);
            System.exit(-1);
        }
        System.out.println("You typed: " + val);
    }
}
```

Here is a sample run of the program:

```
D:\> $ java Read
Type a character: 5
You typed: 53
```

The return type of read method is `int` but it returns a byte value in the range 0 to 255 (yes, it is unintuitive). Hence, for the input 5, the program prints its ASCII value 53. The read method "blocks" (i.e., waits) for the user input; if an I/O exception occurs when reading, the method throws an IOException.

This program illustrates the use of all the three streams – `System.in` is used here to get the input from console, `System.out` is used for printing the read integer value, and `System.err` is used for issuing the error in case an I/O exception occurs.

The overloaded read method is low-level in nature and works in terms of bytes. Reading other types of input such as `Strings` requires using it with Reader or Scanner classes, as in:

```java
BufferedReader br = new BufferedReader(new InputStreamReader(System.in));
String str = br.readLine();

// or use java.util.Scanner, as in:

Scanner scanner = new Scanner(System.in);
String str = scanner.next();
```

We will discuss more about Reader and Scanner classes later in this chapter.

Reassigning Standard Streams

The standard streams are initialized when the JVM starts. Sometimes it is useful to redirect the standard streams by reassigning them. The method System.setIn takes an InputStream object, and the methods System.setOut and System.setError take PrintStream objects as arguments. Here is a code snippet that captures the standard output into a file by reassigning the System.out stream to an output text file:

```java
import java.io.*;

class StreamTest {
    public static void main(String []args ){
        try{
            PrintStream ps = new PrintStream("log.txt");
            System.setOut(ps);
            System.out.println("Test output to System.out");
        } catch(Exception ee){
            ee.printStackTrace();
        }
    }
}
```

When you execute this code segment, the program will create a file named "log.txt" and print the string "Test output to System.out" in that file.

Redirecting the streams is useful in many situations. For example, instead of reading from console, you may want to read the input from a text file for testing purposes. You can achieve that by redirecting the standard input stream to the text file. Similarly, you may want to reassign the error stream to a text file to store all the error messages in a log file. You can achieve that by calling the System.setErr method.

Understanding the Console Class

Using the Console class helps reading the data from the console and writing the data to the console. Note that the word "console" here refers to the character input device (typically a keyboard), and the character display device (typically the screen display). You can obtain a reference to the console using the System.console() method; if the JVM is not associated with any console, this method will return null.

Your first exercise is to implement a simple Echo command that prints back the line of text typed as input when you run this program (Listing 9-2).

Listing 9-2. Echo.java

```java
import java.io.Console;

// simple implementation of Echo command
class Echo {
    public static void main(String []args) {
        // get the System console object
        Console console = System.console();
        if(console == null) {
            System.err.println("Cannot retrieve console object - are you running your
                application from an IDE? Exiting the application ... ");
            System.exit(-1); // terminate the application
        }
```

```
        // read a line and print it through printf
        console.printf(console.readLine());
    }
}
```

Here is how the program behaves for different output (in the first run, we type "hello world" as input and in the second run we terminate the program):

```
D:\>java Echo
hello world
hello world

D:\>java Echo
^Z
Exception in thread "main" java.lang.NullPointerException
        at java.util.regex.Matcher.getTextLength(Matcher.java:1234)
        ... [this part of the stack trace elided to save space]
        at Echo.main(Echo.java:14)
```

For normal text input, this program works fine. If you type no input and try terminating the program with ^z or ^d (Ctrl+Z or Ctrl+D key combinations), then the program receives no input, so the readLine() method returns null; when printf takes a null argument, it throws a NullReferenceException.

Note that you ran this program from the command line. The method System.console() will succeed if the JVM is invoked from a command line without redirecting input or output streams since the JVM will be associated with a console (typically a keyboard and display screen). If the JVM is invoked indirectly by IDE, or if the JVM is invoked from a background process, then the method call System.console() will fail and return null. For example, if you run from IntelliJ IDEA or Eclipse IDEs, the System.console() will fail by returning null.

💣 If the JVM is invoked indirectly by IDE, or if the JVM is invoked from a background process, then the method call System.console() will fail and return null.

Some of the important methods available in the Console class are listed in Table 9-1.

Table 9-1. *Important Methods in the Console Class*

Method	Short description
Reader reader()	Returns the Reader object associated with this Console object; can perform read operations through this returned reference.
PrintWriter writer()	Returns the PrintWriter object associated with this Console object; can perform write operations through this returned reference.
String readLine()	Reads a line of text String (and this returned string object does not include any line termination characters); returns null if it fails (e.g., the user pressed Ctrl+Z or Ctrl+D in the console)
String readLine(String fmt, Object... args)	Same as the readLine() method, but it first prints the string fmt.

(*continued*)

Table 9-1. (*continued*)

Method	Short description
char[] readPassword()	Reads a password text and returns as a char array; echoing is disabled with this method, so when the user types the password, nothing will be displayed in the console.
char[] readPassword(String fmt, Object... args)	Same as the readPassword() method, but it first prints the string given as the format string argument before reading the password string.
Console format(String fmt, Object... args)	Writes the formatted string (created based on values of fmt string and the args passed) to the console.
Console printf(String fmt, Object... args)	Writes the formatted string (created based on values of fmt string and the args passed) to the console. This printf method is the same as the format method: This is a "convenience method"—the method printf and the format specifiers are familiar to most C/C++ programmers, so this method is provided in addition to the format method.
void flush()	Flushes any of the data still remaining to be printed in the console object's buffer.

Formatted Output with the Console Class

The Console class supports formatted I/O in the methods printf() and format() plus the overloaded methods of readPassword() and readLine(). We will now discuss formatted output with methods printf() (and the similar format() method) and later discuss the readPassword() and readLine() methods.

The method printf() uses string-formatting flags to format strings. It is quite similar to the printf() function provided in the library of the C programming language. The first parameter of the printf() method is a format string. A format string may contain string literals and *format specifiers*. The actual arguments are passed after the format string. This method can throw IllegalFormatException if the passed format is not correct.

Format specifiers are the crux of the string formatting concepts. They define the placeholder for a specific data type and its format (such as alignment and width). The remaining parameters of the printf() method are the variables (or literals) that provide the actual data to fill in the placeholders in sequence of the format specifiers.

Let's discuss a detailed example of when and why we need to use the format specifiers. Suppose you want to print a table of soccer players along with their names, played matches, scored goals, and goals per match information. However, there are a few constraints:

- You want to print the name of players to the left (left aligned).

- You want to specify at least 15 characters for the name of the players.

- You want to print each column at a distance of a tab-stop.

- You want to specify only one precision point in goals per match info.

Listing 9-3 shows how to implement this.

Listing 9-3. FormattedTable.java

```java
// This program demonstrates the use of format specifiers in printf
import java.io.Console;

class FormattedTable {
    void line(Console console) {
        console.printf("-------------------------------------------------------------\n");
    }
    void printHeader(Console console) {
        console.printf("%-15s \t %s \t %s \t %s \n", "Player", "Matches", "Goals",
        "Goals per match");

    }

    void printRow(Console console, String player, int matches, int goals) {
        console.printf("%-15s \t %5d \t\t %d \t\t %.1f \n", player, matches, goals,
                        ((float)goals/(float)matches));
    }

    public static void main(String[] str) {
        FormattedTable formattedTable = new FormattedTable();
        Console console = System.console();
        if(console != null) {
            formattedTable.line(console);
            formattedTable.printHeader(console);
            formattedTable.line(console);
            formattedTable.printRow(console, "Demando", 100, 122);
            formattedTable.printRow(console, "Mushi", 80, 100);
            formattedTable.printRow(console, "Peale", 150, 180);
            formattedTable.line(console);
        }
    }
}
```

This program produces following output:

Player	Matches	Goals	Goals per match
Demando	100	122	1.2
Mushi	80	100	1.3
Peale	150	180	1.2

Let's analyze the format string specified in the printRow() method - "%-15s \t %5d \t\t %d \t\t %.1f \n"

- The first part of the format string is "%-15s". Here, the expression starts with %, which indicates the start of a format-specifier string.

- The next symbol is ' - ', which is used to make the string left aligned. The number "15" specifies the width of the string and finally data type specifier of "s" indicates the input data type as String.

- The next format specifier string is "%5d", which signifies it expects an integer that will be displayed in the minimum 5 digits.

- The last format specifier string is "%.1f", which expects a floating-point number that will be displayed with one precision digit.

- All format specifier strings are separated with one or more "\t"s (tab stops) to make space between the columns.

Let's now discuss the template of format specifiers in the printf() method:

%[argument_index][flags][width][.precision]datatype_specifier

- As you can see, each format specifier starts with % sign followed by argument index, flags, width, and precision information and ends with a data type specifier. In this string, the argument index, flags, width, and precision information are optional while the % sign and data type specifiers are mandatory.

- *Argument index* refers to the position of the argument in the argument list; it is an integer followed by $, as in 1$ and 2$ for first and second argument respectively.

- *Flags* are single-character symbols that specify characteristics such as alignment and filling character. For instance, flag "-" specifies left alignment and "0" pads the number with leading zeroes.

- The *width* specifier indicates the minimum number of characters that will span in the final formatted string. If the input data is shorter than the specified width, then it is padded with spaces by default. In case the input data is bigger than the specified width, the full data appears in the output without trimming.

- The *precision field* specifies the number of precision digits in the output. This optional field is particularly useful with floating point numbers.

- Finally, the *data type specifier* indicates the type of expected input data. The field is a placeholder for the specified input data. Table 9-2 provides a list of commonly used data type specifiers.

Table 9-2. *Commonly Used Data Type Specifiers*

Symbol	Description
%b	Boolean
%c	Character
%d	Decimal integer (signed)
%e	Floating point number in scientific format
%f	Floating point number in decimal format
%g	Floating point number in decimal or scientific format (depending on the value passed as argument)
%h	Hashcode of the passed argument
%n	Line separator (new line character)
%o	Integer formatted as an octal value
%s	String
%t	Date/time
%x	Integer formatted as an hexadecimal value

Note that the discussion about `printf()` applies to `format()` method in the `Console` class. In fact, `printf` just invokes `format` method internally:

```
// code from java.io.Console.java
public Console printf(String format, Object ... args) {
    return format(format, args);
}
```

Points to Remember

Here are some points that might prove useful on your OCPJP 8 exam:

- If you do not specify any string formatting specifier, the `printf()` method will not print anything from the given arguments!

- Flags such as `"-"` and "0" make sense only when you specify width with the format specifier string.

- You can also print the % character in a format string; however, you need to use an escape sequence for it. In format specifier strings, % is an escape character, which means you need to use %% to print a single %.

- You can use the argument index feature (an integer value followed by $ symbol) to explicitly refer to the arguments by their index position. For example, the following prints "world hello" because the order of arguments are reversed:

  ```
  console.printf("%2$s %1$s %n", "hello", "world");
  // $2 refers to the second argument ("world") and
  // $1 refers to the first argument ("hello")
  ```

- The < symbol in a format string supports relative index with which you can reuse the argument matched by the previous format specifier. For example, assuming console is a valid Console object, the following code segment prints "10 a 12":
  console.printf("%d %<x %<o", 10);

  ```
  // 10 - the decimal value, a - the hexadecimal value of 10, and
  // 12 - the octal value of 10
  ```

- If you do not provide the intended input data type as expected by the format string, then you can get an IllegalFormatConversionException. For instance, if you provide a string instead of an expected integer in your printRow() method implementation, you will get following exception:

  ```
  Exception in thread "main" java.util.IllegalFormatConversionException:
        d != java.lang.String
  ```

Getting Input with the Console Class

You can get input from console using the overloaded methods of readPassword() and readLine() provided within the Console class. In these methods, the first argument is the format specifier string, and the following arguments are the values that will be passed to the format specifier string. These two methods return the character data read from the console. What's the difference between the readLine() and readPassword() methods? The main difference is that the readPassword() does not display the typed string in the console (for the obvious reason of not displaying the secret password), whereas readLine() displays the input you type in the console. Another minor difference is that the readLine() method returns a String whereas readPassword() returns a char array (see Listing 9-4).

Listing 9-4. Login.java

```java
import java.io.Console;
import java.util.Arrays;

// code to illustrate the use of readPassword method
class Login {
    public static void main(String []args) {
        Console console = System.console();
        if(console != null) {
            String userName = null;
            char[] password = null;
            userName = console.readLine("Enter your username: ");
            // typed characters for password will not be displayed in the screen
            password = console.readPassword("Enter password: ");
            // password is a char[]: convert it to a String first
            // before comparing contents
            if(userName.equals("scrat") && new String(password).equals("nuts")) {
                // we're hardcoding username and password here for
                // illustration, don't do such hardcoding in pratice!
                console.printf("login successful!");
            }
```

```
        else {
            console.printf("wrong user name or password");
        }
        // "empty" the password since its use is over
        Arrays.fill(password, ' ');
    }
  }
}
```

Here is an instance of running this program typing the correct username and password:

```
D:\>java Login
Enter your username: scrat
Enter password:
login successful!
```

Note that nothing was displayed in the console when typing the password. Why is the statement `Arrays.fill(password, ' ');` provided in this program? It is a recommended practice to "empty" the read password string once its use is over; here you use Array's `fill()` method for this purpose. This is a secure programming practice to avoid malicious reads of program data to discover password strings. In fact, unlike the `readLine()` method, which returns a `String`, the `readPassword()` method returns a char array. With a char array, as soon as the password is validated, it is possible to empty it and remove the trace of the password text from memory; with a `String` object, which is garbage collected, it is not as easy as with a char array.

Using Streams to Read and Write Files

Certification Objective

Use BufferedReader, BufferedWriter, File, FileReader, FileWriter, FileInputStream, FileOutputStream, ObjectOutputStream, ObjectInputStream, and PrintWriter in the java.io package

What are streams? Streams are ordered sequences of data. Java deals with input and output in terms of streams. For example, when you read a sequence of bytes from a binary file, you're reading from an *input stream*; similarly, when you write a sequence of bytes to a binary file, you're writing to an *output stream*. Note how we referred to reading or writing *bytes* from *binary files*, but what about reading or writing *characters* from *text files*? Java, similar to other languages and operating systems, differentiates between processing text and binary data. Before delving deeper into streams and reading or writing data from files, you must first understand the difference between the character streams and byte streams, which is essential for understanding the rest of the chapter.

The streams API (covered in Chapter 6) introduced in Java 8 are different from the I/O streams we discuss in this chapter.

Character Streams and Byte Streams

Consider the difference between Java source files and class files generated by the compiler. The Java source files have the extension of ".java" and are meant to be read by humans as well as programming tools such as compilers. However, the Java class files have extension of ".class" and are not meant to be read by humans; they are meant to be processed by low-level tools such as a JVM (the executable java.exe in Windows) and Java disassember (the executable javap.exe in Windows).

Text files are human-readable files containing text (or characters); binary files are machine readable or low-level data storage.

Naturally, how you interpret what is inside text files vs. binary files is different. For example, in text files, you can interpret the data read from the file and differentiate between a tab character, whitespace character, newline character, and so on. However, you don't deal with data from binary files like that; they are low-level values. To give another example, consider a .txt file you create with a text editor such as Notepad in Windows; it contains human-readable text. Now, consider storing your photo in a .bmp or .jpeg file; these files are certainly not human readable. They are meant for processing by photo editing or image manipulation software, and the files contain data in some pre-determined low-level format.

The java.io package has classes that support both character streams and byte streams. You can use character streams for text-based I/O. Byte streams are used for data-based I/O. Character streams for reading and writing are called *readers* and *writers*, respectively (represented by the abstract classes of Reader and Writer). Byte streams for reading and writing are called *input streams* and *output streams*, respectively (represented by the abstract classes of InputStream and OutputStream). Table 9-3 summarizes the differences between character streams and byte streams for your quick reference.

Table 9-3. *Differences Between Character Streams and Byte Streams*

Character streams	Byte streams
Meant for reading or writing to character- or text-based I/O such as text files, text documents, XML, and HTML files.	Meant for reading or writing to binary data I/O such as executable files, image files, and files in low-level file formats such as .zip, .class, .obj, and .exe.
Data dealt with is 16-bit Unicode characters.	Data dealt with is bytes (i.e., units of 8-bit data).
Input and output character streams are called *readers* and *writers*, respectively.	Input and output byte streams are simply called *input streams* and *output streams*, respectively.
The abstract classes of Reader and Writer and their derived classes in the java.io package provide support for character streams.	The abstract classes of InputStream and OutputStream and their derived classes in the java.io package provide support for byte streams.

💣 If you try using a byte stream when a character stream is needed and vice versa, you'll get a nasty surprise in your programs. For example, a bitmap (.bmp) image file must be processed using a byte stream; if you try using character stream, your program won't work. So don't mix up the streams!

Character Streams

In this section, you'll explore I/O with character streams. You'll learn how to read from and write to text files plus some optional features such as buffering to speed up the I/O. For reading and writing text files, you can use the classes derived from the Reader and Writer abstract classes, respectively. For character streams, Figure 9-1 shows important Reader classes, and Table 9-4 provides a short description of these classes. Figure 9-2 shows important Writer classes, and Table 9-5 provides a short description of these classes. Note that we'll cover only a few important classes in this class hierarchy in this chapter.

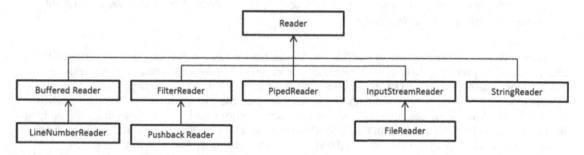

Figure 9-1. *Important classes deriving from the Reader class*

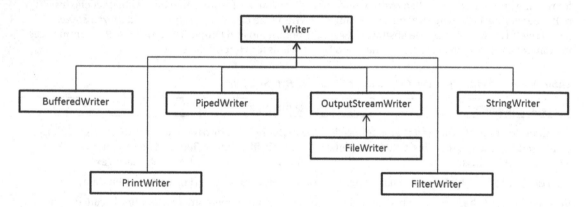

Figure 9-2. *Important classes deriving from the Writer class*

Table 9-4. *Important Classes Deriving from the Reader Class*

Class name	Short description
StringReader	A character stream that operates on a string.
InputStreamReader	This class is a bridge between character streams and byte streams.
FileReader	Derived class of InputStreamReader that provides support for reading character files.
PipedReader	The PipedReader and PipedWriter classes form a pair for "piped" reading/writing of characters.
FilterReader	Abstract base class for streams that support a filtering operation applied on data as characters are read from the stream.
PushbackReader	Derived class of FilterReader that allows read characters to be pushed back into the stream.
BufferedReader	Adds buffering to the underlying character stream so that there is no need to access the underlying file system for each read and write operation.
LineNumberReader	Derived class of BufferedReader that keeps track of line numbers as the characters are read from the underlying character stream.

Table 9-5. *Important Classes Deriving from the Writer Class*

Class name	Short description
StringWriter	A character stream that collects the output in a string buffer, which can be used for creating a string.
OutputStreamWriter	This class is a bridge between character streams and byte streams.
FileWriter	Derived class of OutputStreamWriter that provides support for writing character files.
PipedWriter	The PipedReader and PipedWriter classes form a pair for "piped" reading/writing of characters in character stream.
FilterWriter	Abstract base class for streams that supports a filtering operation applied on data as characters when writing them to a character stream.
PrintWriter	Supports formatted printing of characters to the output character stream.
BufferedWriter	Adds buffering to the underlying character stream so that there is no need to access the underlying file system for each read and write operation.

Reading Text Files

Reader classes read the contents in the stream and try interpreting them as characters, such as a tab, end-of-file, and newline. Listing 9-5 implements a simplified version of the type command in Windows (a similar command is cat command in Linux/Unix/Mac). The type command displays the contents of the file(s) passed as command-line arguments.

Listing 9-5. Type.java

```java
import java.io.FileNotFoundException;
import java.io.FileReader;
import java.io.IOException;

// implements a simplified version of "type" command provided in Windows given
// a text file name(s) as argument, it prints the content of the text file(s) on console
class Type {
    public static void main(String []files) {
        if(files.length == 0) {
            System.err.println("pass the name of the file(s) as argument");
            System.exit(-1);
        }
        // process each file passed as argument
        for(String file : files) {
            // try opening the file with FileReader
            try (FileReader inputFile = new FileReader(file)) {
                int ch = 0;
                // while there are characters to fetch, read, and print the
                // characters when EOF is reached, read() will return -1,
                // terminating the loop
                while( (ch = inputFile.read()) != -1) {
                    // ch is of type int - convert it back to char
                    // before printing
                    System.out.print( (char)ch );
                }
            } catch (FileNotFoundException fnfe) {
                // the passed file is not found ...
                System.err.printf("Cannot open the given file %s ", file);
            }
            catch(IOException ioe) {
                // some IO error occurred when reading the file ...
                System.err.printf("Error when processing file %s... skipping it", file);
            }
            // try-with-resources will automatically release FileReader object
        }
    }
}
```

For a sample text file, here is the output for the type command in Windows and our Type program:

```
D:\> type SaturnMoons.txt
Saturn has numerous icy moons in its rings. Few large moons of Saturn are - Mimas,
Enceladus, Tethys, Dione, Rhea, Titan, Iapetus, and Hyperion.

D:\> java Type SaturnMoons.txt
Saturn has numerous icy moons in its rings. Few large moons of Saturn are - Mimas,
Enceladus, Tethys, Dione, Rhea, Titan, Iapetus, and Hyperion.
```

It works as expected. In this program, you are instantiating the FileReader class and passing the name of the file to be opened. If the file is not found, the FileReader constructor will throw a FileNotFoundException.

Once the file is open, you use the read() method to fetch characters in the underlying file. You are reading character by character. Alternatively, you can use methods such as readLine() to read line by line.

Note that the read() method returns an int instead of a char—it's because when read() reaches End-Of-File (EOF), it returns -1, which is outside the range of char. So, the read() method returns an int to indicate that the end of file has been reached and that you should stop attempting to read any more characters from the underlying stream.

In this program, you only read a text file; you'll now try to read from as well as write to a text file.

Reading and Writing Text Files

In the previous example (Listing 9-5) of reading a text file, you created the character stream as follows:

```
FileReader inputFile = new FileReader(file);
```

This uses unbuffered I/O, which is less efficient when compared to buffered I/O. In other words, the read characters are directly passed instead of using a temporary (internal) buffer, which would speed up the I/O. To programmatically use buffered I/O, you can pass the FileReader reference to a BufferedReader object, as in the following:

```
BufferedReader inputFile = new BufferedReader(new FileReader(file));
```

In the same way, you can also use BufferedWriter for buffered output. (In case of byte streams, you can use BufferedInputStream and BufferedOutputStream, which we'll discuss later in this chapter).

You'll now use buffered I/O to read from and write to a text file. Listing 9-6 contains a simplified version of the copy command in Windows.

Listing 9-6. Copy.java

```
import java.io.BufferedReader;
import java.io.BufferedWriter;
import java.io.FileNotFoundException;
import java.io.FileReader;
import java.io.FileWriter;
import java.io.IOException;

// implements a simplified version of "copy" command provided in Windows
// syntax: java Copy SrcFile DstFile
// copies ScrFile to DstFile; over-writes the DstFile if it already exits
class Copy {
    public static void main(String []files) {
        if(files.length != 2) {
            System.err.println("Incorrect syntax. Correct syntax: Copy SrcFile DstFile");
            System.exit(-1);
        }
        String srcFile = files[0];
        String dstFile = files[1];
```

```
        // try opening the source and destination file
        // with FileReader and FileWriter
        try (BufferedReader inputFile = new BufferedReader(new FileReader(srcFile));
            BufferedWriter outputFile = new BufferedWriter(new FileWriter(dstFile))) {
            int ch = 0;
            // while there are characters to fetch, read the characters from
            // source stream and write them to the destination stream
            while( (ch = inputFile.read()) != -1) {
                // ch is of type int - convert it back to char before
                // writing it
                outputFile.write( (char)ch );
            }
            // no need to call flush explicitly for outputFile - the close()
            // method will first call flush before closing the outputFile stream
        } catch (FileNotFoundException fnfe) {
            // the passed file is not found ...
            System.err.println("Cannot open the file " + fnfe.getMessage());
        }
        catch(IOException ioe) {
            // some IO error occurred when reading the file ...
            System.err.printf("Error when processing file; exiting ... ");
        }
        // try-with-resources will automatically release FileReader object
    }
}
```

Let's first check if this program works. Copy this Java source program itself (Copy.java) into another file (DuplicateCopy.java). You can use the fc (file compare) command provided in Windows (or diff command in Linux/Unix/Mac) to make sure that the contents of the original file and the copied file are the same, to ensure that the program worked correctly.

```
D:\> java Copy Copy.java DuplicateCopy.java
D:\> fc Copy.java DuplicateCopyjava
Comparing files Copy.java and DuplicateCopy.java
FC: no differences encountered
```

Yes, it worked correctly. What if you give it a source file name that does not exist?

```
D:\> java Copy Cpy.java DuplicateCopyjava
Cannot open the file Cpy.java (The system cannot find the file specified)
```

You typed Cpy.java instead of Copy.java and the program terminates with a readable error message, as expected.

Here's how this program works. In the try-with-resources statement, you opened srcFile for reading and dstFile for writing. You wanted to use buffered I/O, so you passed FileReader and FileWriter references to BufferedReader and BufferedWriter, respectively.

```
try (BufferedReader inputFile = new BufferedReader(new FileReader(srcFile));
        BufferedWriter outputFile = new BufferedWriter(new FileWriter(dstFile)))
```

You're using the try-with-resources statement (discussed in Chapter 7), and the close() method for BufferedWriter will first call the flush() method before closing the stream.

💣⃰ When you're using buffered I/O in your programs, it's a good idea to call the flush() method explicitly in places where you want to ensure that all pending characters or data is flushed (i.e., written to the underlying file).

"Tokenizing" Text

In the last two examples (Listings 9-5 and 9-6), you just read or wrote to text files. However, in real-world programs, you may want to perform some processing when reading or writing files. For example, you may want to look out for certain patterns, search for some specific strings, replace one sequence of characters with another sequence of characters, filter out specific words, or format the output in a certain way. You can use existing APIs such as regular expressions and Scanner for such purposes.

For illustration, consider that you want to list all the words in a given text file and eliminate all unnecessary whitespaces, punctuation characters, and so on. Also, you need to print the resulting words in alphabetical order. To solve this problem, you can use a Scanner and pass the regular expression that you want to match or delimit (see Listing 9-7).

Listing 9-7. Tokenize.java

```java
import java.io.FileNotFoundException;
import java.io.FileReader;
import java.util.Scanner;
import java.util.Set;
import java.util.TreeSet;

// read the input file and convert it into "tokens" of words;
// convert the words to same case (lower case), remove duplicates, and print the words
class Tokenize {
    public static void main(String []args) {
        // read the input file
        if(args.length != 1) {
            System.err.println("pass the name of the file to be read as an argument");
            System.exit(-1);
        }
        String fileName = args[0];
        // use a TreeSet<String> which will automatically sort the words
        // in alphabetical order
        Set<String> words = new TreeSet<>();
        try ( Scanner tokenizingScanner = new Scanner(new FileReader(fileName)) ) {
            // set the delimiter for text as non-words (special characters,
            // white-spaces, etc), meaning that all words other than punctuation
            // characters, and white-spaces will be returned
            tokenizingScanner.useDelimiter("\\W");
            while(tokenizingScanner.hasNext()) {
                String word = tokenizingScanner.next();
```

```
                    if(!word.equals("")) { // process only non-empty strings
                        // convert to lowercase and then add to the set
                        words.add(word.toLowerCase());
                    }
                }
                // now words are in alphabetical order without duplicates,
                // print the words separating them with tabs
                for(String word : words) {
                    System.out.print(word + '\t');
                            }
            } catch (FileNotFoundException fnfe) {
                System.err.println("Cannot read the input file - pass a valid file name");
            }
        }
    }
}
```

Let's see if it works:

```
D:\> type limerick.txt
There was a young lady of Niger
Who smiled as she rode on a tiger.
They returned from the ride
With the lady inside
And a smile on the face of the tiger.

D:\> java Tokenize limerick.txt
a       and     as      face    from    inside  lady    niger   of      on      returned ride
rode    she     smile   smiled  the     there   they    tiger   was     who     with     young
```

Yes, it does work correctly. Now let's see what this program does. The program first opens the file using a FileReader and passes it to the Scanner object. The program sets the delimiter for Scanner with useDelimiter("\\W"); the "\W" matches for non-words, so any non-word characters will become delimiters. (Note that you're setting the delimiter and not the pattern that you want to match). The program makes use of a TreeSet<String> to store the read strings. The program reads words from the underlying stream, checks if it is a non-empty string, and adds the lower-case versions of the string to the TreeSet. Since the data structure is a TreeSet, it removes duplicates (remember that a TreeSet is-a Set, which does not allow duplicates). Further, it is also an ordered data structure, meaning that it maintains an "ordering" of values inserted, which in this case is an alphabetical ordering of Strings. Hence the program correctly prints the words from given text file that contained a limerick.

Byte Streams

In this section, you'll explore I/O with byte streams. You'll first learn how to read and write data files, and also how to stream objects, store them in files and then read them back. The class of OutputStream and its derived classes are shown in Figure 9-3; InputStream and its derived classes are shown in Figure 9-4.

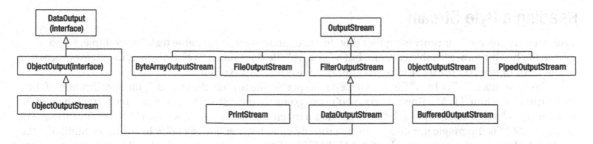

Figure 9-3. *Important classes deriving from the OutputStream abstract class*

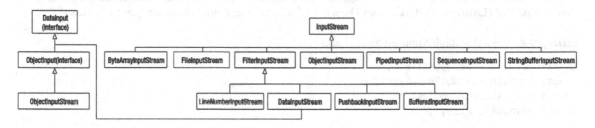

Figure 9-4. *Important classes deriving from the InputStream abstract class*

Table 9-6 summarizes the important classes of InputStream and OutputStream.

Table 9-6. *Important Classes Deriving from the InputStream and OutputStream Classes*

Class name	Short description
PipedInputStream, PipedOutputStream	PipedInputStream and PipedOutputStream create a communication channel on which data can be sent and received. PipedOutputStream sends the data and PipedInputStream receives the data sent on the channel.
FileInputStream, FileOutputStream	FileInputStream receives a byte stream from a file, FileOutputStream writes a byte stream into a file.
FilterInputStream, FilterOutputStream	These filtered streams are used to add functionalities to plain streams. The output of an InputStream can be filtered using FilterInputStream. The output of an OutputStream can be filtered using FilterOutputStream.
BufferedInputStream, BufferedOutputStream	BufferedInputStream adds buffering capabilities to an input stream. BufferedOutputStream adds buffering capabilities to an output stream.
PushbackInputStream	A subclass of FilterInputStream, it adds "pushback" functionality to an input stream.
DataInputStream, DataOutputStream	DataInputStream can be used to read java primitive data types from an input stream. DataOutputStream can be used to write Java primitive data types to an output stream.

Reading a Byte Stream

Byte streams are used for processing files that do not contain human-readable text. For example, a Java source file has human-readable content, but a ".class" file does not. A ".class" file is meant for processing by the JVM, hence you must use byte streams to process the ".class" file.

The contents of a ".class" file are written in a specific file format, described in the specification of the Java Virtual Machine (JVM). Don't worry; you're not going to understand this complex file format, but you'll just check its "magic number." Each file format has a magic number used to quickly check the file format. For example ".MZ" is the magic number (or more properly, magic string) for .exe files in Windows. Similarly, the ".class" files have the magic number "0xCAFEBABE", written as a hexadecimal value. These magic numbers are typically written as first few bytes of a variable length file format.

To understand how byte streams work, you'll just check if the given file starts with the magic number "0xCAFEBABE" (Listing 9-8). If so, it could be a valid ".class" file; if not, it's certainly not a ".class" file.

Listing 9-8. ClassFileMagicNumberChecker.java

```java
import java.io.FileInputStream;
import java.io.FileNotFoundException;
import java.io.IOException;
import java.util.Arrays;

// check if the passed file is a valid .class file or not.
// note that this is an elementary version of a checker that checks if the given file
// is a valid file that is written according to the JVM specification
// it checks only the magic number
class ClassFileMagicNumberChecker {
    public static void main(String []args) {
        if(args.length != 1) {
            System.err.println("Pass a valid file name as argument");
            System.exit(-1);
        }

        String fileName = args[0];
        // create a magicNumber byte array with values for four bytes in 0xCAFEBABE
        // you need to have an explicit down cast to byte since
        // the hex values like 0xCA are of type int
        byte []magicNumber = {(byte) 0xCA, (byte)0xFE, (byte)0xBA, (byte)0xBE};
        try (FileInputStream fis = new FileInputStream(fileName)) {
            // magic number is of 4 bytes -
            // use a temporary buffer to read first four bytes
            byte[] u4buffer = new byte[4];
                // read a buffer full (4 bytes here) of data from the file
                if(fis.read(u4buffer) != -1) { // if read was successful
                    // the overloaded method equals for two byte arrays
                    // checks for equality of contents
                    if(Arrays.equals(magicNumber, u4buffer)) {
                        System.out.printf("The magic number for passed file %s matches
                        that of a .class file", fileName);
                }
```

```
                else {
                    System.out.printf("The magic number for passed file %s does not
                    match that of a .class file", fileName);
                }
            }
        } catch(FileNotFoundException fnfe) {
            System.err.println("file does not exist with the given file name ");
        } catch(IOException ioe) {
            System.err.println("an I/O error occurred while processing the file");
        }
    }
}
```

Let's first see if it works by passing the source (.java) file and the ".class" file for the same program.

```
D:> java ClassFileMagicNumberChecker ClassFileMagicNumberChecker.java
The magic number for passed file ClassFileMagicNumberChecker.java does not match that
of a .class file

D:\> java ClassFileMagicNumberChecker ClassFileMagicNumberChecker.class
The magic number for passed file ClassFileMagicNumberChecker.class matches that of a
.class file
```

Yes, it works. The classes InputStream and OutputStream form the base of the hierarchies for byte streams. You perform file I/O, so open the given file as a FileInputStream. You need to check the first four bytes, so you read four bytes in a temporary buffer. You need to compare the contents of this buffer against the sequence of bytes 0xCA, 0xFE, 0xBA, and 0xBE. If the contents of these two arrays are not equal, then the passed file is not a ".class" file.

In this program, you directly manipulate the underlying byte stream using a FileInputStream. In case you need to speed up the program when you read large number of bytes, you can use a buffered output stream, as in

```
BufferedInputStream bis = new BufferedInputStream(new FileInputStream(fileName));
```

Similar to these input streams, you can use output streams to write a sequence of bytes to a data file. You can use FileOutputStream and BufferedOutputStream for that.

After reading this program, didn't you think that reading an array of four bytes and comparing the contents of the byte arrays was awkward (instead of directly comparing the contents of an integer)? In other words, 0xCAFEBABE is an integer value, and you could read this value directly as an integer value and compare it against the read integer value. For this, you need to use data streams, which provide methods like readInt(), which we'll discuss now.

Data Streams

To understand how to write or read with byte streams, let's write a simple program that writes and then reads constant values to a data file (see Listing 9-9). To keep the problem simple, you will write only the values 0 to 9 in the form of the following primitive type values: byte, short, int, long, float, and double.

Listing 9-9. DataStreamExample.java

```java
import java.io.DataInputStream;
import java.io.DataOutputStream;
import java.io.FileInputStream;
import java.io.FileNotFoundException;
import java.io.FileOutputStream;
import java.io.IOException;

// A simple class to illustrate data streams; write constants 0 and 1 in different
// data type values into a file and read the results back and print them
class DataStreamExample {
    public static void main(String []args) {
        // write some data into a data file with hard-coded name "temp.data"
        try (DataOutputStream dos =
            new DataOutputStream(new FileOutputStream("temp.data"))) {
            // write values 1 to 10 as byte, short, int, long, float and double
            // omitting boolean type because an int value cannot
            // be converted to boolean
            for(int i = 0; i < 10; i++) {
                dos.writeByte(i);
                dos.writeShort(i);
                dos.writeInt(i);
                dos.writeLong(i);
                dos.writeFloat(i);
                dos.writeDouble(i);
            }
        } catch(FileNotFoundException fnfe) {
            System.err.println("cannot create a file with the given file name ");
            System.exit(-1); // don't proceed - exit the program
        } catch(IOException ioe) {
            System.err.println("an I/O error occurred while processing the file");
            System.exit(-1); // don't proceed - exit the program
        }
        // the DataOutputStream will auto-close, so don't have to worry about it
        // now, read the written data and print it to console
        try (DataInputStream dis = new DataInputStream(new FileInputStream("temp.data"))) {
            // the order of values to read is byte, short, int, long, float and
            // double since we've written from 0 to 10,
            // the for loop has to run 10 times
            for(int i = 0; i < 10; i++) {
                // %d is for printing byte, short, int or long
                // %f, %g, or %e is for printing float or double
                // %n is for printing newline
                System.out.printf("%d %d %d %d %g %g %n",
                                                dis.readByte(),
                                                dis.readShort(),
                                                dis.readInt(),
                                                dis.readLong(),
                                                dis.readFloat(),
                                                dis.readDouble());
            }
```

```
        } catch(FileNotFoundException fnfe) {
            System.err.println("cannot create a file with the given file name ");
        } catch(IOException ioe) {
            System.err.println("an I/O error occurred while processing the file");
        } // the DataOutputStream will auto-close, so don't have to worry about it
    }
}
```

First, let's see if it works by executing the program.

```
D:> java DataStreamExample
0 0 0 0 0.000000 0.000000
1 1 1 1 1.000000 1.000000
2 2 2 2 2.000000 2.000000
3 3 3 3 3.000000 3.000000
4 4 4 4 4.000000 4.000000
5 5 5 5 5.000000 5.000000
6 6 6 6 6.000000 6.000000
7 7 7 7 7.000000 7.000000
8 8 8 8 8.000000 8.000000
9 9 9 9 9.000000 9.000000
```

Yes, it works. Now, as mentioned earlier, the contents of data files are not human readable. In this case, you're writing values 0 to 9 as various primitive type values into the temporary file write named temp.data. If you try to open this data file and see the contents, you won't be able to recognize or understand what it contains. Here's an example of its contents:

```
D:>type temp.data
                       ☺   ☺   ☺        ☺?Ç  ?       ●  ●  ●      ●@    @
♥  ♥   ♥       ♥@@      ◆  ◆   ◆        ◆@Ç  @▶      ♣  ♣  ♣      ♣@á   @¶
♠  ♠   ♠       ♠@L  @↑                  @α   @L          A   @
               A▶   @"
```

The typed contents of the file temp.data look like garbage values because the primitive type values like the integer values 0 or 9 are stored in terms of bytes. However, the type command in Windows (or the cat command in Linux/Unix/Mac) tries to convert these bytes into human-readable characters, hence the output does not make any sense. The data will make sense only if we know the format of the data stored in the file and read it according to that format.

Now let's get back to the program and see how it works. The program writes to the data file with a hard-coded file named temp.data in the current directory from which the program is run. This program first writes the data, so it opens the file as an output stream. What does the following statement within the first try block mean?

```
DataOutputStream dos = new DataOutputStream(new FileOutputStream("temp.data"))
```

You can directly perform binary I/O with OutputStream and its derived class of FileOutputStream, but to process data formats such as primitive type values, you need to use DataOutputStream, which acts as a wrapper over the underlying FileOutputStream. So, you use the DataOutputStream here, which provides methods such as writeByte and writeShort. You use these methods to write the primitive type values 0 to 9 into the data file. Note that you don't have to close the streams explicitly since you opened the DataOutputStream in a try-with-resources statement, hence the close() method on dos reference will automatically be invoked. The close() method also flushes the underlying stream; this close() method will also close the underlying reference to the FileOutputStream.

Once the file is written, you read the data file in a similar way. You open a `FileInputStream` and wrap it with a `DataInputStream`. You read the data from the stream and print it in console. You used format specifiers such as `%d` (which is a common format specifier for printing integral values like `byte`, `short`, `int`, or `long`) as well as `%f`, `%g`, or `%e` specifiers for printing floating point values of type `float` or `double`; `%n` is for printing a newline character.

In this program, you wrote and read primitive type values. What about reference type objects, such as Objects, Maps, and so on? Reading and writing objects is achieved through object streams, which we'll discuss now.

Writing to and Reading from Object Streams

Assume that you are creating an online e-commerce web site. You can choose to write data contained in objects such as customers and purchase requests made, to an RDBMS (we'll cover JDBC in Chapter 12). Alternatively, instead of storing the data in a RDBMS, you can store the objects directly in *flat files*: in that case, you must know how to read or write objects into streams. The classes `ObjectInputStream` and `ObjectOutputStream` support reading and writing Java objects that you use in the program.

Listing 9-10 contains a simple example of writing the contents of a Map data structure to a file and reading it back to illustrate the use of the classes `ObjectInputStream` and `ObjectOutputStream` to read or write objects. You store the details of the last three US presidents in this map.

Listing 9-10. ObjectStreamExample.java

```java
import java.io.FileInputStream;
import java.io.FileNotFoundException;
import java.io.FileOutputStream;
import java.io.IOException;
import java.io.ObjectInputStream;
import java.io.ObjectOutputStream;
import java.util.HashMap;
import java.util.Map;

// A simple class to illustrate object streams: fill a data structure, write it to a
// temporary file and read it back and print the read data structure
class ObjectStreamExample {
    public static void main(String []args) {
        Map<String, String> presidentsOfUS = new HashMap<>();
        presidentsOfUS.put("Barack Obama", "2009 to --, Democratic Party, 56th term");
        presidentsOfUS.put("George W. Bush", "2001 to 2009, Republican Party, 54th and 55th
        terms");
        presidentsOfUS.put("Bill Clinton", "1993 to 2001, Democratic Party, 52nd and 53rd
        terms");
        try (ObjectOutputStream oos =
                new ObjectOutputStream(new FileOutputStream("object.data"))) {

            oos.writeObject(presidentsOfUS);
        } catch(FileNotFoundException fnfe) {
            System.err.println("cannot create a file with the given file name ");
        } catch(IOException ioe) {
            System.err.println("an I/O error occurred while processing the file");
        } // the ObjectOutputStream will auto-close, so don't have to worry about it
```

```
        try (ObjectInputStream ois =
              new ObjectInputStream(new FileInputStream("object.data"))) {

            Object obj = ois.readObject();
            // first check if obj is of type Map
            if(obj != null && obj instanceof Map) {
                Map<?, ?> presidents = (Map<?, ?>) obj;
                        System.out.println("President name \t Description");
                for(Map.Entry<?, ?> president : presidents.entrySet()) {
                    System.out.printf("%s \t %s %n", president.getKey(),
                                                      president.getValue());
                }
            }
        } catch(FileNotFoundException fnfe) {
            System.err.println("cannot create a file with the given file name ");
        } catch(IOException ioe) {
            System.err.println("an I/O error occurred while processing the file");
        } catch(ClassNotFoundException cnfe) {
            System.err.println("cannot recognize the class of the object - is the file
                                    corrupted?");
        }
    }
}
```

Before discussing how the program works, let's check if it works.

```
D:\> java ObjectStreamExample
President name    Description
Barack Obama      2009 to --, Democratic Party, 56th term
Bill Clinton      1993 to 2001, Democratic Party, 52nd and 53rd terms
George W. Bush    2001 to 2009, Republican Party, 54th and 55th terms
```

The serialization process converts contents of the objects in memory with the description of the contents (known as *metadata*). When the object has references to other objects, the serialization mechanism also includes them as part of the serialized bytes. If you try to open the file in which the object is persisted, you cannot read these serialized and then persisted objects. For example, if you try to read the object.data file, you'll see numerous unreadable characters.

Now, let's get back to the program and see how it works. In this program, you fill the HashMap container with details of last three US presidents. Then, you open an output stream as follows:

```
ObjectOutputStream oos = new ObjectOutputStream(new FileOutputStream("object.data"))
```

The FileOutputStream opens a temporary file named object.data in the current directory. The ObjectOutputStream is a wrapper over this underlying FileOutputStream. Inside this try-with-resources block, you've only one statement, oos.writeObject(presidentsOfUS), which writes the object to the object.data file.

Reading the object requires a bit more work than writing the object. The readObject() method in ObjectInputStream returns an Object type. You need to convert it back to Map<String, String>. Before downcasting it to this specific type, you check if the obj is of type Map. Note that you don't have to check if it's Map<String, String> because these generic types are lost in the process known as *type erasure*. Hence we are using wildcards for the generic type parameters, as in: Map<?, ?> presidents = (Map<?, ?>) obj. Once the downcast succeeds, you can read the values of the contents in this object. See discussion on type erasure and wildcard character in Chapter 4 Generics and Collections.

Points to Remember

Here are the noteworthy points that may help when you attend the OCPJP 8 exam:

- When you use buffered streams, you should call flush() once you are done with data transmission. The internal buffer might be holding some data that will be cleared and sent to the destination once you call flush(). However, the method close() on the stream will automatically call flush().

- You might have observed that you can combine stream objects. You can create an object of BufferedInputStream that takes a FileInputStream object. In this way, the output of one stream is chained to the filtered stream. This is the important, useful, and beautiful way to customize the stream in a desired way.

- If you want to customize the process of serialization, you can implement readObject() and writeObject(). Note that both of these methods are private methods, which means you are not overriding or overloading these methods. The JVM checks the implementation of these methods and calls them instead of the usual methods. It sounds weird but it is the way the customization of the serialization process is implemented in the JVM.

Summary

Let us briefly review the key points for each certification objective in this chapter. Please read it before appearing for the exam.

Read and write data from the console

- The public static fields in, out, and err in java.lang.System class respectively represent the standard input, output and error streams. System.in is of type java.io.InputStream and System.out and System.err are of type java.io.PrintStream.

- You can redirect standard streams by calling the methods System.setIn, System.setOut and System.setError.

- You can obtain a reference to the console using the System.console() method; if the JVM is not associated with any console, this method will fail and return null.

- Many methods are provided in Console-support formatted I/O. You can use the printf() and format() methods available in the Console class to print formatted text; the overloaded readLine() and readPassword() methods take format strings as arguments.

- The template of format specifiers is: %[flags][width][.precision]datatype_specifier Each format specifier starts with the % sign, followed by flags, width, and precision information, and ending with a data type specifier. In the format string, the flags, width, and precision information are optional but the % sign and data type specifier are mandatory.

- Use the readPassword() method for reading secure strings such as passwords. It is recommended to use Array's fill() method to "empty" the password read into the character array (to avoid malicious access to the typed passwords).

Use BufferedReader, BufferedWriter, File, FileReader, FileWriter, FileInputStream, FileOutputStream, ObjectOutputStream, ObjectInputStream, and PrintWriter in the java.io package

- The java.io package has classes supporting both character streams and byte streams.

- You can use character streams for text-based I/O. Byte streams are used for data-based I/O.

- Character streams for reading and writing are called *readers* and *writers* respectively (represented by the abstract classes of Reader and Writer).

- Byte streams for reading and writing are called *input streams* and *output streams* respectively (represented by the abstract classes of InputStream and OutputStream).

- You should only use character streams for processing text files (or human-readable files), and byte streams for data files. If you try using one type of stream instead of another, your program won't work as you would expect; even if it works by chance, you'll get nasty bugs. So don't mix up streams, and use the right stream for a given task at hand.

- For both byte and character streams, you can use buffering. The buffer classes are provided as wrapper classes for the underlying streams. Using buffering will speed up the I/O when performing bulk I/O operations.

- For processing data with primitive data types and strings, you can use data streams.

- You can use object streams (classes ObjectInputStream and ObjectOutputStream) for reading and writing objects in memory to files and vice versa.

QUESTION TIME

1. Consider the following code segment:

```
OutputStream os = new FileOutputStream("log.txt");
System.setErr(new PrintStream(os)); // SET SYSTEM.ERR
System.err.println("Error");
```

Which one of the following statements is true regarding this code segment?

A. The line with comment SET SYSTEM.ERR will not compile and will result in a compiler error.

B. The line with comment SET SYSTEM.ERR will result in throwing a runtime exception since System.err cannot be programmatically redirected.

C. The program will print the text "Error" in console since System.err by default sends the output to console.

D. This code segment redirects the System.err to the log.txt file and will write the text "Error" to that file.

2. Which one of the following options correctly reads a line of string from the console?

    A. `BufferedReader br = new BufferedReader(System.in);`

        `String str = br.readLine();`

    B. `BufferedReader br =`

        `new BufferedReader(new InputStreamReader(System.in));`
        `String str = br.readLine();`

    C. `InputStreamReader isr =`

        `new InputStreamReader (new BufferedReader(System.in));`
        `String str = isr.readLine();`

    D. `String str = System.in.readLine();`

        `String str;`
        `System.in.scanf(str);`

3. Consider the following code snippet:

    `console.printf("%d %1$x %1$o", 16);`

    Assuming that `console` is a valid `Console` object, what will it print?

    A. This program crashes after throwing an `IllegalFormatException`

    B. This program crashes after throwing `ImproperFormatStringException`

    C. This program prints: 16 16 16

    D. This program prints: 16 10 20

4. There are two kinds of streams in the java.io package: character streams (i.e., those deriving from Reader and Writer interfaces) and byte streams (i.e., those deriving from InputStream and OutputStream). Which of the following statements is true regarding the differences between these two kinds of streams?

    A. In character streams, data is handled in terms of bytes; in byte streams, data is handled in terms of Unicode characters.

    B. Character streams are suitable for reading or writing to files such as executable files, image files, and files in low-level file formats such as .zip, .class, and .jag.

    C. Byte streams are suitable for reading or writing to text-based I/O such as documents and text, XML, and HTML files.

    D. Byte streams are meant for handling binary data that is not human-readable; character streams are meant for human-readable characters.

5. Consider the following code snippet:

```
USPresident usPresident = new USPresident("Barack Obama", "2009 to --", 56);
try (ObjectOutputStream oos =
new ObjectOutputStream(new FileOutputStream("USPresident.data"))) {
    oos.writeObject(usPresident);
    usPresident.setTerm(57);
    oos.writeObject(usPresident);
}
```

If you deserialize the object and print the field term (term is declared as int and is not a transient), what will it print?

A. 56

B. 57

C. null

D. Compiler error

E. Runtime exception

6. Consider the following code segment:

```
FileInputStream findings = new FileInputStream("log.txt");
DataInputStream dataStream = new DataInputStream(findings);
BufferedReader br = new BufferedReader(new InputStreamReader(dataStream));
String line;
while ((line = br.readLine()) != null) {
        System.out.println(line);
}
br.close();
```

Which TWO options are true regarding this code segment?

A. br.close() statement will close only the BufferedReader object, and findings and dataStream will remain unclosed.

B. The br.close() statement will close the BufferedReader object and the underlying stream objects referred by findings and dataStream.

C. The readLine() method invoked in the statement br.readLine() can throw an IOException; if this exception is thrown, br.close() will not be called, resulting in a resource leak.

D. The readLine() method invoked in the statement br.readLine() can throw an IOException; however, there will not be any resource leaks since Garbage Collector collects all resources.

E. In this code segment, no exceptions can be thrown calling br.close(), so there is no possibility of resource leaks.

Answers:

1. D. This code segment redirects the `System.err` to the `log.txt` file and will write the text "Error" to that file.

   Note that you can redirect the `System.err` programmatically using the `setErr()` method. `System.err` is of type `PrintStream`, and the `System.setErr()` method takes a `PrintStream` as an argument. Once the error stream is set, all writes to `System.err` will be redirected to it. Hence, this program will create `log.txt` with the text "Error" in it.

2. B.

   ```
   BufferedReader br =
           new BufferedReader(new InputStreamReader(System.in));
   String str = br.readLine();
   ```

   This is the right way to read a line of a string from the console where you pass a System.in reference to InputStreamReader and pass the returning reference to BufferedReader. From the BufferedReader reference, you can call the readLine() method to read the string from the console.

3. D. This program prints: 16 10 20

   In the format specifier, "1$" refers to first argument, which is 16 in this printf statement. Hence "%1$x" prints the hexadecimal value of 16, which is 10. Further, "%1$o" prints the octal value of 16, which is 20. Hence the output "16 10 20" from this program.

4. D. Byte streams are meant for handling binary data that is not human readable; character streams are for human-readable characters.

   In character streams, data is handled in terms of Unicode characters, whereas in byte streams, data is handled in terms of bytes. Byte streams are suitable for reading or writing to files such as executable files, image files, and files in low-level file formats such as .zip, .class, and .jar. Character streams are suitable for reading or writing to text-based I/O such as documents and text, XML, and HTML files.

5. A. 56

   Yes, it will print 56 even though you changed the term using its setter to 57 and serialized again. At the time of serialization, JVM checks for the duplicate object; if an object is already serialized then JVM do not serialize the object again; instead, JVM stores a reference to the serialized object.

6. Options B and C.

   The `br.close()` statement will close the `BufferedReader` object and the underlying stream objects referred to by `findings` and `dataStream`. The readLine() method invoked in the statement `br.readLine()` can throw an IOException; if this exception is thrown, `br.close()` will not be called, resulting in a resource leak. Note that Garbage Collector will only collect unreferenced memory resources; it is the programmer's responsibility to ensure that all other resources such as stream objects are released.

■ ■ ■

CHAPTER 10

Java File I/O (NIO.2)

Certification Objectives

Use Path interface to operate on file and directory paths

Use Files class to check, read, delete, copy, move, manage metadata of a file or directory

Use Stream API with NIO.2

Java offers a rich set of APIs you can use to manipulate files and directories. Java 7 introduced a set of I/O APIs called NIO.2 that offered convenient ways to perform operations related to a file system. In Java 8, you can use the Stream API (discussed in Chapter 6) with NIO.2.

The previous chapter covered I/O fundamentals; you learned how to read and write from the console and how to use streams to read and write to files. In this chapter, you learn how to operate on file and directory paths using the Path interface. You also learn to perform various file operations such as create, move, copy, and delete using the Files class. Finally, you see how to use the Stream API with NIO.2. This chapter uses functional interfaces in the java.util.function package and the Stream API in the java.util.stream package, and we assume that you have read the Chapters 3, 4, 5, and 6 before reading this chapter.

We give file and directory paths assuming that you are using a Windows machine. If you are on Linux, Mac OS, or any other platform, you may need to make small changes to the path names in order for the programs to work on your machine.

Using the Path Interface

Certification Objective

Use Path interface to operate on file and directory paths

File systems usually form a tree. The file system starts with a root directory that contains files and directories (directories are also called *folders* in Windows). Each directory, in turn, may have subdirectories or hold files. To locate a file, you just need to put together the directories from the root directory to the immediate directory containing the file, along with a file separator, followed by the file name. For instance, if the myfile.txt file resides in a mydocs directory, which resides in root directory C:\, then the path of the file is C:\mydocs\myfile.txt. Every file has a unique path to locate it (apart from symbolic links).

A path can be an *absolute path* (such as C:\mydocs\myfile.txt), which starts from a root element. On the other hand, a path can be specified as a *relative path*. When you try to compile a Java program, you write something like javac programFileName.java; this example specifies the Java source file path relative to the currently selected directory, so this is a relative path. You need a reference path (such as the current directory path, in this case) to interpret a relative path.

Before proceeding, let's talk about *symbolic links*. A symbolic link is like a pointer or reference to an actual file. In general, symbolic links are transparent to applications, which means operations are performed directly on the files rather than on the links (except, of course, for symbolic link-specific operations).

The Path interface is a programing abstraction for a path. A path object contains the names of directories and files that form the full path of the file/directory represented by the Path object; the Path abstraction provides methods to extract path elements, manipulate them, and append them. You see later that almost all the methods that access files/directories to get information about them or manipulate them use Path objects. Table 10-1 summarizes the important methods in this interface.

Table 10-1. *Important Methods in the Path Interface*

Method	Description
Path getRoot()	Returns a Path object representing the root of the given path, or null if the path does not have a root.
Path getFileName()	Returns the file name or directory name of the given path. Note that the file/directory name is the last element or name in the given path.
Path getParent()	Returns the Path object representing the parent of the given path, or null if no parent component exists for the path.
int getNameCount()	Returns the number of file/directory names in the given path; returns 0 if the given path represents the root.
Path getName(int index)	Returns the *i*th file/directory name; the index 0 starts from closest name to the root.
Path subpath(int beginIndex, int endIndex)	Returns a Path object that is part of this Path object; the returned Path object has a name that begins at beginIndex and ends with the element at index endIndex - 1. In other words, beginIndex is inclusive of the name in that index and exclusive of the name in endIndex. This method may throw IllegalArgumentException if beginIndex is >= number of elements, or endIndex <= beginIndex, or endIndex > number of elements.
Path normalize()	Removes redundant elements in the path, such as . (dot symbol that indicates the current directory) and .. (double-dot symbol that indicates the parent directory).
Path resolve(Path other) Path resolve(String other)	Resolves a path against the given path. For example, this method can combine the given path with the other path and return the resulting path.
Boolean isAbsolute()	Returns true if the given path is an absolute path; returns false if not (when the given path is a relative path, for example).
Path startsWith(String path) Path startsWith(Path path)	Returns true if this Path object starts with the given path, or false otherwise.
Path toAbsolutePath()	Returns the absolute path.

Getting Path Information

Let's create a Path object and retrieve the basic information associated with the object. Listing 10-1 shows how to create a Path object and get information about it.

Listing 10-1. PathInfo1.java

```java
import java.nio.file.Path;
import java.nio.file.Paths;

// Class to illustrate how to use Path interface and its methods
public class PathInfo1 {
    public static void main(String[] args) {
        // create a Path object by calling static method get() in Paths class
        Path testFilePath = Paths.get("D:\\test\\testfile.txt");

        // retrieve basic information about path
        System.out.println("Printing file information: ");
        System.out.println("\t file name: " + testFilePath.getFileName());
        System.out.println("\t root of the path: " + testFilePath.getRoot());
        System.out.println("\t parent of the target: " + testFilePath.getParent());

        // print path elements
        System.out.println("Printing elements of the path: ");
        for(Path element : testFilePath) {
            System.out.println("\t path element: " + element);
        }
    }
}
```

The program prints the following:

```
Printing file information:
        file name: testfile.txt
        root of the path: D:\
        parent of the target: D:\test
Printing elements of the path:
        path element: test
        path element: testfile.txt
```

The output is self-explanatory. Let's examine the program:

- First, you create a Path instance using the get() method of the Paths class. The get() method expects a string representing a path as an input. This is the easiest way to create a Path object.

- Note that you use an escape character (\) in Paths.get("D:\\test\\testfile.txt"). In the path, if you gave D:\test, then \t would mean a tab character, and you'd get a java.nio.file.InvalidPathException when you ran the program. Make sure that you provide necessary escape characters in path strings.

- You extract the file name represented by this Path object using the getFilename() method of the Path object.

289

- You also use getRoot() to get the root element of the Path object and getParent() to get the parent directory of the target file.

- You iterate over the elements in the path using a for loop. Alternatively, you can use getNameCount() to get the number of elements or names in the path and getName(index) to iterate over and access elements/names one by one.

Let's try another example. It explores some interesting aspects of a Path object, such as how to get an absolute path from a relative path and how you can *normalize* a path. Before looking at the example, you need to first understand the methods it uses:

- The toUri() method returns the URI (a path that can be opened from a browser) from the path.

- The toAbsolutePath() method returns the absolute path from a given relative path. If the input path is already an absolute path, the method returns the same object.

- The normalize() method performs normalization on the input path. In other words, it removes unnecessary symbols (such as . and ..) from the Path object.

- toRealPath() is an interesting method. It returns an absolute path from the input path object (as toAbsolutepath()). It also normalizes the path (as in normalize()). Further, if linking options are chosen properly, it resolves symbolic links. However, the target file/directory must exist in the file system, which is *not* a prerequisite for other Path methods.

Listing 10-2 shows the example. Assume that the file name Test does not exist in your file system.

Listing 10-2. PathInfo2.java

```java
import java.io.IOException;
import java.nio.file.LinkOption;
import java.nio.file.Path;
import java.nio.file.Paths;

// To illustrate important methods such as normalize(), toAbsolutePath(), and toRealPath()
class PathInfo2 {
    public static void main(String[] args) throws IOException {
        // get a path object with relative path
        Path testFilePath = Paths.get(".\\Test");
        System.out.println("The file name is: " + testFilePath.getFileName());
        System.out.println("Its URI is: " + testFilePath.toUri());
        System.out.println("Its absolute path is: " + testFilePath.toAbsolutePath());
        System.out.println("Its normalized path is: " + testFilePath.normalize());

        // get another path object with normalized relative path
        Path testPathNormalized = Paths.get(testFilePath.normalize().toString());
        System.out.println("Its normalized absolute path is: " +
                testPathNormalized.toAbsolutePath());
        System.out.println("Its normalized real path is: " +
                testFilePath.toRealPath (LinkOption.NOFOLLOW_LINKS));
    }
}
```

On our machine, this code printed the following:

```
The file name is: Test
Its URI is: file:///D:/OCPJP/programs/NIO2/./Test
Its absolute path is: D:\OCPJP\programs\NIO2\.\Test
Its normalized path is: Test
Its normalized absolute path is: D:\OCPJP\programs\NIO2\Test
Exception in thread "main" java.nio.file.NoSuchFileException: D:\OCPJP\programs\NIO2\Test
        at sun.nio.fs.WindowsException.translateToIOException(WindowsException.java:79)
        [... stack trace elided ...]
        at PathInfo2.main(PathInfo2.java:16)
```

Depending on the directory in which you run this program, the directory path will be different for you. This program instantiates a Path object using a relative path. The method getFileName() returns the target file name, as you saw in the last example. The getUri() method returns the URI, which can be used with browsers, and the toAbsolutePath() method returns the absolute path of the given relative path. (Note that we are executing the program from the D:/OCPJP/programs/NIO2/ folder; hence it becomes the current working directory and appears in the absolute path and URI.)

You call the normalize() method to remove redundant symbols from the path, so it removes the leading dot. (In many operating systems, the . [single dot symbol represents the current directory and .. [double dot] represents the parent directory.) You then instantiate another Path object using normalized output and print the absolute path again. Finally, you try to call toRealpath(); however, you get an exception (NoSuchFileException). Why? Because, you have not created the Test directory in the current working directory.

Now, let's create a Test directory in the D:/OCPJP/programs/NIO2/ directory and run this example again. We got the following output:

```
The file name is: Test
Its URI is: file:///D:/OCPJP/programs/NIO2/./Test/
Its absolute path is: D:\OCPJP\programs\NIO2\.\Test
Its normalized path is: Test
Its normalized absolute path is: D:\OCPJP\programs\NIO2\Test
Its normalized real path is: D:\OCPJP\programs\NIO2\Test
```

Now the last call of toRealPath() works fine and returns the absolute normalized path.

Path provides many other useful methods, including those listed earlier in Table 10-1. For example, here's how to use the resolve() method:

```
Path dirName = Paths.get("D:\\OCPJP\\programs\\NIO2\\");
Path resolvedPath = dirName.resolve("Test");
System.out.println(resolvedPath);
```

This code segment prints the following:

```
D:\OCPJP\programs\NIO2\Test
```

This resolve() method considers the given path to be a directory and joins (resolves) the passed path with it, as shown here.

📝 The toPath() method in the java.io.File class returns the Path object; this method was added in Java 7. Similarly, you can use the toFile() method in the Path interface to get a File object.

Comparing Two Paths

The Path interface provides two methods to compare two Path objects: equals() and compareTo(). The equals() method checks the equality of two Path objects and returns a Boolean value, whereas compareTo() compares two Path objects character by character and returns an integer: 0 if both Path objects are equal; a negative integer if this path is lexicographically less than the parameter path; and a positive integer if this path is lexicographically greater than the parameter path. Listing 10-3 contains a small program that demonstrates these methods.

Listing 10-3. PathCompare1.java

```java
import java.nio.file.Path;
import java.nio.file.Paths;

// illustrates how to use compareTo and equals and also shows
// the difference between the two methods
class PathCompare1 {
    public static void main(String[] args) {
        Path path1 = Paths.get("Test");
        Path path2 = Paths.get("D:\\OCPJP\\programs\\NIO2\\Test");
        // comparing two paths using compareTo() method
        System.out.println("(path1.compareTo(path2) == 0) is: "
                + (path1.compareTo(path2) == 0));

        // comparing two paths using equals() method
        System.out.println("path1.equals(path2) is: " + path1.equals(path2));

        // comparing two paths using equals() method with absolute path
        System.out.println("path2.equals(path1.toAbsolutePath()) is "
                            + path2.equals(path1.toAbsolutePath()));
    }
}
```

Intentionally, one path is a relative path and the other is an absolute path. Assume that the current directory from which you are executing this program is D:\\OCPJP\\programs\\NIO2\\Test. Can you guess the output of the program?

It's as follows:

```
(path1.compareTo(path2) == 0) is: false
path1.equals(path2) is: false
path2.equals(path1.toAbsolutePath()) is true
```

Let's examine the program step by step:

- It first compares two paths using the compareTo() method, which compares paths character by character and returns an integer. In this case, because one path is a relative path and another one is an absolute path, you first expect to get a message that says the paths are not equal.

- Then you compare both paths using equals(). The result is the same, which means even if the two Path objects are pointing to the same file/directory, it is possible for equals() to return false. You need to make sure both paths are absolute paths.

- In the next step, you convert the relative path to an absolute path and then compare them using equals(). This time both paths match.

💣 Even if two Path objects point to the same file/directory, it is not guaranteed that the equals() method will return true. You need to make sure both are absolute and normalized paths for an equality comparison to succeed for paths.

Using the Files Class

Certification Objective

Use Files class to check, read, delete, copy, move, manage metadata of a file or directory

The previous section discussed how to create a Path instance and extract useful information from it. In this section, you use Path objects to manipulate files/directories. Java 7 offers a Files class (in the java.nio.file package) that you can use to perform various file-related operations on files or directories. Note that Files is a utility class, meaning it is a final class with a private constructor and consists only of static methods. So you can use the Files class by calling the static methods it provides, such as copy() to copy files. This class provides a wide range of functionality. You can create directories, files, or symbolic links; create streams such as directory streams, byte channels, and input/output streams; examine the attributes of files; walk the file tree; and perform file operations such as read, write, copy, and delete. Table 10-2 provides a sample of the important methods in the Files class.

Table 10-2. *Some Important Methods in the* Files *Class*

Method	Description
`Path createDirectory(Path dirPath, FileAttribute<?>... dirAttrs)` `Path createDirectories(Path dir, FileAttribute<?>... attrs)`	Creates a file given by the dirPath, and sets the attributes given by dirAttributes. May throw an exception such as FileAlreadyExistsException or UnsupportedOperationException (for example, when the file attributes cannot be set as given by dirAttrs). The difference between createDirectory and createDirectories is that createDirectories creates intermediate directories given by dirPath if they are not already present.
`Path createTempFile(Path dir, String prefix, String suffix, FileAttribute<?>... attrs)`	Creates a temporary file with the given prefix, suffix, and attributes in the directory given by dir.
`Path createTempDirectory(Path dir, String prefix, FileAttribute<?>... attrs)`	Creates a temporary directory with the given prefix and directory attributes in the path specified by dir.
`Path copy(Path source, Path target, CopyOption... options)`	Copies the file from source to target. CopyOption can be REPLACE_EXISTING, COPY_ATTRIBUTES, or NOFOLLOW_LINKS. Can throw exceptions such as FileAlreadyExistsException.
`Path move(Path source, Path target, CopyOption... options)`	Similar to the copy operation, but the source file is removed. If the source and target are in the same directory, it is a file-rename operation.
`boolean isSameFile(Path path, Path path2)`	Checks whether the two Path objects locate the same file.
`boolean exists(Path path, LinkOption... options)`	Checks whether a file/directory exists in the given path; can specify LinkOption.NOFOLLOW_LINKS to not to follow symbolic links.
`Boolean isRegularFile(Path path, LinkOption...)`	Returns true if the file represented by path is a regular file.
`Boolean isSymbolicLink(Path path)`	Returns true if the file represented by path is a symbolic link.
`Boolean isHidden(Path path)`	Return true if the file represented by path is a hidden file.
`long size(Path path)`	Returns the size of the file represented by path in bytes.
`UserPrincipal getOwner(Path path, LinkOption...), Path setOwner(Path path, UserPrincipal owner)`	Gets/sets the owner of the file.
`FileTime getLastModifiedTime(Path path, LinkOption...), Path setLastModifiedTime(Path path, FileTime time)`	Gets/sets the last modified time for the specified file.
`Object getAttribute(Path path, String attribute, LinkOption...), Path setAttribute(Path path, String attribute, Object value, LinkOption...)`	Gets/sets the specified attribute of the specified file.

Checking File Properties and Metadata

In the previous section on the Path interface, you tried to figure out whether two paths pointed to the same file (see Listing 10-3). There is another way to find out the same thing: you can use the isSameFile() method from the Files class. Listing 10-4 shows how to do so.

Listing 10-4. PathCompare2.java

```java
import java.io.IOException;
import java.nio.file.Files;
import java.nio.file.Path;
import java.nio.file.Paths;

// illustrates how to use Files class to compare two paths
class PathCompare2 {
    public static void main(String[] args) throws IOException {
        Path path1 = Paths.get("Test");
        Path path2 = Paths.get("D:\\OCPJP\\programs\\NIO2\\Test");

        System.out.println("Files.isSameFile(path1, path2) is: "
                                + Files.isSameFile(path1, path2));
    }
}
```

Assume that the directory D:\\OCPJP\\programs\\NIO2\\Test exists on your machine. The program prints the following:

```
Files.isSameFile(path1, path2) is: true
```

In this case, you have the Test directory in the path D:\OCPJP\programs\NIO2\, so the code worked fine.

If the Test file/directory does not exist in the given path, you get a NoSuchFileException. But how can you figure out whether a file/directory exists on the given path? The Files class offers the exists() method to do that. You can also distinguish between a file and a directory using the isDirectory() method from the Files class. Listing 10-5 uses these methods.

Listing 10-5. PathExists.java

```java
import java.nio.file.Files;
import java.nio.file.LinkOption;
import java.nio.file.Path;
import java.nio.file.Paths;

class PathExists {
    public static void main(String[] args) {
        Path path = Paths.get(args[0]);

        if(Files.exists(path, LinkOption.NOFOLLOW_LINKS)) {
            System.out.println("The file/directory " + path.getFileName() + " exists");
            // check whether it is a file or a directory
            if(Files.isDirectory(path, LinkOption.NOFOLLOW_LINKS)) {
                System.out.println(path.getFileName() + " is a directory");
            }
```

```
        else {
            System.out.println(path.getFileName() + " is a file");
        }
    }
    else {
        System.out.println("The file/directory " + path.getFileName()
                    + " does not exist");
    }
    }
}
```

This program accepts a file/directory name from the command line and creates a Path object. Then, you use the exists() method from the Files class to find out whether the file/directory exists. The second parameter of the exists() method is link option, which is used to specify whether to follow symbolic links; in this case, you are not following symbolic links. If the file/directory associated with the input path exists, then you check whether the input path indicates a file or a directory, using the isDirectory() method of the Files class.

We ran this program with two different command-line arguments and got the following output (assume that PathExists.java is stored in the directory D:\OCPJP\programs\NIO2\src):

```
D:\OCPJP\programs\NIO2\src>java PathExists PathExists.java
The file/directory PathExists.java exists
PathExists.java is a file

D:\OCPJP\programs\NIO2\src>java PathExists D:\OCPJP\
The file/directory OCPJP exists
OCPJP is a directory

D:\OCPJP\programs\NIO2\src>java PathExists D:\
The file/directory null exists
null is a directory
```

In this output, you may have noticed the behavior when the root name (drive name in Windows, in this case) is given as an argument. A root name is a directory, but path.getFileName() returns null if the path is a root name—hence the result.

Existing files may not allow you to read, write, or execute based on your credentials. You can check the ability of a program to read, write, or execute programmatically. The Files class provides the methods isReadable(), isWritable(), and isExecutable() to do that. Listing 10-6 uses these methods: for this program, create a file named readonly.txt with the permissions readable and executable but not writable.

Listing 10-6. FilePermissions.java

```
import java.nio.file.Files;
import java.nio.file.Path;
import java.nio.file.Paths;

class FilePermissions {
    public static void main(String[] args) {
        Path path = Paths.get(args[0]);
        System.out.printf( "Readable: %b, Writable: %b, Executable: %b ",
            Files.isReadable(path), Files.isWritable(path), Files.isExecutable(path));
    }
}
```

Let's execute this program with two different inputs. Here is the output:

```
D:\OCPJP\programs\NIO2\src>java FilePermissions readonly.txt
Readable: true, Writable: false, Executable: true
D:\OCPJP\programs\NIO2\src>java FilePermissions FilePermissions.java
Readable: true, Writable: true, Executable: true
```

For the readonly.txt file, the permissions are readable and executable but not writable. The file FilePermissions.java has all three permissions: readable, writable, and executable.

You can use many other methods to fetch file properties. Let's use the getAttribute() method to get some attributes of a file. The method takes a variable number of parameters: a Path object, an attribute name, and the link options (see Listing 10-7).

Listing 10-7. FileAttributes.java

```java
import java.io.IOException;
import java.nio.file.Files;
import java.nio.file.LinkOption;
import java.nio.file.Path;
import java.nio.file.Paths;

class FileAttributes {
    public static void main(String[] args) {
        Path path = Paths.get(args[0]);
        try {
            Object object = Files.getAttribute(path, "creationTime",
                                   LinkOption.NOFOLLOW_LINKS);
            System.out.println("Creation time: " + object);

            object = Files.getAttribute(path, "lastModifiedTime", LinkOption.NOFOLLOW_LINKS);
            System.out.println("Last modified time: " + object);

            object = Files.getAttribute(path, "size", LinkOption.NOFOLLOW_LINKS);
            System.out.println("Size: " + object);

            object = Files.getAttribute(path, "dos:hidden", LinkOption.NOFOLLOW_LINKS);
            System.out.println("isHidden: " + object);

            object = Files.getAttribute(path, "isDirectory", LinkOption.NOFOLLOW_LINKS);
            System.out.println("isDirectory: " + object);
        } catch (IOException e) {
            e.printStackTrace();
        }
    }
}
```

Let's first execute this program by giving the name of this program and then look at what happens:

```
D:\> java FileAttributes FileAttributes.java
Creation time: 2012-10-06T10:20:10.34375Z
Last modified time: 2012-10-06T10:21:54.859375Z
Size: 914
isHidden: false
isDirectory: false
```

The tricky part of the example is the second parameter of the getAttribute() method. You need to provide a correct attribute name to extract the associated value. The expected string should be specified in view:attribute format, where view is the type of FileAttributeView and attribute is the name of the attribute supported by view. If no view is specified, it is assumed to be basic. In this case, you specify all attributes belonging to a basic view except one attribute from the dos view. If you do not specify the correct view name, you get an UnsupportedOperationException; and if you mess up the attribute name, you get an IllegalArgumentException.

For example, if you type **sized** instead of **size**, you'll get this exception:

```
Exception in thread "main" java.lang.IllegalArgumentException: 'sized' not recognized
[...stack trace elided...]
```

Yyou now know how to read metadata associated with files using the getAttribute() method. However, if you want to read many attributes, calling getAttribute() for each attribute might not be a good idea (from a performance standpoint). In this case, Java 7 offers a solution: an API—readAttributes()—to read the attributes in one shot. The API comes in two flavors:

```
Map<String,Object> readAttributes(Path path, String attributes, LinkOption... options)

<A extends BasicFileAttributes> A readAttributes(Path path, Class<A> type, LinkOption...
options)
```

The first method returns a Map of attribute-value pairs and takes variable-length parameters. The attributes parameter is the key parameter where you specify what you want to retrieve. This parameter is similar to what you use in the getAttribute() method; however, here you can specify a list of attributes, and you can also use an asterisk (*) to specify all attributes. For instance, using * means all attributes of the default FileAttributeView, such as BasicFileAttributes (specified as basic-file-attributes). Another example is dos:*, which refers to all attributes of dos file attributes.

The second method uses generic syntax (Chapter 4). The second parameter here takes a class from the BasicFileAttributes hierarchy, which is discussed shortly. The method returns an instance from the BasicFileAttributes hierarchy.

The file-attributes hierarchy is shown in Figure 10-1. BasicFileAttributes is the base interface from which DosFileAttributes and PosixFileAttributes are derived. Note that these attribute interfaces are provided in the java.nio.file.attribute package.

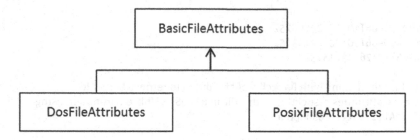

Figure 10-1. *The hierarchy of BasicFileAttributes*

As you can see, the BasicFileAttributes interface defines the basic attributes supported by all common platforms. However, specific platforms define their own file attributes, which are captured by DosFileAttributes and PosixFileAttributes. You can specify any one of these interfaces to retrieve associated file attributes. Listing 10-8 contains a program to retrieve all attributes of a file using BasicFileAttributes.

Listing 10-8. FileAttributes2.java

```java
import java.io.IOException;
import java.nio.file.Files;
import java.nio.file.Path;
import java.nio.file.Paths;
import java.nio.file.attribute.BasicFileAttributes;

class FileAttributes2 {
    public static void main(String[] args) {
        Path path = Paths.get(args[0]);
        try {
            BasicFileAttributes fileAttributes =
                Files.readAttributes(path, BasicFileAttributes.class);
            System.out.println("File size: " + fileAttributes.size());
            System.out.println("isDirectory: " + fileAttributes.isDirectory());
            System.out.println("isRegularFile: " + fileAttributes.isRegularFile());
            System.out.println("isSymbolicLink: " + fileAttributes.isSymbolicLink());
            System.out.println("File last accessed time: " + fileAttributes.lastAccessTime());
            System.out.println("File last modified time: " +
                fileAttributes.lastModifiedTime());
            System.out.println("File creation time: " + fileAttributes.creationTime());
        } catch (IOException e) {
            e.printStackTrace();
        }
    }
}
```

The following is some sample output from the program:

```
D:\>java FileAttributes2 FileAttributes2.java
File size: 904
isDirectory: false
isRegularFile: true
```

```
isSymbolicLink: false
File last accessed time: 2012-10-06T10:28:29.0625Z
File last modified time: 2012-10-06T10:28:22.4375Z
File creation time: 2012-10-06T10:26:39.1875Z
```

You use the readAttribute() method along with BasicFileAttributes to retrieve basic file properties. Similarly, you can retrieve attributes associated with a file in a DOS or Unix environment using DosFileAttributes and PosixFileAttributes, respectively.

Copying a File

Now let's try copying a file/directory from one location to another. This task is easy to accomplish: just call Files.copy() to copy the file from source to target. Here is the signature of this method:

```
Path copy(Path source, Path target, CopyOption... options)
```

Listing 10-9 uses this method to write a simple file-copy program.

Listing 10-9. FileCopy.java

```java
import java.io.IOException;
import java.nio.file.Files;
import java.nio.file.Path;
import java.nio.file.Paths;

public class FileCopy {
    public static void main(String[] args) {
        if(args.length != 2){
            System.out.println("usage: FileCopy <source-path> <destination-path>");
            System.exit(1);
        }
        Path pathSource = Paths.get(args[0]);
        Path pathDestination = Paths.get(args[1]);
        try {
            Files.copy(pathSource, pathDestination);
            System.out.println("Source file copied successfully");
        } catch (IOException e) {
            e.printStackTrace();
        }
    }
}
```

Let's execute it and see whether it works.

```
D:\> java FileCopy FileCopy.java Backup.java
Source file copied successfully
```

Yes, it's working. Try running it again with the same arguments:

```
D:\OCPJP\programs\NIO2\src>java FileCopy FileCopy.java Backup.java
java.nio.file.FileAlreadyExistsException: Backup.java
        at sun.nio.fs.WindowsFileCopy.copy(Unknown Source)
        [...stack trace elided...]
```

Oops! What happened? When you try copying the file for the second time, you get a FileAlreadyExistsException because the destination file already exists. What if you want to overwrite the existing file? The solution: you need to tell the copy() method that you would like to overwrite an existing file. In Listing 10-9, change copy() as follows:

```
Files.copy(pathSource, pathDestination, StandardCopyOption.REPLACE_EXISTING);
```

You specify an additional argument (because the copy() method supports variable arguments) to tell the method that you want to overwrite a file if it already exists. Run this program and see whether it works:

```
D:\>java FileCopy FileCopy.java Backup.java
Source file copied successfully

D:\>java FileCopy FileCopy.java Backup.java
Source file copied successfully
```

Yes, it works. Now, try to copy a file to a new directory:

```
D:\OCPJP\programs\NIO2\src>java FileCopy FileCopy.java bak\Backup.java
java.nio.file.NoSuchFileException: FileCopy.java -> bak\Backup.java
        [...stack trace elided ...]
```

Well, here you tried to copy a file back to a directory that does not exist. So, you got the NoSuchFileException. Not just the given directory but also all intermediate directories on a path must exist for the copy() method to succeed.

All the directories (except the last one, if you are copying a directory) on the specified path must exist to avoid NoSuchFileException.

What if you try copying a directory? It will work, but remember that it will only copy the top-level directory, not the files/directories contained *within* that directory.

If you copy a directory using the copy() method, it does not copy the files/directories contained in the source directory; you need to explicitly copy them to the destination folder.

Moving a File

Moving a file is similar to copying a file; for this purpose, you can use the Files.move() method. The signature of this method is as follows:

```
Path move(Path source, Path target, CopyOption... options)
```

Listing 10-10 contains a small program that uses this method. Note that once the move() method successfully executes, the source file no longer exists.

Listing 10-10. FileMove.java

```java
import java.io.IOException;
import java.nio.file.Files;
import java.nio.file.Path;
import java.nio.file.Paths;
import java.nio.file.StandardCopyOption;

public class FileMove {
    public static void main(String[] args) {
        if(args.length != 2){
            System.out.println("usage: FileMove <source-path> <destination-path>");
            System.exit(-1);
        }
        Path pathSource = Paths.get(args[0]);
        Path pathDestination = Paths.get(args[1]);
        try {
            Files.move(pathSource, pathDestination, StandardCopyOption.REPLACE_EXISTING);
            System.out.println("Source file moved successfully");
        } catch (IOException e) {
            e.printStackTrace();
        }
    }
}
```

This is how to execute this program (assuming that a file named text.txt exists in the current directory):

```
D:\OCPJP\programs\NIO2\src> java FileMove text.txt newtext.txt
Source file moved successfully
```

Here are some observations about the move() method:

- Like the copy() method, the move() method does not overwrite the existing destination file unless you specify that it should do so using REPLACE_EXISTING.

- If you move a symbolic link, the link itself is moved, not the target file of the link. It is important to note that in the case of copy(), if you specify a symbolic link, the target of the link is copied, not the link itself.

- A non-empty directory can be moved if moving the directory does not require moving the containing files/directories. For instance, moving a directory from one physical drive to another may be unsuccessful (an IOException will be thrown). If moving a directory is successful, then all the contained files/directories are also moved.

- You can specify move() as an atomic operation using the ATOMIC_MOVE copy option. When you specify an atomic move, you are assured that either the move completes successfully or the source continues to be present. If move() is performed as a non-atomic operation and it fails while in process, the state of both files is unknown and undefined.

Deleting a File

The Files class provides a delete() method to delete a file/directory/symbolic link. Listing 10-11 contains a simple program to delete a specified file.

Listing 10-11. FileDelete.java

```
import java.io.IOException;
import java.nio.file.Files;
import java.nio.file.Path;
import java.nio.file.Paths;

public class FileDelete {
    public static void main(String[] args) {
        if(args.length != 1){
            System.out.println("usage: FileDelete <source-path>");
            System.exit(1);
        }
        Path pathSource = Paths.get(args[0]);
        try {
            Files.delete(pathSource);
            System.out.println("File deleted successfully");
        } catch (IOException e) {
            e.printStackTrace();
        }
    }
}
```

It prints the following when executed:

```
D:\> java FileDelete log.txt
File deleted successfully
```

There are a few points to remember when using the Files.delete() method. In the case of a directory, the delete() method should be invoked on an empty directory; otherwise, the method will fail. In the case of a symbolic link, the link is deleted, not the target file of the link. The file you intend to delete must exist; otherwise you get a NoSuchFileException. If you silently delete a file and do not want to be bothered with this exception, then you may use the deleteIfExists() method, which does not complain if the file does not exist and deletes the file if it exists. Also, if a file is read-only, some platforms may prevent you from deleting the file.

303

Points to Remember

Remember these points to help you pass the OCPJP 8 exam.

- Do not confuse File with Files, and Path with Paths: they are different. File is an old class (Java 4) that represents file/directory path names, whereas Files was introduced in Java 7 as a utility class with comprehensive support for I/O APIs. The Path interface represents a file/directory path and defines a useful list of methods. However, the Paths class is a utility class that offers only two methods (both to get the Path object).

- The file or directory represented by a Path object may not exist. Other than methods such as toRealPath(), methods in Path do not require that the underlying file or directory be present for a Path object.

- You learned how to perform a copy for files/directories. However, it is not necessary to perform a copy on only two files/directories. You can take input from an InputStream and write to a file, or you can take input from a file and copy to an OutputStream. The methods copy(InputStream, Path, CopyOptions...) and copy(Path, OutputStream, CopyOptions...) can be used here.

Using the Stream API with NIO.2

Certification Objective

Use Stream API with NIO.2

Numerous enhancements to the JDK in Java 8 simplify programming using NIO.2. This section discusses some of the important enhancements to the java.nio package in Java 8.

Using the list() Method in the Files Class

Let's start by using the Files.list() method added in Java 8 to list all the files in the current directory (see Listing 10-12). Underneath, it uses a DirectoryStream, and hence the close() method must be called to release the I/O resource. This program uses the stream with a try-with-resources statement that automatically closes the stream.

Listing 10-12. ListFiles.java

```java
import java.nio.file.Files;
import java.nio.file.Path;
import java.nio.file.Paths;
import java.io.IOException;
import java.util.stream.Stream;

class ListFiles {
    public static void main(String []args) throws IOException {
        try(Stream<Path> entries = Files.list(Paths.get("."))) {
            entries.forEach(System.out::println);
        }
    }
}
```

It printed the files in the current directory:

```
./ListFiles.class
./ListFiles.java
... (rest of the output elided)
```

The list() method is declared as follows:

```
static Stream<Path> list(Path dir) throws IOException
```

Because the list() method returns a Stream, you can use any of the numerous methods provided in the Stream interface, including map(), filter(), findFirst(), findAny(), distinct(), sorted(), allMatch(), noneMatch(), and anyMatch().

This code segment is a modified version of Listing 10-12 that prints the absolute paths of the files:

```
Files.list(Paths.get("."))
    .map(path -> path.toAbsolutePath())
    .forEach(System.out::println);
```

The result is as follows:

```
D:\OCPJP\NIO2\src\ListFiles.class
D:\OCPJP\NIO2\src\ListFiles.java
... (rest of the output elided)
```

Note that the list() method does not recursively traverse the entries in the given Path. To recursively traverse the directories, you can use the Files.walk() method:

```
Files.walk(Paths.get(".")).forEach(System.out::println);
```

The Files.walk() method is an overloaded method:

```
static Stream<Path> walk(Path path, FileVisitOption... options) throws IOException
static Stream<Path> walk(Path path, int maxDepth, FileVisitOption... options) throws
IOException
```

The FileVisitOption has one enumeration value: FileVisitOption.FOLLOW_LINKS. You can pass that to the walk() method. You can also specify maxDepth: the limit on the nesting level for recursively traversing the directory entries (see Listing 10-13).

Listing 10-13. CountEntriesRecur.java

```
import java.nio.file.FileVisitOption;
import java.nio.file.Files;
import java.nio.file.Path;
import java.nio.file.Paths;
import java.io.IOException;
import java.util.stream.Stream;
```

```
class CountEntriesRecur {
    public static void main(String []args) throws IOException {
        try(Stream<Path> entries =
            Files.walk(Paths.get("."), 4, FileVisitOption.FOLLOW_LINKS)) {
                long numOfEntries = entries.count();
                System.out.printf("Found %d entries in the current path", numOfEntries);
        }
    }
}
```

On our machine, this program printed the following:

```
Found 179 entries in the current path
```

This code gives an arbitrary limit of 4 for the nesting depth as the second argument to the Files.walk() method.

Finally, let's use the Files.find() method to list the files that match a given condition (Listing 10-14).

Listing 10-14. FindFiles.java

```
import java.nio.file.Files;
import java.nio.file.Path;
import java.nio.file.Paths;
import java.io.IOException;
import java.nio.file.attribute.BasicFileAttributes;
import java.util.function.BiPredicate;
import java.util.stream.Stream;

class FindFiles {
    public static void main(String []args) throws IOException {
        BiPredicate<Path, BasicFileAttributes> predicate = (path, attrs)
                -> attrs.isRegularFile() && path.toString().endsWith("class");
        try(Stream<Path> entries = Files.find(Paths.get("."), 4, predicate)) {
            entries.limit(100).forEach(System.out::println);
        }
    }
}
```

This program prints long output, so it is not given here.

This example used the limit() method on the Stream<Path> object to limit the number of entries processed when returned from the Files.find() method. The find() method takes the path to start searching from, the maximum depth to search, a BiPredicate, and an optional FileVisitOption as arguments:

```
static Stream<Path> find(Path path, int maxDepth, BiPredicate<Path,BasicFileAttributes>
 matcher, FileVisitOption... options) throws IOException
```

In this example, you are looking for files that end with a class extension, and you limit the number of entries to 100.

Using the lines() Method in the Files Class

Files.lines() is a very convenient method to read the contents of a file:

static Stream<String> lines(Path path)

Internally, it uses a Reader and hence must be closed after use. You use try-with-resources in Listing 10-15 to print the contents of the file whose name is passed as the argument.

Listing 10-15. Type.java

```java
import java.io.IOException;
import java.nio.file.Paths;
import java.nio.file.Files;
import java.util.Arrays;
import java.util.stream.Stream;

// implements a simplified version of "type" command provided in Windows;
// given a text file name(s) as argument, it prints the content of the file(s)

class Type {
    private static void processFile(String file) {
        try(Stream<String> lines = Files.lines(Paths.get(file))) {
            lines.forEach(System.out::println);
        } catch (IOException ioe) {
            System.err.println("IOException occurred when reading the file... exiting");
            System.exit(-1);
        }
    }

    public static void main(String[] files) throws IOException {
        if (files.length == 0) {
            System.err.println("pass the name of the file(s) as argument");
            System.exit(-1);
        }
        // process each file passed as argument
        Arrays.stream(files).forEach(Type::processFile);
    }
}
```

This code is much concise than the version you saw in the chapter on IO fundamentals (Listing 9-5 in Chapter 9).

Summary

Let's briefly review the key points from each certification objective in this chapter. Please read this section before you appear for the exam.

Use Path interface to operate on file and directory paths

- A Path object is a programming abstraction to represent the path of a file/directory.

- You can get an instance of Path using the get() method of the Paths class.

- Path provides two methods to compare Path objects: equals() and compareTo(). Even if two Path objects point to the same file/directory, the equals() method is not guaranteed to return true.

Use Files class to check, read, delete, copy, move, manage metadata of a file or directory

- You can check the existence of a file using the exists() method of the Files class.

- The Files class provides the methods isReadable(), isWritable(), and isExecutable() to check the ability of the program to read, write, and execute programmatically, respectively.

- You can retrieve the attributes of a file using the getAttributes() method.

- You can use the readAttributes() method of the Files class to read file attributes in bulk.

- The copy() method can be used to copy a file from one location to another. Similarly, the move() method moves a file from one location to another.

- While copying, all the directories (except the last one, if you are copying a directory) on the specified path must exist to avoid a NoSuchFileException.

- Use the delete() method to delete a file; use the deleteIfExists() method to delete a file only if it exists.

Use Stream API with NIO.2

- The Files.list() method returns a Stream<Path>. It does not recursively traverse the directories in the given Path.

- The Files.walk() method returns a Stream<Path> by recursively traversing the entries from the given Path; in one of its overloaded versions, you can also pass the maximum depth for such traversal and provide FileVisitOption.FOLLOW_LINKS as the third option.

- The Files.find() method returns a Stream<Path> by recursively traversing the entries from the given Path; it also takes the maximum depth to search, a BiPredicate, and an optional FileVisitOption as arguments.

- Files.lines() is a very convenient method to read the contents of a file. It returns a Stream<String>.

QUESTION TIME

1. **Consider the following program:**

```java
import java.nio.file.*;

public class PathInfo {
        public static void main(String[] args) {
                Path aFilePath = Paths.get("D:\\directory\\file.txt");
                // FILEPATH

                while(aFilePath.iterator().hasNext()) {
                        System.out.println("path element: " + aFilePath.
                        iterator().next());
                }
        }
}
```

   Assume that the file D:\directory\file.txt **exists in the underlying file system. Which one of the following options correctly describes the behavior of this program?**

   A. The program gives a compiler error in the line marked with the comment FILEPATH because the checked exception FileNotFoundException is not handled.

   B. The program gives a compiler error in the line marked with the comment FILEPATH because the checked exception InvalidPathException is not handled.

   C. The program gets into an infinite loop, printing "path element: directory" forever.

   D. The program prints the following:

   ```
   path element: directory
   path element: file.txt
   ```

2. **Consider the following program:**

```java
import java.nio.file.*;

class SubPath {
        public static void main(String []args) {
                Path aPath = Paths.get("D:\\OCPJP\\programs\\..\\NIO2\
                \src\\.\\SubPath.java");
                aPath = aPath.normalize();
                System.out.println(aPath.subpath(2, 3));
        }
}
```

This program prints the following:

A. ..

B. src

C. NIO2

D. NIO2\src

E. ..\NIO2

3. **Consider the following program:**

```java
import java.nio.file.*;
import java.io.IOException;

class PathExists {
        public static void main(String []args) throws IOException {
                Path aFilePath = Paths.get("D:\\directory\\file.txt");
                System.out.println(aFilePath.isAbsolute());
        }
}
```

Assuming that the file D:\\directory\\file.txt **does not exist, what will be the behavior of this program?**

A. This program prints `false`.

B. This program prints `true`.

C. This program crashes by throwing a `java.io.IOException`.

D. This program crashes by throwing a `java.nio.file.NoSuchFileException`.

4. **Given this code segment (assume that necessary `import` statements are provided in the program that contains this code segment)**

```java
Stream<String> lines = Files.lines(Paths.get("./text.txt"))
// line n1
```

If a file named text.txt **exists in the current directory in which you are running this code segment, which one of the following statements will result in printing the first line of the file's contents?**

A. `lines.limit(1).forEach(System.out::println);`

B. `lines.forEach(System.out::println);`

C. `lines.println();`

D. `lines.limit(1).println();`

E. `lines.forEach(1);`

5. **Consider the following code segment:**

```
try(Stream<Path> entries = Files.find(Paths.get("."), 4, predicate)) {
    entries.forEach(System.out::println);
}
```

Which one of the following is a valid definition of the variable predicate that can be used in this code segment?

A. `BiPredicate<Path, BasicFileAttributes> predicate = (path, attrs)`
   `-> true;`

B. `Predicate<Path> predicate = (path) -> true`

C. `Predicate<BasicFileAttributes> predicate = (attrs) -> attrs.`
   `isRegularFile();`

D. `Predicate predicate = FileVisitOption.FOLLOW_LINKS;`

Answers:

1. C. The program gets into an infinite loop, printing "path element: directory" forever.

   In the `while` loop, you use `iterator()` to get a temporary iterator object. So, the call to `next()` on the temporary variable is lost, and the `while` loop gets into an infinite loop. In other words, the following loop terminates after printing the directory and `file.txt` parts of the path:

   ```
   Iterator<Path> paths = aFilePath.iterator();
   while(paths.hasNext()) {
       System.out.println("path element: " + paths.next());
   }
   ```

   Option A is wrong because the `Paths.get` method does not throw `FileNotFoundException`.

   Option B is wrong because `InvalidPathException` is a `RuntimeException`. Also, even if the file path does not exist in the underlying file system, this exception will not be thrown when the program is executed.

   Option D is wrong because the program gets into an infinite loop.

2. B. src

   The `normalize()` method removes redundant name elements in the given path, so after the call to the `normalize()` method, the `aPath` value is `D:\OCPJP\NIO2\src\SubPath.java`.

   The `subpath(int beginIndex, int endIndex)` method returns a path based on the values of `beginIndex` and `endIndex`. The name that is closest to the root has index 0; note that the root itself (in this case, `D:\`) is not considered an element in the path. Hence, the name elements "OCPJP", "NIO2", "src", and "SubPath.java" are in index positions 0, 1, 2, and 3, respectively.

Note that `beginIndex` is the index of the first element, inclusive of that element; `endIndex` is the index of the last element, exclusive of that element. Hence, the subpath is `src`, which is at index position 2 in this path.

3. B. This program prints: true

   To use methods such as `isAbsolute()`, the actual file need not exist. Because the path represents an absolute path (and not a relative path), this program prints true.

4. A. `lines.limit(1).forEach(System.out::println);`

   The `limit(1)` method truncates the result to one line; and the `forEach()` method, when passed with the `System.out::println` method reference, prints that line to the console. Option B prints all the lines in the given file and thus is the wrong answer. The code segments given in the other three options will result in compiler errors.

5. A. `BiPredicate<Path, BasicFileAttributes> predicate = (path, attrs) -> true;`

   The `find()` method takes the path to start searching from, the maximum depth to search, a `BiPredicate`, and an optional `FileVisitOption` as arguments:

   ```
   static Stream<Path> find(Path path, int maxDepth, BiPredicate<Path,
   BasicFileAttributes>
   matcher, FileVisitOption... options) throws IOException
   ```

   Option A provides a definition of `BiPredicate` and hence it is the correct answer. Using the other options will result in a compiler error.

■ ■ ■

CHAPTER 11

Java Concurrency

Certification Objectives

Create worker threads using Runnable, Callable, and use an ExecutorService to concurrently execute tasks

Identify potential threading problems among deadlock, starvation, livelock, and race conditions

Use synchronized keyword and java.util.concurrent.atomic package to control the order of thread execution

Use java.util.concurrent collections and classes including CyclicBarrier and CopyOnWriteArrayList

Use parallel Fork/Join Framework

Use parallel Streams including reduction, decomposition, merging processes, pipelines, and performance

Concurrency is gaining importance with more widespread use of multicore processors. The Latin root of the word *concurrency* means "running together." In programming, you can have multiple threads running in parallel in a program executing different tasks at the same time. When used correctly, concurrency can improve the performance and responsiveness of the application, and hence it is a powerful and useful feature. In this chapter, we use the terms multi-threading and concurrency interchangeably.

From the beginning, Java supported concurrency in the form of low-level threads management, locks, synchronization, and APIs for concurrency. Since 5.0, Java also supports high-level concurrency APIs in its java.util.concurrent package. From version 8.0, Java has gotten even better support for concurrency with the introduction of parallel streams.

The OCPJP 8 exam objectives cover a wide range of topics related to concurrency, including different ways of creating worker threads to using parallel streams. You can expect many questions from this topic in your exam. For this reason, we will discuss Java's concurrency support in detail in this chapter.

Creating Threads to Execute Tasks Concurrently

Certification Objective

Create worker threads using Runnable, Callable, and use an ExecutorService to concurrently execute tasks

The Thread and Object classes and the Runnable interface provide the necessary support for concurrency in Java. The Thread class has methods such as run(), start(), and sleep() that are useful for multi-threading (Table 11-1 lists important methods in the Thread class). The Object class has methods such as wait() and notify() that support concurrency. Since every class in Java derives from the Object class, all the objects have some basic multi-threading capabilities. For example, you can acquire a lock on *any* object in Java (using synchronized keyword, which we'll discuss later in this chapter). However, to *create* a thread, this basic support from Object is not useful. For that, a class should extend the Thread class or implement the Runnable interface. Both Thread and Runnable are in the java.lang package, so you don't have to import these classes explicitly for writing multi-threaded programs.

Table 11-1. *Important Methods in the Thread Class*

Method	Method Type	Short Description
Thread currentThread()	Static method	Returns reference to the current thread.
String getName()	Instance method	Returns the name of the current thread.
int getPriority()	Instance method	Returns the priority value of the current thread.
void join(), void join(long), void join(long, int)	Overloaded instance methods	The current thread invoking join on another thread waits until the other thread completes. You can optionally give the timeout in milliseconds (given in long) or timeout in milliseconds as well as nanoseconds (given in long and int).
void run()	Instance method	Once you start a thread (using the start() method), the run() method will be called when the thread is ready to execute.
void setName(String)	Instance method	Changes the name of the thread to the given name in the argument.
void setPriority(int)	Instance method	Sets the priority of the thread to the given argument value.
void sleep(long) void sleep(long, int)	Overloaded static methods	Makes the current thread sleep for given milliseconds (given in long) or for given milliseconds and nanoseconds (given in long and int).
void start()	Instance method	Starts the thread; JVM calls the run() method of the thread.
String toString()	Instance method	Returns the string representation of the thread; the string has the thread's name, priority, and its group.

Creating Threads

Let us now create threads using the Thread class and Runnable interface. We will discuss how to create worker threads using Callable and ExecutorService later in this chapter.

Creating Threads by Extending the Thread Class

To extend the Thread class, you need to override the run() method. If you don't override the run() method, the default run() method from the Thread class will be called, which does nothing. To override the run() method, you need to declare it as public; it takes no arguments and has a void return type; in other words, it should be declared as public void run().

You can create a thread by invoking the start() method on an object of the Thread class (Listing 11-1). When the JVM schedules the thread, it will move the thread to a *runnable* state and then execute the run() method. When the run() method completes its execution and returns, the thread will terminate.

Listing 11-1. MyThread.java

```java
class MyThread extends Thread {
    public void run() {
        try {
            sleep(1000);
        }
        catch (InterruptedException ex) {
            ex.printStackTrace();
            // ignore the InterruptedException - this is perhaps the one of the
            // very few of the exceptions in Java which is acceptable to ignore
        }
        System.out.println("In run(); thread name is: " + getName());
    }
    public static void main(String args[])  {
        Thread myThread = new MyThread();
        myThread.start();
        System.out.println("In main(); thread name: " +
                Thread.currentThread().getName());
    }
}
```

This program prints the following:

```
In main(); thread name is: main
In run(); thread name is: Thread-0
```

In this example, the MyThread class extends the Thread class. You have overridden the run() method in this class. This run() method will be called when the thread runs. In the main() function, you create a new thread and start it using the start() method. An important note: you do not invoke the run() method directly. Instead you start the thread using the start() method; the run() method is invoked automatically by the JVM.

For printing the name of the thread, you can use the instance method getName(), which returns a String. Since main() is a static method, you don't have access to this reference. So you get the current thread name using the static method currentThread() in the Thread class (which returns a Thread object). Now you can call getName on that returned object. As you'll see later, the main() method is also executed as a thread! However, inside the run() method, you can directly call the getName() method: MyThread extends Thread, so all base class members are available in MyThread also.

Creating Threads by Implementing Runnable Interface

Another way to create a thread is to implement the Runnable interface. The Thread class itself implements the Runnable interface. The Runnable interface declares a sole method, run().Hence, when you implement the Runnable interface, you need to define the run() method. Remember Runnable does not declare the start() method. So, how do you create a thread if you implement the Runnable interface? Thread has an overloaded constructor, which takes a Runnable object as an argument. Listing 11-2 implements the Runnable interface and creates a Thread.

Listing 11-2. RunnableImpl.java

```java
class RunnableImpl implements Runnable {
    public void run() {
        System.out.println("In run(); thread name is: " +
                Thread.currentThread().getName());
    }

    public static void main(String args[]) throws Exception {
        Thread myThread = new Thread(new RunnableImpl());
        myThread.start();
        System.out.println("In main(); thread name is: " +
                Thread.currentThread().getName());
    }
}
```

This program prints:

```
In main(); thread name is: main
In run(); thread name is: Thread-0
```

You are implementing the run() method in this program. However, to get the name of the string, you must follow a round-about route and get the thread name with Thread.currentThread().getName(). In the main() method, to create a thread you must pass the object of the RunnableImpl class to the Thread constructor. The start() method starts the thread and the JVM later calls the run() method of the thread.

Thread Synchronization With synchronized Keyword

Certification Objective

Use synchronized keyword and java.util.concurrent.atomic package to control the order of thread execution

Java's synchronized keyword helps in thread synchronization. You can use it in two forms: synchronized blocks and synchronized methods. Why do we need to use the synchronized keyword? To avoid the problem of race conditions. Let us discuss this topic now.

Race Conditions

Threads share memory, and they can concurrently modify data. Since the modification can be done at the same time without safeguards, this can lead to unintuitive results.

When two or more threads are trying to access a variable and one of them wants to modify it, you get a problem known as a *race condition* (also known as *data race* or *race hazard*). Listing 11-3 shows an example of a race condition.

Listing 11-3. RaceCondition.java

```java
// This class exposes a publicly accessible counter
// to help demonstrate race condition problem
class Counter {
    public static long count = 0;
}

// This class implements Runnable interface
// Its run method increments the counter three times
class UseCounter implements Runnable {
    public void increment() {
        // increments the counter and prints the value
        // of the counter shared between threads
        Counter.count++;
        System.out.print(Counter.count + "  ");
    }
    public void run() {
        increment();
        increment();
        increment();
    }
}

// This class creates three threads
public class RaceCondition {
    public static void main(String args[]) {
        UseCounter c = new UseCounter();
        Thread t1 = new Thread(c);
        Thread t2 = new Thread(c);
        Thread t3 = new Thread(c);
        t1.start();
        t2.start();
        t3.start();
    }
}
```

In this program, there is a Counter class that has a static variable count. In the run() method of the UseCounter class, you increment the count three times by calling the increment() method. You create three threads in the main() function in the RaceCondition class and start it. You expect the program to print 1 to 9 sequentially as the threads run and increment the counters. However, when you run this program, it does print nine integer values, but the output looks like garbage! In a sample run, we got these values:

3 3 5 6 3 7 8 4 9

Note that the values will usually be different every time you run this program; when we ran it two more times, we got these outputs:

3 3 5 6 3 4 7 8 9

3 3 3 6 7 5 8 4 9

317

So, what is the problem?

The expression `Counter.count++` is a write operation, and the next `System.out.print` statement has a read operation for `Counter.count`. When the three threads execute, each of them has a local copy of the value `Counter.count` and when they update the `counter` with `Counter.count++`, they need not immediately reflect that value in the main memory (see Figure 11-1). In the next read operation of `Counter.count`, the local value of `Counter.count` is printed.

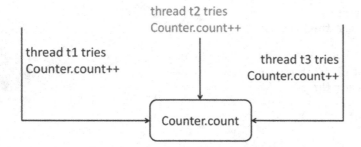

Figure 11-1. *Threads t1, t2, and t3 trying to change Counter.count, causing a race condition*

Therefore, this program suffers from the race condition problem. To avoid this problem, you need to ensure that a single thread does the write and read operations together (*atomically*). The section of code that is commonly accessed and modified by more than one thread is known as *critical section*. To avoid the race condition problem, you need to ensure that the critical section is executed by only one thread at a time.

How do you do that? By acquiring a lock on the object using the `synchronized` keyword, which we'll discuss now. Only a single thread can acquire a lock on an object at a time, and only that thread can execute the block of code (i.e., the critical section) protected by the lock. Until then, the other threads have to wait.

Synchronized Blocks

In synchronized blocks, you use the `synchronized` keyword for a reference variable and follow it by a block of code. A thread has to acquire a lock on the synchronized variable to enter the block; when the execution of the block completes, the thread releases the lock. For example, you can acquire a lock on `this` reference if the block of code is within a non-static method:

```
synchronized(this) {
        // code segment guarded by the mutex lock
}
```

What if an exception gets thrown inside the synchronized block? Will the lock get released? Yes, regardless of whether the block is executed fully or an exception is thrown, the lock will be automatically released by the JVM. With synchronized blocks, you can acquire a lock on a reference variable only. If you use a primitive type, you will get a compiler error.

Let us fix the race condition problem in Listing 11-3 by adding a synchronized block in the `increment()` method, as in:

```
// within the UseCounter class
public void increment() {
    // increments the counter and prints the value
    // of the counter shared between threads
```

```
    synchronized(this) {
        Counter.count++;
        System.out.print(Counter.count + "  ");
    }
}
```

With this change, the program prints value count incremented correctly:

```
1  2  3  4  5  6  7  8  9
```

In the increment() method, you acquire a lock on the this reference before reading and writing to Counter.count. So, it is not possible for more than one thread to execute these statements at the same time. Since only one thread can acquire a lock and execute the "critical section" code block, the counter is incremented by only one thread at a given time; as a result, the program prints the values 1 to 9 correctly. Without the synchronized block, three different threads would freely modify the variable and hence you will not get the values 1 to 9 printed correctly (because of the *race condition* problem which we discussed earlier).

Synchronized Methods

An entire method can be declared synchronized. In that case, when the method declared as synchronized is called, a lock is obtained on the object on which the method is called, and it is released when the method returns to the caller. Here is an example:

```
public synchronized void assign(int i) {
    val = i;
}
```

Now the assign() method is a synchronized method. If you call the assign() method, it will acquire the lock on the this reference implicitly and then execute the statement val = i;. What happens if some other thread acquired the lock already? Just like synchronized blocks, if the thread cannot get the lock, it will be *blocked* and the thread will wait until the lock becomes available.

A synchronized method is equivalent to a synchronized block if you enclose the whole method body in a synchronized(this) block. So, the equivalent assign() method using synchronized blocks is,

```
public void assign(int i) {
    synchronized(this) {
        val = i;
    }
}
```

You can declare static methods synchronized. However, what is the reference variable on which the lock is obtained? Remember that static methods do not have the implicit this reference. Static synchronized methods acquire locks on the class object. Every class is associated with an object of Class type, and you can access it using ClassName.class syntax. For example,

```
class SomeClass {
    private static int val;
    public static synchronized void assign(int i) {
        val = i;
    }
    // more members ...
}
```

In this case, the `assign` method acquires a lock on the `SomeClass.class` object when it is called. Now the equivalent `assign()` method using synchronized blocks can be written as

```
class SomeClass {
    private static int val;
    public static void assign(int i) {
        synchronized(SomeClass.class) {
            val = i;
        }
    }
    // more members ...
}
```

You cannot declare constructors synchronized; it will result in a compiler error. For example, for

```
class Synchronize {
    public synchronized Synchronize() { /* constructor body */}
    // more methods
}
```

you get this error:

```
Synchronize.java:2: modifier synchronized not allowed here
        public synchronized Synchronize() { /* constructor body */}
```

Why can't you declare constructors synchronized? The JVM ensures that only one thread can invoke a constructor call (for a specific constructor) at a given point in time. So, there is no need to declare a constructor synchronized. However, if you want, you can use synchronized blocks inside constructors.

Let's get back to the RaceCondition example in Listing 11-3. The `increment()` method in the UseCounter class can be rewritten as a synchronized method also:

```
// declaring the increment synchronized instead of using
// a synchronized statement for a block of code inside the method
public synchronized void increment() {
    Counter.count++;
    System.out.print(Counter.count + "  ");
}
```

This program prints:

```
1 2 3 4 5 6 7 8 9
```

The program prints the expected output correctly.

Beginners commonly misunderstand that a synchronized block obtains a lock for a block of code. Actually, the lock is obtained for an object and not for a piece of code. The obtained lock is held until all the statements in that block complete execution.

Threading Problems

Certification Objective

Identify potential threading problems among deadlock, starvation, livelock, and race conditions

Concurrent programming in threads is fraught with pitfalls and problems. We have already discussed race conditions that occur when we don't use locks in the previous section. In this section, let us discuss three more threading problems: deadlock, starvation, and livelock.

Deadlocks

Obtaining and using locks is tricky, and it can lead to lots of problems. One of the difficult (and common) problems is known as a *deadlock*. *A deadlock arises when locking threads result in a situation where they cannot proceed and thus wait indefinitely for others to terminate.* Say, one thread acquires a lock on resource r1 and waits to acquire another on resource r2. At the same time, say there is another thread that has already acquired r2 and is waiting to obtain a lock on r1. Neither of the threads can proceed until the other one releases the lock, which never happens—so they are stuck in a deadlock. Listing 11-4 shows how this situation can arise (using the example from the Cricket game).

Listing 11-4. DeadLock.java

```java
// Balls class has a globally accessible data member to hold the number of balls thrown
class Balls {
    public static long balls = 0;
}

// Runs class has a globally accessible data member to hold the number of runs scored
class Runs {
    public static long runs = 0;
}

// Counter class has two methods - IncrementBallAfterRun and IncrementRunAfterBall.
// For demonstrating deadlock, we call these two methods in the run method, so that
// locking can be requested in opposite order in these two methods
class Counter implements Runnable {
    // this method increments runs variable first and then increments the balls variable
    // since these variables are accessible from other threads,
    // we need to acquire a lock before processing them
    public void IncrementBallAfterRun() {
        // since we're updating runs variable first, first lock the Runs.class
        synchronized(Runs.class) {
            // lock on Balls.class before updating balls variable
            synchronized(Balls.class) {
                Runs.runs++;
                Balls.balls++;
            }
        }
    }
}
```

```java
    public void IncrementRunAfterBall() {
        // since we're updating balls variable first; so first lock Balls.class
        synchronized(Balls.class) {
            // acquire lock on Runs.class before updating runs variable
            synchronized(Runs.class) {
                Balls.balls++;
                Runs.runs++;
            }
        }
    }

    public void run() {
        // call these two methods which acquire locks in different order
        // depending on thread scheduling and the order of lock acquision,
        // a deadlock may or may not arise
        IncrementBallAfterRun();
        IncrementRunAfterBall();
    }
}

public class DeadLock {
    public static void main(String args[]) throws InterruptedException {
        Counter c = new Counter();
        // create two threads and start them at the same time
        Thread t1 = new Thread(c);
        Thread t2 = new Thread(c);
        t1.start();
        t2.start();
        System.out.println("Waiting for threads to complete execution...");
        t1.join();
        t2.join();
        System.out.println("Done.");
    }
}
```

If you execute this program, the program might run fine, or it might deadlock and never terminate (the occurrence of deadlock in this program depends on how threads are scheduled).

```
D:\> java DeadLock
Waiting for threads to complete execution...
Done.

D:\> java DeadLock
Waiting for threads to complete execution...
[deadlock - user pressed ctrl + c to terminate the program]

D:\> java DeadLock
Waiting for threads to complete execution...
Done.
```

In this example, there are two classes, Balls and Runs, with static members called balls and runs. The Counter class has two methods, IncrementBallAfterRun() and IncrementRunAfterBall(). They acquire locks on the Balls.class and Runs.class in the opposite order. The run() method calls these two methods consecutively. The main() method in the Dead class creates two threads and starts them.

When the threads t1 and t2 execute, they invoke the methods IncrementBallAfterRun and IncrementRunAfterBall. In these methods, locks are obtained in opposite order. It might happen that t1 acquires a lock on Runs.class and then waits to acquire a lock on Balls.class. Meanwhile, t2 might have acquired the Balls.class and now will be waiting to acquire a lock on the Runs.class. Therefore, this program can lead to a deadlock (Figure 11-2).

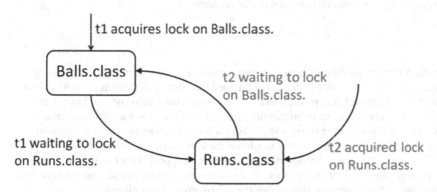

Figure 11-2. Deadlock between threads t1 and t2

It cannot be assured that this program will lead to a deadlock every time you execute this program. Why? You never know the sequence in which threads execute and the order in which locks are acquired and released. For this reason, such problems are said to be non-deterministic, and such problems cannot be reproduced consistently.

There are different strategies to deal with deadlocks, such as deadlock prevention, avoidance, or detection. For exam purposes, this is what you need to know about deadlocks:

- Deadlocks can arise in the context of multiple locks.

- If multiple locks are acquired in the same order, then a deadlock will not occur; however, if you acquire them in a different order, then deadlocks may occur.

- Deadlocks (just like other multi-threading problems) are non-deterministic; you cannot consistently reproduce deadlocks.

Avoid acquiring multiple locks. If you want to acquire multiple locks, make sure that they are acquired in the same order everywhere to avoid deadlocks.

Livelocks

To help understand livelocks, let's consider an analogy. Assume that there are two robotic cars that are programmed to automatically drive in the road. There is a situation where two robotic cars reach the two opposite ends of a narrow bridge. The bridge is so narrow that only one car can pass through at a time. The robotic cars are programmed such that they wait for the other car to pass through first. When both the cars attempt to enter the bridge at the same time, the following situation could happen: each car starts to enter the bridge, notices that the other car is attempting to do the same, and reverses! Note that the cars keep moving forward and backward and thus appear as if they're doing lots of work, but there is no progress made by either of the cars. This situation is called a *livelock*.

Consider two threads t1 and t2. Assume that thread t1 makes a change and thread t2 undoes that change. When both the threads t1 and t2 work, it will appear as though lots of work is getting done, but no progress is made. This situation is called a livelock in threads.

The similarity between livelocks and deadlocks is that the process "hangs" and the program never terminates. However, in a deadlock, the threads are stuck in the same state waiting for other thread(s) to release a shared resource; in a livelock, the threads keep executing a task, and there is continuous change in the process states, but the application as a whole does not make progress.

Lock Starvation

Consider the situation in which numerous threads have different priorities assigned to them (in the range of lowest priority, 1, to highest priority, 10, which is the range allowed for priority of threads in Java). When a lock is available, the thread scheduler will give priority to the threads with high priority over low priority. If there are many high-priority threads that want to obtain the lock and also hold the lock for long time periods, when will the low-priority threads get a chance to obtain the lock? In other words, in a situation where low-priority threads "starve" for a long time trying to obtain the lock is known as *lock starvation*.

There are many techniques available for detecting or avoiding threading problems like livelocks and starvation, but they are not within the scope of OCPJP 8 exam. From the exam perspective, you are expected to know the different kinds of threading problems that we've already covered in this chapter.

Using java.util.concurrent.atomic Package

Certification Objective

Use synchronized keyword and java.util.concurrent.atomic package to control the order of thread execution

The java.util.concurrent package has two subpackages: java.util.concurrent.atomic and java.util.concurrent.locks. In this section we discuss atomic variables in java.util.concurrent.atomic package from the OCPJP 8 exam perspective.

Often you can see code that acquires and releases locks for implementing primitive/simple operations like incrementing a variable, decrementing a variable, and so on? (We have already seen an example on incrementing an integer variable when we discussed synchronized keyword earlier in this chapter.) Acquiring and releasing locks for such primitive operations is not efficient. In such cases, Java provides an efficient alternative in the form of atomic variables.

Here is a list of some of the classes in this package and their short description:

- AtomicBoolean: Atomically updatable Boolean value.

- AtomicInteger: Atomically updatable int value; inherits from the Number class.

- AtomicIntegerArray: An int array in which elements can be updated atomically.

- AtomicLong: Atomically updatable long value; inherits from Number class.

- AtomicLongArray: A long array in which elements can be updated atomically.

- AtomicReference<V>: An atomically updatable object reference of type V.

- AtomicReferenceArray<E>: An atomically updatable array that can hold object references of type E (E refers to the base type of elements).

Only AtomicInteger and AtomicLong extend from Number class but not AtomicBoolean. All other classes in the java.util.concurrent.atomic subpackage inherit directly from the Object class.

Of the classes in the java.util.concurrency.atomic subpackage, AtomicInteger and AtomicLong are the most important. Table 11-2 lists important methods in the AtomicInteger class. (The methods in AtomicLong are analogous to these.)

Table 11-2. *Important Methods in the AtomicInteger Class*

Method	Short Description
AtomicInteger()	Creates an instance of AtomicInteger with initial value 0.
AtomicInteger(int initVal)	Creates an instance of AtomicInteger with initial value initVal.
int get()	Returns the integer value held in this object.
void set(int newVal)	Resets the integer value held in this object to newVal.
int getAndSet(int newValue)	Returns the current int value held in this object and sets the value held in this object to newVal.
boolean compareAndSet(int expect, int update)	Compares the int value of this object to the expect value, and if they are equal, sets the int value of this object to the update value.
int getAndIncrement()	Returns the current value of the integer value in this object and increments the integer value in this object. Similar to the behavior of i++ where i is an int.
int getAndDecrement()	Returns the current value of the integer value in this object and decrements the integer value in this object. Similar to the behavior of i-- where i is an int.
int getAndAdd(int delta)	Returns the integer value held in this object and adds given delta value to the integer value.
int incrementAndGet()	Increments the current value of the integer value in this object and returns that value. Similar to the behavior of ++i where i is an int.
int decrementAndGet()	Decrements the current integer value in this object and returns that value. Similar to behavior of --i where i is an int.
int addAndGet(int delta)	Adds the delta value to the current value of the integer in this object and returns that value.
int intValue() long longValue() float floatValue() double doubleValue()	Casts the current int value of the object and returns it as int, long, float, or double values.

Let's try out an example to understand how to use `AtomicInteger` or `AtomicLong`. Assume that you have a counter value that is public and accessible by all threads. How do you update or access this common counter value safely without introducing the race condition problem (discussed earlier in this chapter)? Obviously, you can use the synchronized keyword to ensure that the critical section (the code that modifies the counter value) is accessed by only one thread at a given point in time. The critical section will be very small, as in

```java
public void run() {
        synchronized(SharedCounter.class) {
                SharedCounter.count++;
        }
}
```

However, this code is inefficient since it acquires and releases the lock every time just to increment the value of count. Alternatively, if you declare count as `AtomicInteger` or `AtomicLong` (whichever is suitable). The classes such as AtomicInteger do not use a lock; rather, they internally use volatile variables and a low-level mechanism known as Compare-And-Set (CAS). For this reason, using AtomicInteger and related classes is faster than using locks using synchronized keyword.

Listing 11-5 shows how to use `AtomicLong` in practice.

Listing 11-5. AtomicVariableTest.java

```java
import java.util.concurrent.atomic.AtomicInteger;

// Class to demonstrate how mutating "normal" (i.e., thread unsafe) integers
// and mutating "atomic" (i.e., thread safe) integers are different:
// Mutating a shared Integer object without locks can result in a race condition;
// however, mutating a shared AtomicInteger will not result in a race conditiond.

class Counter {
    public static Integer integer = new Integer(0);
    public static AtomicInteger atomicInteger = new AtomicInteger(0);
}

class AtomicVariableTest {
    static class Incrementer extends Thread {
        public void run() {
            Counter.integer++;
            Counter.atomicInteger.incrementAndGet();
        }
    }
    static class Decrementer extends Thread {
        public void run() {
            Counter.integer--;
            Counter.atomicInteger.decrementAndGet();
        }
    }
    public static void main(String []args) throws InterruptedException {
        Thread incrementerThread[] = new Incrementer[1000];
        Thread decrementerThread[] = new Decrementer[1000];
```

```
    for(int i = 0; i < 1000; i++) {
        incremeterThread[i] = new Incrementer();
        decrementerThread[i] = new Decrementer();
        incremeterThread[i].start();
        decrementerThread[i].start();
    }
    for(int i = 0; i < 1000; i++) {
        incremeterThread[i].join();
        decrementerThread[i].join();
    }
    System.out.printf("Integer value = %d AtomicInteger value = %d ",
        Counter.integer, Counter.atomicInteger.get());
    }
}
```

The actual output depends on thread scheduling. In different runs it printed the following outputs:

```
Integer value = -2 AtomicInteger value = 0
Integer value = 2 AtomicInteger value = 0
Integer value = -1 AtomicInteger value = 0
Integer value = -1 AtomicInteger value = 0
Integer value = 0 AtomicInteger value = 0
```

Let's analyze this program. The Counter class has two data members—one of type Integer and the other of type AtomicInteger—with the same initial value 0.

There are two Thread classes. The Incrementer class has run() method that increments Integer and AtomicInteger values. On the other hand, Decrementer class has run() method that decrements Integer and AtomicInteger values.

In this output, notice that incrementing the Integer object could result in a race condition: the final value of Integer or AtomicInteger after incrementing and decrementing an equal number of times should always be 0–if not we have a race condition. As you can observe from the output, sometimes for Integer object it is 0 (meaning no race condition), but most of the time it is not equal to 0 (which means it has race condition). However, for AtomicInteger, the result is always zero (meaning that it has no race condition). In other words, this program shows that it is safe to manipulate an AtomicInteger value without any locks.

Use java.util.concurrent Collections

Certification Objective

Use java.util.concurrent collections and classes including CyclicBarrier and CopyOnWriteArrayList

There are many classes and interfaces in the java.util.concurrent package that provide high-level APIs for concurrent programming. In this section, we will mainly discuss synchronizer classes provided in this package. Following that, we will briefly cover the important concurrent collection classes provided in the java.util.concurrent package.

You already understand the low-level concurrency constructs such as the use of the synchronized keyword and using Runnable interfaces for creating threads. In the case of a shared resource that needs to be accessed by multiple threads, access and modifications to the shared resource need to be protected.

When you use the synchronized keyword, you employ mutexes to synchronize between threads for safe shared access. Threads also often needed to coordinate their executions to complete a bigger higher-level task. It is possible to build higher-level abstractions for thread synchronization. These high-level abstractions for synchronizing activities of two or more threads are known as *synchronizers*. Synchronizers internally make use of the existing low-level APIs for thread coordination.

The synchronizers provided in the java.util.concurrent library and their uses are:

- A Semaphore controls access to shared resources. A semaphore maintains a counter to specify number of resources that the semaphore controls.

- CountDownLatch allows one or more threads to wait for a countdown to complete.

- The Exchanger class is meant for exchanging data between two threads. This class is useful when two threads need to synchronize between each other and continuously exchange data.

- CyclicBarrier helps provide a synchronization point where threads may need to wait at a predefined execution point until all other threads reach that point.

- Phaser is a useful feature when few independent threads have to work in phases to complete a task.

The OCPJP 8 exam objective covers only the CyclicBarrier class and we discuss it with the help of an example in this section.

CyclicBarrier

There are many situations in concurrent programming where threads may need to wait at a predefined execution point until all other threads reach that point. CyclicBarrier helps provide such a synchronization point; see Table 11-3 for the important methods in this class.

Table 11-3. *Important Methods in the CyclicBarrier Class*

Method	Short Description
CyclicBarrier(int numThreads)	Creates a CyclicBarrier object with the number of threads waiting on it specified. Throws IllegalArgumentException if numThreads is negative or zero.
CyclicBarrier(int parties, Runnable barrierAction)	Same as the previous constructor; this constructor additionally takes the thread to call when the barrier is reached.
int await() int await(long timeout, TimeUnit unit)	Blocks until the specified number of threads have called await() on this barrier. The method returns the arrival index of this thread. This method can throw an InterruptedException if the thread is interrupted while waiting for other threads or a BrokenBarrierException if the barrier was broken for some reason (for example, another thread was timed-out or interrupted).The overloaded method takes a time-out period as an additional option; this overloaded version throws a TimeoutException if all other threads aren't reached within the time-out period.
boolean isBroken()	Returns true if the barrier is broken. A barrier is broken if at least one thread in that barrier was interrupted or timed-out, or if a barrier action failed throwing an exception.
void reset()	Resets the barrier to the initial state. If there are any threads waiting on that barrier, they will throw the BrokenBarrier exception.

Listing 11-6 is an example that makes use of CyclicBarrier class.

Listing 11-6. CyclicBarrierTest.java

```java
import java.util.concurrent.CyclicBarrier;
import java.util.concurrent.BrokenBarrierException;

// The run() method in this thread should be called only when
// four players are ready to start the game
class MixedDoubleTennisGame extends Thread {
    public void run() {
        System.out.println("All four players ready, game starts \n Love all...");
    }
}

// This thread simulates arrival of a player.
// Once a player arrives, he/she should wait for other players to arrive
class Player extends Thread {
    CyclicBarrier waitPoint;
    public Player(CyclicBarrier barrier, String name) {
        this.setName(name);
        waitPoint = barrier;
        this.start();
    }
    public void run() {
        System.out.println("Player " + getName() + " is ready ");
        try {
            waitPoint.await(); // await for all four players to arrive
        } catch(BrokenBarrierException | InterruptedException exception) {
            System.out.println("An exception occurred while waiting... "
                    + exception);
        }
    }
}

// Creates a CyclicBarrier object by passing the number of threads and the thread to run
// when all the threads reach the barrier
class CyclicBarrierTest {
    public static void main(String []args) {
        // a mixed-double tennis game requires four players;
        // so wait for four players
        // (i.e., four threads) to join to start the game
        System.out.println("Reserving tennis court \n"
                + "As soon as four players arrive, game will start");
        CyclicBarrier barrier = new CyclicBarrier(4, new MixedDoubleTennisGame());
        new Player(barrier, "G I Joe");
        new Player(barrier, "Dora");
        new Player(barrier, "Tintin");
        new Player(barrier, "Barbie");
    }
}
```

The program prints the following:

```
Reserving tennis court
As soon as four players arrive, game will start
Player Dora is ready
Player G I Joe is ready
Player Tintin is ready
Player Barbie is ready
All four players ready, game starts
  Love all...
```

Now let's see how this program works. In the main() method you create a CyclicBarrier object. The constructor takes two arguments: the number of threads to wait for, and the thread to invoke when all the threads reach the barrier. In this case, you have four players to wait for, so you create four threads, with each thread representing a player. The second argument for the CyclicBarrier constructor is the MixedDoubleTennisGame object since this thread represents the game, which will start once all four players are ready.

Inside the run() method for each Player thread, you call the await() method on the CyclicBarrier object. Once the number of awaiting threads for the CyclicBarrier object reaches four, the run() method in MixedDoubleTennisGame is called.

Concurrent Collections

The java.util.concurrent package provides a number of classes that are thread-safe equivalents of the ones provided in the collections framework classes in the java.util package. For example, java.util.concurrent.ConcurrentHashMap is a concurrent equivalent to java.util.HashMap. The main difference between these two containers is that you need to explicitly synchronize insertions and deletions with HashMap, whereas such synchronization is built into the ConcurrentHashMap. If you know how to use HashMap, you know how to use ConcurrentHashMap implicitly. From the OCPJP 8 exam perspective, you only need to have an overall understanding of the classes in Table 11-4, so we won't delve into details on how to make use of these classes. We'll only cover a detailed example of using CopyOnWriteArrayList.

Table 11-4. *Some Concurrent Collection Classes/Interfaces in the java.util.concurrent Package*

Class/Interface	Short Description
BlockingQueue	This interface extends the Queue interface. In BlockingQueue, if the queue is empty, it waits (i.e., blocks) for an element to be inserted, and if the queue is full, it waits for an element to be removed from the queue.
ArrayBlockingQueue	This class provides a fixed-sized array based implementation of the BlockingQueue interface.
LinkedBlockingQueue	This class provides a linked-list-based implementation of the BlockingQueue interface.
DelayQueue	This class implements BlockingQueue and consists of elements that are of type Delayed. An element can be retrieved from this queue only after its delay period.
PriorityBlockingQueue	Equivalent to java.util.PriorityQueue, but implements the BlockingQueue interface.

(continued)

Table 11-4. (*continued*)

Class/Interface	Short Description
SynchronousQueue	This class implements BlockingQueue. In this container, each insert() by a thread waits (blocks) for a corresponding remove() by another thread and vice versa.
LinkedBlockingDeque	This class implements BlockingDeque where insert and remove operations could block; uses a linked-list for implementation.
ConcurrentHashMap	Analogous to Hashtable, but with safe concurrent access and updates.
ConcurrentSkipListMap	Analogous to TreeMap, but provides safe concurrent access and updates.
ConcurrentSkipListSet	Analogous to TreeSet, but provides safe concurrent access and updates.
CopyOnWriteArrayList	Similar to ArrayList, but provides safe concurrent access. When the container is modified, it creates a fresh copy of the underlying array.
CopyOnWriteArraySet	A Set implementation, but provides safe concurrent access and is implemented using CopyOnWriteArrayList. When the container is modified, it creates a fresh copy of the underlying array.

CopyOnWriteArrayList Class

Both ArrayList and CopyOnWriteArrayList implement the List interface. There are three main differences between ArrayList and CopyOnWriteArrayList:

- ArrayList is not thread-safe but CopyOnWriteArrayList is thread-safe. That means, it is unsafe to use ArrayList in contexts where multiple threads are executing (especially when some of the threads modify the container) but it is safe to use CopyOnWriteArrayList in this context.

- Methods in ArrayList such as remove(), add(), and set() methods can throw java.util.ConcurrentModificationException if another thread modifies the ArrayList when one thread is accessing it. However, it is safe to perform these operations from multiple threads in CopyOnWriteArrayList, and hence methods such as remove(), add(), and set() do not throw this exception. How? All the active iterators will still have access to the unmodified version of the container and hence they remain unaffected; if you try to create an iterator after the modification, you will get the iterator for the modified container.

- You can get an iterator by calling the Iterator() method on a List object. If you call remove() method when the underlying container is modified, you may get a ConcurrentModificationException. However, you cannot call the remove() method on an Iterator of a CopyOnWriteArrayList: it always throws the UnsupportedOperationException.

The behavior of CopyOnWriteArrayList is sometimes useful even in contexts where multithreading is not used. For instance, Listing 11-7 shows an ArrayList that is being modified when the iterator executes.

Listing 11-7. ModifyingList.java

```java
import java.util.ArrayList;
import java.util.Iterator;
import java.util.List;

public class ModifyingList {
    public static void main(String []args) {
        List<String> aList = new ArrayList<>();
        aList.add("one");
        aList.add("two");
        aList.add("three");

        Iterator listIter = aList.iterator();
        while(listIter.hasNext()) {
            System.out.println(listIter.next());
            aList.add("four");
        }
    }
}
```

This program crashes by throwing java.util.ConcurrentModificationException. Why? Because the iterators of ArrayList are fail-fast; it fails by throwing ConcurrentModificationException if it detects that the underlying container has changed when it is iterating over the elements in the container. This behavior is useful in concurrent contexts when one thread modifies the underlying container when another thread is iterating over the elements of the container.

You can use CopyOnWriteArrayList for making such changes to the underlying container when iteration is happening. Listing 11-8 is the modified version of Listing 11-7. This version uses a CopyOnWriteArrayList.

Listing 11-8. COWList.java

```java
import java.util.Iterator;
import java.util.List;
import java.util.concurrent.CopyOnWriteArrayList;

public class COWList {
    public static void main(String []args) {
        List<String> aList = new CopyOnWriteArrayList<>();
        aList.add("one");
        aList.add("two");
        aList.add("three");

        Iterator listIter = aList.iterator();
        while(listIter.hasNext()) {
            System.out.println(listIter.next());
            aList.add("four");
        }
    }
}
```

Now the program does not crash, it prints:

```
one
two
three
```

Observe that the element "four" added three times is not printed as part of the output. This is because the iterator still has access to the original (unmodified) container that had three elements. If you create a new iterator and access the elements, you will find that new elements have been added to aList.

Using Callable and ExecutorService Interfaces

Certification Objective

Create worker threads using Runnable, Callable, and use an ExecutorService to concurrently execute tasks

You can directly create and manage threads in the application by creating Thread objects. However, if you want to abstract away the low-level details of multi-threaded programming, you can make use of the Executor interface.

Figure 11-3 shows the important classes and interfaces in the Executor hierarchy. In this section, you'll focus on using the Executor and the ExecutorService Interfaces. We'll cover ForkJoinPool later in this chapter.

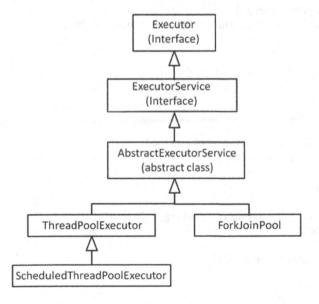

Figure 11-3. *Important Classes/Interfaces in the Executor hierarchy*

Executor

Executor is an interface that declares only one method: void execute(Runnable). This may not look like a significant interface by itself, but its derived classes (or interfaces), such as ExecutorService, ThreadPoolExecutor, and ForkJoinPool, support useful functionality. We will discuss some of the derived classes of Executor in more detail later in this chapter. For now, check out Listing 11-9 for a simple example of the Executor interface to understand how to implement this interface and use it in practice.

Listing 11-9. ExecutorTest.java

```java
import java.util.concurrent.Executor;

// This Task class implements Runnable, so its a Thread object
class Task implements Runnable {
    public void run() {
        System.out.println("Calling Task.run() ");
    }
}

// This class implements Executor interface and should override execute(Runnable) method.
// We provide an overloaded execute method with an additional argument 'times' to create and
// run the threads for given number of times
class RepeatedExecutor implements Executor {
    public void execute(Runnable runnable) {
        new Thread(runnable).start();
    }
    public void execute(Runnable runnable, int times) {
        System.out.printf("Calling Task.run() %d times thro' Executor.execute() %n",
                times);
        for(int i = 0; i < times; i++) {
            execute(runnable);
        }
    }
}

// This class spawns a Task thread and explicitly calls start() method.
// It also shows how to execute a Thread using Executor
class ExecutorTest {
    public static void main(String []args) {
        Runnable runnable = new Task();
        System.out.println("Calling Task.run() by directly creating a Thread");
        Thread thread = new Thread(runnable);
        thread.start();
        RepeatedExecutor executor = new RepeatedExecutor();
        executor.execute(runnable, 3);
    }
}
```

Here is the output of this program:

```
Calling Task.run() by directly creating a Thread
Calling Task.run()
Calling Task.run() 3 times thro' Executor.execute()
Calling Task.run()
Calling Task.run()
Calling Task.run()
```

In this program, you have a Task class that implements Runnable by providing the definition of the run() method. The class RepeatedExecutor implements the Executor interface by providing the definition of the execute(Runnable) method.

Both Runnable and Executor are similar in the sense that they provide a single method for implementation. In this definition you may have noticed that Executor by itself is not a thread, and you must create a Thread object to execute the Runnable object passed in the execute() method. However, the main difference between Runnable and Executor is that Executor is meant to abstract how the thread is executed. For example, depending on the implementation of the Executor, an Executor may schedule a thread to run at a certain time, or execute the thread after a certain delay period.

In this program, you have overloaded the execute() method with an additional argument to create and execute threads a certain number of times. In the main() method, you first create a Thread object and schedule it for running. After that, you instantiate RepeatedExecutor to execute the thread three times.

Callable and ExecutorService

Callable is an interface that declares only one method: call(). Its full signature is V call() throws Exception. It represents a task that needs to be completed by a thread. Once the task completes, it returns a value. For some reason, if the call() method cannot execute or fails, it throws an Exception.

To execute a task using the Callable object, you first create a thread pool. A thread pool is a collection of threads that can execute tasks. You create a thread pool using the Executors utility class. This class provides methods to get instances of thread pools, thread factories, and so on.

The ExecutorService interface extends the Executor interface and provides services such as termination of threads and production of Future objects. Some tasks may take considerable execution time to complete. So, when you submit a task to the executor service, you get a Future object.

Future represents objects that contain a value that is returned by a thread in the future (i.e., it returns the value once the thread terminates in the "future"). You can use the isDone() method in the Future class to check if the task is complete and then use the get() method to fetch the task result. If you call the get() method directly while the task is not complete, the method blocks until it completes and returns the value once available.

Here is a simple example to see how these classes work together (Listing 11-10).

Listing 11-10. CallableTest.java

```
import java.util.concurrent.Callable;
import java.util.concurrent.ExecutorService;
import java.util.concurrent.Future;
import java.util.concurrent.Executors;
```

```
// Factorial implements Callable so that it can be passed to a ExecutorService
// and get executed as a task.
class Factorial implements Callable<Long> {
    long n;
    public Factorial(long n) {
        this.n = n;
    }
    public Long call() throws Exception {
        if(n <= 0) {
            throw new Exception("for finding factorial, N should be > 0");
        }
        long fact = 1;
        for(long longVal = 1; longVal <= n; longVal++) {
            fact *= longVal;
        }
        return fact;
    }
}


// Illustrates how Callable, Executors, ExecutorService, and Future are related;
// also shows how they work together to execute a task
class CallableTest {
    public static void main(String []args) throws Exception {
        // the value for which we want to find the factorial
        long N = 20;
        // get a callable task to be submitted to the executor service
        Callable<Long> task = new Factorial(N);
        // create an ExecutorService with a fixed thread pool having one thread
        ExecutorService es = Executors.newSingleThreadExecutor();
        // submit the task to the executor service and store the Future object
        Future<Long> future = es.submit(task);
        // wait for the get() method that blocks until the computation is complete.
        System.out.printf("factorial of %d is %d", N, future.get());
        // done. shutdown the executor service since we don't need it anymore
        es.shutdown();
    }
}
```

The program prints the following:

```
factorial of 20 is 2432902008176640000
```

In this program, you have a Factorial class that implements Callable. Since the task is to compute the factorial of a number N, the task needs to return a result. You use Long type for the factorial value, so you implement Callable<Long>. Inside the Factorial class, you define the call() method that actually performs the task (the task here is to compute the factorial of the given number). If the given value N is negative or zero, you don't perform the task and throw an exception to the caller. Otherwise, you loop from 1 to N and find the factorial value.

In the CallableTest class, you first create an instance of the Factorial class. You then need to execute this task. For the sake of simplicity, you get a singled-threaded executor by calling the newSingleThreadExecutor() method in the Executors class. Note that you could use other methods such as newFixedThreadPool(nThreads) to create a thread pool with multiple threads depending on the level of parallelism you need.

Once you get an ExecutorService, you submit the task for execution. ExecutorService abstracts details such as when the task is executed and how the task is assigned to the threads. You get a reference to Future<Long> when you call the submit(task) method. From this future reference, you call the get() method to fetch the result after completing the task. If the task is still executing when you call future.get(), this get() method will block until the task execution completes. Once the execution is complete, you need to manually release the ExecutorService by calling the shutdown() method.

Use Parallel Fork/Join Framework

Certification Objective

Use parallel Fork/Join Framework

The Fork/Join framework in the java.util.concurrent package helps simplify writing parallelized code. The framework is an implementation of the ExecutorService interface and provides an easy-to-use concurrent platform in order to exploit multiple processors. This framework is very useful for modeling divide-and-conquer problems. This approach is suitable for tasks that can be divided recursively and computed on a smaller scale; the computed results are then combined. Dividing the task into smaller tasks is *forking*, and merging the results from the smaller tasks is *joining*.

The Fork/Join framework uses the work-stealing algorithm: when a worker thread completes its work and is free, it takes (or "steals") work from other threads that are still busy doing some work. Initially, it will appear to you that using Fork/Join is a complex task. Once you get familiar with it, however, you'll realize that it is conceptually easy and that it significantly simplifies your job. The key is to recursively subdivide the task into smaller chunks that can be processed by separate threads.

Briefly, the Fork/Join algorithm is designed as follows:

```
forkJoinAlgorithm() {
    fork (split) the tasks;
    join the tasks;
    compose the results;
}
```

Here is the pseudo-code of how these steps work:

```
doRecursiveTask(input) {
    if (the task is small enough to be handled by a thread) {
        compute the small task;
        if there is a result to return, do so
    }
    else {
        divide (i.e., fork) the task into two parts
        call compute() on first task, join() on second task, return combined results
    }
}
```

Figure 11-4 visualizes how the task is recursively subdivided into smaller tasks and how the partial results are combined. As shown by the figure, a task is split into two subtasks, and then each subtask is again split in two subtasks, and so on until each split subtask is computable by each thread. Once a thread completes the computation, it returns the result for combining it with other results; in this way all the computed results are combined back.

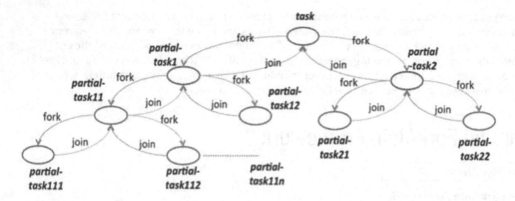

Figure 11-4. *The Fork/Join Framework Uses Divide-and-Conquer to Complete the Task*

Useful Classes in the Fork/Join Framework

The following classes play key roles in the Fork/Join framework: ForkJoinPool, ForkJoinTask, RecursiveTask, and RecursiveAction. Let's consider these classes in more detail.

- ForkJoinPool is the most important class in the Fork/Join framework. It is a thread pool for running fork/join tasks and it executes an instance of ForkJoinTask. It executes tasks and manages their lifecycle. Table 11-5 lists the important methods belonging to this abstract class.

Table 11-5. *Important Methods in the ForkJoinPool Class*

Method	Short Description
void execute(ForkJoinTask<?> task)	Executes a given task asynchronously.
<T> T invoke(ForkJoinTask<T> task)	Executes the given task and returns the computed result.
<T> List<Future<T>> invokeAll(Collection<? extends Callable<T>> tasks)	Executes all the given tasks and returns a list of future objects when all the tasks are completed.
boolean isTerminated()	Returns true if all the tasks are completed.
int getParallelism() int getPoolSize() long getStealCount() int getActiveThreadCount()	These are status-checking methods.
<T> ForkJoinTask<T> submit(Callable<T> task) <T> ForkJoinTask<T> submit(ForkJoinTask<T> task) ForkJoinTask<?> submit(Runnable task) <T> ForkJoinTask<T> submit(Runnable task, T result)	These methods are executing a submitted task. Overloaded versions take different types of tasks; returns a Task object or a Future object.

- ForkJoinTask<V> is a lightweight thread-like entity representing a task that defines methods such as fork() and join(). Table 11-6 lists the important methods of this class.

Table 11-6. *Important Methods in the ForkJoinTask Class*

Method	Short Description
`boolean cancel(boolean mayInterruptIfRunning)`	Attempts to cancel the execution of the task.
`ForkJoinTask<V> fork()`	Executes the task asynchronously.
`V join()`	Returns the result of the computation when the computation is done.
`V get()`	Returns the result of the computation; waits if the computation is not complete.
`V invoke()` `static <T extends ForkJoinTask<?>> Collection<T> invokeAll(Collection<T> tasks)`	Starts the execution of the submitted tasks; waits until computation complete, and returns results.
`boolean isCancelled()`	Returns `true` if the task is cancelled.
`boolean isDone()`	Returns `true` if the task is completed.

- `RecursiveTask<V>` is a task that can run in a `ForkJoinPool`; the `compute()` method returns a value of type V. It inherits from `ForkJoinTask`.

- `RecursiveAction` is a task that can run in a `ForkJoinPool`; its `compute()` method performs the actual computation steps in the task. It is similar to `RecursiveTask`, but does not return a value.

Using the Fork/Join Framework

Let's ascertain how you can use Fork/Join framework in problem solving. Here are the steps to use the framework:

- First, check whether the problem is suitable for the Fork/Join framework or not. Remember: the Fork/Join framework is not suitable for all kinds of tasks. This framework is suitable if your problem fits this description:

    - The problem can be designed as a recursive task where the task can be subdivided into smaller units and the results can be combined together.

    - The subdivided tasks are independent and can be computed separately without the need for communication between the tasks when computation is in process. (Of course, after the computation is over, you will need to join them together.)

- If the problem you want to solve can be modeled recursively, then define a task class that extends either `RecursiveTask` or `RecursiveAction`. If a task returns a result, extend from `RecursiveTask`; otherwise extend from `RecursiveAction`.

- Override the `compute()` method in the newly defined task class. The `compute()` method actually performs the task if the task is small enough to be executed; or splits the task into subtasks and invoke them. The subtasks can be invoked either by `invokeAll()` or `fork()` method (use `fork()` when the subtask returns a value). Use the `join()` method to get the computed results (if you used `fork()` method earlier).

- Merge the results, if computed from the subtasks.

- Then instantiate ForkJoinPool, create an instance of the task class, and start the execution of the task using the invoke() method on the ForkJoinPool instance.

- That's it—you are done.

Now let's try solving the problem of how to sum 1..N where N is a large number. You can solve this problem rescursively using the Fork/Join framework (Listing 11-11).

Listing 11-11. SumOfNUsingForkJoin.java

```java
import java.util.concurrent.RecursiveTask;
import java.util.concurrent.ForkJoinPool;

// This class illustrates how we can compute sum of 1..N numbers using fork/join framework.
// The range of numbers are divided into half until the range can be handled by a thread.
// Once the range summation completes, the result gets summed up together.

class SumOfNUsingForkJoin {

    private static long N = 1000_000; // one million - we want to compute sum
    // from 1 .. one million

    private static final int NUM_THREADS = 10;
    // number of threads to create for
    // distributing the effort

    // This is the recursive implementation of the algorithm; inherit from RecursiveTask
    // instead of RecursiveAction since we're returning values.
    static class RecursiveSumOfN extends RecursiveTask<Long> {
        long from, to;
        // from and to are range of values to sum-up

        public RecursiveSumOfN(long from, long to) {
            this.from = from;
            this.to = to;
        }

        // the method performs fork and join to compute the sum if the range
        // of values can be summed by a threadremember that we want to divide
        // the summation task equally among NUM_THREADS) then, sum the range
        // of numbers from..to  using a simple for loop;
        // otherwise, fork the range and join the results
        public Long compute() {

            if( (to - from) <= N/NUM_THREADS) {
                // the range is something that can be handled
                // by a thread, so do summation
```

```java
        long localSum = 0;
        // add in range 'from' .. 'to' inclusive of the value 'to'
        for(long i = from; i <= to; i++) {
            localSum += i;
        }
        System.out.printf("\tSum of value range %d to %d is %d %n",
                from, to, localSum);
        return localSum;
    }
    else {
        // no, the range is too big for a thread to handle,
        // so fork the computation
        // we find the mid-point value in the range from..to
        long mid = (from + to)/2;
        System.out.printf("Forking computation into two ranges: " +
                "%d to %d and %d to %d %n", from, mid, mid, to);

        // determine the computation for first half
        // with the range from..mid
        RecursiveSumOfN firstHalf = new RecursiveSumOfN(from, mid);

        // now, fork off that task
        firstHalf.fork();
        // determine the computation for second half
        // with the range mid+1..to
        RecursiveSumOfN secondHalf
                = new RecursiveSumOfN(mid + 1, to);
        long resultSecond = secondHalf.compute();

        // now, wait for the first half of computing sum to
        // complete, once done, add it to the remaining part
        return firstHalf.join() + resultSecond;
    }
    }
}

public static void main(String []args) {
    // Create a fork-join pool that consists of NUM_THREADS
    ForkJoinPool pool = new ForkJoinPool(NUM_THREADS);

    // submit the computation task to the fork-join pool
    long computedSum = pool.invoke(new RecursiveSumOfN(0, N));

    // this is the formula sum for the range 1..N
    long formulaSum = (N * (N + 1)) / 2;

    // Compare the computed sum and the formula sum
    System.out.printf("Sum for range 1..%d; computed sum = %d, " +
            "formula sum = %d %n", N, computedSum, formulaSum);
    }
}
```

The program prints the following:

```
Forking computation into two ranges: 0 to 500000 and 500000 to 1000000
Forking computation into two ranges: 500001 to 750000 and 750000 to 1000000
Forking computation into two ranges: 0 to 250000 and 250000 to 500000
Forking computation into two ranges: 500001 to 625000 and 625000 to 750000
Forking computation into two ranges: 750001 to 875000 and 875000 to 1000000
Forking computation into two ranges: 500001 to 562500 and 562500 to 625000
Forking computation into two ranges: 625001 to 687500 and 687500 to 750000
Forking computation into two ranges: 0 to 125000 and 125000 to 250000
Forking computation into two ranges: 250001 to 375000 and 375000 to 500000
        Sum of value range 562501 to 625000 is 37109406250
Forking computation into two ranges: 0 to 62500 and 62500 to 125000
        Sum of value range 687501 to 750000 is 44921906250
Forking computation into two ranges: 250001 to 312500 and 312500 to 375000
Forking computation into two ranges: 750001 to 812500 and 812500 to 875000
        Sum of value range 250001 to 312500 is 17578156250
Forking computation into two ranges: 875001 to 937500 and 937500 to 1000000
        Sum of value range 750001 to 812500 is 48828156250
        Sum of value range 812501 to 875000 is 52734406250
        Sum of value range 312501 to 375000 is 21484406250
Forking computation into two ranges: 125001 to 187500 and 187500 to 250000
        Sum of value range 625001 to 687500 is 41015656250
Forking computation into two ranges: 375001 to 437500 and 437500 to 500000
        Sum of value range 187501 to 250000 is 13671906250
        Sum of value range 62501 to 125000 is 5859406250
        Sum of value range 500001 to 562500 is 33203156250
        Sum of value range 437501 to 500000 is 29296906250
        Sum of value range 125001 to 187500 is 9765656250
        Sum of value range 875001 to 937500 is 56640656250
        Sum of value range 0 to 62500 is 1953156250
        Sum of value range 937501 to 1000000 is 60546906250
        Sum of value range 375001 to 437500 is 25390656250
Sum for range 1..1000000; computed sum = 500000500000, formula sum = 500000500000
```

Let's analyze how this program works. In this program, you want to compute the sum of the values in the range 1..1,000,000. For the sake of simplicity, you decide to use ten threads to execute the tasks. The class RecursiveSumOfN extends RecursiveTask<Long>. In RecursiveTask<Long>, you use <Long> because the sum of numbers in each sub-range is a Long value. In addition, you chose RecursiveTask<Long> instead of plain RecursiveAction because each subtask returns a value. If the subtask does not return a value, you can use RecursiveAction instead.

In the compute() method, you decide whether to compute the sum for the range or subdivide the task further using following condition:

```
(to - from) <= N/NUM_THREADS)
```

You use this "threshold" value in this computation. In other words, if the range of values is within the threshold that can be handled by a task, then you perform the computation; otherwise you recursively divide the task into two parts. You use a simple for loop to find the sum of the values in that range. In the other case, you divide the range similarly to how you divide the range in a binary search algorithm: for the range from .. to, you find the mid-point and create two sub-ranges from .. mid and mid + 1 .. to. Once you call fork(), you wait for the first task to complete the computation of the sum and spawn another task for the second half of the computation.

In the main() method, you create a ForkJoinPool with number of threads given by NUM_THREADS. You submit the task to the fork/join pool and get the computed sum for 1..1,000,000. Now you also calculate the sum using the formula to sum N continuous numbers.

From the output of the program, you can observe how the task got subdivided into subtasks. You can also verify from the output that the computed sum and sum computed from the formula are the same, indicating that your division of tasks for summing the sub-ranges is correct.

In this program, you arbitrarily assumed the number of threads to use was ten threads. This was to simplify the logic of this program. A better approach to decide the threshold value is to divide the data size length by the number of available processors. In other words,

```
threshold value = (data length size) / (number of available processors);
```

How do you programmatically get the number of available processors? For that you can use the method Runtime.getRuntime().availableProcessors()).

In Listing 11-11, you used RecursiveTask; however, if a task is not returning a value, then you should use RecursiveAction. There will be several differences in the program if you use RecursiveAction instead of RecursiveTask. One change is that you need to extend the task class from RecursiveAction. Also, compute() method does not return anything. Another change is that you need to use the invokeAll() method to submit the subtasks to execute. Finally, an obvious change is that you need to carry out the search in the compute() method instead of summation in the earlier case.

Points to Remember

Remember these points for your OCPJP 8 exam:

- It is possible to achieve what the Fork/Join framework offers using basic concurrency constructs such as start() and join(). However, the Fork/Join framework abstracts many lower-level details and thus is easier to use. In addition, it is much more efficient to use the Fork/Join framework instead of handling the threads at lower levels. Furthermore, using ForkJoinPool efficiently manages the threads and performs much better than conventional threads pools. For all these reasons, you are encouraged to use the Fork/Join framework.

- Each worker thread in the Fork/Join framework has a work queue, which is implemented using a Deque. Each time a new task (or subtask) is created, it is pushed to the head of its own queue. When a task completes a task and executes a join with another task that is not completed yet, it works smart. The thread pops a new task from the head of its queue and starts executing rather than sleeping (in order to wait for another task to complete). In fact, if the queue of a thread is empty, then the thread pops a task from the tail of the queue belonging to another thread. This is nothing but a work-stealing algorithm.

- It looks obvious to call fork() for both the subtasks (if you are splitting in two subtasks) and call join() two times. It is correct—but inefficient. Why? Well, basically you are creating more parallel tasks than are useful. In this case, the original thread will be waiting for the other two tasks to complete, which is inefficient considering task creation cost. That is why you call fork() once and call compute() for the second task.

- The placement of fork() and join() calls are very important. For instance, let's assume that you place the calls in the following order:

```
first.fork();
resultFirst = first.join();
resultSecond = second.compute();
```

  This usage is a serial execution of two tasks, since the second task starts executing only after the first is complete. Thus, it is less efficient even than its sequential version since this version also includes cost of the task creation. The take-away: watch your placement of fork/join calls.

- Performance is not always guaranteed while using the Fork/Join framework. One of the reasons we mentioned earlier is the placement of fork/join calls.

Use Parallel Streams

Certification Objective

Use parallel Streams including reduction, decomposition, merging processes, pipelines, and performance

Streams can be sequential or parallel. When we discussed Stream API (in Chapter 6), we discussed only sequential streams. In this section, let us discuss parallel streams.

What are parallel streams? Parallel streams split the elements into multiple chunks, process each chunk with different threads, and (if necessary) combine the results from those threads to evaluate the final result.

In the last section, we discussed the fork/join framework: tasks are executed by recursively splitting them into sub-tasks and then the sub-tasks are executed in parallel. Parallel streams internally use this fork/join framework. The process steps should consist of stateless and independent tasks.

Here is an example of counting number of primes from 1 to N. The logic used for checking if a given number is straightforward is that we check if there is any number divisible from 2 to N/2. Of course we can simplify the logic to speed-up the computation but our objective here is to show how the parallel streams work, so we have retained using this simple logic to check if a given number is prime or not. First, let us see the sequential version of this program (Listing 11-12).

Listing 11-12. PrimeNumbers.java

```
import java.util.stream.LongStream;

class PrimeNumbers {
    private static boolean isPrime(long val) {
        for(long i = 2; i <= val/2; i++) {
            if((val % i) == 0) {
                return false;
            }
        }
        return true;
    }
```

```
    public static void main(String []args) {
        long numOfPrimes = LongStream.rangeClosed(2, 100_000)
                    .filter(PrimeNumbers::isPrime)
                    .count();
        System.out.println(numOfPrimes);
    }
}
```

This program prints:

9592

This program correctly reports that there are 9,592 prime numbers till 1,00,000. When we timed it, it took 2.510 seconds to run (in my machine that has a 2.4 GHz Intel Core i5 dual core processor).

It is very easy to make the computation parallel: we have to call parallel() method provided in the LongStream interface. The code segment with this change is:

```
long numOfPrimes = LongStream.rangeClosed(2, 100_000)
                            .parallel()
                            .filter(PrimeNumbers::isPrime)
                            .count();
System.out.println(numOfPrimes);
```

Because of the call to parallel(), the stream becomes a parallel stream, and the work to be executed is split and dispatched to be executed by threads available in the fork/join pool. When the computation of the number of prime numbers is performed in parallel, the time taken now reduces to 1.235 seconds. This is almost half the time taken when compared to the 2.510 seconds it took when the computation was performed in the sequential stream.

If you compare the complexity of the code to use fork/join framework (check the code example in Listing 11-9), the code that uses parallel streams is very simple: all we have to do is just call parallel() method in the stream!

When you call the stream() method of the Collection class, you will get a sequential stream. When you call parallelStream() method of the Collection class, you will get a parallel stream.

You can check if the stream is sequential or parallel by calling the isParallel() method. Here is a simple code segment that illustrates using is method in a stream:

```
System.out.println(IntStream.range(1, 10).filter(i -> (i % 2) == 0).isParallel());
```

This code segment prints: false. Why? Because the underlying stream (is by default) sequential, and hence the isParallel() method returns false. How about this code segment?

```
List<Integer> ints = Arrays.asList(1, 2, 3, 4, 5);
System.out.println(ints.parallelStream().filter(i -> (i % 2) == 0).isParallel());
```

Because the underlying stream is parallel (because of the parallelStream() method call), the isParallel() method returns true.

✏️ You can convert a sequential stream to a parallel stream by calling the `parallel()` method; similarly, you can convert a parallel stream to a sequential stream by calling the `sequential()` method.

What will this code segment print?

```
List<Integer> ints = Arrays.asList(1, 2, 3, 4, 5);
System.out.println(ints.parallelStream().filter(i -> (i % 2) == 0).sequential().
isParallel());
```

This code segment prints: false. Why? Though the created stream is a parallel stream, the call to the `sequential()` method has made the stream sequential. Hence, the call `isParallel()` prints `false`.

Performing Correct Reductions

To use parallel streams correctly, it is important not to depend on global state. In other words, the computations should be "side-effect" free. To give an example of wrong use of streams, here is an example (Listing 11-13).

Listing 11-13. StringSplitAndConcatenate.java

```
import java.util.Arrays;

class StringConcatenator {
    public static String result = "";
    public static void concatStr(String str) {
        result = result + " " + str;
    }
}

class StringSplitAndConcatenate {
    public static void main(String []args) {
        String words[] = "the quick brown fox jumps over the lazy dog".split(" ");
        Arrays.stream(words).forEach(StringConcatenator::concatStr);
        System.out.println(StringConcatenator.result);
    }
}
```

This program prints:

```
the quick brown fox jumps over the lazy dog
```

In this program, we are splitting the words in the string `"the quick brown fox jumps over the lazy dog"` and then combining it again. For combining the words, we are using a global variable result and modifying it by passing the `StringConcatenator::concatStr()` method reference in the `forEach()` method of the stream. Because the underlying stream is a sequential stream, we don't seem to get into trouble and we were able to reconstruct the string correctly. However, here is a modified version of the program that converts the stream to a parallel stream by calling `parallel()`.

```
Arrays.stream(words).parallel().forEach(StringConcatenator::concatStr);
```

With this single change, we get garbled string! When we ran this program it printed:

```
quick the fox brown lazy dog the jumps
```

When we ran it again, it printed:

```
fox quick the jumps lazy dog
```

Clearly, there is something seriously going wrong when we used the parallel() method. What is happening?

When the stream is parallel, the task is split into multiple sub-tasks and different threads execute it. The calls to forEach(StringConcatenator::concatStr) now access the globally accessible variable result in StringConcatenator class. Hence this program suffers from a race condition problem (discussed earlier in this chapter). How do we fix this problem? We need to get rid of modifying the global state and keep the reduction localized. We can use the reduce() method instead, as in Listing 11-14. Remember that you can use reduce() method on a stream when you want to perform repeated operations on stream elements to compute a result.

Listing 11-14. CorrectStringSplitAndConcatenate.java

```
import java.util.Arrays;
import java.util.Optional;

class CorrectStringSplitAndConcatenate {
    public static void main(String []args) {
        String words[] = "the quick brown fox jumps over the lazy dog".split(" ");
        Optional<String> originalString =
                (Arrays.stream(words).parallel().reduce((a, b) -> a + " " + b));
        System.out.println(originalString.get());
    }
}
```

This program correctly prints:

```
the quick brown fox jumps over the lazy dog
```

If you remove the parallel() method or retain it (it does not matter), this program will correctly concatenate the words to print the original string because we have used the reduce operation correctly without depending on global state changes.

Parallel Streams and Performance

An important note of caution on using parallel streams: it is not always the case that the performance with parallel streams is better than sequential streams. Only if the operations are performed on a significantly large number of elements, the operations are computationally expensive, and the data structures are efficiently splittable, you will see performance improvements with parallel streams; otherwise, execution with a parallel stream may be slower than with sequential streams!

By default, the fork/join thread pool has the number of threads is typically equal to the number of processors you have in your machine. You can get the number of processors in your machine using this call: `Runtime.getRuntime().availableProcessors()`. This default configuration is good enough for most uses of parallel streams. Alternatively, you can check the default parallelism by using the `getParallelism()` method in the ForkJoinPool:

```
System.out.println(ForkJoinPool.commonPool().getParallelism());
// it printed 3 in my machine
```

The `getParallelism()` method gets the value from the system property `java.util.concurrent.ForkJoinPool.common.parallelism`. You can use the `System.setProperty` method to modify the value of this system property (Listing 11-15).

Listing 11-15. Parallelism.java

```java
import java.util.concurrent.ForkJoinPool;

public class Parallelism {
    public static void main(String []args) {
        System.setProperty("java.util.concurrent.ForkJoinPool.common.parallelism", "8");
        System.out.println(ForkJoinPool.commonPool().getParallelism());
    }
}
```

When executed, this program prints: 8. An alternative to using `System.setProperty()` is to set this property by passing it as a JVM parameter when invoking the JVM, as in:

```
java -Djava.util.concurrent.ForkJoinPool.common.parallelism=8 GetParallelism
```

Summary

Let us briefly review the key points for each certification objective in this chapter. Please read it before appearing for the exam.

Create worker threads using Runnable, Callable, and use an ExecutorService to concurrently execute tasks

- You can create classes that are capable of multi-threading by implementing the Runnable interface or by extending the Thread class.

- Always implement the `run()` method. The default `run()` method in Thread does nothing.

- Call the `start()` method and not the `run()` method directly in code. (Leave it to the JVM to call the `run()` method.)

- The Callable interface represents a task that needs to be completed by a thread. Once the task completes, the `call()` method of a Callable implementation returns a value.

- The Executor hierarchy abstracts the lower-level details of multi-threaded programming and offers high-level user-friendly concurrency constructs.

Identify potential threading problems among deadlock, starvation, livelock, and race conditions

- Concurrent reads and writes to resources may lead to the *race condition* problem.

- You must use thread synchronization (i.e., locks) to access shared values and avoid race conditions. Java provides thread synchronization features to provide protected access to shared resources—namely, synchronized blocks and synchronized methods.

- Using locks can introduce problems such as deadlocks. When a deadlock happens, the process will *hang* and will never terminate.

- A deadlock typically happens when two threads acquire locks in opposite order. When one thread has acquired one lock and waits for another lock, another thread has acquired that other lock and waits for the first lock to be released. So, no progress is made and the program deadlocks.

- When a change done by a thread is repeatedly undone by another thread, both the threads are busy but the application as a whole does not make progress; this situation is known as a livelock.

- The situation in which low-priority threads "starve" for a long time trying to obtain the lock is known as lock starvation.

Use synchronized keyword and java.util.concurrent.atomic package to control the order of thread execution

- In synchronized blocks, you use the synchronized keyword for a reference variable and follow it by a block of code. A thread has to acquire a lock on the synchronized variable to enter the block; when the execution of the block completes, the thread releases the lock.

- Java provides an efficient alternative in the form of atomic variables where one needs to acquire and release a lock just to carry out primitive operations on variables.

- A lock ensures that only one thread accesses a shared resource at a time.

- Performing locking and unlocking for performing operations on primitive types is inefficient. A better alternative is to use atomic variables provided in java.util.concurrent.atomic package including AtomicBoolean, AtomicInteger, AtomicIntegerArray, AtomicLong, AtomicLongArray, AtomicReference<V>, and AtomicReferenceArray<E>.

Use java.util.concurrent collections and classes including CyclicBarrier and CopyOnWriteArrayList

- Semaphore controls access to one or more shared resources.

- CountDownLatch allows threads to wait for a countdown to complete.

- Exchanger supports exchanging data between two threads.

- Phaser is used to support a synchronization barrier.

- CyclicBarrier enables threads to wait at a predefined execution point.

- The java.util.concurrent package provides a number of classes that are thread-safe equivalents of the ones provided in the collections framework classes in the java.util package; for example, java.util.concurrent.ConcurrentHashMap is a concurrent equivalent to java.util.HashMap.

- CopyOnWriteArrayList is similar to ArrayList, but provides safe concurrent access. When you modify a CopyOnWriteArrayList, a fresh copy of the underlying array is created.

Use Parallel Fork/Join Framework

- The Fork/Join framework is a portable means of executing a program with decent parallelism.

- The framework is an implementation of the ExecutorService interface and provides an easy-to-use concurrent platform in order to exploit multiple processors.

- This framework is very useful for modeling divide-and-conquer problems.

- The Fork/Join framework uses the work-stealing algorithm: when a worker thread completes its work and is free, it takes (or "steals") work from other threads that are still busy doing some work.

- The work-stealing technique results in decent load balancing thread management with minimal synchronization cost.

- ForkJoinPool is the most important class in the Fork/Join framework. It is a thread pool for running fork/join tasks—it executes an instance of ForkJoinTask. It executes tasks and manages their lifecycles.

- ForkJoinTask<V> is a lightweight thread-like entity representing a task that defines methods such as fork() and join().

Use parallel Streams including reduction, decomposition, merging processes, pipelines, and performance

- Parallel streams split the elements into multiple chunks, process each chunk with different threads, and (if necessary) combine the results from those threads to evaluate the final result.

- When you call the stream() method of the Collection class, you will get a sequential stream. When you call the parallelStream() method of the Collection class, you will get a parallel stream.

- Parallel streams internally use the fork/join framework. To use parallel streams correctly, the process steps should consist of stateless and independent tasks.

- You can convert a sequential stream to a parallel stream by calling the parallel() method; similarly, you can convert a parallel stream to a sequential stream by calling the sequential() method.

- You can check if the stream is sequential or parallel by calling the isParallel() method.

Q0075ESTION TIME

1. Here is a class named PingPong that extends the Thread class. Which of the
   following PingPong class implementations correctly prints "ping" from the
   worker thread and then prints "pong" from the main thread?

   A.

   ```
   class PingPong extends Thread {
       public void run() {
           System.out.println("ping ");
       }
       public static void main(String []args) {
           Thread pingPong = new PingPong();
           System.out.print("pong");
       }
   }
   ```

   B.

   ```
   class PingPong extends Thread {
       public void run() {
           System.out.println("ping ");
       }
       public static void main(String []args) {
           Thread pingPong = new PingPong();
           pingPong.run();
           System.out.print("pong");
       }
   }
   ```

   C.

   ```
   class PingPong extends Thread {
       public void run() {
           System.out.println("ping");
       }
       public static void main(String []args) {
           Thread pingPong = new PingPong();
           pingPong.start();
           System.out.println("pong");
       }
   }
   ```

   D.

   ```
   class PingPong extends Thread {
       public void run() {
           System.out.println("ping");
       }
   ```

```
        public static void main(String []args) throws InterruptedException{
            Thread pingPong = new PingPong();
            pingPong.start();
            pingPong.join();
            System.out.println("pong");
        }
    }
```

2. You've written an application for processing tasks. In this application, you've separated the critical or urgent tasks from the ones that are not critical or urgent. You've assigned high priority to critical or urgent tasks.

   In this application, you find that the tasks that are not critical or urgent are the ones that keep waiting for an unusually long time. Since critical or urgent tasks are high priority, they run most of the time. Which one of the following multi-threading problems correctly describes this situation?

   A. Deadlock

   B. Starvation

   C. Livelock

   D. Race condition

3. Which of the following two definitions of Sync (when compiled in separate files) will compile without errors?

   A.

```
class Sync {
    public synchronized void foo() {}
}
```

   B.
```
abstract class Sync {
    public synchronized void foo() {}
}
```

   C.

```
abstract class Sync {
    public abstract synchronized void foo();
}
```
   D.

```
interface Sync {
    public synchronized void foo();
}
```

4. **Consider the following program:**

```java
import java.util.concurrent.atomic.*;

class AtomicIntegerTest {
    static AtomicInteger ai = new AtomicInteger(10);
    public static void check() {
        assert (ai.intValue() % 2) == 0;
    }
    public static void increment() {
        ai.incrementAndGet();
    }
    public static void decrement() {
        ai.getAndDecrement();
    }
    public static void compare() {
        ai.compareAndSet(10, 11);
    }
    public static void main(String []args) {
        increment();
        decrement();
        compare();
        check();
        System.out.println(ai);
    }
}
```

The program is invoked as follows:

`java -ea AtomicIntegerTest`

What is the expected output of this program?

A. It prints 11

B. It prints 10

C. It prints 9

D. It crashes throwing an `AssertionError`

5. **Which one of the following options correctly makes use of Callable that will compile without any errors?**

A. `import java.util.concurrent.Callable;`

```java
class CallableTask implements Callable {
    public int call() {
        System.out.println("In Callable.call()");
        return 0;
    }
}
```

B. ```
    import java.util.concurrent.Callable;

    class CallableTask extends Callable {
        public Integer call() {
            System.out.println("In Callable.call()");
            return 0;
        }
    }
    ```

C.  ```
    import java.util.concurrent.Callable;

    class CallableTask implements Callable<Integer> {
        public Integer call() {
            System.out.println("In Callable.call()");
            return 0;
        }
    }
    ```

D. ```
    import java.util.concurrent.Callable;

    class CallableTask implements Callable<Integer> {
        public void call(Integer i) {
            System.out.println("In Callable.call(i)");
        }
    }
    ```

6.  **Choose the correct option based on this program:**

    ```
    import java.util.concurrent.*;
    import java.util.*;
    class COWArrayListTest {
        public static void main(String []args) {
            ArrayList<Integer> aList =
                            new CopyOnWriteArrayList<Integer>(); // LINE A
            aList.addAll(Arrays.asList(10, 20, 30, 40));
            System.out.println(aList);
        }
    }
    ```

    A. When executed the program prints the following: [10, 20, 30, 40].

    B. When executed the program prints the following: CopyOnWriteArrayList.class.

    C. The program does not compile and results in a compiler error in line marked with comment LINE A.

    D. When executed the program throws a runtime exception ConcurrentModificationException.

    E. When executed the program throws a runtime exception InvalidOperationException.
    ```

7. **Which one of the following methods return a Future object?**

   A. The overloaded `replace()` methods declared in the `ConcurrentMap` interface

   B. The `newThread()` method declared in the `ThreadFactory` interface

   C. The overloaded `submit()` methods declared in the `ExecutorService` interface

   D. The `call()` method declared in the `Callable` interface

Answers:

1. D.

```
class PingPong extends Thread {
    public void run() {
        System.out.println("ping");
    }
    public static void main(String []args) throws InterruptedException{
        Thread pingPong = new PingPong();
        pingPong.start();
        pingPong.join();
        System.out.println("pong");
    }
}
```

The `main` thread creates the worker thread and waits for it to complete (which prints "ping"). After that it prints "pong". So, this implementation correctly prints "ping pong".

Why are the other options wrong?

Option a) The `main()` method creates the worker thread, but doesn't start it. So, the code given in this option only prints "pong".

Option b) The program always prints "ping pong", but it is misleading. The code in this option directly calls the `run()` method instead of calling the `start()` method. So, this is a single threaded program: both "ping" and "pong" are printed from the main thread.

Option c) The `main` thread and the `worker` thread execute independently without any coordination. (Note that it does not have a call to `join()` in the `main` method.) So, depending on which thread is scheduled first, you can get "ping pong" or "pong ping" printed.

2. B. Starvation

The situation in which low-priority threads keep waiting for a long time to acquire the lock and execute the code in critical sections is known as starvation.

3. A. and B.

Abstract methods (in abstract classes or interfaces) cannot be declared `synchronized`, hence the options C and D are incorrect.

4. D. It crashes throwing an `AssertionError`.

The initial value of `AtomicInteger` is 10. Its value is incremented by 1 after calling `incrementAndGet()`. After that, its value is decremented by 1 after calling `getAndDecrement()`. The method `compareAndSet(10, 11)` checks if the current value is 10, and if so sets the atomic integer variable to value 11. Since the assert statement checks if the atomic integer value % 2 is zero (that is, checks if it is an even number), the assert fails and the program results in an `AssertionError`.

5. C.

```
import java.util.concurrent.Callable;

class CallableTask implements Callable<Integer> {
    public Integer call() {
        System.out.println("In Callable.call()");
        return 0;
    }
}
```

The `Callable` interface is defined as follows:

```
public interface Callable<V> {
    V call() throws Exception;
}
```

In option A), the `call()` method has the return type `int`, which is incompatible with the return type expected for overriding the `call` method and so will not compile.

In option B), the `extends` keyword is used, which will result in a compiler (since `Callable` is an interface, the `implements` keyword should be used).

Option C) correctly defines the `Callable` interface providing the type parameter `<Integer>`. The same type parameter `Integer` is also used in the return type of the `call()` method that takes no arguments, so it will compile without errors.

In option D), the return type of `call()` is `void` and the `call()` method also takes a parameter of type `Integer`. Hence, the method declared in the interface `Integer call()` remains unimplemented in the `CallableTask` class, so the program will not compile.

6. C. The program does not compile and results in a compiler error in the line marked with comment LINE A.

The class `CopyOnWriteArrayList` does not inherit from `ArrayList`, so an attempt to assign a `CopyOnWriteArrayList` to an `ArrayList` reference will result in a compiler error. Note that the `ArrayList` suffix in the class named `CopyOnWriteArrayList` could be misleading as these two classes do not share an IS-A relationship.

7. C. The overloaded `submit()` methods declared in `ExecutorService` interface

   Option A) The overloaded `replace()` methods declared in the `ConcurrentMap` interface remove an element from the map and return the success status (a Boolean value) or the removed value.

   Option B) The `newThread()` is the only method declared in the `ThreadFactory` interface and it returns a `Thread` object as the return value.

   Option C) The `ExecutorService` interface has overloaded `submit()` method that takes a task for execution and returns a Future representing the pending results of the task.

   Option D) The `call()` method declared in `Callable` interface returns the result of the task it executed.

CHAPTER 12

■ ■ ■

Building Database Applications with JDBC

Certification Objectives

Describe the interfaces that make up the core of the JDBC API including the Driver, Connection, Statement, and ResultSet interfaces and their relationship to provider implementations

Identify the components required to connect to a database using the DriverManager class including the JDBC URL

Submit queries and read results from the database including creating statements, returning result sets, iterating through the results, and properly closing result sets, statements, and connections

JDBC (Java Database Connectivity) is an important Java API that defines how a client accesses a database. As such, it is critical in building large-scale enterprise Java solutions.

At a high level, interacting with a database involves the following steps:

1. Establish a connection to a database.

2. Execute SQL queries to retrieve, create, or modify tables in the database.

3. Close the connection to the database.

Java provides a set of APIs (JDBC) to carry out these activities with databases. You can use JDBC to establish a connection to a database, execute your SQL query, and close the connection with the database. The benefit of JDBC is that you are not writing a program for a specific database. JDBC creates a loose coupling between your Java program and the type of database used. For instance, databases may differ in how they establish a connection (the API name may differ, and so on). JDBC hides all the heterogeneity of these databases and offers a single set of APIs you can use to interact with all types of databases. Note that JDBC supports only relational databases such as MySQL, Oracle, Microsoft SQL, and DB2. It does not support new-generation databases (also known as NoSQL databases) such as MongoDB and Neo4j.

From an OCPJP 8 exam perspective, you are expected to know how to connect to a database using JDBC and perform database operations such as inserting, updating, and creating database entities. You are also expected to know how to submit queries and read results from the database and properly release database resources.

The JDBC classes and interfaces are part of the packages `java.sql.*` and `javax.sql.*`. This chapter assumes that you're already familiar with SQL queries and have some basic understanding of database concepts. The chapter describes JDBC 4.2, which is part of the Java SE 8 release.

Introduction to JDBC

Certification Objective

Describe the interfaces that make up the core of the JDBC API including the Driver, Connection, Statement, and ResultSet interfaces and their relationship to provider implementations

Let's examine the vital components of JDBC and how these components work together to achieve seamless integration with databases. A simplified architecture of JDBC is represented in Figure 12-1. A Java application uses JDBC APIs to interact with databases. JDBC APIs interact with the JDBC driver manager to transparently connect and perform various database activities with different types of databases. The JDBC driver manager uses various JDBC drivers to connect to their specific DBMSs.

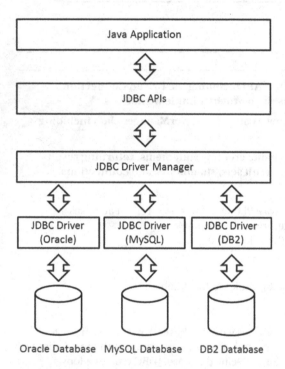

Figure 12-1. *JDBC architecture*

JDBC drivers and the driver manager play a key role in realizing the objective of JDBC. JDBC drivers are specifically designed to interact with their respective DBMSs. The driver manager works as a directory of JDBC drivers—it maintains a list of available data sources and their drivers. The driver manager chooses an appropriate driver to communicate with the respective DBMS. It can manage multiple concurrent drivers connected to their respective data sources.

You can see in the figure that the complexity of heterogeneous interactions is delegated to the JDBC driver manager and JDBC drivers. Low-level details and the associated complexity are hidden from the application developer by the JDBC API.

Setting Up the Database

Before you begin exploring JDBC APIs and their usage, you must set up a database with which to work. The database needs to be configured properly before you can start writing JDBC programs. You can use any database. The examples in this chapter use MySQL to explain various aspects of JDBC APIs because this database is free and widely available. This section shows the steps to set up a MySQL database on your machine, assuming that you use Windows (if you are using a different operating system, the steps will slightly differ):

1. Download the latest MySQL installer from the MySQL download page (www.mysql.com/downloads/mysql).

2. Invoke the MySQL installer, and follow all the steps shown by the installation wizard. Keep the default values, and complete the installation. The installer asks you to provide a root/admin password; remember it, because it's used in the examples.

3. Invoke the MySQL command-line client (in our case, it is MySQL 5.5 Command Line Client, shown on the Start menu). You see a MySQL prompt once you provide the root/admin password.

The following code sets up a database and creates two records:

```
Enter password: ********
Welcome to the MySQL monitor. Commands end with ; or \g.
Your MySQL connection id is 1
Server version: 5.5.27 MySQL Community Server (GPL)

Copyright (c) 2000, 2011, Oracle and/or its affiliates. All rights reserved.

Oracle is a registered trademark of Oracle Corporation and/or its affiliates. Other names
may be trademarks of their respective owners.

Type 'help;' or '\h' for help. Type '\c' to clear the current input statement.

mysql> /* Let's create a database for our use.*/

mysql> create database addressBook;
Query OK, 1 row affected (0.01 sec)

mysql> /* Now, let's create a table in this database and insert two records for our use
later. */

mysql> use addressBook;
Database changed

mysql> create table contact (id int not null auto_increment, firstName varchar(30) Not null,
lastName varchar(30), email varchar(30), phoneNo varchar(13), primary key (id));
Query OK, 0 rows affected (0.20 sec)

mysql> insert into contact values (default, 'Michael', 'Taylor', 'michael@abc.com',
'+919876543210');
Query OK, 1 row affected (0.10 sec)
```

```
mysql> insert into contact values (default, 'William', 'Becker', 'william@abc.com',
'+449876543210');
Query OK, 1 row affected (0.03 sec)

mysql> select * from contact;
+----+-----------+----------+------------------+----------------+
| id | firstName | lastName | email            | phoneNo        |
+----+-----------+----------+------------------+----------------+
|  1 | Michael   | Taylor   | michael@abc.com  | +919876543210  |
|  2 | William   | Becker   | william@abc.com  | +449876543210  |
+----+-----------+----------+------------------+----------------+
2 rows in set (0.00 sec)

mysql> /* That's it. Our database is ready to use now.*/
```

Connecting to a Database

This section discusses how to programmatically connect to a database. First, let's briefly cover the Connection interface.

The Connection Interface

The Connection interface of the java.sql package represents a connection from application to the database. It is a channel through which your application and the database communicate. Table 12-1 lists important methods in the Connection interface. All of these methods throw SQLExceptions, so this isn't mentioned in the table.

Table 12-1. *Important Methods in the Connection Interface*

Method	Description
Statement createStatement()	Creates a Statement object that can be used to send SQL statements to the database.
PreparedStatement prepareStatement(String sql)	Creates a PreparedStatement object that can contain SQL statements. The SQL statement can have IN parameters; they may contain ? symbol(s), which are used as placeholders for passing actual values later.
CallableStatement prepareCall(String sql)	Creates a CallableStatement object for calling stored procedures in the database. The SQL statement can have IN or OUT parameters; they may contain ? symbol(s), which are used as placeholders for passing actual values later.
DatabaseMetaData getMetaData()	Gets the DataBaseMetaData object. This metadata contains database schema information, table information, and so on, which is especially useful when you don't know the underlying database.
Clob createClob()	Returns a Clob object (Clob is the name of the interface). Character Large Object (CLOB) is a built-in type in SQL; it can be used to store a column value in a row of a database table.

(continued)

Table 12-1. (*continued*)

Method	Description
Blob createBlob()	Returns a Blob object (Blob is the name of the interface). Binary Large Object (BLOB) is a built-in type in SQL; it can be used to store a column value in a row of a database table.
void setSchema(String schema)	When passed the schema name, sets this Connection object to the database schema to access.
String getSchema()	Returns the schema name of the database associated with this Connection object; returns null if no schema is associated with it.

Connecting to the Database Using DriverManager

Certification Objective

Identify the components required to connect to a database using the DriverManager class including the JDBC URL

The first step in communicate with your database is to set up a connection between your application and the database server. Establishing a connection requires understanding the database URL, so let's discuss it now.

Here is the general format of the JDBC URL:

```
jdbc:<subprotocol>:<subname>
```

An example of a URL string is `jdbc:mysql://localhost:3306/`:

- jdbc (`<protocol>`) is the same for all DBMSs.

- `<subprotocol>` differs for each DBMS—it is mysql in this case. Sometimes it includes the vendor name (absent in this example).

- The format of `<subname>` depends on the database, but its general format is `//<server>:<port>/database`. `<server>` depends on the location in which you host the database. Each DBMS uses a specific `<port>` number (3306 in the case of MySQL). Finally, the database name is provided

Here are few more examples:

```
jdbc:postgresql://localhost/test
jdbc:oracle://127.0.0.1:44000/test
jdbc:microsoft:sqlserver://himalaya:1433
```

Now, let's write a simple application to acquire a connection (see Listing 12-1).

Listing 12-1. DbConnect.java

```java
import java.sql.Connection;
import java.sql.DriverManager;

// The class attempts to acquire a connection with the database
class DbConnect {
    public static void main(String[] args) {
        // URL points to JDBC protocol: mysql subprotocol;
        // localhost is the address of the server where we installed our
        // DBMS (i.e. on local machine) and 3306 is the port on which
        // we need to contact our DBMS
          String url = "jdbc:mysql://localhost:3306/";

        // we are connecting to the addressBook database we created earlier
        String database = "addressBook";
        // we login as "root" user with password "mysql123"
        String userName = "root";
        String password = "mysql123";

        try (Connection connection = DriverManager.getConnection
                (url + database, userName, password)){
                System.out.println("Database connection: Successful");
        } catch (Exception e) {
                System.out.println("Database connection: Failed");
                e.printStackTrace();
        }
    }
}
```

Let's analyze the program step by step:

1. The URL jdbc:mysql://localhost:3306/ indicates that jdbc is the protocol and mysql is a subprotocol; localhost is the address of the server where we installed our DBMS (the local machine), and 3306 is the port on which to contact the DBMS. (Note that this port number is different when you use some other database. We used the default port number provided by the MySQL database, which can be changed if required. Additionally, if you are using another database, the subprotocol also changes.) You need to use the addressBook database with root credentials.

2. You can get a connection object by invoking the DriverManager.getConnection() method. The method expects the URL of the database along with a database name, username, and password.

3. You need to close the connection before exiting the program. This example uses a try-with-resources statement; hence the close() method for the connection is automatically called.

4. If anything goes wrong, you get an exception. In that case, the program prints the exception's stack trace.

Go ahead and run the program. Here is the output:

```
Database connection: Failed
java.sql.SQLException: No suitable driver found for jdbc:mysql://localhost:3306/addressBook
        at java.sql.DriverManager.getConnection(DriverManager.java:604)
        at java.sql.DriverManager.getConnection(DriverManager.java:221)
        at DbConnect.main(DbConnect.java:16)
```

Oops! Why did you get this SQLException? When you attempt to connect to the database using JDBC, the DriverManager searches for the MySQL driver. You need to explicitly install the relevant drivers—they are not part of JDK.

You can download the connector for MySQL from its download page (http://dev.mysql.com/downloads/connector/j). Do not forget to add the path of the connector to the CLASSPATH. If the connector name is mysql-connector-java-5.1.21-bin.jar, stored in C:\mysql-connector-java-5.1.21, then add c:\ mysql-connector-java-5.1.21\mysql-connector-java-5.1.21-bin.jar to the CLASSPATH.

It is a common mistake to forget to add the path of the jar in the CLASSPATH environment variable. In this case, the JDBC API will not be able to locate the JDBC driver and will throw an exception. Remember, entering the path of the jar is not enough: you need to add the jar name along with the full path to the CLASSPATH variable or pass the jar file's path with the -cp command when invoking the JVM.

Update the CLASSPATH variable and then try again. You may get another exception:

```
Database connection: Failed
java.sql.SQLException: Access denied for user 'root'@'localhost' (using password: YES)
    at com.mysql.jdbc.SQLError.createSQLException(SQLError.java:1074)
    [... rest of the stack trace elided ...]
```

This program gives the username "root" and password "mysql123". If you've set the root user password to something else, you'll get this exception with the message "access denied for user." There are two ways to fix this problem. The first way is to change the program to give your password instead of the "mysql123" used in this program. The second way is to reset the password in your database. For MySQL, you can reset the password as follows for the user "root":

```
UPDATE mysql.user SET Password=PASSWORD('mysql123') WHERE User='root';
FLUSH PRIVILEGES;
```

Here is the output when the program runs successfully:

```
Database connection: Successful
```

When you see this output, it means you are able to establish a connection with the database. If you want to try the programs in the rest of this chapter, you should get this program working in your system; you need to establish a connection to query or update the database.

You've already seen two examples of SQLException thrown from the JDBC API. When you get a SQLException, you can rarely do anything in the program to recover from it. In a real-world application, you can wrap it as a higher-level exception and rethrow it to the calling component. To save space in the chapter's code segments, we print the stack trace of the exception and ignore it in the programs.

Understanding he DriverManager Class

The DriverManager class helps establish the connection between the program (the user) and the JDBC drivers. This class also keeps track of different data sources and JDBC drivers. Hence, there is no need to explicitly load the JDBC driver: DriverManager searches for a suitable driver and, if found, automatically loads it when you call the getConnection() method. Listing 12-1 contains the following code to get the connection (given within a try-with-resources statement) when you don't explicitly load the JDBC driver:

```
Connection connection = DriverManager.getConnection(url + database, userName, password);
```

The driver manager also manages multiple concurrent drivers connected to their respective data sources. Table 12-2 lists other important methods provided in the DriverManager class, including the overloaded versions of getConnection().

Table 12-2. Important Methods in the DriverManager Class

Method	Description
static Connection getConnection(String url) static Connection getConnection(String url, Properties info) static Connection getConnection(String url, String user, String password) ()	Attempts to establish a connection given the database URL. Additionally, you can provide Information such as a username and password directly as String arguments or through a Properties file. This method throws an SQLException if the connection can't be established.
static Driver getDriver(String url)	Searches the list of registered JDBC drivers and, if found, returns the appropriate Driver object matching the database URL.
static void registerDriver(Driver driver)	Add to the list of registered Driver objects in the DriverManager.
static void deregisterDriver(Driver driver)	Deregisters a driver from the list of registered Driver objects in the DriverManager

Using the getDriver() method, you can load the driver by passing the database URL:

```
String url = "jdbc:mysql://localhost:3306/";
Driver driver = DriverManager.getDriver(url);
System.out.println(driver.getClass().getName());
```

This code segment prints com.mysql.jdbc.Driver—this is the fully qualified name of the MySQL JDBC driver, and DriverManager was able to load it. From this Driver object, you can establish a connection by calling the connect() method and passing the database URL and the optional Properties file reference:

```
Connection connection = driver.connect(url, /*properties = */ null);
```

In the Properties file, you can provide the username and password in addition to any other details.

Querying and Updating the Database

Certification Objective

Submit queries and read results from the database including creating statements, returning result sets, iterating through the results, and properly closing result sets, statements, and connections

Once you establish a connection to the desired database, you can perform various operations on it. Common operations are known by the acronym CRUD (create, read, update, delete). You can read data using a SELECT SQL statement and modify the database using INSERT, UPDATE, and DELETE. JDBC provides two important interfaces to support queries: Statement and ResultSet. The next two subsections discuss these interfaces.

Statement Interface

As the name suggests, Statement is a SQL statement that can be used to communicate a SQL statement to the connected database and receive results from the database. You can form SQL queries using Statement and execute it using APIs provided in the Statement interface (or one of its derived interfaces). Statement comes in three flavors: Statement, PreparedStatement, and CallableStatement; these are shown in the inheritance hierarchy in Figure 12-2.

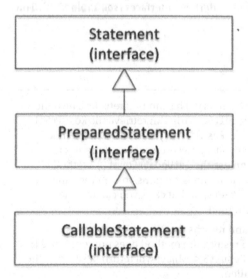

Figure 12-2. The Statement interface and its subinterfaces

How do you choose from these three Statement interfaces for a given situation? Let's look at the differences:

- Statement: Sends a SQL statement to the database without any parameters. For typical uses, you need to use this interface. You can create an instance of Statement using the createStatement() method in the Connection interface.

- PreparedStatement: Represents a *precompiled SQL statement* that can be customized using IN parameters. Usually, it is more efficient than a Statement object; hence, it is used to improve performance, especially if a SQL statement is executed multiple times. You can get an instance of PreparedStatement by calling the preparedStatement() method in the Connection interface.

- CallableStatement: Executes *stored procedures*. CallableStatement instances can handle IN as well as OUT and INOUT parameters. You need to call the prepareCall() method in the Connection interface to get an instance of this class.

Once you have created an appropriate Statement object, you are ready to execute a SQL statement. The Statement interface provides three execute methods: executeQuery(), executeUpdate(), and execute(). If your SQL statement is a SELECT query, use the executeQuery() method, which returns a ResultSet (discussed in the next section). When you want to update a database using an INSERT, UPDATE, or DELETE statement, you should use the executeUpdate() method, which returns an integer reflecting the updated number of rows. If you don't know the type of SQL statement, you can use the execute() method, which may return multiple resultsets or multiple update counts or a combination of both. From the OCPJP 8 exam perspective, you need to know about the Statement interface and its derived interfaces (see Table 12-3). The rest of this chapter uses the Statement interface.

Table 12-3. *Important Methods of the Statement Interface*

Method	Description
boolean execute(String sql)	Executes the given SQL query. This method returns true if the query resulted in a ResultSet. You can retrieve the ResultSet object by calling the getResultSet() method. This method returns false if the SQL query has no results or if there is an update count. You can use the getUpdateCount() method to get the update count. In rare situations, this method may return multiple ResultSets; in that case, you can call the getMoreResults() method.
ResultSet executeQuery(String sql)	Executes the query and returns the ResultSet object as the result. If there are no results, the method does not return null; rather, the returned ResultSet object will return false when the next() method is called.
int executeUpdate(String sql)	Executes CREATE, INSERT, UPDATE, or DELETE SQL queries. It returns the number of rows updated (or zero if there is no result, such as with the CREATE statement).
Connection getConnection()	Returns the Connection object with which the Statement object was created.
void close()	Closes the database and other JDBC resources associated with this Statement object. Calling close() on an already-closed Statement object has no effect.

📝 Choose the relevant execute method based on the type of the SQL statement. Remember that each execute method returns different output. The method executeQuery() returns a ResultSet, executeUpdate() returns an update count, and execute() method may return multiple ResultSets or multiple update counts or a combination of both.

ResultSet Interface

Relational databases contain tables. Each table has a set of attributes (properties of an object modeled by the table) that are represented by columns; rows are records containing values for those properties. When you query a database, it results in tabular data: a certain number of rows containing the columns requested by the query. This tabular data is referred to as *resultset*. A *resultset* is a table with column headings and associated values requested by the query.

A resultset maintains a cursor pointing to the current row. You can read only one row at a time, so you must change the position of the cursor to read/navigate through the entire resultset. Initially, the cursor is set to just before the first row. You need to call the next() method on the resultset to advance the cursor position by one row. This method returns a Boolean value; hence you can use it in a while loop to iterate over the entire resultset. Table 12-4 shows other methods supported by ResultSet for moving the cursor.

Table 12-4. Useful ResultSet Methods to Move the Cursor

Method	Description
void beforeFirst()	Sets the cursor just before the first row in the resultset.
void afterLast()	Sets the cursor just after the last row of the resultset.
boolean absolute(int rowNumber)	Sets the cursor to the requested row number (absolute position in the table—not relative to the current position).
boolean relative(int rowNumber)	Sets the cursor to the requested row number relative to the current position. rowNumber can be a positive or negative value: a positive value moves forward, and a negative value moves backward relative to the current position.
boolean next()	Sets the cursor to the next row of the resultset.
boolean previous()	Sets the cursor to the previous row of the resultset.

Figure 12-3 illustrates these methods with an example. The figure has five rows, with the cursor pointing to the row with ID 3. If you call beforeFirst(), the cursor is moved to the position before row ID 1. If you call afterLast(), the cursor is moved to the position after row ID 5. If you call relative(-2), because the current position is at row ID 3, the cursor moves two position backward and points to the position with row ID 1. Calling previous() and next() moves the cursor to positions with row ID 2 and row ID 4, respectively. Finally, calling absolute(5) moves the cursor to the position with row ID 5.

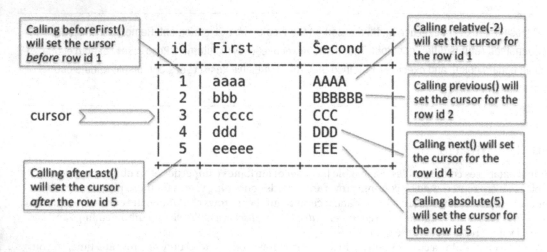

Figure 12-3. *Moving the cursor by calling ResultSet methods*

ResultSet also provides a set of methods to read the value at the desired column in the current row. In general, these methods come in two flavors: the first flavor takes a column number as the input, and the second flavor accepts a column name as the input. For instance, the methods to read a double value are `double getDouble(int columnNumber)` and `double getDouble(String columnName)`. In a similar way, `ResultSet` provides `get()` methods for all basic types.

Similarly, `ResultSet` provides a set of methods to update values at the desired column in the selected row. These methods also come in two variants: `void updateXXX(int columnNumber, XXX x)` and `void updateXXX(String columnName, XXX x)`, where the update methods are defined for various data types represented as XXX.

Querying the Database

Now you know all the necessary interfaces that are used to execute a simple SQL query on a database: `Connection`, `Statement`, and `ResultSet`. Figure 12-4 shows the high-level steps for establishing connection to the database, executing SQL queries, and processing the results.

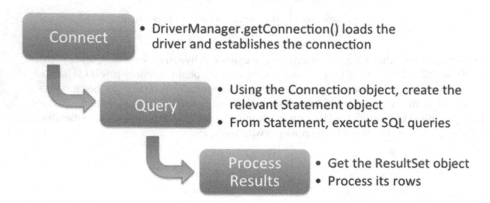

Figure 12-4. *Connecting to, querying, and processing results from a database*

Let's query a database and print the output. Recollect that you created a database named addressBook and a table named contact in this database, and inserted two rows in the table. Assume that you want to print the table contents; Listings 12-2 and 12-3 contain the program to do so

Listing 12-2. DbConnector.java

```java
import java.sql.Connection;
import java.sql.DriverManager;
import java.sql.SQLException;

// Utility class with method connectToDb() that will be used by other programs in this
chapter
public class DbConnector {
    public static Connection connectToDb() throws SQLException {
        String url = "jdbc:mysql://localhost:3306/";
        String database = "addressBook";
        String userName = "root";
        String password = "mysql123";
        return DriverManager.getConnection(url + database, userName, password);
    }
}
```

Listing 12-3. DbQuery.java

```java
import java.sql.Connection;
import java.sql.Statement;
import java.sql.ResultSet;
import java.sql.SQLException;

// Program to illustrate how to query a database
class DbQuery {
    public static void main(String[] args) {
        // Get connection, execute query, get the result set
        // and print the entries from the result rest
        try (Connection connection = DbConnector.connectToDb();
            Statement statement = connection.createStatement();
            ResultSet resultSet = statement.executeQuery("SELECT * FROM contact")){
                System.out.println("ID \tfName \tlName \temail \t\tphoneNo");
                while (resultSet.next()) {
                    System.out.println(resultSet.getInt("id") + "\t"
                        + resultSet.getString("firstName") + "\t"
                        + resultSet.getString("lastName") + "\t"
                        + resultSet.getString("email") + "\t"
                        + resultSet.getString("phoneNo"));
                }
        }
        catch (SQLException sqle) {
            sqle.printStackTrace();
            System.exit(-1);
        }
    }
}
```

The output of the program is as follows:

```
ID      fName       lName       email                       phoneNo
1       Michael     Taylor      michael@abc.com         +919876543210
2       William     Becker      william@abc.com         +449876543210
```

Let's look at what is happening in this code step by step:

- In the main() method, there is a try-with-resources statement. The first statement is a call to the connectToDb() method, which is defined in the program. The connectToDb() method simply connects to the database (which you saw in the last example) and returns a Connection object if it succeeds.

- The next statement creates a Statement object from the connection.

- The Statement object is now used to execute a query. You want to fetch all the columns in the contact table; hence you write SELECT * FROM contact as a SQL query. You execute the query using the executeQuery() method of the Statement object. The outcome of the query is stored in a ResultSet object.

- The ResultSet object is used to print the fetched data. You read all column values in the current row and do the same for each row in the ResultSet object.

- Because you've created the Connection, Statement, and ResultSet objects within a try-with-resources statement, there is no need to explicitly call close() on these resources. However, if you are not using try-with-resources, you need to release them explicitly in a finally block.

Here, you are using column names to read the associated values. You can use column numbers instead to do the same job. Here is the modified code in the while loop to use column numbers:

```
while (resultSet.next()) {
        System.out.println(resultSet.getInt(1)
                + "\t" + resultSet.getString(2)
                + "\t" + resultSet.getString(3)
                + "\t" + resultSet.getString(4)
                + "\t" + resultSet.getString(5));
}
```

This code produces exactly the same result as the last example. However, it's important to observe that here the column index starts from 1, not 0.

 The column index in the ResultSet object starts from 1, not 0.

While referring to columns by column index, if you refer to a column by an index that is more than the total number of columns, you get an exception. For instance, if you change one of the column indices used in the previous example to 6, you get the following exception:

```
java.sql.SQLException: Column Index out of range, 6 > 5.
        at com.mysql.jdbc.SQLError.createSQLException(SQLError.java:1074)
        [... this part of the stack trace elided ...]
        at DbQuery.main(DbQuery.java:18)
```

Be careful to always provide the correct column indices.

In this example, you know the number of columns as well as the data types in the columns. What if you know neither the number of columns in each row nor the data types in the columns? In that case, you first need to call the getMetaData() method on the ResultSet object that returns a ResultMetaData object; on that ResultMetaData object, you can use the getColumnCount() method to get the column count. When you don't know the data type of a column entry, you can use the getObject() method on the ResultSet object. You can pass the column index to getObject() to get the value in the corresponding column. Here is the modified code that uses these methods:

```
// from resultSet metadata, find out how many columns there are
// and then read the column entries
int numOfColumns = resultSet.getMetaData().getColumnCount();
while (resultSet.next()) {
    // remember that the column index starts from 1 not 0
    for(int i = 1; i <= numOfColumns; i++) {
        // since we do not know the data type of the column, we use getObject()
        System.out.print(resultSet.getObject(i) + "\t");
    }
    System.out.println("");
}
```

The output of the program is

ID	+Name	‐Name	email	phoneNo
1	Michael	Taylor	michael@abc.com	+919876543210
2	William	Becker	william@abc.com	+449876543210

Let's carry out another exercise. This time, you just want to print the name and e-mail address of records where the first name matches "Michael" (see Listing 12-4).

Listing 12-4. DbQuery4.java

```
import java.sql.Connection;
import java.sql.Statement;
import java.sql.ResultSet;
import java.sql.SQLException;

class DbQuery4 {
    public static void main(String[] args) throws SQLException {
        try (Connection connection = DbConnector.connectToDb();
            Statement statement = connection.createStatement();
            ResultSet resultset = statement.executeQuery("SELECT firstName, email FROM
            contact WHERE firstName=\"Michael\"")) {
            System.out.println("fName \temail");
            while (resultset.next()){
                System.out.println(resultset.getString("firstName") + "\t"
                            + resultset.getString("email"));
            }
```

```
        } catch (SQLException e) {
            e.printStackTrace();
            System.exit(-1);
        }
    }
}
```

This program prints the following:

```
fName    email
Michael  michael@abc.com
```

Updating the Database

Now let's update the database. You can do so in two ways: you can use SQL queries to update the database directly, or you can fetch a resultset using a SQL query and then change it and the database. JDBC supports both of these methods. Let's focus on retrieving the resultset and modifying it and the database.

In order to modify the resultset and the database, the ResultSet class provides a set of update methods for each data type. There are also other supporting methods, such as updateRow() and deleteRow(), to make the task simpler. It's time to get your hands dirty: assume that one of the contacts in your addressBook database has changed their phone number, and you need to update the phone number in the database using a JDBC program (see Listing 12-5).

Listing 12-5. DbUpdate.java

```
import java.sql.Connection;
import java.sql.Statement;
import java.sql.ResultSet;
import java.sql.SQLException;

// To illustrate how we can update a database
class DbUpdate {
    public static void main(String[] args) throws SQLException {
        try (Connection connection = DbConnector.connectToDb();
            Statement statement = connection.createStatement();
            ResultSet resultSet = statement.executeQuery("SELECT * FROM contact WHERE
            firstName=\"Michael\"")) {
                // first fetch the data and display it before the update operation
                System.out.println("Before the update");
                System.out.println("id \tfName \tlName \temail \t\tphoneNo");
                while (resultSet.next()) {
                    System.out.println(resultSet.getInt("id") + "\t"
                                + resultSet.getString("firstName") + "\t"
                                + resultSet.getString("lastName") + "\t"
                                + resultSet.getString("email") + "\t"
                                + resultSet.getString("phoneNo"));
                }
                // now update the resultset and display the modified data
                resultSet.absolute(1);
                resultSet.updateString("phoneNo", "+919976543210");
                System.out.println("After the update");
```

```
        System.out.println("id \tfName \tlName \temail \t\tphoneNo");
        resultSet.beforeFirst();
        while (resultSet.next()) {
                System.out.println(resultSet.getInt("id") + "\t"
                                + resultSet.getString("firstName") + "\t"
                                + resultSet.getString("lastName") + "\t"
                                + resultSet.getString("email") + "\t"
                                + resultSet.getString("phoneNo"));
        }
    } catch (SQLException e) {
        e.printStackTrace();
        System.exit(-1);
    }
  }
}
```

Let's pick out the nitty-gritty of the program, step by step:

- You establish the connection using the DbConnector.connectToDb() method.

- After creating a Statement object, you execute a query on the database to find the record associated with *Michael*. (For the sake of simplicity, assume that the resultset will contain exactly one record.)

- You print the retrieved record.

- You use the absolute() method to move the cursor to the first row in the ResultSet object; then you update the phone number using the updateString() method.

- Finally, you print the modified resultset.

That looks straightforward. Execute the program and see what it prints:

```
Before the update
id      fName  lName   email           phoneNo
1       Michael Taylor  michael@abc.com +919876543210
com.mysql.jdbc.NotUpdatable: Result Set not updatable.(...rest of the text elided)
        at com.mysql.jdbc.ResultSetImpl.updateString(ResultSetImpl.java:8618)
        at com.mysql.jdbc.ResultSetImpl.updateString(ResultSetImpl.java:8636)
        at DbUpdate.main(DbUpdate.java:34)
```

Oops—the program crashed after throwing an exception! What happened?

You are trying to update a ResultSet object that is not updatable. In order to make the update in the resultset and the database, you need to make this resultset updatable. You can do that by creating a proper Statement object; while calling the createStatement() method, you can pass inputs such as whether you want a scrollable resultset that is sensitive to changes or an updatable resultset.

Make this single change to the call to createStatement() in Listing 12-5:

```
Statement statement = connection.createStatement(ResultSet.TYPE_SCROLL_SENSITIVE,
ResultSet.CONCUR_UPDATABLE);
```

Now run the changed program to see if it works:

```
Before the update
id      fName  lName  email            phoneNo
1       Michael Taylor michael@abc.com +919876543210
After the update
id      fName  lName  email            phoneNo
1       Michael Taylor michael@abc.com +919876543210
```

Good, the program did not result in an exception. But wait—the phone number is not updated! What happened? You forgot a vital statement after the update: the updateRow() method. Every time you make a change in the resultset using the appropriate updateXXX() method, you need to call updateRow() to make sure all the values are actually updated in the database. Make this change, and try again (see Listing 12-6).

Listing 12-6. DbUpdate2.java

```java
import java.sql.Connection;
import java.sql.Statement;
import java.sql.ResultSet;
import java.sql.SQLException;

// To illustrate how we can update a database
class DbUpdate2 {
    public static void main(String[] args) throws SQLException {
        try (Connection connection = DbConnector.connectToDb();
            // create a statement from which the created ResultSets
            // are "scroll sensitive" as well as "updatable"
            Statement statement = connection.createStatement(ResultSet.TYPE_SCROLL_
            SENSITIVE, ResultSet.CONCUR_UPDATABLE);
            ResultSet resultSet = statement.executeQuery("SELECT * FROM contact WHERE
            firstName=\"Michael\"")) {
                // first fetch the data and display it before the update operation
                System.out.println("Before the update");
                System.out.println("id \tfName \tlName \temail \t\tphoneNo");
                while (resultSet.next()) {
                        System.out.println(resultSet.getInt("id") + "\t"
                                + resultSet.getString("firstName") + "\t"
                                + resultSet.getString("lastName") + "\t"
                                + resultSet.getString("email") + "\t"
                                + resultSet.getString("phoneNo"));
                }
                // now update the resultset and display the modified data
                resultSet.absolute(1);
                resultSet.updateString("phoneNo", "+919976543210");
                // reflect those changes back to the database
                // by calling updateRow() method
                resultSet.updateRow();
                System.out.println("After the update");
                System.out.println("id \tfName \tlName \temail \t\tphoneNo");
                resultSet.beforeFirst();
```

```
                while (resultSet.next()) {
                    System.out.println(resultSet.getInt("id") + "\t"
                            + resultSet.getString("firstName") + "\t"
                            + resultSet.getString("lastName") + "\t"
                            + resultSet.getString("email") + "\t"
                            + resultSet.getString("phoneNo"));
                }
            } catch (SQLException e) {
                e.printStackTrace();
                System.exit(-1);
            }
        }
    }
}
```

The revised program prints the following:

```
Before the update
id      fName   lName   email           phoneNo
1       Michael Taylor  michael@abc.com +919876543210
After the update
id      fName   lName   email           phoneNo
1       Michael Taylor  michael@abc.com +919976543210
```

It is working fine. Now you know the requirements and steps required to update a row in a database.

 Always call updateRow after modifying the row contents; otherwise, you will lose the changes.

Next, how about inserting a record in the resultset and the database? Try the example shown in Listing 12-7.

Listing 12-7. DbInsert.java

```java
import java.sql.Connection;
import java.sql.Statement;
import java.sql.ResultSet;
import java.sql.SQLException;

// To illustrate how to insert a row in a resultset and in the database
class DbInsert {
    public static void main(String[] args) throws SQLException {
        try (Connection connection = DbConnector.connectToDb();
            Statement statement = connection.createStatement(
                    ResultSet.TYPE_SCROLL_SENSITIVE, ResultSet.CONCUR_UPDATABLE);
            ResultSet resultSet =
                    statement.executeQuery("SELECT * FROM contact")) {
            System.out.println("Before the insert");
            System.out.println("id \tfName \tlName \temail \t\tphoneNo");
```

```
            while (resultSet.next()){
                    System.out.println(resultSet.getInt("id") + "\t"
                            + resultSet.getString("firstName") + "\t"
                            + resultSet.getString("lastName") + "\t"
                            + resultSet.getString("email") + "\t"
                            + resultSet.getString("phoneNo"));
            }
            resultSet.moveToInsertRow();
            resultSet.updateString("firstName", "John");
            resultSet.updateString("lastName", "K.");
            resultSet.updateString("email", "john@abc.com");
            resultSet.updateString("phoneNo", "+19753186420");
            resultSet.insertRow();
            System.out.println("After the insert");
            System.out.println("id \tfName \tlName \temail \t\tphoneNo");
            resultSet.beforeFirst();
            while (resultSet.next()){
                    System.out.println(resultSet.getInt("id") + "\t"
                            + resultSet.getString("firstName") + "\t"
                            + resultSet.getString("lastName") + "\t"
                            + resultSet.getString("email") + "\t"
                            + resultSet.getString("phoneNo"));
            }
    } catch (SQLException e) {
            e.printStackTrace();
    }
  }
}
```

What happens in this example? After printing the current records, you call the moveToInsertRow() method. This method sets the cursor to a new record and prepares the resultset for the insertion of a row (it creates a buffer to hold the column values). After that, you use updateString() to modify each column value in the newly added row. And finally, you call insertRow() to insert the new row into the resultset and the database. One important thing to note here is that you need to provide the correct type of values for each column. Also, you cannot leave a column blank (not provide any value) if the column value cannot be left unfilled. In the case of either of these violations, you may get a SQLException.

Let's see what this program prints:

```
Before the insert
id      fName   lName   email           phoneNo
1       Michael Taylor  michael@abc.com +919976543210
2       William Becker  william@abc.com +449876543210
After the insert
id      fName   lName   email           phoneNo
1       Michael Taylor  michael@abc.com +919976543210
2       William Becker  william@abc.com +449876543210
3       John    K.      john@abc.com    +19753186420
```

Looks good! Now let's try another operation: deleting a record from the database. Take a look at the program in Listing 12-8.

Listing 12-8. DbDelete.java

```java
import java.sql.Connection;
import java.sql.Statement;
import java.sql.ResultSet;
import java.sql.SQLException;

// To illustrate how to delete a row in a resultset and in the database
class DbDelete {
    public static void main(String[] args) throws SQLException {
        try (Connection connection = DbConnector.connectToDb();
            Statement statement = connection.createStatement(
            ResultSet.TYPE_SCROLL_SENSITIVE, ResultSet.CONCUR_UPDATABLE);
            ResultSet resultSet1 = statement.executeQuery
                    ("SELECT * FROM contact WHERE firstName=\"John\"")) {
                if(resultSet1.next()){
                        // delete the first row
                        resultSet1.deleteRow();
                }
                resultSet1.close();

                // now fetch again from the database
                try (ResultSet resultSet2 = statement.executeQuery("SELECT * FROM contact")) {
                        System.out.println("After the deletion");
                        System.out.println("id \tfName \tlName \temail \t\tphoneNo");
                        while (resultSet2.next()){
                                System.out.println(resultSet2.getInt("id") + "\t"
                                            + resultSet2.getString("firstName") + "\t"
                                            + resultSet2.getString("lastName") + "\t"
                                            + resultSet2.getString("email") + "\t"
                                            + resultSet2.getString("phoneNo"));
                        }
                }
        } catch (SQLException e) {
            e.printStackTrace();
            System.exit(-1);
        }
    }
}
```

This program simply selects a proper row to delete and calls the deleteRow() method on the current selected row. Here's the output of the program:

```
After the deletion
id      fName  lName   email           phoneNo
1       Michael Taylor  michael@abc.com +919976543210
2       William Becker  william@abc.com +449876543210
```

The program works fine and correctly removes the row where the person's first name is John.

You may remember that you created a table named contact in your database. At that time, you created the table from the MySQL command prompt. The same task can be done using a JDBC program. Let's create a new table named familyGroup in the database programmatically (see Listing 12-9).

Listing 12-9. DbCreateTable.java

```
import java.sql.Connection;
import java.sql.Statement;
import java.sql.SQLException;

class DbCreateTable {
    public static void main(String[] args) {
        try (Connection connection = DbConnector.connectToDb();
            Statement statement = connection.createStatement()){
                // use CREATE TABLE SQL statement to
                // create table familyGroup
                statement.executeUpdate("CREATE TABLE familyGroup (id int not null
                auto_increment, nickName varchar(30) not null, primary key(id));");
                System.out.println("Table created successfully");
        }
        catch (SQLException sqle) {
            sqle.printStackTrace();
                System.exit(-1);
        }
    }
}
```

The program prints the following:

```
Table created successfully
```

The program is working as expected. You connect to the database and get the Statement object as you did earlier. Then, you issue a SQL statement using the executeUpdate() method. Using the SQL statement, you declare that a table called familyGroup needs to be created along with two columns: id and nickName. Also, you declare that id should be treated as the primary key. That's it; the SQL statement creates a new table in your database.

What happens when you pass a SQL statement that has syntax errors? For example, if you misspell "TABLE" as "TABL", you get this exception:

```
com.mysql.jdbc.exceptions.jdbc4.MySQLSyntaxErrorException: You have an error in your SQL
syntax; check the manual that corresponds to your MySQL server version for the right syntax
to use near 'TABL familyGroup (id int not null auto_increment, nickName varchar(30) not
null,' at line 1
```

Passing correct SQL statements (without syntax errors) is your responsibility.

Points to Remember

Here is a list of points that may be helpful on your OCPJP 8 exam:

- The boolean absolute(int) method in ResultSet moves the cursor to the passed row number in that ResultSet object. If the row number is positive, it moves to that position from the beginning of the ResultSet object; if the row number is negative, it moves to that position from the end of the ResultSet object. Assume that there are ten entries in the ResultSet object. Calling absolute(3) moves the cursor to the third row. Calling absolute(-bs) moves the cursor to the eighth row. If you give out-of-range values, the cursor moves to either the beginning or the end.

- In a ResultSet object, calling absolute(1) is equivalent to calling first(), and calling absolute(-1) is equivalent to calling last().

- You can use a column name or column index with ResultSet methods. The index you use is the index of the ResultSet object, not the column number in the database table.

- A Statement object closes the current ResultSet object if the Statement object is closed, re-executed, or made to retrieve the next set of results. That means it is not necessary to call close() explicitly with a ResultSet object; however, it is good practice to call close() once you are done with the object.

- You may use the column name of a ResultSet object without worrying about the case: getXXX() methods accept case-insensitive column names to retrieve the associated value.

- Think of a case in which you have two columns in a ResultSet object with the same name. How you can retrieve the associated values using the column name? If you use a column name to retrieve the value, it always points to the first column that matches the given name. Hence, you have to use column index in this case to retrieve values associated with both columns.

- You may remember that the PreparedStatement interface inherits from Statement. However, PreparedStatement overrides all flavors of execute methods. For instance, the behavior of executeUpdate() may be different from its base method.

- You may cancel any update you made using the method cancelRowUpdates(). However, you must call this method before calling updateRow(). In all other cases, it has no impact on the row.

- While connecting to the database, you need to specify the correct username and password. If the provided username or password is not correct, you get a SQLException.

Summary

Let's briefly review the key points for each certification objective in this chapter. Please read this section before appearing for the exam.

Identify the components required to connect to a database using the DriverManager class including the JDBC URL

- JDBC hides the heterogeneity of all the DBMSs and offers a single set of APIs to interact with all types of databases. The complexity of heterogeneous interactions is delegated to the JDBC driver manager and JDBC drivers.

- The getConnection() method in the DriverManager class takes three arguments: a URL string, a username string, and a password string.

- The syntax of the URL (which needs to be specified to get the Connection object) is jdbc: <subprotocol>:<subname>.

- If the JDBC API is not able to locate the JDBC driver, it throws a SQLException. If jars for the drivers are available, they need to be included in the classpath to enable the JDBC API to locate the driver.

Describe the interfaces that make up the core of the JDBC API including the Driver, Connection, Statement, and ResultSet interfaces and their relationship to provider implementations

- The java.sql.Connection interface provides a channel through which the application and the database communicate.

- JDBC supports two classes for querying and updating: Statement and Resultset.

- A Statement is a SQL statement that can be used to communicate a SQL statement to the connected database and receive results from the database. There are three types of Statements:

  - Statement: Sends a SQL statement to the database without any parameters

  - PreparedStatement: Represents a precompiled SQL statement that can be customized using IN parameters

  - CallableStatement: Executes stored procedures; can handle IN as well as OUT and INOUT parameters

- A resultset is a table with column heading and associated values requested by the query.

Submit queries and read results from the database including creating statements, returning result sets, iterating through the results, and properly closing result sets, statements, and connections

- A ResultSet object maintains a cursor pointing to the current row. Initially, the cursor is set to just before the first row; calling the next() method advances the cursor position by one row.

- The column index in the ResultSet object starts from 1 (*not* from 0).

- You need to call updateRow() after modifying the row contents in a resultset; otherwise, changes made to the ResultSet object are lost.

- You can use a try-with-resources statement to close resources (Connection, ResultSet, and Statement) automatically.

QUESTION TIME

1. Which one of the given options is *not* correct with respect to the driver manager belonging to the JDBC architecture?

   A. A driver manager maintains a list of available data sources and their drivers.

   B. A driver manager chooses an appropriate driver to communicate to the respective DBMS.

   C. A driver manager ensures the atomic properties of a transaction.

   D. A driver manager manages multiple concurrent drivers connected to their respective data sources.

2. Consider the following code segment. Assume that the connection object is valid and the `statement.executeQuery()` method successfully returns a ResultSet object with a few rows in it:

```
Statement statement = connection.createStatement();
ResultSet resultSet = statement.executeQuery("SELECT * FROM contact"));

int numOfColumns = resultSet.getMetaData().getColumnCount();

while (resultSet.next()) {
    // traverse the columns by index values
    for(int i = 0; i < numOfColumns; i++) {
        // since we do not know the data type of the column, we use getObject()
        System.out.print(resultSet.getObject(i) + "\t");
    }
    System.out.println("");
}
```

Which of the following statements is true regarding this code segment?

A. The code segment will successfully print the contents of the rows in the ResultSet object.

B. The looping header is wrong. To traverse all the columns, it should be

```
for(int i = 0; i <= numOfColumns; i++) {
```

C. The looping header is wrong. To traverse all the columns, it should be

```
for(int i = 1; i <= numOfColumns; i++) {
```

D. The looping header is wrong. To traverse all the columns, it should be

```
for(int i = 1; i < numOfColumns; i++) {
```

3. Consider this program, and choose the best option describing its behavior (assume that the connection is valid):

```
try (Statement statement = connection.createStatement();
     ResultSet resultSet = statement.executeQuery("SELECT * FROM contact")){
    System.out.println(resultSet.getInt("id") + "\t"
        + resultSet.getString("firstName") + "\t"
        + resultSet.getString("lastName") + "\t"
        + resultSet.getString("email") + "\t"
        + resultSet.getString("phoneNo"));
}
catch (SQLException sqle) {
    System.out.println("SQLException");
}
```

A. This program will print the following: SQLException.

B. This program will print the first row from contact.

C. This program will print all the rows from contact.

D. This program will report compiler errors.

4. Which *two* of the following statements are *true* regarding Statement and its derived types?

A. Statement can handle SQL queries with IN, OUT, and INOUT parameters.

B. PreparedStatement is used to execute stored procedures.

C. You can get an instance of PreparedStatement by calling the preparedStatement() method in the Connection interface.

D. CallableStatement extends the PreparedStatement class; PreparedStatement in turn extends the Statement class.

E. The Statement interface and its derived interfaces implement the AutoCloseable interface, hence Statement objects can be used with the try-with-resources statement.

5. Which one of the following statements is a correct way to instantiate a Statement object?

A. Statement statement = connection.getStatement();

B. Statement statement = connection.createStatement();

C. Statement statement = connection.newStatement();

D. Statement statement = connection.getStatementInstance();

6. Consider the following code snippet:

```
try(ResultSet resultSet = statement.executeQuery("SELECT * FROM contact")) {

        // Stmt #1

        resultSet.updateString("firstName", "John");
        resultSet.updateString("lastName", "K.");
        resultSet.updateString("email", "john@abc.com");
        resultSet.updateString("phoneNo", "+19753186420");

        // Stmt #2

        // rest of the code elided
}
```

Assume that resultSet and statement are legitimate instances of the ResultSet and Statement interfaces, respectively. Which one of the following statements is correct with respect to Stmt #1 and Stmt #2 for successfully inserting a new row?

A. Replacing Stmt #1 with `resultSet.moveToInsertRow()` will make the program work.

B. Replacing Stmt #1 with `resultSet.insertRow()` will make the program work.

C. Replacing Stmt #1 with `resultSet.moveToInsertRow()` and Stmt #2 with `resultSet.insertRow()` will make the program work.

D. Replacing Stmt #1 with `resultSet.insertRow()` and Stmt #2 with `resultSet.moveToInsertRow()` will make the program work.

7. Which one of the following statements is *true* with respect to `ResultSet`?

A. Calling `absolute(1)` on a `ResultSet` instance is equivalent to calling `first()`, and calling `absolute(-1)` is equivalent to calling `last()`.

B. Calling `absolute(0)` on a `ResultSet` instance is equivalent to calling `first()`, and calling `absolute(-1)` is equivalent to calling `last()`.

C. Calling `absolute(-1)` on a `ResultSet` instance is equivalent to calling `first()`, and calling `absolute(0)` is equivalent to calling `last()`.

D. Calling `absolute(1)` on a `ResultSet` instance is equivalent to calling `first()`, and calling `absolute(0)` is equivalent to calling `last()`.

8. Consider the following code snippet. Assume that `DbConnector.connectToDb()` returns a valid `Connection` object and that the `contact` table has an entry with the value "Michael" in the `firstName` column:

```
ResultSet resultSet = null;
try (Connection connection = DbConnector.connectToDb()) {
    Statement statement = connection.createStatement();
    resultSet = statement.executeQuery("SELECT * FROM contact WHERE firstName
    LIKE 'M%'"); // #LINE1
}
while (resultSet.next()){      //#LINE2
    // print the names by calling resultSet.getString("firstName"));
}
```

A. This program results in a compiler error in the statement marked with comment #LINE1.

B. This program results in a compiler error in the statement marked with comment #LINE2.

C. This program crashes by throwing an `SQLException`.

D. This program crashes by throwing a `NullPointerException`.

E. This program prints `firstName` column values that start with the character "M".

Answers:

1. C. A driver manager ensures the atomic properties of a transaction.

   The other three options A, B, and D are true. A driver manager maintains a list of available data sources and their drivers. Given a database URL, the driver manager chooses an appropriate driver to communicate with the respective DBMS. Further, a driver manager manages multiple concurrent drivers connected to their respective data sources. However, it is not responsible for maintaining atomicity properties when performing transactions.

2. C. The looping header is wrong. To traverse all the columns, it should be

   ```
   for(int i = 1; i <= numOfColumns; i++) {
   ```

   Given *N* columns in a table, the valid column indexes are from 1 to *N*, not 0 to *N* - 1.

3. A. This program will print the following: `SQLException`.

   The statement `while (resultSet.next())` is missing.

4. The correct options are C and E.

   You can get an instance of `PreparedStatement` by calling the `preparedStatement()` method in the `Connection` interface. The `Statement` interface and its derived interfaces implement the `AutoCloseable` interface, so `Statement` objects can be used with the `try-with-resources` statement.

   The other three options A, B, and D are incorrect for the following reasons:

   A: `Statement` objects can be used for SQL queries that have no parameters. Only a `CallableStatement` can handle `IN`, `OUT`, and `INOUT` parameters.

   B: `PreparedStatement` is used for precompiled SQL statements. The `CallableStatement` type is used for stored procedures.

   D: `CallableStatement` implements the `PreparedStatement` interface. `PreparedStatement` in turn implements the `Statement` interface. Further, these three types are interfaces, not classes.

5. B. `Statement statement = connection.createStatement();`

6. C. Replacing Stmt #1 with `resultSet.moveToInsertRow();` and Stmt #2 with `resultSet.insertRow();` will make the program work.

   You need to call the `moveToInsertRow()` method in order to insert a new row: this method prepares the resultset for creating a new row. Once the row is updated, you need to call `insertRow()` to insert the row into the resultset and the database.

7. A. Calling `absolute(1)` on a `ResultSet` instance is equivalent to calling `first()`, and calling `absolute(-1)` is equivalent to calling `last()`.

8. C. This program crashes by throwing a `SQLException`.

    The `try-with-resources` block is closed before the `while` statement executes. Calling `resultSet.next()` results in making a call on the closed `ResultSet` object. Hence, this program results in throwing a `SQLException` ("Operation not allowed after ResultSet closed").

CHAPTER 13

Localization

Certification Objectives

Read and set the locale by using the Locale object

Create and read a Properties file

Build a resource bundle for each locale and load a resource bundle in an application

Computers and software have become so prevalent today that they are used everywhere in the world for human activities. For any software to be relevant and useful to these users, it needs to be localized. The process in which we adapt the software to the local language and customs is known as *localization*.

Localization is all about making the software relevant and usable for the users from different cultures—in other words, customizing software for people from different countries or languages. How do you localize a software application? Two important guidelines should be heeded when you localize a software application:

- Do not hardcode text (such as messages to the users, textual elements in GUIs, etc.) and separate them into external files or dedicated classes. With this accomplished there is usually minimal effort to add support for a new locale in your software.

- Handle cultural-specific aspects such as date, time, currency, and formatting numbers with localization in mind. Instead of assuming a default locale, design in such a way that the current locale is fetched and customized.

In this chapter, you'll learn how to localize your software. Localization mainly involves creating *resource bundles* for different locales, as well as making the software culture-aware by adapting it for use in different locales. You will also learn how to create and use these resource bundles in this chapter.

Locales

Certification Objective

Read and set the locale by using the Locale object

A locale is "a place representing a country, language, or culture." Consider the Canada-French locale. French is spoken in many parts of Canada, and this could be a locale. In other words, if you want to sell software that is customized for Canadians who speak French, then you need to facilitate your software for this locale. In Java, this locale is represented by the code fr_CA where fr is short for French and CA is short for Canada; we'll discuss the naming scheme for locales in more detail later in this section.

389

The Locale Class

In Java, the java.util.Locale class provides programming support for locales. Table 13-1 lists important methods in this class.

Table 13-1. *Important Methods in the Locale Class*

Method	Short Description
static Locale[] getAvailableLocales()	Returns a list of available locales (i.e., installed locales) supported by the JVM.
static Locale getDefault()	Returns the default locale of the JVM.
static void setDefault(Locale newLocale)	Sets the default locale of the JVM.
String getCountry()	Returns the country *code* for the locale object.
String getDisplayCountry()	Returns the country *name* for the locale object.
String getLanguage()	Returns the language *code* for the locale object.
String getDisplayLanguage()	Returns the language *name* for the locale object.
String getVariant()	Returns the variant *code* for the locale object.
String getDisplayVariant()	Returns the *name* of the variant code for the locale object.
String toString()	Returns a String composed of the codes for the locale's language, country, variant, etc.

The code in Listing 13-1 detects the default locale and checks the available locales in the JVM.

Listing 13-1. AvailableLocales.java

```java
import java.util.Locale;
import java.util.Arrays ;

class AvailableLocales {
        public static void main(String []args) {
                System.out.println("The default locale is: " + Locale.getDefault());
                Locale [] locales = Locale.getAvailableLocales();
                System.out.printf("No. of other available locales is: %d, and they are: %n",
                        locales.length);
                Arrays.stream(locales).forEach(
                        locale -> System.out.printf("Locale code: %s and it stands for %s %n",
                        locale, locale.getDisplayName()));
        }
}
```

It prints the following:

```
The default locale is: en_US
No. of other available locales is: 160, and they are:
Locale code: ms_MY and it stands for Malay (Malaysia)
Locale code: ar_QA and it stands for Arabic (Qatar)
Locale code: is_IS and it stands for Icelandic (Iceland)
Locale code: sr_RS_#Latn and it stands for Serbian (Latin,Serbia)
Locale code: no_NO_NY and it stands for Norwegian (Norway,Nynorsk)
Locale code: th_TH_TH_#u-nu-thai and it stands for Thai (Thailand,TH)
Locale code: fr_FR and it stands for French (France)
Locale code: tr and it stands for Turkish
Locale code: es_CO and it stands for Spanish (Colombia)
Locale code: en_PH and it stands for English (Philippines)
Locale code: et_EE and it stands for Estonian (Estonia)
Locale code: el_CY and it stands for Greek (Cyprus)
Locale code: hu and it stands for Hungarian
 [...rest of the output elided...]
```

Let's look at the methods in the program before analyzing the output. You use the method getDefault() in Locale to get the code of the default locale. After that you use getAvailableLocales() in the Locale class to get the list of locales supported by the JVM. Now, for each locale you print the code for the locale and also print the descriptive name using the getDisplayName() method of Locale.

The program prints the default locale as en_US for this JVM, which means the default is the English language spoken in US. Then it prints a very long list of available locales; to save space, we've shown only small part of the output. From this program, you know that there are many locales available and supported, and there is a default locale associated with every JVM.

There are four different kinds of locale codes in this output:

- "hu and it stands for Hungarian": just one code where hu stands for Hungarian

- "ms_MY and it stands for Malay (Malaysia)": two codes separated by underscore where ms stands for Malay and MY stands for Malaysia

- "no_NO_NY and it stands for Norwegian (Norway,Nynorsk)": three codes separated by underscores, as in no_NO_NY where no stands for Norwegian, NO for Norway, and NY for Nynorsk

- "th_TH_TH_#u-nu-thai and it stands for Thai (Thailand,TH)": two or three initial codes separated by underscores and the final one by # or _#, as in th_TH_TH_#u-nu-thai, which we'll discuss now.

Here is how these locale names are encoded:

```
language + "_" + country + "_" + (variant + "_#" | "#") + script + "-" + extensions
```

This locale coding scheme allows combining different variations to create a locale. For the locale code of "th_TH_TH_#u-nu-thai",

- The language code is "th" (Thai) and it is always written in lowercase

- The country code is "TH" (Thailand) and it is always written in uppercase

- The variant name is "TH"; here it repeats the country code, but it could be any string

- The script name is an empty string here; if given, it will be a four-letter string with the first letter in uppercase and the rest in lowercase (e.g., Latn)

- The extension follows the # or _# character (since script is an empty string); it is "u-nu-thai" in this example

To give another example, consider the locale code "sr_RS_#Latn",

- The language code is "sr" (Serbian)

- The country code is "RS" (Serbia)

- The variant name is empty here

- The script name is "Latn" (Latin) which is a four-letter string with the first letter in uppercase and the rest in lowercase

- The extension is empty here

Consider English, which is spoken in many countries. There are variations in English based on the country in which the language is spoken. We all know that American English is different from British English, but there are many such versions. Here is the code (Listing 13-2) that filters only English locales from all the available locales:

Listing 13-2. AvailableLocalesEnglish.java

```java
import java.util.Locale;
import java.util.Arrays;

class AvailableLocalesEnglish {
    public static void main(String []args) {
        Arrays.stream(Locale.getAvailableLocales())
                .filter(locale -> locale.getLanguage().equals("en"))
                .forEach(locale ->
                        System.out.printf("Locale code: %s and it stands for %s %n",
                                    locale, locale.getDisplayName()));
    }
}
```

It prints the following (the output and order may change in your machine):

```
Locale code: en_MT and it stands for English (Malta)
Locale code: en_GB and it stands for English (United Kingdom)
Locale code: en_CA and it stands for English (Canada)
Locale code: en_US and it stands for English (United States)
Locale code: en_ZA and it stands for English (South Africa)
Locale code: en and it stands for English
Locale code: en_SG and it stands for English (Singapore)
Locale code: en_IE and it stands for English (Ireland)
Locale code: en_IN and it stands for English (India)
Locale code: en_AU and it stands for English (Australia)
Locale code: en_NZ and it stands for English (New Zealand)
Locale code: en_PH and it stands for English (Philippines)
```

The output refers to different locales in English and makes use of only language code and the country code. We used the getLanguage() method in Locale, which returns the locale code. What are other such methods? Let's explore the methods available in the Locale class now.

Getting Locale Details and Setting Locales

The getter methods in the Locale class such as getLanguage(), getCountry(), and getVariant() return *codes*, whereas the similar methods getDisplayCountry(), getDisplayLanguage(), and getDisplayVariant() return *names*. Listing 13-3 illustrates how to use these methods for the locale Locale.CANADA_FRENCH.

Listing 13-3. LocaleDetails.java

```java
import java.util.Locale;

public class LocaleDetails {
    public static void main(String args[]) {
        Locale.setDefault(Locale.CANADA_FRENCH);
        Locale defaultLocale = Locale.getDefault();
        System.out.printf("The default locale is %s %n", defaultLocale);
        System.out.printf("The default language code is %s and the name is %s %n",
                    defaultLocale.getLanguage(), defaultLocale.getDisplayLanguage());
        System.out.printf("The default country code is %s and the name is %s %n",
                defaultLocale.getCountry(), defaultLocale.getDisplayCountry());
        System.out.printf("The default variant code is %s and the name is %s %n",
                defaultLocale.getVariant(), defaultLocale.getDisplayVariant());
    }
}
```

It prints the following:

```
The default locale is fr_CA
The default language code is fr and the name is français
The default country code is CA and the name is Canada
The default variant code is  and the name is
```

Let's understand the program. The setDefault() method takes a Locale object as argument. In this program, you set the default locale as Locale.CANADA_FRENCH with this statement:

```java
Locale.setDefault(Locale.CANADA_FRENCH);
```

The Locale class has many static Locale objects representing common locales so that you don't have to instantiate them and use them directly in your programs. In this case, Locale.CANADA_FRENCH is a static Locale object.

Instead of using this static Locale object, you can choose to instantiate a Locale object. Here is an alternative way to set the default locale by creating a new Canada (French) locale object:

```java
Locale.setDefault(new Locale("fr", "CA", ""));
```

The getDefault() method in Locale returns the default locale object set in the JVM. The next statement uses methods to get information related to the country. The difference between the getCountry() and getDisplayCountry() methods is that the former method returns the country code (which is not very readable for us), and the latter returns the country name, which is human readable. The country code is a two or three letter code (this code comes from an international standard: ISO 3166).

The behavior of getLanguage() and getDisplayLanguage() is similar to getting country details. The language code consists of two or three letters (this code comes from another international standard: ISO 639).

There was no variant in this locale, so nothing got printed when you used the getVariant() and getDisplayVariant() methods. However, for some other locale, there could be variant values, and those values would get printed for that locale. The variant could be any extra details such as operating environments (like MAC for Macintosh machine) or name of the company (such as Sun or Oracle).

Other than these, you also have less widely used methods such as getScript() and getDisplayCountry() that returns the script code and the country name for the locale.

Instead of calling Locale's getDisplayCountry() method, which takes no arguments, you can choose the overloaded version of getDisplayCountry(Locale), which takes a Locale object as an argument. This will print the name of the country *as in the passed locale*. For example, for the call Locale.GERMANY. getDisplayCountry(), you'll get the output "Deutschland" (that's how Germans refer to their country); however, for the call Locale.GERMANY.getDisplayCountry(Locale.ENGLISH), you'll get the output "Germany" (that's how British refer to the country name Germany)

DIFFERENT WAYS TO CREATE A LOCALE OBJECT

There are many ways to get or create a Locale object. We list four options here for creating an instance of Italian locale that corresponds to the language code of it.

Option 1: Use the constructor of the Locale class: Locale(String language, String country, String variant):

```
Locale locale1 = new Locale("it", "", "");
```

Option 2: Use the forLanguageTag(String languageTag) method in the Locale class:

```
Locale locale2 = Locale.forLanguageTag("it");
```

Option 3: Build a Locale object by instantiating Locale.Builder and then call setLanguageTag() from that object:

```
Locale locale3 = new Locale.Builder().setLanguageTag("it").build();
```

Option 4: Use the predefined static final constants for locales in the Locale class:

```
Locale locale4 = Locale.ITALIAN;
```

You can choose the way to create a Locale object based on your need. For example, the Locale class has only a few predefined constants for locales. If you want a Locale object from one of the predefined ones, you can straightaway use it, or you'll have to check which other option to use.

Resource Bundles

Certification Objective

Build a resource bundle for each locale and load a resource bundle in an application

In the last section, we discussed the Locale class and the way to get details of the default locale and the list of available locales. How do you *use* this locale information to customize the behavior of your programs? Let's take a simple example of greeting someone: in English, you say "Hello," but if the locale is different, how do you change this greeting to say, for example, "Ciao" if the locale is Italian (Italy)?

One obvious solution is to get the default locale, check if the locale is Italy and print "Ciao." It will work, but this approach is neither flexible nor extensible. How about customizing to other locales like Saudi Arabia (Arabic) or Thailand (Thai)? You have to find and replace all the locale specific strings for customizing for each locale. This task will be a nightmare if your application consists of thousands of such strings spread over a million lines of code and there are many locales to support.

In Java, resource bundles provide a solution to this problem of how to customize the application to locale-specific needs. So, what is a resource bundle? A resource bundle is a set of classes or property files that help define a set of keys and map those keys to locale specific values.

The abstract class java.util.ResourceBundle provides an abstraction of resource bundles in Java. It has two derived classes: java.util.PropertyResourceBundle and java.util.ListResourceBundle (see Figure 13-1). The two derived classes provide support for resource bundles using two different mechanisms:

- **The PropertyResourceBundle Class:** This concrete class provides support for multiple locales in the form of property files. For each locale, you specify the keys and values in a property file for that locale. For a given locale, if you use the ResourceBundle.getBundle() method, the relevant property file will be automatically loaded. Of course, there is no magic in it; you have to follow certain naming conventions for creating the property files, which we'll discuss in the section dedicated to discussing property files. You can use only Strings as keys and values when you use property files.

- **The ListResourceBundle Class:** For adding support to a locale, you can extend this abstract class. In your derived class, you have to override the getContents() method, which returns an Object [][]. This array must have the list of keys and values. The keys must be Strings. Typically the values are also Strings, but values can be anything: sound clips, video clips, URLs, or pictures.

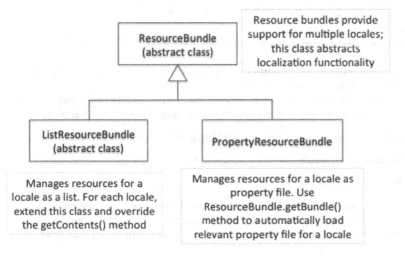

Figure 13-1. ResourceBundle and its two derived classes

Let's take a quick look at the methods supported by the ResourceBundle abstract class. Table 13-2 summarizes the important methods of this class. We'll now discuss localization support using these two derived classes of ResourceBundle.

Table 13-2. *Important Methods in the ResourceBundle Abstract Class*

Method	Short Description
Object getObject(String key)	Returns the value mapped to the given key. Throws a MissingResourceException if no object for a given key is found.
static ResourceBundle getBundle (String baseName), static final ResourceBundle getBundle (String baseName, Locale locale) final ResourceBundle getBundle (String baseName, Locale targetLocale, Control control)	Returns the ResourceBundle for the given baseName, locale, and control; throws a MissingResourceException if no matching resource bundle is found. The Control parameter is meant for controlling or obtaining info about the resource bundle loading process
String getString(String key)	Returns the value mapped to the given key; equivalent to casting the return value from getObject() to String. Throws a MissingResourceException if no object for a given key is found. Throws ClassCastException if the object returned is not a String.

Using PropertyResourceBundle

Certification Objective

Create and read a Properties file

If you design your application with localization in mind using property files, you can add support for new locales to the application *without changing anything in the code*!

We'll now look at an example using resource files and it will become clear to you. Let's start with a very simple program that prints "Hello" to the user. This program has three property file resource bundles:

1. The default resource bundle that assumes the English (US) locale.

2. A resource bundle for the Arabic locale.

3. A resource bundle for the Italian locale.

As discussed above, property files define strings as key value pairs in a file. Here is an example of a classpath that can be mapped to an actual path in your machine: classpath=C:\Program Files\Java\jre8. Property files will usually contain numerous such key value pairs, with each such pair in separate lines, as in the following:

```
classpath=C:\Program Files\Java\jre8
temp=C:\Windows\Temp
windir=C:\Windows
```

In the case of localization, you use property files to map the same key strings to different value strings. In the program, you'll refer the key strings, and by loading the matching property file for the locale, the corresponding values for the keys will be fetched from the property files for use in the program.

The naming of these property files is important (you'll see why soon) and below is the content of these bundles. To keep this example simple, there is only one key-value pair in these property files; in real-world programs, there could be a few hundred or even thousands of pairs present in each property file.

```
D:\> type ResourceBundle.properties
Greeting=Hello

D:\> type ResourceBundle_ar.properties
Greeting=As-Salamu Alaykum

D:\> type ResourceBundle_it.properties
Greeting=Ciao
```

As you can see, the default bundle is named ResourceBundle.properties. The resource bundle for Arabic is named ResourceBundle_ar.properties. Note the suffix "_ar", indicating Arabic as a local language. Similarly, the resource bundle for Italian is named ResourceBundle_it.properties, which makes use of the "_it" suffix to indicate the Italian as the associated language with this property file. Listing 13-4 makes use of these resource bundles.

Listing 13-4. LocalizedHello.java

```java
import java.util.Locale;
import java.util.ResourceBundle;

public class LocalizedHello {
    public static void main(String args[]) {
        Locale currentLocale = Locale.getDefault();
        ResourceBundle resBundle =
                        ResourceBundle.getBundle("ResourceBundle", currentLocale);
        System.out.printf(resBundle.getString("Greeting"));
    }
}
```

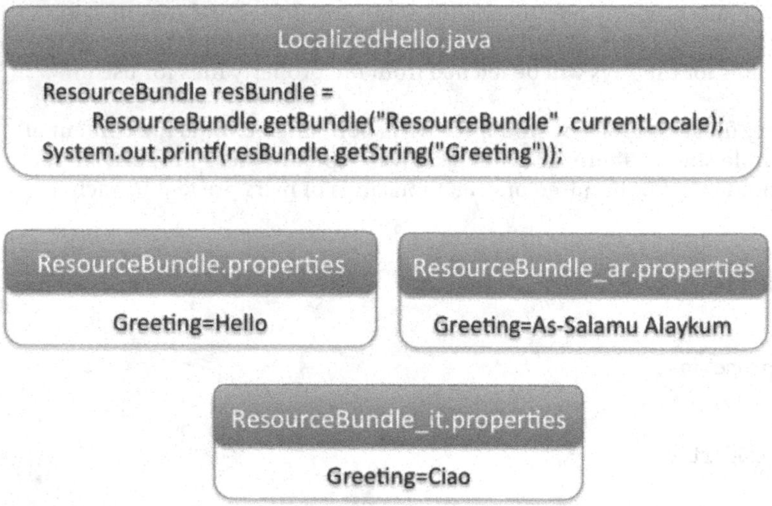

```
                    LocalizedHello.java
ResourceBundle resBundle =
     ResourceBundle.getBundle("ResourceBundle", currentLocale);
System.out.printf(resBundle.getString("Greeting"));
```

```
ResourceBundle.properties          ResourceBundle_ar.properties

     Greeting=Hello                   Greeting=As-Salamu Alaykum
```

```
          ResourceBundle_it.properties

                 Greeting=Ciao
```

Figure 13-2. *Getting relevant strings from ResourceBundles based on the locale*

There are two options to run this program in the desired way:

- **Option I:** Change the default locale in the program by calling the setDefault() method:

```
Locale.setDefault(Locale.ITALY);
```

This option is not recommended since it will require changing the program to set the locale.

- **Option II:** Change the default locale when invoking the JVM from the command line (if you're invoking the JVM from an IDE, provide the command line arguments to the JVM in the IDE settings):

```
D:\> java -Duser.language=it -Duser.region=IT LocalizedHello
```

Let's try the program by setting the locale with Option II (passing arguments to the command line when invoking the JVM).

```
D:\> java LocalizedHello
Hello
D:\> java -Duser.language=it LocalizedHello
Ciao
D:\> java -Duser.language=ar LocalizedHello
As-Salamu Alaykum
```

As you can see, depending on the locale that you explicitly set (Italian or Arabic in this example), or the default locale (US English in this example), the corresponding property file is loaded and the message string is resolved.

If you forget to create property files or they are not in the path, you will get a `MissingResourceException`.

In the program, first you get the current locale in the statement.

```
Locale currentLocale = Locale.getDefault();
```

After that, you load the resource bundle that starts with the name ResourceBundle and pass the locale for loading the resource bundle.

```
ResourceBundle resBundle = ResourceBundle.getBundle("ResourceBundle", currentLocale);
```

Finally, from the resource bundle, you look for the key "Greeting" and use the value of that key based on the loaded resource bundle.

```
System.out.printf(resBundle.getString("Greeting"));
```

Using ListResourceBundle

Support for a new locale can be added using `ListResourceBundle` by extending it. While extending the ListResourceBundle, you need to override the abstract method getContents(); the signature of this method is:

```
protected Object[][] getContents();
```

Note that the keys are Strings, but values can be of any type, hence the array type is Object; further, the method returns a list of key and value pairs. As a result, the getContents() method returns a two-dimensional array of Objects.

You create resource bundles by extending the `ListResourceBundle` class, whereas with `PropertyResourceBundle`, you create the resource bundle as property files. Furthermore, when extending `ListResourceBundle`, you can have any type of objects as values, whereas values in a properties file can only be Strings.

Listing 13-5 shows an example of extending the ListResourceBundle, which returns the largest box-office movie hit for that particular locale. It defines a resource bundle named ResBundle. Since the name of the class does not have any suffix (such as "_it" or "_en_US"), it is the default implementation of the resource bundle. When looking for a matching ResBundle for any locale, this default implementation will be used in case no match is found.

Listing 13-5. ResBundle.java

```java
import java.util.ListResourceBundle;

// default US English version
public class ResBundle extends ListResourceBundle {
    public Object[][] getContents() {
        return contents;
    }
    static final Object[][] contents = {
        { "MovieName", "Avatar" },
        { "GrossRevenue", (Long) 2782275172L }, // in US dollars
        { "Year", (Integer)2009 }
    };
}
```

Now, let's define a ResBundle for the Italian locale. You give the class the suffix "_it_IT". The language code "it" stands for Italian and the country code "IT" stands for Italy (Listing 13-6).

Listing 13-6. ResBundle_it_IT.java

```java
import java.util.ListResourceBundle;

// Italian version
public class ResBundle_it_IT extends ListResourceBundle {
    public Object[][] getContents() {
        return contents;
    }
    static final Object[][] contents = {
        { "MovieName", "Che Bella Giornata" },
        { "GrossRevenue", (Long) 43000000L }, // in euros
        { "Year", (Integer)2011 }
    };
}
```

As you can see, the implementations for ResBundle and ResBundle_it_IT are similar except for the values mapped to the keys. Now how do you know if your resource bundles are working or not? Listing 13-7 loads ResBundle for both default and Italian locales.

Listing 13-7. LocalizedBoxOfficeHits.java

```java
import java.util.ResourceBundle;
import java.util.Locale;

public class LocalizedBoxOfficeHits {
    public void printMovieDetails(ResourceBundle resBundle) {
        String movieName = resBundle.getString("MovieName");
        Long revenue = (Long)(resBundle.getObject("GrossRevenue"));
        Integer year = (Integer) resBundle.getObject("Year");

        System.out.println("Movie " + movieName + "(" + year + ")" + " grossed "
                        + revenue );
    }
```

```
    public static void main(String args[]) {
        LocalizedBoxOfficeHits localizedHits = new LocalizedBoxOfficeHits();
        // print the largest box-office hit movie for default (US) locale
        Locale locale = Locale.getDefault();
        localizedHits.printMovieDetails(ResourceBundle.getBundle("ResBundle", locale));

        // print the largest box-office hit movie for Italian locale
        locale = new Locale("it", "IT", "");
        localizedHits.printMovieDetails(ResourceBundle.getBundle("ResBundle", locale));
    }
}
```

It prints the following:

```
Movie Avatar (2009) grossed 2782275172
Movie Che Bella Giornata (2011) grossed 43000000
```

It loaded the default and Italian resource bundles successfully. However, there are problems with this output. The value 2782275172 is a US dollar value and the value 43000000 is in Euros. Moreover, the numbers are printed without commas, so it is difficult to make sense of these figures. It is possible to localize formatting these currency values. But handling number format, decimal format and currency difference between locales is not covered as part of the OCPJP 8 exam, so we are not discussing it further in this book.

Now, consider the following statement from this program:

```
Long revenue = (Long)(resBundle.getObject("GrossRevenue"));
```

This statement returns the value mapping to the key named GrossRevenue in the resource bundle. You have defined it as a Long object in the classes ResBundle and ResBundle_it_IT—so it worked. If you cast the types incorrectly, for example, as an Integer, you'll get a ClassCastException, as in:

```
Integer revenue = (Integer)(resBundle.getObject("GrossRevenue"));
// This code change will result in throwing this exception:
// Exception in thread "main" java.lang.ClassCastException:
//      java.lang.Long cannot be cast to java.lang.Integer
```

Here is another situation: if you mistype GrossRevenu instead of GrossRevenue as the key name, the program will crash with this exception, as in:

```
Long revenue = (Long)(resBundle.getObject("GrossRevenu"));
// This code will crash with this exception:
// Exception in the thread "main" java.util.MissingResourceException:
//      Can't find resources for bundle ResBundle, key GrossRevenu
```

You need to be careful in providing the keyname to get an object from a resource bundle: the keyname is case sensitive and the key name should exactly match—or else you'll get a MissingResourceException.

Loading a Resource Bundle

Certification Objective

Build a resource bundle for each locale and load a resource bundle in an application

You've already loaded resource bundles in the programs you've written using ResourceBundle or its two derived classes. From the exam perspective, you need to understand this loading process thoroughly, so we'll cover it in more detail in this section.

The process of finding a matching resource bundle is same for classes extended from ListResourceBundles as for property files defined for PropertyResourceBundles.

💣 For the resource bundles implemented as classes extended from ListResourceBundles, Java uses the reflection mechanism to find and load the class. You need to make sure that the class is public so that the reflection mechanism will find the class.

Naming Convention for Resource Bundles

Java enforces a predefined naming convention to be followed for creating resource bundles. Only through the names of the property bundles does the Java library load the relevant locales. Hence, it is important to understand and follow this naming convention when creating the property bundles for localizing Java applications.

You already saw how a locale name is encoded. Understanding this locale name encoding is important for naming the resource bundles because it makes use of the same encoding scheme. A fully qualified resource bundle has the following form:

```
packagequalifier.bundlename + "_" + language + "_" + country + "_" + (variant + "_#" | "#") +
script + "-" + extensions
```

Here is the description of the elements in this fully qualified name:

- **packagequalifier**: The name of the package (or the subpackages) in which the resource bundle is provided.

- **bundlename**: The name of the resource bundle that you'll use in the program to refer and load it.

- **language**: A two-letter abbreviation typically given in lowercase for the locale's language (in rare cases, it could be three letters as well).

- **country**: A two-letter abbreviation typically given in uppercase for the locale's country (in rare cases, it could be three letters as well).

- **variant**: An arbitrary list of variants (in lowercase or uppercase) to differentiate locales when you need more than one locale for a language and country combination.

We've omitted describing script and extension since they are rarely used.

For example, consider this fully qualified name:

`localization.examples.AppBundle_ en_US_Oracle_exam`

In this case, `localization.examples` is the package, `AppBundle` is the name of the resource bundle, en is language (which stands for English), US is the country, and `Oracle_exam` is the variant.

The two (or sometimes three) letter abbreviations for the locale's language and country are predefined since they are based on international standards. We don't provide the detailed list and there is also no need to know or remember all of them from the exam. You can look at the documentation of the `Locale` class to understand that.

On the OCPJP 8 exam, you're not expected to memorize language codes or country codes that are used for naming resource bundles. However, you are expected to *remember the naming convention* and recognize the constituents of a fully qualified resource bundle name.

Given that there could be many resource bundles for a bundle name, what is the search sequence to determine the resource bundle to be loaded? To clarify, we present the sequence as a series of steps. The search starts from Step 1. If at any step the search finds a match, the resource bundle is loaded. Otherwise, the search proceeds to the next step (see Figure 13-3).

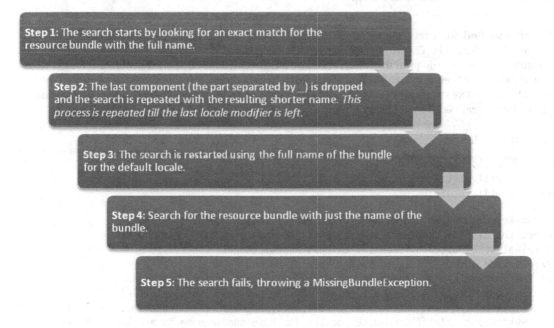

Figure 13-3. *Seach sequence for ResourceBundles*

The search starts with the given locale details and if not found, proceeds with checking for default locale, as in:

```
BundleName + "_" + language + "_" + country + "_" + variant
BundleName + "_" + language + "_" + country
BundleName + "_" + language
BundleName + "_" + defaultLanguage + "_" + defaultCountry
BundleName + "_" + defaultLanguage
```

Consider an example to find out how the matching resource bundle is found, and it will become clear to you. Assume that you have the following five entries in the search path, and your default locale is US English.

```
ResourceBundle.properties           -- Global bundle
ResourceBundle_ar.properties        -- Arabic language bundle
ResourceBundle_en.properties        -- English bundle (assuming en_US is the default locale)
ResourceBundle_it.properties        -- Italian language bundle
ResourceBundle_it_IT_Rome.properties -- Italian (Italy, Rome) bundle
```

📋 The getBundle() method takes a ResourceBundle.Control object as an additional parameter. By extending this ResourceBundle.Control class and passing the instance of that extended class to the getBundle() method, you can change the default resource bundle search process or read from non-standard resource bundle formats (such as XML files).

How can we find out what is the sequence of locales that Java is searching for? For that, let us extend the ResourceBundle.Control class and override the getCandidateLocales() method: this is to programmatically access and print the list of candidate locales and finally display the matching locale. Note that "candidate locale" refers to locales being considered by Java during the search process. Assume that property files named ResourceBundle_it_IT_Rome.properties and ResourceBundle_en.properties are available. The program is given in Listing 13-8.

Listing 13-8. CandidateLocales.java

```java
import java.util.ResourceBundle;
import java.util.List;
import java.util.Locale;

// Extend ResourceBundle.Control and override getCandidateLocales method
// to get the list of candidate locales that Java searches for
class TalkativeResourceBundleControl extends ResourceBundle.Control {
    // override the default getCandidateLocales method to print
    // the candidate locales first
    public List<Locale> getCandidateLocales(String baseName, Locale locale) {
        List<Locale> candidateLocales = super.getCandidateLocales(baseName, locale);
        System.out.printf("Candidate locales for base bundle name %s and locale %s %n",
                            baseName, locale.getDisplayName());
        candidateLocales.forEach(System.out::println);
        return candidateLocales;
    }
}
```

```
// Use a helper method loadResourceBundle to load a bundle given the bundle name and locale
class CandidateLocales {
    public static void loadResourceBundle(String resourceBundleName, Locale locale) {
        // Pass an instance of TalkativeResourceBundleControl
        // to print candidate locales
        ResourceBundle resourceBundle = ResourceBundle.getBundle(resourceBundleName,
                            locale, new TalkativeResourceBundleControl());
        String rbLocaleName = resourceBundle.getLocale().toString();
        // if the resource bundle locale name is empty,
        // it means default property file
        if(rbLocaleName.equals("")) {
                System.out.println("Loaded the default property file with name: "
                                + resourceBundleName);
        } else {
                System.out.println("Loaded the resource bundle for the locale: "
                                + resourceBundleName + "." + rbLocaleName);
        }
    }

    public static void main(String[] args) {
        // trace how ResourceBundle_it_IT_Rome.properties is resolved
        loadResourceBundle("ResourceBundle", new Locale("it", "IT", "Rome"));
    }
}
```

It prints the following:

```
Candidate locales for base bundle name ResourceBundle and locale Italian (Italy, Rome)
it_IT_Rome
it_IT
it

Loaded the resource bundle for the locale: ResourceBundle.it_IT_Rome
```

Now, before trying with other locales, consider how the program works. To trace how Java resolves the resource bundle to be finally loaded, you need to get the list of candidate locales. With the ResourceBundle.getBundle() method, you can pass an additional argument that is an instance of the ResourceBundle.Control class. For this reason, you define the TalkativeResourceBundleControl class.

The TalkativeResourceBundleControl class extends the ResourceBundle.Control class and overrides the getCandidateLocales() method. This getCandidateLocales() method returns a List<Locale> instance that contains the list of candidate locales for the given locale. You invoke super.getCandidateLocales() and traverse the resulting List<Locale> object to print the candidate locales so that you can examine the output later. From this overridden getCandidateLocales() method, you simply return this List<Locale> object. So, the behavior of TalkativeResourceBundleControl is identical to ResourceBundle.Control except that the overridden getCandidateLocales() in TalkativeResourceBundleControl prints the candidate locales.

The `CandidateLocales` class makes use of the `TalkativeResourceBundleControl`. It has a helper method called `loadResourceBundle()` that takes the resource bundle name and the name of the locale as arguments. This method simply passes these argument values to the `ResourceBundle.getBundle()` method; additionally it instantiates `TalkativeResourceBundleControl` and passes that object as the third argument to this method. The `getBundle()` method returns a `ResourceBundle` object. If the locale of the `ResourceBundle.getLocale()` name is empty, it means Java has loaded the global resource bundle. (Remember that the global resource bundle for that bundle name does not have any associated locale details.) If the name of the locale is not empty, it means Java has resolved to that particular locale.

Now, consider the code in the `main()` method. It calls `loadResourceBundle()` for the locale `it_IT_Rome`. There are three candidate locales and of that it correctly loaded the matching property file for the locale `it_IT_Rome`. So you know that it loaded the property file `ResourceBundle_it_IT_Rome.properties` correctly.

To continue this experiment, let's change the code inside the `main()` method of Listing 13-8 to this code:

```
loadResourceBundle("ResourceBundle", new Locale("fr", "CA", ""));
```

Now the program prints the following:

```
Candidate locales for base bundle name ResourceBundle and locale French (Canada)
fr_CA
fr
Candidate locales for base bundle name ResourceBundle and locale English (United States)
en_US
en
Loaded the resource bundle for the locale: ResourceBundle.en
```

Why does the program print the above output? Note that there is no corresponding property file for the `fr_CA` locale in the list of property files. So, the search continues to check the property files for the default locale. In this case, the default locale is `en_US`, and there is a property file for the `en` (English) locale. So, from the candidate locales, Java resolves to load the property file `ResourceBundle_en.properties` correctly.

Here is the final example. Replace the code in the `main()` method with this statement:

```
loadResourceBundle("ResBundl", Locale.getDefault());
```

The program prints the following:

```
Candidate locales for base bundle name ResBundl and locale English (United States)
en_US
en

The exception in thread "main" java.util.MissingResourceException: Can't find bundle for
base name ResBundl, locale en_US
        [... thrown stack trace elided ...]
```

You don't have any resource bundle named `ResBundl` and you've given the default locale (`en_US` in this case). Java searches for the bundle for this locale, and you know that you have not provided any bundle with name `ResBundl`. So, the program crashes after throwing a `MissingResourceException`.

Summary

Let us briefly review the key points from each certification objective in this chapter. Please read it before appearing for the exam.

Read and set the locale by using the Locale object

- A *locale* represents a language, culture, or country; the Locale class in Java provides an abstraction for this concept.

- Each locale can have three entries: the language, country, and variant. You can use standard codes available for language and country to form locale tags. There are no standard tags for variants; you can provide variant strings based on your need.

- The getter methods in the Locale class—such as getLanguage(), getCountry(), and getVariant()—return *codes*; whereas the similar methods of getDisplayCountry(), getDisplayLanguage(), and getDisplayVariant() return *names*.

- The getDefault() method in Locale returns the default locale set in the JVM. You can change this default locale to another locale by using the setDefault() method.

- There are many ways to create or get a Locale object corresponding to a locale:

  - Use the constructor of the Locale class.

  - Use the forLanguageTag(String languageTag) method in the Locale class.

  - Build a Locale object by instantiating Locale.Builder and then call setLanguageTag() from that object.

  - Use the predefined static final constants for locales in the Locale class.

Create and read a Properties file

- A resource bundle is a set of classes or property files that help define a set of keys and map those keys to locale-specific values.

- The class ResourceBundle has two derived classes: PropertyResourceBundle and ListResourceBundle. You can use ResourceBundle.getBundle() to get the bundle for a given locale.

- The PropertyResourceBundle class provides support for multiple locales in the form of property files. For each locale, you specify the keys and values in a property file for that locale. You can use only Strings as keys and values.

- To add support for a new locale, you can extend the ListResourceBundle class. In this derived class, you have to override the Object [][] getContents() method. The returned array must have the list of keys and values. The keys must be Strings, and values can be any objects.

- When passing the key string to the getObject() method to fetch the matching value in the resource bundle, make sure that the passed keys and the key in the resource bundle exactly match (the keyname is case sensitive). If they don't match, you'll get a MissingResourceException.

- The naming convention for a fully qualified resource bundle name is packagequalifier.bundlename + "_" + language + "_" + country + "_" + (variant + "_#" | "#") + script + "-" + extensions.

Build a resource bundle for each locale and load a resource bundle in an application

- The process of finding a matching resource bundle is same for classes extended from ListResourceBundles as for property files defined for PropertyResourceBundles.

- Here is the search sequence to look for a matching resource bundle. Search starts from Step 1. If at any step the search finds a match, the resource bundle is loaded. Otherwise, the search proceeds to the next step.

  - **Step 1:** The search starts by looking for an exact match for the resource bundle with the full name.

  - **Step 2:** The last component (the part separated by _) is dropped and the search is repeated with the resulting shorter name. *This process is repeated till the last locale modifier is left.*

  - **Step 3:** The search is continued using the full name of the bundle for the default locale.

  - **Step 4:** Search for the resource bundle with just the name of the bundle.

  - **Step 5:** The search fails, throwing a MissingBundleException.

- The getBundle() method takes a ResourceBundle.Control object as an additional parameter. By extending this ResourceBundle.Control class and passing that object, you can control or customize the resource bundle searching and loading process.

QUESTION TIME

1. Which one of the following statements makes use of a factory method?

   A. `Locale locale1 = new Locale("it", "", "");`

   B. `NumberFormat.getInstance(Locale.GERMANY);`

   C. `Locale locale3 = new Locale.Builder().setLanguageTag("it").build();`

   D. `Date today = new Date();`

   E. `Locale locale4 = Locale.ITALIAN;`

2. Consider the following program and choose the correct option:

```java
import java.util.Locale;

class Test {
    public static void main(String []args) {
        Locale locale1 = new Locale("en");                //#1
        Locale locale2 = new Locale("en", "in");          //#2
        Locale locale3 = new Locale("th", "TH", "TH");    //#3
        Locale locale4 = new Locale(locale3);             //#4
        System.out.println(locale1 + " " + locale2 + " " + locale3 + " " + locale4);
    }
}
```

A. This program will print the following: en en_IN th_TH_TH_#u-nu-thai th_TH_ TH_#u-nu-thai.

B. This program will print the following: en en_IN th_TH_TH_#u-nu-thai (followed by a runtime exception).

C. This program results in a compiler error at statement #1.

D. This program results in a compiler error at statement #2.

E. This program results in a compiler error at statement #3.

F. This program results in a compiler error at statement #4.

3. Choose the best option based on this program:

```
import java.util.Locale;

class LocaleTest {
    public static void main(String []args) {
            Locale locale = new Locale("navi", "pandora");   //#1
            System.out.println(locale);
    }
}
```

A. The program results in a compiler error at statement #1.

B. The program results in a runtime exception of NoSuchLocaleException.

C. The program results in a runtime exception of MissingResourceException.

D. The program results in a runtime exception of IllegalArgumentException.

E. The program prints the following: navi_PANDORA.

4. For localization, resource bundle property files are created that consist of key-value pairs. Which one of the following is a valid key value pair as provided in a resource bundle property file for some strings mapped to German language?

A.

```
<pair> <key>from</key> <value>von</value> </pair>
<pair> <key>subject</key> <value> betreff </value> </pair>
```

B.

```
from=von
subject=betreff
```

C.

```
key=from; value=von
key=subject; value=betreff
```

D.

```
pair<from,von>
pair<subject,betreff>
```

5. Assume that you've the following resource bundles in your classpath:

   ResourceBundle.properties

   ResourceBundle_ar.properties

   ResourceBundle_en.properties

   ResourceBundle_it.properties

   ResourceBundle_it_IT_Rome.properties

   Also assume that the default locale is English (US), where the language code is en and country code is US. Which one of these five bundles will be loaded for the call

   loadResourceBundle("ResourceBundle", new Locale("fr", "CA", ""));?

   A.   ResourceBundle.properties

   B.   ResourceBundle_ar.properties

   C.   ResourceBundle_en.properties

   D.   ResourceBundle_it.properties

   E.   ResourceBundle_it_IT_Rome.properties

6. Which of the following is a correct override for extending the ListResourceBundle class?

   A.   ```
        public HashMap<String, String> getContents() {
                Map<String, String> contents = new HashMap<>();
                contents.add("MovieName", "Avatar");
                return contents;
        }
        ```

   B.   ```
        public Object[] getContents() {
                return new Object[] { { "MovieName" } , { "Avatar" } };
        }
        ```

   C.   ```
        public Object[][] getContents() {
                return new Object[][] { { "MovieName", "Avatar" } };
        }
        ```

   D.   ```
        public String[] getKeysAndValues() {
                return new String[] { { "MovieName" } , { "Avatar" } };
        }
        ```

   E.   ```
        public String[] getProperties() {
                return new String[] { { "MovieName" }, { "Avatar" } };
        }
        ```
        ```

Answers:

1. B. `NumberFormat.getInstance(Locale.GERMANY);`

   A factory method creates an instance and returns back. Using a constructor directly to create an object is not related to a factory method, so A) and D) are not correct. C) builds a locale and is an example for using the Builder pattern. E) merely accesses the predefined `Locale` object; so it's not a method.

2. F. This program results in a compiler error at #4.

   The `Locale` class supports three constructors that are used in statements #1, #2, and #3; however, there is no constructor in the `Locale` class that takes another `Locale` object as argument, so the compiler gives an error for statement #4.

3. E. The program prints the following: navi_PANDORA.

   To create a `Locale` object using the constructor `Locale(String language, String country)`, any `String` values can be passed. Just attempting to create a Locale object will not result in throwing exceptions other than a `NullPointerException`, which could be raised for passing null `Strings`.

   The `toString()` method of `Locale` class returns a string representation of the `Locale` object consisting of language, country, variant, etc.)

4. B.

   `from=von`

   `subject=betreff`

   In the resource bundle property files, the key values are separated using the = symbol, with each line in the resource file separated by a newline character.

5. C. ResourceBundle_en.properties

   Java looks for candidate locales for a base bundle named `ResourceBundle` and locale French (Canada), and checks for the presence of the following property files:

   `ResourceBundle_fr_CA.properties`

   `ResourceBundle_fr.properties`

   Since both of them are not there, Java searches for candidate locales for the base bundle named `ResourceBundle` and a default locale (English - United States):

   `ResourceBundle_en_US.properties`

   `ResourceBundle_en.properties`

   `Java finds that there is a matching resource bundle,`
   `ResourceBundle_en.properties. Hence it loads this resource bundle.`

6. C.

```
public Object[][] getContents() {
    return new Object[][] { { "MovieName", "Avatar" } };
}
```

The return type of the `getContents()` method is `Object[][]`. Further, the method should return a new object of type `Object [][]` from the `method body`. Hence, option C) is the correct answer.

CHAPTER 14

■ ■ ■

Mock Exam

The prospect of taking the OCPJP 8 exam raises many questions in your mind.

- "What types of questions are asked in the exam?"
- "What is the format of the questions?"
- "How hard are the questions?"
- "How do I know if I'm ready to take the exam?"

This chapter presents a *mock exam* that helps answer these questions. Use this mock exam as a mental dipstick to gauge how prepared you are to pass the OCPJP 8 exam.

The questions in this mock exam closely mimic the actual questions you will encounter on your OCPJP 8 exam. For instance, you will find these aspects in the actual OCPJP 8 exam: the questions will assume that necessary import statements are included; most questions will contain only relevant code segments (and not complete programs); and questions will appear in random order (and not according to the sequence of exam topics given in the exam syllabus). In this mock exam, we have adopted a similar approach to make this mock exam closely mimic the question format in the actual OCPJP 8 exam.

Before you get started, take a print out of the answer sheet given at the end of this exam. Take this exam as if it were your real OCPJP 8 exam by simulating real test conditions. Find a quiet place where you can take this mock exam without interruption or distraction. Mark your start and finish times, and stop if you cross the exam time limit (2.5 hours). Observe closed-book rules: do not consult the answer key or any other any print, human, or web resources during this mock exam. Check the answers only after you complete the exam. Out of 85 questions, you need to answer at least 55 questions correctly to pass this exam (the passing score is 65%).

Best of luck!

TIME: 2 HOURS 30 MINUTES   NO. OF QUESTIONS: 85

1.   **What will be the result of executing this code segment?**

```
Stream.of("ace ", "jack ", "queen ", "king ", "joker ")
        .mapToInt(card -> card.length())
        .filter(len -> len > 3)
        .peek(System.out::print)
        .limit(2);
```

a)   This code segment prints: jack queen king joker

b)   This code segment prints: jack queen

c)   This code segment prints: king joker

d)   This code segment does not print anything on the console

2.   **Consider the following snippet:**

```
int ch = 0;
try (FileReader inputFile = new FileReader(file)) {
        // #1
        System.out.print( (char)ch );
    }
}
```

**Which one of the following statements can be replaced with statement #1
so that the contents of the file are correctly printed on the console and the
program terminates.**

a)   while((ch = inputFile.read()) != null) {

b)   while((ch = inputFile.read()) != -1) {

c)   while((ch = inputFile.read()) != 0) {

d)   while((ch = inputFile.read()) != EOF) {

3.   **What will be the output of the following program?**

```
class Base {
    public Base() {
        System.out.println("Base");
    }
}

class Derived extends Base {
    public Derived() {
        System.out.println("Derived");
    }
}
```

```
class DeriDerived extends Derived {
    public DeriDerived() {
        System.out.println("DeriDerived");
    }
}

class Test {
    public static void main(String []args) {
        Derived b = new DeriDerived();
    }
}
```

a) Base

    Derived

    DeriDerived

b) Derived

    DeriDerived

c) DeriDerived

    Derived

    Base

d) DeriDerived

    Derived

e) DeriDerived

4. Given this code segment:

```
final CyclicBarrier barrier =
        new CyclicBarrier(3, () -> System.out.println("Let's play"));
            // LINE_ONE

Runnable r = () -> {                              // LINE_TWO
    System.out.println("Awaiting");
    try {
        barrier.await();
    } catch(Exception e) { /* ignore */ }
};

Thread t1 = new Thread(r);
Thread t2 = new Thread(r);
Thread t3 = new Thread(r);

t1.start();
t2.start();
t3.start();
```

Choose the correct option based on this code segment.

a) This code segment results in a compiler error in line marked with the comment `LINE_ONE`

b) This code segment results in a compiler error in line marked with the comment `LINE_TWO`

c) This code prints:

```
Let's play
```

d) This code prints:

```
Awaiting
Awaiting
Awaiting
Let's play
```

e) This code segment does not print anything on the console

5. **Given this class definition:**

```
class Point {
    private int x = 0, y;
    public Point(int x, int y) {
        this.x = x;
        this.y = y;
    }
    // DEFAULT_CTOR
}
```

Which one of the following definitions of the `Point` constructor can be replaced without compiler errors in place of the comment `DEFAULT_CTOR`?

```
a) public Point() {
        this(0, 0);
        super();
    }

b) public Point() {
        super();
        this(0, 0);
    }

c) private Point() {
        this(0, 0);
    }

d) public Point() {
        this();
    }
```

```
    e) public Point() {
            this(x, 0);
        }
```

6. **Consider the following program:**

```
class Base {
    public Base() {
        System.out.print("Base ");
    }
    public Base(String s) {
        System.out.print("Base: " + s);
    }
}

class Derived extends Base {
    public Derived(String s) {
        super();          // Stmt-1
        super(s);         // Stmt-2
        System.out.print("Derived ");
    }
}

class Test {
    public static void main(String []args) {
        Base a = new Derived("Hello ");
    }
}
```

Select three correct options from the following list:

a) Removing only Stmt-1 will make the program compilable and it will print the following: Base Derived

b) Removing only Stmt-1 will make the program compilable and it will print the following: Base: Hello Derived

c) Removing only Stmt-2 will make the program compilable and it will print the following: Base Derived

d) Removing both Stmt-1 and Stmt-2 will make the program compilable and it will print the following: Base Derived

e) Removing both Stmt-1 and Stmt-2 will make the program compilable and it will print the following: Base: Hello Derived

7. **Consider the following program and choose the right option from the given list:**

```
class Base {
    public void test() {
        protected int a = 10;    // #1
    }
}
```

```
class Test extends Base {                    // #2
    public static void main(String[] args) {
        System.out.printf(null);        // #3
    }
}
```

a) The compiler will report an error at statement marked with the comment #1

b) The compiler will report an error at statement marked with the comment #2

c) The compiler will report errors at statement marked with the comment #3

d) The program will compile without any error

8. **Given this code segment:**

```
LocalDate joiningDate = LocalDate.of(2014, Month.SEPTEMBER, 20);
LocalDate now = LocalDate.of(2015, Month.OCTOBER, 20);
// GET_YEARS
System.out.println(years);
```

Which one of the following statements when replaced by the comment GET_YEARS will print 1 on the console?

a) `Period years = Period.between(joiningDate, now).getYears();`

b) `Duration years = Period.between(joiningDate, now).getYears();`

c) `int years = Period.between(joiningDate, now).getYears();`

d) `Instant years = Period.between(joiningDate, now).getYears();`

9. **Consider the following program:**

```
class Outer {
    class Inner {
        public void print() {
            System.out.println("Inner: print");
        }
    }
}

class Test {
    public static void main(String []args) {
        // Stmt#1
        inner.print();
    }
}
```

Which one of the following statements will you replace with // Stmt#1 to make the program compile and run successfully to print "Inner: print" in console?

a) `Outer.Inner inner = new Outer.Inner();`

b) `Inner inner = new Outer.Inner();`

c) `Outer.Inner inner = new Outer().Inner();`

d) `Outer.Inner inner = new Outer().new Inner();`

10. **Consider the following program:**

```
public class Outer {
    private int mem = 10;
    class Inner {
        private int imem = new Outer().mem;                  // ACCESS1
    }

    public static void main(String []s) {
        System.out.println(new Outer().new Inner().imem); // ACCESS2
    }
}
```

Which one of the following options is correct?

a) When compiled, this program will result in a compiler error in line marked with comment ACCESS1

b) When compiled, this program will result in a compiler error in line marked with comment ACCESS2

c) When executed, this program prints 10

d) When executed, this program prints 0

11. **Consider the following program:**

```
interface EnumBase { }

enum AnEnum implements EnumBase {      // IMPLEMENTS_INTERFACE
    ONLY_MEM;
}

class EnumCheck {
    public static void main(String []args) {
        if(AnEnum.ONLY_MEM instanceof AnEnum) {
            System.out.println("yes, instance of AnEnum");
        }
        if(AnEnum.ONLY_MEM instanceof EnumBase) {
            System.out.println("yes, instance of EnumBase");
        }
        if(AnEnum.ONLY_MEM instanceof Enum) {    // THIRD_CHECK
            System.out.println("yes, instance of Enum");
        }
    }
}
```

Which one of the following options is correct?

a) This program results in a compiler error in the line marked with comment
`IMPLEMENTS_INTERFACE`

b) This program results in a compiler in the line marked with comment
`THIRD_CHECK`

c) When executed, this program prints the following:

```
yes, instance of AnEnum
```

d) When executed, this program prints the following:

```
yes, instance of AnEnum
yes, instance of EnumBase
```

e) When executed, this program prints the following:

```
yes, instance of AnEnum
yes, instance of EnumBase
yes, instance of Enum
```

12. **Which of the following statements are true with respect to enums? (Select all that apply.)**

a) An enum can have `private` constructor

b) An enum can have `public` constructor

c) An enum can have `public` methods and fields

d) An enum can implement an interface

e) An enum can extend a class

13. **Choose the correct option based on this program:**

```
class base1 {
    protected int var;
}

interface base2 {
    int var = 0; // #1
}

class Test extends base1 implements base2 { // #2
    public static void main(String args[]) {
        System.out.println("var:" + var);    // #3
    }
}
```

a) The program will report a compilation error at statement marked with the comment #1

b) The program will report a compilation error at statement marked with the comment #2

c) The program will report a compilation error at statement marked with the comment #3

d) The program will compile without any errors

14. **Consider the following program:**

```
class WildCard {
    interface BI {}
    interface DI extends BI {}
    interface DDI extends DI {}

    static class C<T> {}
    static void foo(C<? super DI> arg) {}

    public static void main(String []args) {
        foo(new C<BI>());       // ONE
        foo(new C<DI>());       // TWO
        foo(new C<DDI>());      // THREE
        foo(new C());           // FOUR
    }
}
```

Which of the following options are correct?

a) Line marked with comment ONE will result in a compiler error

b) Line marked with comment TWO will result in a compiler error

c) Line marked with comment THREE will result in a compiler error

d) Line marked with comment FOUR will result in a compiler error

15. **Consider the following definitions:**

```
interface BI {}
interface DI extends BI {}
```

The following options provide definitions of a template class X. Which one of the options specifies class X with a type parameter whose upper bound declares DI to be the super type from which all type arguments must be derived?

a) `class X <T super DI> { }`

b) `class X <T implements DI> { }`

c) `class X <T extends DI> { }`

d) `class X <T extends ? & DI> { }`

16. **In the context of Singleton pattern, which one of the following statements is true?**

    a) A Singleton class must not have any static members

    b) A Singleton class has a public constructor

    c) A Factory class may use Singleton pattern

    d) All methods of the Singleton class must be private

17. **Consider the following program:**

```
class ClassA {}

interface InterfaceB {}

class ClassC {}

class Test extends ClassA implements InterfaceB {
    String msg;
    ClassC classC;
}
```

    Which one of the following statements is true?

    a) Class Test is related with ClassA with a HAS-A relationship.

    b) Class Test is related to ClassC with a composition relationship.

    c) Class Test is related with String with an IS-A relationship.

    d) Class ClassA is related with InterfaceB with an IS-A relationship.

18. **Choose the correct option based on the following code segment:**

```
Comparator<String> comparer =
        (country1, country2) ->
                country2.compareTo(country2); // COMPARE_TO

String[] brics = {"Brazil", "Russia", "India", "China"};
Arrays.sort(brics, null);
Arrays.stream(brics).forEach(country -> System.out.print(country + " "));
```

    a) The program results in a compiler error in the line marked with the comment COMPARE_TO

    b) The program prints the following: Brazil Russia India China

    c) The program prints the following: Brazil China India Russia

    d) The program prints the following: Russia India China Brazil

    e) The program throws the exception InvalidComparatorException

f) The program throws the exception `InvalidCompareException`

g) The program throws the exception `NullPointerException`

19. **Which one of the following class definitions will compile without any errors?**

a) ```
    class P<T> {
        static T s_mem;
    }
    ```

b)  ```
    class Q<T> {
        T mem;
        public Q(T arg) {
            mem = arg;
        }
    }
    ```

c) ```
    class R<T> {
        T mem;
        public R() {
            mem = new T();
        }
    }
    ```

d)  ```
    class S<T> {
        T []arr;
        public S() {
            arr = new T[10];
        }
    }
    ```

20. **In a class that extends `ListResourceBundle`, which one of the following method definitions correctly overrides the `getContents()` method of the base class?**

a) ```
    public String[][] getContents() {
        return new Object[][] { { "1", "Uno" }, { "2", "Duo" }, { "3", "Trie" }};
    }
    ```

b)  ```
    public Object[][] getContents() {
        return new Object[][] { { "1", "Uno" }, { "2", "Duo" }, { "3", "Trie" }};
    }
    ```

c) ```
    private List<String> getContents() {
        return new ArrayList (Arrays.AsList({ { "1", "Uno" }, { "2", "Duo" },
        { "3", "Trie" }}));
    }
    ```

d)  ```
    protected Object[] getContents(){
        return new String[] { "Uno", "Duo", "Trie" };
    }
    ```

21. **Which one of the following interfaces declares a single abstract method named `iterator()`? (Note: Implementing this interface allows an object to be the target of the for-each statement.)**

    a) `Iterable<T>`

    b) `Iterator<T>`

    c) `Enumeration<E>`

    d) `ForEach<T>`

22. **Choose the correct option based on this program:**

```java
import java.util.stream.Stream;

public class Reduce {
    public static void main(String []args) {
        Stream<String> words = Stream.of("one", "two", "three");
        int len = words.mapToInt(String::length).reduce(0, (len1, len2) ->
        len1 + len2);
        System.out.println(len);
    }
}
```

    a) This program does not compile and results in compiler error(s)

    b) This program prints: onetwothree

    c) This program prints: 11

    d) This program throws an `IllegalArgumentException`

23. **Which one of the following options is best suited for generating random numbers in a multi-threaded application?**

    a) Using `java.lang.Math.random()`

    b) Using `java.util.concurrent.ThreadLocalRandom`

    c) Using `java.util.RandomAccess`

    d) Using `java.lang.ThreadLocal<T>`

24. **Given this code segment:**

```java
DateTimeFormatter fromDateFormat = DateTimeFormatter.ofPattern("MM/dd/yyyy");
// PARSE_DATE
DateTimeFormatter toDateFormat = DateTimeFormatter.ofPattern("dd/MMM/YY");
System.out.println(firstOct2015.format(toDateFormat));
```

Which one of the following statements when replaced with the comment PARSE_DATE will result in the code to print "10/Jan/15"?

a) DateTimeFormatter firstOct2015 = DateTimeFormatter. parse("01/10/2015", fromDateFormat);

b) LocalTime firstOct2015 = LocalTime.parse("01/10/2015", fromDateFormat);

c) Period firstOct2015 = Period.parse("01/10/2015", fromDateFormat);

d) LocalDate firstOct2015 = LocalDate.parse("01/10/2015", fromDateFormat);

25. Consider the following program:

```java
import java.util.*;

class ListFromVarargs {
    public static <T> List<T> asList1(T... elements) {
        ArrayList<T> temp = new ArrayList<>();
        for(T element : elements) {
            temp.add(element);
        }
        return temp;
    }

    public static <T> List<?> asList2(T... elements) {
        ArrayList<?> temp = new ArrayList<>();
        for(T element : elements) {
            temp.add(element);
        }
        return temp;
    }

    public static <T> List<?> asList3(T... elements) {
        ArrayList<T> temp = new ArrayList<>();
        for(T element : elements) {
            temp.add(element);
        }
        return temp;
    }

    public static <T> List<?> asList4(T... elements) {
        List<T> temp = new ArrayList<T>();
        for(T element : elements) {
            temp.add(element);
        }
        return temp;
    }
}
```

Which of the `asList` definitions in this program will result in a compiler error?

a) The definition of asList1 will result in a compiler error

b) The definition of asList2 will result in a compiler error

c) The definition of asList3 will result in a compiler error

d) The definition of asList4 will result in a compiler error

e) None of the definitions (asList1, asList2, asList3, asList4) will result in a compiler error

26. **Given this code segment:**

```
IntFunction<UnaryOperator<Integer>> func = i -> j -> i * j;
// LINE
System.out.println(apply);
```

Which one of these statements when replaced by the comment marked with LINE will print 200?

a) `Integer apply = func.apply(10).apply(20);`

b) `Integer apply = func.apply(10, 20);`

c) `Integer apply = func(10 , 20);`

d) `Integer apply = func(10, 20).apply();`

27. **Given this code segment:**

```
List<Map<List<Integer>, List<String>>> list = new ArrayList<>(); // ADD_MAP
Map<List<Integer>, List<String>> map = new HashMap<>();
list.add(null);                                     // ADD_NULL
list.add(map);
list.add(new HashMap<List<Integer>, List<String>>()); // ADD_HASHMAP
list.forEach(e -> System.out.print(e + " "));        // ITERATE
```

Which one of the following options is correct?

a) This program will result in a compiler error in line marked with comment ADD_MAP

b) This program will result in a compiler error in line marked with comment ADD_HASHMAP

c) This program will result in a compiler error in line marked with comment ITERATE

d) When run, this program will crash, throwing a NullPointerException in line marked with comment ADD_NULL

e) When run, this program will print the following: null {} {}

28. **Given this code snippet:**

```
LocalDate dateOfBirth = LocalDate.of(1988, Month.NOVEMBER, 4);
MonthDay monthDay =
        MonthDay.of(dateOfBirth.getMonth(), dateOfBirth.getDayOfMonth());
boolean ifTodayBirthday =
        monthDay.equals(MonthDay.from(LocalDate.now())); // COMPARE
System.out.println(ifTodayBirthday ? "Happy birthday!" : "Yet another day!");
```

Assume that today's date is 4ᵗʰ November 2015. Choose the correct answer based on this code segment.

a) This code will result in a compiler error in the line marked with the comment COMPARE

b) When executed, this code will throw DateTimeException

c) This code will print: Happy birthday!

d) This code will print: Yet another day!

29. **Consider the following program:**

```
class Base<T> { }

class Derived<T> { }

class Test {
    public static void main(String []args) {
        // Stmt #1
    }
}
```

Which statements can be replaced with // Stmt#1 and the program remains compilable (choose two):

a) Base<Number> b = new Base<Number>();

b) Base<Number> b = new Derived<Number>();

c) Base<Number> b = new Derived<Integer>();

d) Derived<Number> b = new Derived<Integer>();

e) Base<Integer> b = new Derived<Integer>();

f) Derived<Integer> b = new Derived<Integer>();

30. **Which of the following classes in the java.util.concurrent.atomic package inherit from java.lang.Number? (Select all that apply.)**

a) AtomicBoolean

b) AtomicInteger

c) AtomicLong

d) AtomicFloat

e) AtomicDouble

31. **Given the class definition:**

```
class Student{
        public Student(int r) {
                rollNo = r;
        }
        int rollNo;
}
```

Choose the correct option based on this code segment:

```
HashSet<Student> students = new HashSet<>();
students.add(new Student(5));
students.add(new Student(10));
System.out.println(students.contains(new Student(10)));
```

a) This program prints the following: true

b) This program prints the following: false

c) This program results in compiler error(s)

d) This program throws NoSuchElementException

32. **Which of the following statements are true regarding resource bundles in the context of localization? (Select ALL that apply.)**

a) java.util.ResourceBundle is the base class and is an abstraction of resource bundles that contain locale-specific objects

b) java.util.PropertyResourceBundle is a concrete subclass of java.util. ResourceBundle that manages resources for a locale using strings provided in the form of a property file

c) Classes extending java.util.PropertyResourceBundle must override the getContents() method which has the return type Object [][]

d) java.util.ListResourceBundle defines the getKeys() method that returns enumeration of keys contained in the resource bundle

33. **Which of the following statements is true regarding the classes or interfaces defined in the java.util.concurrent package? (Select ALL that apply.)**

a) The Executor interface declares a single method execute(Runnable command) that executes the given command at sometime in the future

b) The Callable interface declares a single method call() that computes a result

c) The CopyOnWriteArrayList class is not thread-safe unlike ArrayList that is thread-safe

d) The CyclicBarrier class allows threads to wait for each other to reach a common barrier point

34. **Given these two class declarations:**

```
class CloseableImpl implements Closeable {
    public void close() throws IOException {
        System.out.println("In CloseableImpl.close()");
    }
}

class AutoCloseableImpl implements AutoCloseable {
    public void close() throws Exception {
        System.out.println("In AutoCloseableImpl.close()");
    }
}
```

Choose the correct option based on this code segment:

```
try (Closeable closeableImpl = new CloseableImpl();
        AutoCloseable autoCloseableImpl = new AutoCloseableImpl()) {
} catch (Exception ignore) {
    // do nothing
}
finally {
    // do nothing
}
```

a) This code segment does not print any output in console

b) This code segment prints the following output:

```
In AutoCloseableImpl.close()
```

c) This code segment prints the following output:

```
In AutoCloseableImpl.close()
In CloseableImpl.close()
```

d) This code segment prints the following output:

```
In CloseableImpl.close()
In AutoCloseableImpl.close()
```

35. **Choose the correct option based on this code segment:**

```
List<Integer> ints = Arrays.asList(1, 2, 3, 4, 5);
ints.replaceAll(i -> i * i); // LINE
System.out.println(ints);
```

a) This code segment prints: [1, 2, 3, 4, 5]

b) This program prints: [1, 4, 9, 16, 25]

c) This code segment throws java.lang.UnsupportedOperationException

d) This code segment results in a compiler error in the line marked with the comment LINE

36. **Choose the correct option for this code snippet:**

```
public static void main(String []files) {
    try (FileReader inputFile = new FileReader(new File(files[0]))) { // #1
            inputFile.close();                                        // #2
    }
    catch (FileNotFoundException | IOException e) {                   // #3
            e.printStackTrace();
    }
}
```

a) The code snippet will compile without any errors

b) The compiler will report an error at statement marked with the comment #1

c) The compiler will report an error at statement marked with the comment #2

d) The compiler will report an error at statement marked with the comment #3

37. **Given this program:**

```
import java.time.*;
import java.time.temporal.ChronoUnit;

class DecadeCheck {
    public static void main(String []args) {
        Duration tenYears = ChronoUnit.YEARS.getDuration().multipliedBy(10);
        Duration aDecade = ChronoUnit.DECADES.getDuration();
        assert tenYears.equals(aDecade) : "10 years is not a decade!";
    }
}
```

Assume that this program is invoked as follows:

```
java DecadeCheck
```

Choose the correct option based on this program:

a) This program does not compile and results in compiler error(s)

b) When executed, this program prints: 10 years is not a decade!

c) When executed, this program throws an AssertionError with the message "10 years is not a decade!"

d) When executed, this program does not print any output and terminates normally

38. **Consider the following code segment:**

```
while( (ch = inputFile.read()) != VALUE) {
        outputFile.write( (char)ch );
}
```

Assume that **inputFile** is of type **FileReader**, and **outputFile** is of type **FileWriter**, and **ch** is of type **int**. The method **read()** returns the character if successful, or **VALUE** if the end of the stream has been reached. What is the correct value of this **VALUE** checked in the **while** loop for end-of-stream?

a)   -1

b)   0

c)   255

d)   Integer.MAX_VALUE

e)   Integer.MIN_VALUE

39. **Consider the following code snippet.**

```
String srcFile = "Hello.txt";
String dstFile = "World.txt";

try (BufferedReader inputFile = new BufferedReader(new FileReader(srcFile));
     BufferedWriter outputFile = new BufferedWriter(new FileWriter(dstFile))) {
    int ch = 0;
    inputFile.skip(6);
    while( (ch = inputFile.read()) != -1) {
        outputFile.write( (char)ch );
    }
    outputFile.flush();
} catch (IOException exception) {
    System.err.println("Error " + exception.getMessage());
}
```

Assume that you have a file named Hello.txt in the current directory with the following contents:

Hello World!

Which one of the following options correctly describes the behavior of this code segment (assuming that both srcFile and dstFile are opened successfully)?

a)   The program will throw an IOException because skip() is called before calling read()

b)   The program will result in creating the file World.txt with the contents "World!" in it

c) This program will result in throwing CannotSkipException

d) This program will result in throwing IllegalArgumentException

40. **Consider the following code segment:**

```
try (BufferedReader inputFile = new BufferedReader(new FileReader(srcFile));
    BufferedWriter outputFile
        = new BufferedWriter(new FileWriter(dstFile))) {  // TRY-BLOCK
    int ch = 0;
    while( (ch = inputFile.read()) != -1) {              // COND-CHECK
        outputFile.write( (char)ch );
    }
} catch (Exception exception) {
    System.err.println("Error in opening or processing file "
        + exception.getMessage());
}
```

Assume that srcFile and dstFile are Strings. Choose the correct option.

a) This program will get into an infinite loop because the condition check for
    end-of-stream (checking != -1) is incorrect

b) This program will get into an infinite loop because the variable ch is declared
    as int instead of char

c) This program will result in a compiler error in line marked with comment
    TRY-BLOCK because you need to use , (comma) instead of ; (semi-colon) as
    separator for opening multiple resources

d) This program works fine and copies srcFile to dstFile

41. **Given the following definitions:**

```
interface InterfaceOne<T> {
    void foo();
}

interface InterfaceTwo<T> {
    T foo();
}

interface InterfaceThree<T> {
    void foo(T arg);
}

interface InterfaceFour<T> {
    T foo(T arg);
}
```

```
public class DateLambda {
    public static void main(String []args) {
        // STATEMENT
        System.out.println(val.foo());
    }
}
```

Which one of the following statements can be replaced with the line marked with the comment STATEMENT that the program will print the result that is same as the call LocalDateTime.now()?

a) InterfaceOne<LocalDateTime> val = LocalDateTime::now;

b) InterfaceTwo<LocalDateTime> val = LocalDateTime::now;

c) InterfaceThree<LocalDateTime> val = LocalDateTime::now;

d) InterfaceFour<LocalDateTime> val = LocalDateTime::now;

42. **Which one of the following statements will compile without errors?**

a) Locale locale1 = new Locale.US;

b) Locale locale2 = Locale.US;

c) Locale locale3 = new US.Locale();

d) Locale locale4 = Locale("US");

e) Locale locale5 = new Locale(Locale.US);

43. **Choose the correct option based on this code segment:**

```
String []exams = { "OCAJP 8", "OCPJP 8", "Upgrade to OCPJP 8" };
Predicate isOCPExam = exam -> exam.contains("OCP");          // LINE-1
List<String> ocpExams = Arrays.stream(exams)
                        .filter(exam -> exam.contains("OCP"))
                        .collect(Collectors.toList());      // LINE-2
boolean result =
        ocpExams.stream().anyMatch(exam -> exam.contains("OCA")); // LINE-3
System.out.println(result);
```

a) This code results in a compiler error in line marked with the comment LINE-1

b) This code results in a compiler error in line marked with the comment LINE-2

c) This code results in a compiler error in line marked with the comment LINE-3

d) This program prints: true

e) This program prints: false

44. **Which one of the following code snippets shows the correct usage of try-with-resources statement?**

a)
```java
public static void main(String []files) {
    try (FileReader inputFile
            = new FileReader(new File(files[0]))) {
                //...
    }
    catch(IOException ioe) {}
}
```

b)
```java
public static void main(String []files) {
    try (FileReader inputFile
            = new FileReader(new File(files[0]))) {
                //...
    }
    finally { }
    catch(IOException ioe) {}
}
```

c)
```java
public static void main(String []files) {
    try (FileReader inputFile
            = new FileReader(new File(files[0]))) {
                //...
    }
    catch(IOException ioe) {}
    finally { inputFile.close(); }
}
```

d)
```java
public static void main(String []files) {
    try (FileReader inputFile
            = new FileReader(new File(files[0]))) {
                //...
    }
}
```

45. **Two friends are waiting for some more friends to come so that they can go to a restaurant for dinner together. Which synchronization construct could be used here to programmatically simulate this situation?**

a) java.util.concurrent.RecursiveTask

b) java.util.concurrent.locks.Lock

c) java.util.concurrent.CyclicBarrier

d) java.util.concurrent.RecursiveAction

46. **Choose the correct option based on this program:**

```
import java.util.*;

public class ResourceBundle_it_IT extends ListResourceBundle {
    public Object[][] getContents() {
        return contents;
    }
    static final Object[][] contents = {
                { "1", "Uno" },
                { "2", "Duo" },
                { "3", "Trie" },
    };
    public static void main(String args[]) {
        ResourceBundle resBundle =
                ResourceBundle.getBundle("ResourceBundle",
                new Locale("it", "IT", ""));
        System.out.println(resBundle.getObject(new Integer(1).toString()));
    }
}
```

a) This program prints the following: Uno

h) This program prints the following: 1

c) This program will throw a MissingResourceException

d) This program will throw a ClassCastException

47. **Given this code segment:**

```
Set<String> set = new CopyOnWriteArraySet<String>(); // #1
set.add("2");
set.add("1");
Iterator<String> iter = set.iterator();
set.add("3");
set.add("-1");
while(iter.hasNext()) {
    System.out.print(iter.next() + " ");
}
```

Choose the correct option based on this code segment.

a) This code segment prints the following: 2 1

b) This code segment the following: 1 2

c) This code segment prints the following: -1 1 2 3

d) This code segment prints the following: 2 1 3 -1

e) This code segment throws a ConcurrentModificationException

f) This code segment results in a compiler error in statement #1

48. **Choose the correct option based on this code segment:**

```
Stream<Integer> ints = Stream.of(1, 2, 3, 4);
boolean result = ints.parallel().map(Function.identity()).isParallel();
System.out.println(result);
```

a)   This code segment results in compiler error(s)

b)   This code segment throws `InvalidParallelizationException` for
     the call `parallel()`

c)   This code segment prints: `false`

d)   This code segment prints: `true`

49. **Choose the correct option based on this code segment:**

```
Path currPath = Paths.get(".");
try (DirectoryStream<Path> javaFiles = Files.newDirectoryStream(currPath,
"*.{java}")) {
    for(Path javaFile : javaFiles) {
        System.out.println(javaFile);
    }
} catch (IOException ioe) {
    System.err.println("IO Error occurred");
    System.exit(-1);
}
```

a)   This code segment throws a `PatternSyntaxException`

b)   This code segment throws an `UnsupportedOperationException`

c)   This code segment throws an `InvalidArgumentException`

d)   This code segment lists the files ending with suffix `.java` in the
     current directory

50. **Given this code segment:**

```
Path aFilePath = Paths.get("D:\\dir\\file.txt");
Iterator<Path> paths = aFilePath.iterator();
while(paths.hasNext()) {
    System.out.print(paths.next() + " ");
}
```

Choose the correct option assuming that you are using a Windows machine and the
file `D:\dir\file.txt` does not exist in the underlying file system.

a)   The program throws a `FileNotFoundException`

b)   The program throws an `InvalidPathException`

c)   The program throws an `UnsupportedOperationException`

d) The program gets into an infinite loop and keeps printing: `path element: dir`

e) The program prints the following: `dir file.txt`

51. **Which of the following is NOT a problem associated with thread synchronization using mutexes?**

a) Deadlock

b) Lock starvation

c) Type erasure

d) Livelock

52. **Assume that a thread acquires a lock on an object obj; the same thread again attempts to acquire the lock on the same object obj. What will happen?**

a) If a thread attempts to acquire a lock again, it will result in throwing an `IllegalMonitorStateException`

b) If a thread attempts to acquire a lock again, it will result in throwing an `AlreadyLockAcquiredException`

c) It is okay for a thread to acquire lock on `obj` again, and such an attempt will succeed

d) If a thread attempts to acquire a lock again, it will result in a deadlock

53. **Which one of the following interfaces is empty (i.e., an interface that does not declare any methods)?**

a) `java.lang.AutoCloseable` interface

b) `java.util.concurrent.Callable<T>` interface

c) `java.lang.Cloneable` interface

d) `java.lang.Comparator<T>` interface

54. **Consider the following program and choose the correct option that describes its output:**

```
import java.util.concurrent.atomic.AtomicInteger;

class Increment {
    public static void main(String []args) {
        AtomicInteger i = new AtomicInteger(0);
        increment(i);
        System.out.println(i);
    }
    static void increment(AtomicInteger atomicInt){
        atomicInt.incrementAndGet();
    }
}
```

a)   0

b)   1

c)   This program throws an UnsafeIncrementException

d)   This program throws a NonThreadContextException

55.   **What is the output of the following program?**

```
class EnumTest {
    enum Directions { North, East, West, South };
    enum Cards { Spade, Hearts, Club, Diamond };
    public static void main(String []args) {
        System.out.println("equals: " + Directions.East.equals(Cards.Hearts));
        System.out.println("ordinals: " +
                        (Directions.East.ordinal() == Cards.Hearts.ordinal()));
    }
}
```

a)

```
equals: false
ordinals: false
```

b)

```
equals: true
ordinals: false
```

c)

```
equals: false
ordinals: true
```

d)

```
equals: true
ordinals: true
```

56.   **Consider the following program and choose the correct option:**

```
import java.util.concurrent.atomic.AtomicInteger;

class AtomicVariableTest {
    private static AtomicInteger counter = new AtomicInteger(0);
    static class Decrementer extends Thread {
        public void run() {
            counter.decrementAndGet(); // #1
        }
    }
```

```
        static class Incrementer extends Thread {
            public void run() {
                counter.incrementAndGet(); // #2
            }
        }
        public static void main(String []args) {
            for(int i = 0; i < 5; i++) {
                new Incrementer().start();
                new Decrementer().start();
            }
            System.out.println(counter);
        }
    }
```

a) This program will always print 0

b) This program will print any value between -5 to 5

c) If you make the `run()` methods in the `Incrementer` and `Decrementer` classes synchronized, this program will always print 0

d) The program will report compilation errors at statements #1 and #2

57. **Which one of the following statements will compile without any errors?**

a) `Supplier<LocalDate> now = LocalDate::now();`

b) `Supplier<LocalDate> now = () -> LocalDate::now;`

c) `String now = LocalDate::now::toString;`

d) `Supplier<LocalDate> now = LocalDate::now;`

58. **For the following enumeration definition, which one of the following prints the value 2 in the console?**

`enum Pets { Cat, Dog, Parrot, Chameleon };`

a) `System.out.print(Pets.Parrot.ordinal());`

b) `System.out.print(Pets.Parrot);`

c) `System.out.print(Pets.indexAt("Parrot"));`

d) `System.out.print(Pets.Parrot.value());`

e) `System.out.print(Pets.Parrot.getInteger());`

59. **Assume that the current directory is "D:\workspace\ch14-test". Choose the correct option based on this code segment:**

```
Path testFilePath = Paths.get(".\\Test");
System.out.println("file name:" + testFilePath.getFileName());
System.out.println("absolute path:" + testFilePath.toAbsolutePath());
System.out.println("Normalized path:" + testFilePath.normalize());
```

a) file name:Test

absolute path:D:\workspace\ch14-test\.\Test
Normalized path:Test

b) file name:Test

absolute path:D:\workspace\ch14-test\Test
Normalized path:Test

c) file name:Test

absolute path:D:\workspace\ch14-test\.\Test
Normalized path:D:\workspace\ch14-test\.\Test

d) file name:Test

absolute path:D:\workspace\ch14-test\.\Test
Normalized path:D:\workspace\ch14-test\Test

60. **Given this code segment:**

```
BufferedReader br = new BufferedReader(new FileReader("names.txt"));
System.out.println(br.readLine());
br.mark(100);    // MARK
System.out.println(br.readLine());
br.reset();      // RESET
System.out.println(br.readLine());
```

Assume that `names.txt` exists in the current directory, and opening the file succeeds, and `br` points to a valid object. The content of the names.txt is the following:

```
olivea
emma
margaret
emily
```

Choose the correct option.

a) This code segment prints the following:

```
olivea
emma
margaret
```

b) This code segment prints the following:

```
olivea
emma
olivea
```

c) This code segment prints the following:

```
olivea
emma
emma
```

d) This code segment throws an IllegalArgumentException in the line MARK

e) This code segment throws a CannotResetToMarkPositionException in the line RESET

61. **Given this class definition:**

```
abstract class Base {
    public abstract Number getValue();
}
```

Which of the following two options are correct concrete classes extending Base class?

a)

```
class Deri extends Base {
    protected Number getValue() {
        return new Integer(10);
    }
}
```

b)

```
class Deri extends Base {
    public Integer getValue() {
        return new Integer(10);
    }
}
```

c)

```
class Deri extends Base {
    public Float getValue(float flt) {
        return new Float(flt);
    }
}
```

d)

```
class Deri extends Base {
    public java.util.concurrent.atomic.AtomicInteger getValue() {
        return new java.util.concurrent.atomic.AtomicInteger(10);
    }
}
```

62. **Which TWO of the following classes are defined in the `java.util.concurrent.atomic` package?**

    a) `AtomicBoolean`

    b) `AtomicDouble`

    c) `AtomicReference<V>`

    d) `AtomicString`

    e) `AtomicObject<V>`

63. **Given the following class and interface definitions:**

```
class CannotFlyException extends Exception {}

interface Birdie {
    public abstract void fly() throws CannotFlyException;
}

interface Biped {
    public void walk();
}

abstract class NonFlyer {
    public void fly() { System.out.print("cannot fly ");  }  // LINE A
}

class Penguin extends NonFlyer implements Birdie, Biped {    // LINE B
    public void walk() { System.out.print("walk "); }
}
```

    Select the correct option for this code segment:

```
Penguin pingu = new Penguin();
pingu.walk();
pingu.fly();
```

    a) Compiler error in line with comment LINE A because `fly()` does not declare to throw `CannotFlyException`

    b) Compiler error in line with comment LINE B because `fly()` is not defined and hence need to declare it abstract

    c) It crashes after throwing the exception `CannotFlyException`

    d) When executed, the program prints "walk cannot fly"

64. **Given this class definition:**

```
class Outer {
    static class Inner {
        public final String text = "Inner";
    }
}
```

Which one of the following expressions when replaced for the text in place of the comment /*CODE HERE*/ will print the output "Inner" in console?

```
class InnerClassAccess {
    public static void main(String []args) {
        System.out.println(/*CODE HERE*/);
    }
}
```

a) new Outer.Inner().text

b) Outer.new Inner().text

c) Outer.Inner.text

d) new Outer().Inner.text

65. **Given this code snippet:**

```
String[] fileList = { "/file1.txt", "/subdir/file2.txt", "/file3.txt" };
for (String file : fileList) {
    try {
        new File(file).mkdirs();
    }
    catch (Exception e) {
        System.out.println("file creation failed");
        System.exit(-1);
    }
}
```

Assume that the underlying file system has the necessary permissions to create files, and that the program executed successfully without printing the message "file creation failed." (In the answers, note that the term "current directory" means the directory from which you execute this program, and the term "root directory" in Windows OS means the root path of the current drive from which you execute this program.)

Choose the correct option:

a) This code segment will create file1.txt and file3.txt files in the current directory, and file2.txt file in the subdir directory of the current directory

b) This code segment will create file1.txt and file3.txt directories in the current directory and the file2.txt directory in the "subdir" directory in the current directory

c) This code segment will create file1.txt and file3.txt files in the root directory, and a file2.txt file in the "subdir" directory in the root directory

d) This code segment will create file1.txt and file3.txt directories in the root directory, and a file2.txt directory in the "subdir" directory in the root directory

66. **Given these class definitions:**

```java
class Book {
    public void read() {
        System.out.println("read!");
    }
}

public class BookUse {
    // DEFINE READBOOK HERE
    public static void main(String []args) {
        new BookUse().readBook(Book::new);
    }
}
```

Which one of the following code segments when replaced with the comment "DEFINE READBOOK HERE" inside the BookUse class will result in printing "read!" on the console?

a)

```java
private void readBook(Supplier<? extends Book> book) {
    book.get().read();
}
```

b)

```java
private static void readBook(Supplier<? extends Book> book) {
    Book::read;
}
```

c)

```java
private void readBook(Consumer<? extends Book> book) {
    book.accept();
}
```

d)

```java
private void readBook(Function<? extends Book> book) {
    book.apply(Book::read);
}
```

67. **Given the class definition:**

```java
class Employee {
    String firstName;
    String lastName;
    public Employee (String fName, String lName) {
        firstName = fName;
        lastName = lName;
    }
```

```
        public String toString() { return firstName + " " + lastName; }
        String getFirstName() { return firstName; }
        String getLastName() { return lastName; }
}
```

Here is a code segment:

```
Employee[] employees = { new Employee("Dan", "Abrams"),
                         new Employee("Steve", "Nash"),
                         new Employee("John", "Nash"),
                         new Employee("Dan", "Lennon"),
                         new Employee("Steve", "Lennon")
                       };
Comparator<Employee> sortByFirstName =
                ((e1, e2) -> e1.getFirstName().compareTo(e2.getFirstName()));
Comparator<Employee> sortByLastName =
                ((e1, e2) -> e1.getLastName().compareTo(e2.getLastName()));
// SORT
```

The sorting needs to be performed in descending order of the first names; when first names are the same, the names should then be sorted in ascending order of the last names. For that, which one of the following code segment will you replace for the line marked by the comment SORT?

a) ```
    Stream.of(employees)
        .sorted(sortByFirstName.thenComparing(sortByLastName))
        .forEach(System.out::println);
    ```

b)  ```
    Stream.of(employees)
        .sorted(sortByFirstName.reversed().thenComparing(sortByLastName))
        .forEach(System.out::println);
    ```

c) ```
    Stream.of(employees)
        .sorted(sortByFirstName.thenComparing(sortByLastName).reversed())
        .forEach(System.out::println);
    ```

d)  ```
    Stream.of(employees)
        .sorted(sortByFirstName.reversed().thenComparing(sortByLastName).reversed())
        .forEach(System.out::println);
    ```

68. **Given this code snippet:**

```
Statement statement = connection.createStatement
        (ResultSet.TYPE_SCROLL_SENSITIVE, ResultSet.CONCUR_UPDATABLE);
ResultSet resultSet = statement.executeQuery
        ("SELECT * FROM EMPLOYEE WHERE EMPNAME = \"John\"");
resultSet.updateString("EMPNAME", "Jonathan");
// UPDATE
```

Assume that the variable connection points to a valid `Connection` object and there exists an employee record with EMPNAME value "John". The `resultSet` is updated by changing the value of EMPNAME column with the value "Jonathan" instead of "John". For this change to be reflected in the underlying database, which one of the following statements will you replace with the comment UPDATE?

a) `connection.updateAllResultSets();`

b) `resultSet.updateRow();`

c) `statement.updateDB();`

d) `connection.updateDatabase();`

69. **Given these class definitions:**

```java
class ReadDevice implements AutoCloseable {
    public void read() throws Exception {
        System.out.print("read; ");
        throw new Exception();
    }
    public void close() throws Exception {
        System.out.print("closing ReadDevice; ");
    }
}

class WriteDevice implements AutoCloseable {
    public void write() {
        System.out.print("write; ");
    }
    public void close() throws Exception {
        System.out.print("closing WriteDevice; ");
    }
}
```

What will this code segment print?

```java
try(ReadDevice rd = new ReadDevice();
    WriteDevice wd = new WriteDevice()) {
    rd.read();
    wd.write();
} catch(Exception e) {
    System.out.print("Caught exception; ");
}
```

a) read; closing WriteDevice; closing ReadDevice; Caught exception;

b) read; write; closing WriteDevice; closing ReadDevice;
   Caught exception;

c) read; write; closing ReadDevice; closing WriteDevice;
   Caught exception;

d) read; write; Caught exception; closing ReadDevice; closing WriteDevice;

e) read; Caught exception; closing ReadDevice; closing WriteDevice;

70. **Select all the statements that are true about streams (supported in java.util.stream.Stream interface)?**

a) Computation on source data is performed in a stream only when the terminal operation is initiated, i.e., streams are "lazy"

b) Once a terminal operation is invoked on a stream, it is considered consumed and cannot be used again

c) Once a stream is created as a sequential stream, its execution mode cannot be changed to parallel stream (and vice versa)

d) If the stream source is modified when the computation in the stream is being performed, then it may result in unpredictable or erroneous results

71. **Given the code segment:**

```
List<Integer> integers = Arrays.asList(15, 5, 10, 20, 25, 0);
// GETMAX
```

Which of the code segments can be replaced for the comment marked with GETMAX to return the maximum value?

a) `Integer max = integers.stream().max((i, j) -> i - j).get();`

b) `Integer max = integers.stream().max().get();`

c) `Integer max = integers.max();`

d) `Integer max = integers.stream().mapToInt(i -> i).max();`

72. **Given the class definition:**

```
class NullableBook {
    Optional<String> bookName;
    public NullableBook(Optional<String> name) {
        bookName = name;
    }
    public Optional<String> getName() {
        return bookName;
    }
}
```

Choose the correct option based on this code segment:

```
NullableBook nullBook = new NullableBook(Optional.ofNullable(null));
Optional<String> name = nullBook.getName();
name.ifPresent(System.out::println).orElse("Empty"); // NULL
```

a) This code segment will crash by throwing `NullPointerException`

b) This code segment will print: `Empty`

c) This code segment will print: `null`

d) This code segment will result in a compiler error in line marked with `NULL`

73. **Choose the correct option for this code segment:**

```
List<String> lines = Arrays.asList("foo;bar;baz", "", "qux;norf");
lines.stream()
        .flatMap(line -> Arrays.stream(line.split(";"))) // FLAT
        .forEach(str -> System.out.print(str + ":"));
```

a) This code will result in a compiler error in line marked with the comment `FLAT`

b) This code will throw a `java.lang.NullPointerException`

c) This code will throw a `java.util.regex.PatternSyntaxException`

d) This code will print `foo:bar:baz::qux:norf:`

74. **Choose the correct option based on this code segment:**

```
LocalDate feb28th = LocalDate.of(2015, Month.FEBRUARY, 28);
System.out.println(feb28th.plusDays(1));
```

a) This program prints: `2015-02-29`

b) This program prints: `2015-03-01`

c) This program throws a `java.time.DateTimeException`

d) This program throws a `java.time.temporal.UnsupportedTemporalTypeException`

75. **Choose the correct option based on this code segment:**

```
List<Integer> ints = Arrays.asList(1, 2, 3, 4, 5);
ints.removeIf(i -> (i % 2 ==0)); // LINE
System.out.println(ints);
```

a) This code segment prints: `[1, 3, 5]`

b) This code segment prints: `[2, 4]`

c) This code segment prints: `[1, 2, 3, 4, 5]`

d) This code segment throws `java.lang.UnsupportedOperationException`

e) This code segment results in a compiler error in the line marked with the comment `LINE`

76. Given the class definition:

```
class Point {
        public int x, y;
        public Point(int x, int y) {
                this.x = x;
                this.y = y;
        }
        public int getX() { return x; }
        public int getY() { return y; }
        // other methods elided
}
```

Which one of the following enforces encapsulation? (Select all that apply.)

a) Make data members x and y private

b) Make the Point class public

c) Make the constructor of the Point class private

d) Remove the getter methods getX() and getY() methods from the Point class

e) Make the Point class static

77. **Given the definition:**

```
class Sum implements Callable<Long> {    // LINE_DEF
    long n;
    public Sum(long n) {
        this.n = n;
    }
    public Long call() throws Exception {
        long sum = 0;
        for(long longVal = 1; longVal <= n; longVal++) {
            sum += longVal;
        }
        return sum;
    }
}
```

Given that the sum of 1 to 5 is 15, select the correct option for this code segment:

```
Callable<Long> task = new Sum(5);
ExecutorService es = Executors.newSingleThreadExecutor(); // LINE_FACTORY
Future<Long> future = es.submit(task);                    // LINE_CALL
System.out.printf("sum of 1 to 5 is %d", future.get());
es.shutdown();
```

a) This code results in a compiler error in the line marked with the comment `LINE_DEF`

b) This code results in a compiler error in the line marked with the comment `LINE_FACTORY`

c) This code results in a compiler error in the line marked with the comment `LINE_CALL`

d) This code prints: `sum of 1 to 5 is 15`

78. **Given this class definition:**

```java
public class AssertCheck {
    public static void main(String[] args) {
        int score = 0;
        int num = 0;
        assert ++num > 0 : "failed";
        int res = score / num;
        System.out.println(res);
    }
}
```

Choose the correct option assuming that this program is invoked as follows:

```
java -ea AssertCheck
```

a) This program crashes by throwing `java.lang.AssertionError` with the message "`failed`"

b) This program crashes by throwing `java.lang.ArithmeticException` with the message "`/ by zero`"

c) This program prints: `0`

d) This program prints "`failed`" and terminates normally

79. **Given this code segment:**

```java
BufferedReader br = new BufferedReader(new InputStreamReader(System.in));
String integer = br.readLine();
// CODE
System.out.println(val);
```

Which one of the following statements when replaced by the comment CODE will successfully read an integer value from console?

a) `int val = integer.getInteger();`

b) `int val = Integer.parseInt(integer);`

c) `int val = String.parseInt(integer);`

d) `int val = Number.parseInteger(integer);`

80. **Which one of the following definitions of the AR
source class implementation is correct so that it can be used with try-with-resources statement?**

   a) class AResource implements Closeable {
       protected void close() /* throws IOException */ {
           // body of close to release the resource
       }
   }

   b) class AResource implements Closeable {
       public void autoClose() /* throws IOException */ {
           // body of close to release the resource
       }
   }

   c) class AResource implements AutoCloseable {
       void close() /* throws IOException */ {
           // body of close to release the resource
       }
   }

   d) class AResource implements AutoCloseable {
       public void close() throws IOException {
           // body of close to release the resource
       }
   }

81. **Which of the following are functional interfaces? (Select all that apply.)**

   a) @FunctionalInterface
      interface Foo {
         void execute();
      }

   b) @FunctionalInterface
      interface Foo {
         void execute();
         boolean equals(Object arg0);
      }

   c) @FunctionalInterface
      interface Foo {
         boolean equals(Object arg0);
      }

   d) interface Foo{}

82. **Choose the correct option based on this code segment:**

```
Stream<String> words = Stream.of("eeny", "meeny", "miny", "mo");
// LINE_ONE
String boxedString = words.collect(Collectors.joining(", ", "[", "]"));
// LINE_TWO
System.out.println(boxedString);
```

a) This code results in a compiler error in line marked with the comment `LINE_ONE`

b) This code results in a compiler error in line marked with the comment `LINE_TWO`

c) This program prints: `[eeny, meeny, miny, mo]`

d) This program prints: `[eeny], [meeny], [miny], [mo]`

83. **Choose the correct option based on the following code snippet. Assume that `DbConnector.connectToDb()` returns a valid `Connection` object and that the `EMPLOYEE` table has a column named `CUSTOMERID` of type `VARCHAR(3)`.**

```
ResultSet resultSet = null;
try (Connection connection = DbConnector.connectToDb()) {
            // LINE_ONE
    Statement statement = connection.createStatement();
    resultSet = statement.executeQuery
                ("SELECT * FROM CUSTOMER WHERE CUSTOMERID = 1212"); // LINE_TWO
}
while (resultSet.next()){      // LINE_THREE
    resultSet.getString("CUSTOMERID");
}
```

a) This code results in a compiler error in line marked with the comment
LINE_ONE

b) This code results in a compiler error in line marked with the comment
LINE_TWO

c) This code results in a compiler error in line marked with the comment
LINE_THREE

d) This code prints "1212" on the console and terminates

e) This code gets into an infinite loop and keeps printing "1212" on the console

f) This code throws SQLException

84. **Given this code snippet:**

```java
public static Connection connectToDb() throws SQLException {
    String url = "jdbc:mysql://localhost:3306/";
    String database = "addressBook";
    String userName = "root";
    String password = "mysql123";
    // CONNECT_TO_DB
}
```

Which one of the following statements will you replace with the comment CONNECT_TO_DB to create a Connection object?

a) return DatabaseManager.getConnection(url, database, userName, password);

b) return Connection.getConnection(url, database, userName, password);

c) return DriverManager.getConnection(url + database, userName, password);

d) return DatabaseDriver.getConnection(url + database, userName, password);

85. **Choose the correct option based on this code segment:**

```java
Path path = Paths.get("file.txt");
// READ_FILE
lines.forEach(System.out::println);
```

Assume that a file named "file.txt" exists in the directory in which this code segment is run and has the content "hello". Which one of these options can be replaced by the text READ_FILE that will successfully read the "file.txt" and print "hello" on the console?

a) List<String> lines = Files.lines(path);

b) Stream<String> lines = Files.lines(path);

c) Stream<String> lines = File.readLines(path);

d) Stream<String> lines = Files.readAllLines(path);

Answer Sheet

Question No	Answer	Question No	Answer	Question No	Answer
1		31		61	
2		32		62	
3		33		63	
4		34		64	
5		35		65	
6		36		66	
7		37		67	
8		38		68	
9		39		69	
10		40		70	
11		41		71	
12		42		72	
13		43		73	
14		44		74	
15		45		75	
16		46		76	
17		47		77	
18		48		78	
19		49		79	
20		50		80	
21		51		81	
22		52		82	
23		53		83	
24		54		84	
25		55		85	
26		56			
27		57			
28		58			
29		59			
30		60			

Answers and Explanations

1.

d) This code segment does not print anything on the console

The limit() method is an intermediate operation and not a terminal operation. Since there is no terminal operation in this code segment, elements are not processed in the stream and hence it does not print anything on the console.

2.

b) while((ch = inputFile.read()) != -1) {

The read() method returns -1 when the file reaches the end.

Why other options are wrong:

Option a) Since ch is of type int, it cannot be compared with null.

Option c) With the check != 0, the program will never terminate since inputFile.read() returns -1 when it reaches end of the file.

Option d) Using the identifier EOF will result in a compiler error.

3.

a) Base
   Derived
   DeriDerived

Whenever a class gets instantiated, the constructor of its base classes (the constructor of the root of the hierarchy gets executed first) gets invoked before the constructor of the instantiated class.

4.

d) This code prints:

Awaiting
Awaiting
Awaiting
Let's play

There are three threads expected in the CyclicBarrier because of the value 3 given as the first argument to the CyclicBarrier constructor. When a thread executes, it prints "Awaiting" and awaits for the other threads (if any) to join. Once all three threads join, they cross the barrier and the message "Let's play" gets printed on the console.

5.

```
c) private Point() {
        this(0, 0);
    }
```

Options a) and b) Both the calls super() and this() cannot be provided in a constructor

Option d) The call this(); will result in a recursive constructor invocation for Point() constructor (and hence the compiler will issue an error)

Option e) You cannot refer to an instance field x while explicitly invoking a constructor using this keyword

6.

b) Removing Stmt-1 will make the program compilable and it will print the following: Base: Hello Derived.

c) Removing Stmt-2 will make the program compilable and it will print the following: Base Derived

d) Removing both Stmt-1 and Stmt-2 will make the program compilable and it will print the following: Base Derived

Why other options are wrong:

Option a) If you remove Stmt-1, a call to super(s) will result in printing Base: Hello, and then constructor of the Derived class invocation will print Derived. Hence it does not print: Base Derived.

Option e) If you remove Stmt-1 and Stmt-2, you will get a compilable program but it will result in printing: Base Derived and not Base: Hello Derived.

7.

a) The compiler will report an error at statement line marked with the comment #1

Statement #1 will result in a compiler error since the keyword protected is not allowed inside a method body. You cannot provide access specifiers (public, protected, or private) inside a method body.

Why other options are wrong:

Option b) It is acceptable to extend a base class and hence there is no compiler error in line marked with comment #2.

Option c) It is acceptable to pass null to printf function hence there is no compiler error in line marked with comment #2.

Option d) This program will not compile cleanly and hence this option is wrong.

8.

c) int years = Period.between(joiningDate, now).getYears();

The between() method in Period returns a Period object. The getYears() method called on the returned Period returns an int. Hence, option c) that declares years as int is the correct option.

Using the other three options will result in compiler errors because the getYears() method of Period return an int.

9.

d) `Outer.Inner inner = new Outer().new Inner();`

Option d) uses the correct syntax for instantiating Outer and Inner classes. The other three options will result in compiler error(s).

10.

c) This program runs and prints 10

An inner class can access even the private members of the outer class. Similarly, the private variable belonging to the inner class can be accessed in the outer class.

Why other options are wrong:

Options a) and b) are wrong because this program compiles without any errors. The variable mem is initialized to value 10 and that gets printed by the program (and not 0) and hence Option d) is wrong.

11.

e) When executed, this program prints the following:

```
yes, instance of AnEnum
yes, instance of EnumBase
yes, instance of Enum
```

An enumeration can implement an interface (but cannot extend a class, or cannot be a base class). Each enumeration constant is an object of its enumeration type. An enumeration automatically extends the abstract class `java.util.Enum`. Hence, all the three `instanceof` checks succeed.

Why other options are wrong:

This program compiles cleanly and hence options a) and b) are wrong. Options c) and d) do not provide the complete output of the program and hence they are also incorrect.

12.

a) An enum can have `private` constructor

c) An enum can have `public` methods and fields

d) An enum can implement an interface

Why other options are wrong:

Option b) An enum cannot have `public` constructor(s)

Option e) An enum cannot extend a class

13.

c) The program will report a compilation error at statement marked with the comment #3

Statements marked with the comment #1 and #2 will not result in any compiler errors; only access to the variable var will generate a compiler error since the access is ambiguous (since the variable is declared in both base1 and base2).

14.

c) The line marked with comment THREE will result in a compiler error

Options a) and b) For the substitution to succeed, the type substituted for the wildcard ? should be DI or one of its super types.

Option c) The type DDI is not a super type of DI, so it results in a compiler error.

Option d) The type argument is not provided, meaning that C is a raw type in the expression new C(). Hence, this will elicit a compiler warning, but not an error.

15.

c) class X <T extends DI> { }

The keyword extends is used to specify the upper bound for type T; with this, only the classes or interfaces implementing the interface DI can be used as a replacement for T. Note that the extends keyword is used for any base type—irrespective of whether the base type is a class or an interface.

16.

c) A Factory class may use Singleton pattern

A Factory class generates the desired type of objects on demand. Hence, it might be required that only one Factory object exists; in this case, Singleton can be employed in a Factory class.

Why other options are wrong:

a) A Singleton class needs to have a static member to return a singleton instance

b) A Singleton class must declare its constructor(s) private to ensure that they are not instantiated

d) A static method (typically named getInstance()) with public access may need to be provided to get the instance of the Singleton class.

17.

b) Class Test is related with ClassC with a composition relationship.

When a class inherits from another class, they share an IS-A relationship. On the other hand, if a class uses another class (by declaring an instance of another class), then the first class has a HAS-A relationship with the used class.

18.

c) The program prints the following: Brazil China India Russia.

For the sort() method, null value is passed as the second argument, which indicates that the elements' "natural ordering" should be used. In this case, natural ordering for Strings results in the strings sorted in ascending order. Note that passing null to the sort() method does not result in a NullPointerException.

The statement marked with COMPARE_TO will compile without errors. Note that the variable comparer is unused in this code segment.

19.

```
b) class Q<T> {
       T mem;
       public Q(T arg) {
           mem = arg;
       }
   }
```

Option a) You cannot make a static reference of type T in a generic class.

Option c) and d) You cannot instantiate the type T or T[] using new operator in a generic class.

20.

```
b)  public Object[][] getContents() {
        return new Object[][] { { "1", "Uno" }, { "2", "Duo" }, { "3", "Trie" }};
    }
```

The getContents() method is declared in ListResourceBundle as follows:

```
protected abstract Object[][] getContents()
```

The other three definitions are incorrect overrides and will result in compiler error(s).

21.

a) Iterable<T>

The interface Iterable<T> declares this single method:

```
Iterator<T> iterator();
```

This iterator() method returns an object of type Iterator<T>. A class must implement Iterable<T> for using its object in a for-each loop. Though Iterable interface (in Java 8) defines forEach() and spliterator() methods, they are default methods and not static methods.

Why other options are wrong:

Option b) The `Iterator<T>` interface declares abstract methods `hasNext()` and `next()`, and defines default methods `remove()` and `forEachRemaining()`.

Option c) The `Enumeration<T>` interface declares hasMoreElements() and `nextElement()` methods.

Option d) There is no interface named `ForEach<T>` in the Java core library.

22.

c) This program prints: 11

This program compiles without any errors. The variable words point to a stream of `String`s. The call `mapToInt(String::length)` results in a stream of `Integer`s with the length of the strings. One of the overloaded versions of `reduce()` method takes two arguments:

`T reduce(T identity, BinaryOperator<T> accumulator);`

The first argument is the `identity` value, which is given as the value 0 here. The second operand is a `BinaryOperator` match for the lambda expression `(len1, len2) -> len1 + len2`. The `reduce()` method thus adds the length of all the three strings in the stream, which results in the value 11.

23.

b) Using `java.util.concurrent.ThreadLocalRandom`

`java.lang.Math.random()` is not efficient for concurrent programs. Using `ThreadLocalRandom` results in less overhead and contention when compared to using `Random` objects in concurrent programs (and hence using this class type is the best option in this case).

`java.util.RandomAccess` is unrelated to random number generation. This interface is the base interface for random access data structures and is implemented by classes such as `Vector` and `ArrayList`. `java.lang.ThreadLocal<T>` class provides support for creating thread-local variables.

24.

d) `LocalDate firstOct2015 = LocalDate.parse("01/10/2015", fromDateFormat);`

You need to use `LocalDate` for parsing the date string given in the `DateTimeFormatter` variable `fromDateFormat` (with the format string `MM/dd/yyyy`"). Other options will not compile.

25.

b) The definition of `asList2` will result in a compiler error.

In the `asList2` method definition, `temp` is declared as `ArrayList<?>`. Since the template type is a wild-card, you cannot put any element (or modify the container). Hence, the method call `temp.add(element);` will result in a compiler error.

26.

a) `Integer apply = func.apply(10).apply(20);`

The `IntFunction<R>` takes an argument of type `int` and returns a value of type `R`. The `UnaryOperator<T>` takes an argument of type `T` and returns a value of type `T`.

The correct way to invoke `func` is to call `func.apply(10).apply(10)` (the other three options do not compile). The first call `apply(10)` results in an `Integer` object that is passed to the lambda expression; calling `apply(20)` results in executing the expression (`i * j`) that evaluates to 200.

The other three options will result in compiler error(s).

27.

e) When run, this program will print the following: `null {} {}`

The lines marked with comments `ADD_MAP` and `ADD_HASHMAP` are valid uses of the diamond operator to infer type arguments. Calling the `add()` method passing `null` does not result in a `NullPointerException`. The program, when run, will successfully print the output `null {} {}` (null output indicates a null value was added to the list, and the {} output indicates that `Map` is empty).

28.

c) This code will print: `Happy birthday!`

This code gets the month-and-day components from the given `LocalDate` and creates a `MonthDay` object. Another way to create a `MonthDay` object is to call the `from()` method and pass a `LocalDate` object. The `equals()` method compares if the month and date components are equal and if so returns true. Since the month and day components are equal in this code (assuming that the today's date is 4th November 2015 as given in the question), it results in printing "Happy birthday!".

29.

a) `Base<Number> b = new Base<Number>();`

f) `Derived<Integer> b = new Derived<Integer>();`

Note that `Base` and `Derived` are not related by an inheritance relationship. Further, for generic type parameters, subtyping doesn't work: you cannot assign a derived generic type parameter to a base type parameter.

30.

b) `AtomicInteger`

c) `AtomicLong`

Classes `AtomicInteger` and `AtomicLong` extend `Number` class.

Why other options are wrong:

Option a) `AtomicBoolean` does not extend `java.lang.Number`.

Options d) and e) Classes named as `AtomicFloat` or `AtomicDouble` do not exist in the `java.util.concurrent.atomic` package.

31.

b) This program prints the following: `false`

Since methods `equals()` and `hashcode()` methods are not overridden in the `Student` class, the `contains()` method will not work as intended and prints false.

32.

a) `ResourceBundle` is the base class and is an abstraction of resource bundles that contain locale-specific objects

b) `java.util.PropertyResourceBundle` is a concrete subclass of `java.util.ResourceBundle` that manages resources for a locale using strings provided in the form of a property file

d) `java.util.ListResourceBundle` defines the `getKeys()` method that returns enumeration of keys contained in the resource bundle

The option c) is not to be selected. There is no such method named `getContents()` method that has the return type `Object [][]`. It has the method `getKeys()` that returns an enumeration of keys contained in the resource bundle. It is classes that extend `java.util.ListResourceBundle` (and not `java.util.PropertyResourceBundle` as given in this option) that must override the `getContents()` method that has the return type `Object [][]`.

33.

a) The `Executor` interface declares a single method `execute(Runnable command)` that executes the given command at some time in the future

b) The `Callable` interface declares a single method `call()` that computes a result

d) The `CyclicBarrier` class allows threads to wait for each other to reach a common barrier point

These three options are true.

Option c) is incorrect because the `CopyOnWriteArrayList` class is thread-safe whereas `ArrayList` class is not thread-safe.

34.

c) This code segment prints the following output:

```
In AutoCloseableImpl.close()
In CloseableImpl.close()
```

The types implementing `AutoCloseable` can be used with a try-with-resources statement. The `Closeable` interface extends `AutoCloseable`, so classes implementing `Closeable` can also be used with a try-with-resources statement.

The `close()` methods are called in the opposite order when compared to the order of resources acquired in the try-with-resources statement. So, this program calls the `close()` method of `AutoCloseableImpl` first, and after that calls the `close()` method on the `CloseableImpl` object.

35.

b) This program prints: [1, 4, 9, 16, 25]

The `replaceAll()` method (added in Java 8 to the `List` interface) takes an `UnaryOperator` as the argument. In this case, the unary operator squares the integer values. Hence, the program prints [1, 4, 9, 16, 25]. The underlying `List` object returned by `Arrays.asList()` method can be modified using the `replaceAll()` method and it does not result in throwing `java.lang.UnsupportedOperationException`.

36.

d) The compiler will report an error at the statement marked with the comment #3

Both of the specified exceptions belong to the same hierarchy (`FileNotFoundException` derives from an `IOException`), so you cannot specify both exceptions together in the multi-catch handler block.

It is not a compiler error to explicitly call `close()` method for a `FileReader` object inside a try-with-resources block.

37.

d) When executed, this program does not print any output and terminates normally

The program compiles cleanly without any errors. Assertions are disabled by default. Since assertions are not enabled when invoking this program, it does not evaluate the `assert` expression. Hence, the program terminates normally without printing any output on the console.

38.

a) -1

The `read()` method returns the value -1 if end-of-stream (EOS) is reached, which is checked in this `while` loop.

39.

b) The program will result in creating the file `World.txt` with the contents "World!" in it.

The method call `skip(n)` skips n bytes (i.e., moves the buffer pointer by n bytes). In this case, 6 bytes need to be skipped, so the string "Hello" is not copied in the `while` loop while reading and writing the file contents.

Why other options are wrong:

Option a) The `skip()` method can be called before the `read()` method.

Option c) No exception named `CannotSkipException` exists.

Option d) The `skip()` method will throw an `IllegalArgumentException` only if a negative value is passed.

40.

d) This program works fine and copies `srcFile` to `dstFile`

Why other options are wrong:

Options a) and b) This program does not get into an infinite loop because the condition check for end-of-stream (checking `!= -1`) is correct and the variable `ch` needs to be declared as `int` (and not `char`).

Option c) You can use ; (semi-colon) as separator for opening multiple resources in try-with-resources statement.

41.

b) `InterfaceTwo<LocalDateTime> val = LocalDateTime::now;`

The method `now()` in `LocalDateTime` is declared with the signature:

`LocalDateTime now()`

The matching functional interface should also have an abstract method that takes no argument and returns value of type `T`. Since `InterfaceTwo` has the abstract method declared as `T foo()`, the statement `InterfaceTwo<LocalDateTime> val = LocalDateTime::now;` succeeds. From the interface, the method can be invoked with `val.foo();` since `val` refers to `LocalDateTime::now`, and it is equivalent to making the call `LocalDateTime.now()`.

42.

b) `Locale locale2 = Locale.US;`

The `static public final Locale US` member in the `Locale` class is accessed using the expression `Locale.US`, as in option b).

The other options will result in compiler error(s).

43.

a) This code results in a compiler error in line marked with the comment `LINE-1`

The functional interface `Predicate<T>` takes type `T` as the generic parameter that is not specified in `LINE-1`. This results in a compiler error because the lambda expression uses the method `contains()` in the call `exam.contains("OCP")`.

If `Predicate<String>` were specified (as in `Predicate isOCPExam = exam -> exam.contains("OCP")`), this code segment would compile without errors, and when executed will print "false".

44.

```
a) public static void main(String []files) {
        try (FileReader inputFile
                = new FileReader(new File(files[0]))) {
                //...
        }
        catch(IOException ioe) {}
    }
```

Why other options are wrong:

- Option b) provides finally before the catch block, it will result in a compiler error.

- Option c) uses the variable inputFile in the statement inputFile.close() that is not accessible in the finally block and hence results in a compiler error. Option d) the required catch block in this context is missing in the code (because the try block code may throw IOException), and hence it is incorrect usage.

45.

c) java.util.concurrent.CyclicBarrier

CyclicBarrier is used when threads may need to wait at a predefined execution point until all other threads reach that point. This construct matches the given requirements.

Why other options are wrong:

- Options a) and d) java.util.concurrent.RecursiveTask and java.util.concurrent.RecursiveAction are used in the context of executing tasks in fork-join framework.

- Option b) The java.util.concurrent.locks.Lock class provides better abstraction for locking and unlocking than using the synchronized keyword.

46.

a) This program prints the following: Uno

This program correctly extends ListResourceBundle and defines a resource bundle for the locale it_IT.

The getObject() method takes String as an argument; this method returns the value of the matching key. The expression new Integer(1).toString() is equivalent of providing the key "1", so the program prints Uno in the console.

47.

a) This code segment prints the following: 2 1

This code segment modifies the underlying CopyOnWriteArrayList container object using the add() method. After adding the elements "2" and "1", the iterator object is created. After creating this iterator object, two more elements are added, so internally a copy of the underlying container is created due to this modification to the container. But the iterator still refers to the original container that had two elements. So, this program results in printing 2 and 1. If a new iterator is created after adding these four elements, it will iterate over all those four elements.

48.

d) This code segment prints: `true`

The stream pointed by ints is a sequential stream because sequential is the default execution mode. The call to `parallel()` method changes the execution mode to parallel stream. The `isParallel()` method returns true because the current execution mode of the stream is parallel.

Why other options are wrong:

Option a) This code compiles without errors. The call to `map(Function.identity())` is acceptable because the argument `Function.identity()` just returns the same stream element it is passed with.

Option b) It is possible to change the execution mode of a stream after it is created, and it does not result in throwing any exceptions.

Option c) The `isParallel()` method returns the current execution mode and not the execution mode when the stream was created. So the `isParallel()` method returns true in this code (and not false as given in this option).

49.

d) This code segment lists the files ending with suffix `.java` in the current directory

The path "." specifies the current directory. The pattern "`*.{java}`" matches file names with suffix `.java`.

50.

e) This code segment prints the following: `dir file.txt`

The name elements in a `path` object are identified based on the separators. Note: To iterate name elements of the `Path` object does not actually require that the corresponding files/directories must exist, so it will not result in throwing any exceptions.

51.

c) Type erasure

Deadlocks, lock starvation, and livelocks are problems that arise when using mutexes for thread synchronization. Type erasure is a concept related to generics where the generic type information is lost once the generic type is compiled.

52.

c) It is okay for a thread to acquire lock on `obj` again, and such an attempt will succeed

Java locks are reentrant: a Java thread, if it has already acquired a lock, can acquire it again, and such an attempt will succeed. No exception is thrown and no deadlock occurs for this case.

53.

c) `java.lang.Cloneable` interface

From the documentation of `clone()` method: "By *convention*, classes that implement this interface should override the `Object.clone()` method. Note that this interface does *not* contain the `clone` method."

Why other options are wrong:

- Option a) The `AutoCloseable` interface declares the `close()` method.

- Option b) `Callable` declares `call()` method.

- Option d) The `Comparator<T>` interface declares `compare()` and `equals()` methods.

54.

b) 1

The call `atomicInt.incrementAndGet();` mutates the integer value passed through the reference variable `atomicInt`, so the changed value is printed in the `main()` method. Note that `AtomicInteger` can be used in thread or non-thread context though it is not of any practical use when used in single-threaded programs.

55.

c)

```
equals: false
ordinals: true
```

The `equals()` method returns true only if the enumeration constants are the same. In this case, the enumeration constants belong to different enumerations, so the `equals()` method returns `false`. However, the ordinal values of the enumeration constants are equal since both are second elements in their respective enumerations.

56.

b) This program will print any value between −5 to 5

You have employed `AtomicInteger`, which provides a set of `atomic` methods such as `incrementAndGet()` and `decrementAndGet()`. Hence, you will always get 0 as the final value of counter. However, depending on thread scheduling, the intermediate counter values may be anywhere between −5 to +5, Hence the output of the program can range between −5 and +5.

57.

d) `Supplier<LocalDate> now = LocalDate::now;`

The `now()` method defined in `LocalDate` does not take any arguments and returns a `LocalDate` object. Hence, the signature of `now()` method matches that of the only abstract method in the `Supplier` interface: `T get()`. Hence, the method reference `Local::now` can be assigned to `Supplier<LocalDate>` and the statement compiles without any errors.

Other options show improper use of method reference and they will result in compiler error(s).

58.

a) `System.out.print(Pets.Parrot.ordinal());`

The `ordinal()` method prints the position of the enumeration constant within an enumeration and hence it prints 2 for this program.

Why other options are wrong:

- Option b) The call `print(Pets.Parrot);` prints the string "Parrot" to console

- Options c), d) and e) There are no methods named `indexAt()`, `value()`, or `getInteger()` in `Enum`

59.

a)

```
file name:Test
absolute path:D:\workspace\ch14-test\.\Test
Normalized path:Test
```

The absolute path adds the path from the root directory; however, it does not normalize the path. Hence, ".\" will be retained in the resultant path. On the other hand, the `normalize()` method normalizes the path but does not make it absolute.

60.

c) This code segment prints the following:

```
olivea
emma
emma
```

The method `void mark(int limit)` in `BufferedReader` marks the current position for resetting the stream to the marked position. The argument limit specifies the number of characters that may be read while still preserving the mark. This code segment marks the position after "olivea" is read, so after reading "emma," when the marker is reset and the line is read again, it reads "emma" once again.

61.

b)

```
class Deri extends Base {
    public Integer getValue() {
        return new Integer(10);
    }
}
```

d)

```
class Deri extends Base {
    public java.util.concurrent.atomic.AtomicInteger getValue() {
        return new java.util.concurrent.atomic.AtomicInteger(10);
    }
}
```

Option b) makes use of a co-variant return type (note that Integer extends Number), and defines the overriding method correctly.

Option d) makes use of co-variant return type (note that AtomicInteger extends Number), and defines the overriding method correctly.

Why the other two options are wrong:

- Option a) attempts to assign a weaker access privilege by declaring the method protected when the base method is public, and thus is incorrect (results in a compiler error).

- In option c) the method Float getValue(float flt) does not override the getValue() method in Base since the signature does not match, so it is incorrect (results in a compiler error).

62.

a) AtomicBoolean and c) AtomicReference<V>

The class AtomicBoolean supports atomically updatable Boolean values. The class AtomicReference<V> supports atomically updatable references of type V. Classes AtomicDouble, AtomicString, and AtomicObject are not part of the java.util. concurrent.atomic package.

63.

d) When executed, the program prints "walk cannot fly"

In order to override a method, it is not necessary for the overridden method to specify an exception. However, if the exception is specified, then the specified exception must be the same or a subclass of the specified exception in the method defined in the super class (or interface).

64.

a) `new Outer.Inner().text`

The correct way to access fields of the static inner class is to use the inner class instance along with the outer class, so `new Outer.Inner().text` will do the job.

65.

d) This code segment will create file1.txt and file3.txt directories in the root directory, and a file2.txt directory in the "subdir" directory in the root directory.

The `mkdirs()` method creates a directory for the given name. Since the file names have / in them, the method creates directories in the root directory (or root path for the Windows drive based on the path in which you execute this program).

66.

a)

```
private void readBook(Supplier<? extends Book> book) {
    book.get().read();
}
```

The `Supplier<T>` interface declares the abstract method `get()`. The `get()` method does not take any arguments and returns an object of type `T`. Hence, the call `book.get().read()` succeeds and prints "read!" on the console.

Why other options are wrong:

- Option b) Method references can be used in places where lambda expressions can be used. Hence, this code segment will result in a compiler error.

- Option c) The `accept()` method in the `Consumer<T>` interface requires an argument to be passed – since it is missing here, it will result in a compiler error.

- Option d) The `Function<T, R>` interface takes two type parameters and hence this method definition will result in a compiler error.

67.

b)

```
Stream.of(employees)
        .sorted(sortByFirstName.reversed().thenComparing(sortByLastName))
        .forEach(System.out::println);
```

The `sortByFirstName` is a `Comparator` that sorts names by the `Employee`'s first name. Because we need to sort the names in descending order, we need to call the `reversed()` method. After that, we need to sort the last names in ascending order, and hence we can call `thenComparing(sortByLastName)`.

68.

b) `resultSet.updateRow();`

The call `updateRow()` on the `ResultSet` object updates the database. Other options will not compile.

69.

a) `read; closing WriteDevice; closing ReadDevice; Caught exception;`

The `read()` method of `ReadDevice` throws an exception, and hence the `write()` method of `WriteDevice` is not called. The try-with-resources statement releases the resources in the reverse order from which they were acquired. Hence, the `close()` for `WriteDevice` is called first, followed by the call to the `close()` method for `ReadDevice`. Finally, the `catch` block prints "`Caught exception;`" to the console.

70.

a) Computation on source data is performed in a stream only when the terminal operation is initiated, i.e., streams are "lazy"

b) Once a terminal operation is invoked on a stream, it is considered consumed and cannot be used again

d) If the stream source is modified when the computation in the stream is being performed, then it may result in unpredictable or erroneous results

These three statements are true about streams.

Option c) is not correct. Once a stream is created as a sequential its execution mode can be changed to parallel stream by calling `parallel()` method. Similarly, once a parallel stream is created, you can make it a sequential stream by calling `sequential()` method.

71.

a) `Integer max = integers.stream().max((i, j) -> i - j).get();`

Calling `stream()` method on a `List<Integer>` object results in a stream of type `Stream<Integer>`. The `max()` method takes a `Comparator` as the argument that is provided by the lambda expression `(i, j) -> i - j`. The `max()` method returns an `Optional<Integer>` and the `get()` method returns an `Integer` value.

Why other options are wrong:

- Option b) The `max()` method in `Stream` requires a `Comparator` to be passed as the argument

- Option c) There is no `max()` method in `List<Integer>`

- Option d) The `mapToInt()` method returns an `IntStream`, but the `max()` method returns an `OptionalInt` and hence it cannot be assigned to `Integer` (as required in this context)

72.

d) This program will result in a compiler error in line marked with NULL

The ifPresent() method for Optional takes a Consumer as the argument and returns void. Hence, it is not possible to chain the orElse() method after calling the ifPresent() method.

73.

d) This code will print foo:bar:baz::qux:norf:

The flatMap() method flattens the streams by taking the elements in the stream. The elements in the given strings are split using the separator ";" and the elements from the resulting string stream are collected. The forEach() method prints the resulting strings.

Why other options are wrong:

- Option a) This code does not issue any compiler errors

- Option b) This Splitting an empty string does not result in a null, and hence this code does not throw NullPointerException.

- Option c) The syntax of the given regular expression is correct and hence it does not result in PatternSyntaxException.

74.

b) This program prints: 2015-03-01

Since 2015 is not a leap year, there are only 28 days in February. Hence adding a day from 28th February 2015 results in 1st March 2015 and that is printed.

75.

d) This code segment throws java.lang.UnsupportedOperationException

The underlying List object returned by Arrays.asList() method is a fixed-size list and hence we cannot remove elements from that list. Hence calling removeIf() method on this list results in throwing an UnsupportedOperationException.

76.

a) Make data members x and y private

Publicly visible data members violate encapsulation since any code can modify the x and y values of a Point object directly. It is important to make data members private to enforce encapsulation.

Why other options are wrong:

- Options b), c), and d) Making the Point class public, making the constructor of the class private or removing the getter methods will not help enforce encapsulation.

- Option e) You cannot declare a class static.

77.

d) This code prints: sum of 1 to 5 is 15

This code correctly uses Callable<T>, ExecutorService, and Future<T> interfaces and the Executors class to calculate the sum of numbers from 1 to 5.

78.

c) This program prints: 0

The condition within the assert statement ++num > 0 holds true because num's value is 1 with the pre-increment expression ++num. The expression 0 / 1 results in the value 0 and hence the output.

Why other options are wrong:

- Options a) and d) The assertion condition holds true; hence neither java.lang.AssertionError is thrown nor the message "failed" get printed

- Since the assertions are enabled by passing the option "-ea" this does not result in divide-by-zero. If the assertion were not disabled, it would have crashed by throwing java.lang.ArithmeticException with the message "/ by zero"

79.

b) int val = Integer.parseInt(integer);

Using the method Integer.parseInt(String) is the correct way to get an int value from a String object. The other three options will not compile.

80.

d)

```
class AResource implements AutoCloseable {
    public void close() throws IOException {
        // body of close to release the resource
    }
}
```

AutoCloseable is the base interface of the Closeable interface; AutoCloseable declares close as void close() throws Exception; In Closeable, it is declared as public void close() throws IOException;. For a class to be used with try-with-resources, it should both implement Closeable or AutoCloseable and correctly override the close() method.

Option a) declares close() protected; since the close() method is declared public in the base interface, you cannot reduce its visibility to protected, so this will result in a compiler error.

Option b) declares autoClose(); a correct implementation would define the close() method.

Option c) declares `close()` with default access; since the close method is declared public in the base interface, you cannot reduce its visibility to default accesses, so it will result in a compiler error.

Option d) is a correct implementation of the `AResource` class that overrides the `close()` method.

81.

a)
```
@FunctionalInterface
    interface Foo {
        void execute();
}
```

b)
```
@FunctionalInterface
    interface Foo {
        void execute();
        boolean equals(Object arg0);
}
```

The interface in option a) declares exactly one abstract method and hence it is a functional interface. In option b) note that `equals()` method belongs to `Object` class, which is not counted as an abstract method required for a functional interface. Hence, the interface in option b) has only one abstract method and it qualifies as a functional interface.

Why other options are wrong:

- Option c) the interface does not have an abstract method declared and hence it is not a functional interface.

- Option d) the interface does not have any methods and hence it is not a functional interface.

82.

c) This program prints: [eeny, meeny, miny, mo]

`Stream.of()` method takes a variable length argument list of type `T` and it returns a `Stream<T>`. The `joining()` method in `Collectors` class takes `delimiter`, `prefix`, and `suffix` as arguments:

`joining(CharSequence delimiter, CharSequence prefix, CharSequence suffix)`

Hence, the expression `Collectors.joining(", ", "[", "]")` joins the strings with commas and encloses the resulting string within '[' and ']'.

83.

f) This code throws SQLException

The try-with-resources block is closed before the while statement executes. Hence, call resultSet.next() results in making a call on the closed ResultSet object, thereby throwing an SQLException.

84.

c) return DriverManager.getConnection(url + database, userName, password);

The getConnection() method in DriverManager takes three String arguments and returns a Connection:

Connection getConnection(String url, String user, String password)

Hence, option c) is the correct answer.

The other three options will result in compiler errors.

85.

b) Stream<String> lines = Files.lines(path);

The lines(Path) method in Files class takes a Path and returns Stream<String>. Hence option b) is the correct answer.

Option a) The code segment results in a compiler error because the return type of lines() method is Stream<String> and not List<String>.

Option c) There is no such method named readLines(Path) in Files that returns a Stream<String> and hence it results in a compiler error.

Option d) The readAllLines(Path) method returns a List<String> and not Stream<String> and hence the given statement results in a compiler error.

Index

P, Q

■ U, V

■ W, X, Y, Z

Get the eBook for only $5!

Why limit yourself?

Now you can take the weightless companion with you wherever you go and access your content on your PC, phone, tablet, or reader.

Since you've purchased this print book, we're happy to offer you the eBook in all 3 formats for just $5.

Convenient and fully searchable, the PDF version enables you to easily find and copy code—or perform examples by quickly toggling between instructions and applications. The MOBI format is ideal for your Kindle, while the ePUB can be utilized on a variety of mobile devices.

To learn more, go to www.apress.com/companion or contact support@apress.com.

Printed in the United States
By Bookmasters